Introduction

Charles T. Brown

With drawings by ABNER DEAN

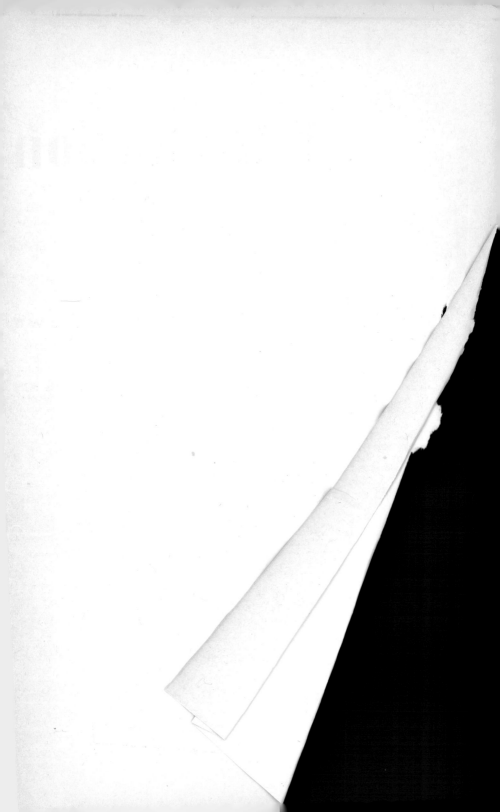

to
Speech

WESTERN MICHIGAN COLLEGE OF EDUCATION

HOUGHTON MIFFLIN COMPANY · *Boston*

New York · Chicago · Dallas · Atlanta · San Francisco

The Riverside Press Cambridge

PN
4121
B73

To My Wife
Partner in the Project

Preface

In the past we have taught speech as spoken rhetoric and artistic achievement. We have developed our courses and our books around thinking, organization, language, voice, action, and audience analysis. This has been all to the good. More and more, we have come to think of speech as a social process, and to see speaker and listener as whole individuals interacting. This book is an attempt to give added depth and effectiveness to both traditional and evolving disciplines of speech training by applying new insights from psychology and semantics, and from concepts developed by those who have worked with communicating machines. To weld the old and the new into a practicable, teachable text, the plan of the book takes account of the natural order of speech learning; it assumes that in every area of training, the student's first somewhat random efforts are gradually guided, refined, and fixed by recognition and stimulating practice. In short, the book covers the accepted areas of speech training, but treats them so as to sharpen the student's focus on his growth as a speaker and listener, and indeed as a human being.

A few words about arrangement. The first two chapters give an overall view of the text, showing how speech is an integral part of every social experience, and how the echoes of our own speech guide and control our growth and behavior. The three remaining chapters in Part One sketch first considerations for mastering speech situations and so equip the student with flexibility — a kind of first aid for emergencies and a condition needed for further development.

The four chapters in Part Two deal with speech composition. Stressing the nature of mature thought as a structure of assertion and support, they apply this principle to the planning and organization of speeches and to the variety of purposes and audiences which a speaker may meet.

Part Three considers other typical speech activities besides those of the formal public speaking situation, and develops an understanding of the nature of that speech which makes sense to listeners.

Part Four is an extended treatment of expressive action and voice. Recent research has shed a great deal of light on the problems of voice and voice production, and the three chapters on that subject present in a non-technical way the most cogent of these findings for student use. The final chapter in this part, "The Faults of Voice and Their Correction," suggests practice for every major voice problem likely to be met in a first course in speech. This is a chapter for reference rather than for general study.

Part Five explores the relationships between speech and personality, the mixture of traits and forces which shape our speech. A secondary purpose running through the book, and a primary purpose in these chapters, is to teach the student to listen so that he may increase his understanding of himself and others, and adjust his speech accordingly. For instance, most speech texts treat stage fright, one of the main problems of beginning speakers, in an almost cursory fashion. Here a chapter is devoted to the nature, causes, and reduction of speech fear, discussed against the background of the more general malady. The teacher is in no sense expected to be a therapist, or to spend an undue amount of valuable class time on discussions more appropriate to the purposes of a course in psychology. However, many students need information and techniques for reducing their speech fears beyond what may be achieved by the conditioning of early assignments, and this need we have tried to meet. The other three chapters of Part Five are related and deal with other significant forces that mold our speech.

While the book is written to be taught straight through, the parts can be taken up in almost any order, depending on the instructor's preference and the needs of a class, or indeed an individual — except that Part One offers several kinds of help most valuable early in the course. The skillful teacher knows when his class is ready for a given kind of learning, and the book is flexible enough to suit a variety of needs. In the main, however, the parts should probably be taken up as units.

The book provides adequate material for a year's work, though by selection it can be readily adapted for a half-year course. There are more assignments and suggested kinds of practice than any one student or instructor could hope to use. This was intentional, for we are all individuals, each with his peculiar needs, strengths, and weaknesses. And the greater the variety of suggested approaches to a problem, the better the chances of solving it.

Finally, an underlying aim of the book is worth mentioning. Western culture has distinguished itself by a relentless effort to master, exploit, and harness the earth, and our daily comforts are obvious evidence of the success of the struggle. We have attacked our social problems with the same aggressive vigor, but not with the same success. In taking stock of Western civilization, Arnold Toynbee concludes that the continued existence of our society depends on developing the ability to alter the attitudes that produce human conflict, and to work out techniques whereby those who disagree may still live side by side. But coexistence is dangerous existence, and if we are to be equal to it, we must understand our speech for what it is, a mirror of ourselves. Without this objectivity we lack the power to make the kind of sense our age demands. It is hoped that this book may help students see themselves, and others, a bit more clearly as they are.

I am indebted to a host of authors, but no less to a patient stream of students who have passed through my hands. Many students have read parts of the manuscript and made helpful evaluations. My colleagues, Dr. Albert Becker and Dr. John Murphy, have been sounding boards since the beginning of the idea. Mrs. Jean Malmstrom and Dr. Robert Limpus of our English Department helped me with matters of style. Dean James H. McBurney of Northwestern University and Dr. Orville Pence of the University of Washington made profound suggestions that sharpened the emphases of the book. Dr. Charles Van Riper of Western Michigan College has been of inestimable aid; his experience, insight, and lively imagination have stimulated me at many points. A man's family affects what and how he writes. My wife has been a patient, and sometimes long-suffering, partner in the project, and my children have had their somewhat different part — but I love them dearly. I am sincerely grateful to those authors, speakers, and students who have permitted me to quote their work.

CHARLES T. BROWN

Contents

Part Four · *The Mechanics of Speech*

Part Five · *Speech and Personality*

Index   451

Part One

The Nature of Speech and How We Learn It

———

1

The Urge to Talk

To SPEAK is to be human. Other creatures bark, roar, howl, whinny, or chirp, thus releasing their satisfaction or disapproval of life and their environment. But the discriminations of the "dumb" animals are few and almost entirely emotional. Man is unique in that somewhere along the trail he developed a more refined appraisal of things. With his increased brain power came a like refinement in his code of communication. It appears also that with these developments there emerged a greater *need* to communicate. The very fact that men live in complex communities argues that man, more than any other creature, is a social animal. Did a larger brain produce speech and did speech produce society? Or was it the other way around? Whatever was cause and result, the facts of present-day existence show that brain, speech, and society are interdependent.

*Without speech we would be unassembled
parts of the machine we call society.*

3

Brawn has its limits: brain (we hope) has not.

Speech and Society

Imagination suggests that community — common action among people — is no stronger and no weaker than the intelligence of their communication. In a society without communication, human interaction would be no more complex than that of a congregation of cattle in the shade of maples on a summer day. People would in fact be unassembled parts of the machine we call society. It is through speech that men have evolved the structure, organization, or pattern of relationships called community.

Perhaps it was an awareness that we could achieve more and be more secure when organized than when working independently that led man to develop the symbols for mental commerce. We can imagine that, one day in the gray past, a brighter member of *homo*

Speech wins cooperation — and
cooperation gets results.

sapiens perceived that two could move a log more easily than one. Perhaps, then, by impulsive trial-and-error gestures and haphazard sounds, he aroused the same idea in one of his more intelligent comrades. Once men found that they could work and think together, speech and all other forms of human communication slowly grew more precise and convenient. We can only guess how all this happened. The point here is that speech was born in, if not of, social need.

Speaking and Living

Like any action, speech is a product of energy. Energy is expended to remove tension and restore balance. But as we shall see, the variation in expressive behavior cannot be explained by energy alone. Energy produces action but has of itself no discrimination. The variation in expression is determined by *information*, the way organisms see things. Animals search for food; they eat, play, and raise young. Satisfaction in a given act transmitted back to the brain of the organism is a *message* which ensures a repeat performance when imbalance builds up again. The peculiar thing about man is that his ability to act is so much more various than that of other animals. It is not enough for him to know the satisfaction of food. He wants also to know why he eats, the values of the things he eats, why he sometimes does not want to eat, and why to be well-fed is not enough. Each new bit of information momentarily satisfies the urge that set up the question and magnifies his power to see into the distance. But sharper vision sees new questions, too, and reveals the existence of still more space for the ego to explore.

Children give proof of the place of the quest in life, and the range of their questions indicates the reaches of human unrest. "Why does it get dark?" "Why does it rain?" "Where does the rain come from?" "Where does it go?" "Why does the wind blow?" "Who makes it stop?" All the "why's," "where's," and "who's" bubble up out of the drive to establish a community of the self, others, and the physical environment, and to seek out the meaning of existence.

From one point of view, life is simply the perpetual movement of the individual to restore balance through communication. Questions are neutralized by information, and this brings satisfaction. But information suggests new questions, new questions create new imbalance, and this in turn begins the search for further information. A basic

Our speech is our shadow,
revealing our weakness . . .

motive of human life is thus to be found in the communicative
process.[1]

Understanding Through Speech

*Since speech is the primary channel of communication, listening
to man's talk is the direct road to understanding him.* Indeed, a man's
speech is his shadow, cast out before him. It is made of himself, and
he is destined to follow it. If (as is too often true) a man is hypnotized by his own words, he has no choice in life, no self-control, no
self-management or power to lead himself. Like the children of Hame-
lin who skipped away to the entrancing music of the Piper, man
marches out of reality when he becomes immersed in the rhythm of
his own song. This is most clearly seen in primitive peoples, who
chant an endless chain of mumbo-jumbo that wells up out of ignorance and fear

The Dobuans of the Pacific believe that good and evil are controlled by mystical words which may be obtained from the medicine
man. The Dobuan plants his yams, then leaves them to the mercy of
weeds and drought. Meantime he chants magic words to drive away
the evil spirits, which otherwise would "ghost" away his crop. One
time a missionary rigged an experiment to prove the value of caring
for a garden. He planted his alongside a Dobuan's, watering and tend-

---

[1] Norbert Wiener, *Cybernetics*, New York, John Wiley & Sons, Inc., 1949.

. . . and our strength.

ing it, while the native's withered. When harvest came, the white man called the people together to show them the difference, explaining how he had produced a bumper crop. They were impressed and amazed — and made fabulous offers for the white man's magic words!

Lest we dismiss the Dobuan too quickly, let us remember that western man condemns, beats, starves, and even kills his fellows under the trance of magic words — democracy, communism, isolationism, reactionary, Republican, Democrat, free enterprise, Christian, Catholic, Protestant, Negro, Jew. The words "mean" infinitely more than the objective reality to which they refer.

FIVE REASONS WHY WE TALK

Only as we detect the tendency to follow our own reflection — our speech — do we gain the first tool of self-prediction and control. To this end let us look into some of the reasons why we talk. People talk for five reasons. Two of these are exploratory, and the remaining three are geared to action.

Self-Exploration

Often we talk to find out what we mean. Agitated by a fuzzy idea, we probe with words to make it clear, and thus to see whether the notion fits in with other things we think are so — to see if the idea "makes sense." In addition, we often argue because we are disturbed by a situation which does not suit us. Having talked it out, we may reaffirm our position or shift to another, finding the original solution no longer acceptable.

In such speech our listeners, though indispensable (since we taboo openly talking to ourselves), are but mirrors. They interrupt our train of vocal thought, reinforcing our views with a nod or a comment, or checking us by a shake of the head. We send out messages and watch their effect on our listeners in order to test our verbal problem-solving.

Some time ago a colleague of the writer, a woman teacher, was killed in an automobile accident. After her death the writer found people saying what he too had trouble in understanding about himself. The comment would go something like this: "I have the most unusual reaction to Ruth's death. I didn't know her very well. But suddenly I am haunted by the feeling that a part of me is gone. I never thought of her much; I can't figure it out."

Obviously Ruth did mean much to the group. She was social interaction. She was communication, communion, relationship with people, more than she was a separate entity, a person, or a self. And so she became a part of others without their knowing it. In saying, "Strange, I really never knew her," they were talking to find their own thoughts. Haltingly, they were trying to understand themselves. The tragedy in most of us is that so much experience is below the verbal level. We might otherwise plan our lives more satisfactorily.

Yet man has always tried to make sense to himself, varying his technique from culture to culture. The Mexican talks aloud to his saints. The Zuñi Indians in their kiva carry out the search in group fashion. The prayer, so universal to religion, is a striking form of self-inquiry; we even close our eyes to deal more effectively with our innermost meanings.

A good many of us have a person or two upon whom we pour out our flow of chatter and with whom we share our troubles. These are our true friends, and they become a part of our most meaningful experience. The significance of communication to human existence is revealed in the fact that when we talk frankly to a friend we gain a firmer hold on the helm of life. He may not tell us what is right and wrong, or what we ought to do. In solving any puzzle, after a time we keep making the same mistakes over and over again. Our friend keeps us from going in circles by feeding into our thinking and talking just enough new messages to freshen and redirect our attempts to solve our problem.

In this self-talk we wander among all the motives that make us what we are — testing, weighing, trying to find what we believe, what we value and are endowed with. We all speak "to hear ourselves talk," and it is important that we do. The more a man understands himself, the better he is prepared to meet his world. Self-search is the means of directing our own growth. It can also be the source of some fascinating and creative speeches.

Social Exploration

But men speak for other reasons, too. Much of our speech is motivated to gain and maintain a proper relation with others, noise designed to keep the lines of communication open.[2] The chatter of bridge clubs, parties, dances, soda fountains, and street corners is an expression of this urge. Discussion of the weather, ceremonies, rallies, group singing, group speaking, praying in unison, all arise from the drive for group cohesion. We want the pleasure of association with people of kindred sympathies. A man in the writer's neighborhood would gleefully announce upon entering a house, "Well, we're here because we're here!" The comment is hardly exciting, but it does express a mood. "Hi! Whata ya know?" "Be seeing you," "Take it easy," "What's the pitch?" "Lovely day," "Good evening, Sir!" "Don't take any wooden nickels," "Charming," are the language of social exploration. An interesting example of this speech motive is cited by Hayakawa.

> Let us suppose that we are on the roadside struggling with a flat tire. A not-very-bright-looking but friendly youth comes up and asks, "Got a flat tire?" If we insist upon interpreting his words literally, we will regard this as an extremely silly question and our answer may be, "Can't you see I have, you dumb ox?" [3]

Dr. Karl Menninger, commenting on the "stupid" question, "Got a flat tire?" says the boy really means

> "Hello, I see you are in trouble. I'm a stranger to you but I might be your friend. . . . Are you approachable? Are you a decent fellow?

[2] S. I. Hayakawa, *Language in Thought and Action*, New York, Harcourt, Brace and Company, 1949, chapter 5. Also, by permission of George Allen & Unwin Ltd.
[3] *Ibid.*, p. 78.

Would you appreciate it if I helped you? I would like to do so, but I don't want to be rebuffed. That is what my voice sounds like. What does your voice sound like?"

Dr. Menninger says, "But people are too timid and mutually distrustful to be so direct. They want to hear one another's voices. People need assurance that others are just like themselves." [4] Much of our expression is like a blind man's tapping of his cane to test the next step, for we cannot see into the turbulent hearts of those with whom we live.

We have a tendency to ridicule the social exploratory speech of any group to which we do not belong. The speeches of political conventions (except of the party we favor) sound superficial and disgustingly sentimental. The chatter of teas, unless we are having a good time, suggests that everybody present is a perfect fool. But this reaction is rationalization, defense against the knowledge of isolation. There is no pain equal to the sense of not belonging. In a culture where we are not encouraged to look for our frustrations in our own lines of communication, we put the blame for this self-consciousness on the stupid fellow beside us.

Men talk to belong — to belong to the groups they love. This is "small talk," but it is important talk, for with it we learn to relate ourselves to others, to appreciate them and to be appreciated by them.

Control

Not all talk is exploratory. Speech, we have found, is a magic lamp. Aladdin's had the power to change and direct things, to send the carpet flying through the air. The enchantment of speech is comparable, except that it works on animate creatures, particularly human beings. Through speech we can control the thoughts and acts of others. Or, as will be explained later, we can cooperate with them, or we can adapt ourselves to their purposes and submit to their wills. All these reasons for talking go beyond exploration into the realm of action.

One of the commonest reasons students give for taking a course in speech is to improve their skill in controlling the acts and thoughts of others. They frequently phrase this aim as wanting to "put across

[4] Karl Menninger, *Love Against Hate*, New York, Harcourt, Brace and Company, 1942, pp. 268–69.

a point," or "sell themselves." Now, control, in the best sense of the word, is essential to the existence of organized human life as we know it. Our lives are made up of a complex network of activities channeled and conditioned by natural law and man-made law, custom, tradition, and ethical belief. We are controlled by "the best that has been thought and said" through the centuries of human civilization, and these controls are not bonds or shackles; they are the framework which man has slowly and painstakingly created in order that he may be a social being.

Unfortunately, it is not usually this kind of control which students have in mind when they describe their purpose in taking a course in speech. Rather, what they have in mind is likely to be a much narrower concept, which may better be described as dominating, or at least directing, the thought and behavior of others. They wish to make clients sign on the dotted line, build a house with a second bathroom, buy an extra insurance policy. Or they may wish only mental acceptance and the sense of power that comes from winning others to their views. This kind of control — or domination — is all too often exercised for the primary good of the speaker; or to put this the other way about, the good of the listener is a secondary consideration.

Speech for control is inseparable from ethical considerations. By its very nature it implies a reward to the listener who submits: "Vote for me and I'll keep you out of war." "Buy my soap and be beautiful." "Date me and enjoy a dance." The ethical question is, How sure is the persuader that he can produce the promised reward in return for the desired behavior? The future about which the persuader usually speaks is obscure, and every breach of promise is a blow to the lines of communication.[5]

Men speak to control, and often it is good for all concerned that they do. But the speaker who would dominate should be sure that he can deliver what he promises, and that getting what he wants is good for the other fellow as well as for himself.

Cooperation

Another reason we talk is to cooperate with others. When this is our objective, our speech is generally informative, dynamic but flexible. We are then interested in contributing what we know to the

---

[5] Hayakawa, *op. cit.*, p. 104.

pool of common knowledge; we do not urge unduly a view we have already formulated, but compare it with others to find out the best. Cooperative speech is organized social exploratory speech; it is a systematic move toward agreement. Since many social problems remain unsolved because of some failure in cooperation, it has become fashionable to question the value and even the existence of this amiable quality. However, an inventory of our speech soon shows that much of it is designed to notify others of our hopes and beliefs, and to find bases for agreement and cooperation.

Cooperative and democratic speech grows out of common interest, mutual influence, mutual suggestion, and reciprocal action. Speech that reaches agreement must employ tact, gracious concession, and the courage to hear the other fellow. In view of our usual ways of solving problems, all this may sound idealistic and a bit naive. If so, that is because we tend to accept common practices even when they do not achieve the best results. Basically, there are two ways in which people can live together. One is founded on the principle that order is best effected under a powerful individual or group. The other is based in the belief that the best will prevail when control rests with the group as a whole. Under the first view we expect coercive speech and action, and the techniques of power are of the highest value. Under the second, we mistrust the speech of those who would enforce their views without giving due consideration to the views of men who disagree. If we believe in group control, we believe that democracy is not to be served by emphasizing the skills of persuasiveness and dominance as the chief benefits of training in speech; rather, we place greater weight on releasing the self-governing abilities of all. Or to put this crucial concept still another way, the power to control is one of the finest of human urges. Those who also believe in the dignity of the individual, therefore, would divide control, allowing every man at least enough to govern his own life. This belief is the heart of democracy and the source of cooperative speech. Speech is the primary tool of human interaction and social growth, and it is important that we recognize and learn the kind of speech that helps to create the kind of society we want.

Submission or Adaptation

Men talk for one more reason. Sometimes we cannot and do not desire to control others, or even to work out a compromise on a give-and-take basis. When this is so, speech is entirely adaptive in its purpose. We search for the submission we must make to gain mutual action. If your roommate does not want to study and cannot be induced to, you, if you are an adaptive personality, may be persuaded to amble down to the corner with him for a cup of coffee.

If your speech is adaptive, somebody else's speech (understood or stated) controls. When yours controls, somebody else adapts. When neither person seeks control, speech and action are cooperative. When both are aggressive, argument, misunderstanding, charge, and counter-charge are likely to be the order of the day.

Shifts of Purpose

In most speech, and especially in conversation, we shift constantly among these five objectives. This is inevitable *in a free society where one retains status by social acceptance.* Self and social exploration are always in process. If we push too much, the pain of excessive or unjustified adaptation on the part of others causes them to reject us. On the other hand, over-submissiveness on our part may provoke the aggression of others. A proper balance achieves cooperation.

Notice the shifts of purpose in this typical conversation:

Social exploratory	A.	"Hi!"
Social exploratory	B.	"Hi! Sorta warm."
Control and social exploratory	A.	"Yeh! What did you think of tonight's meeting?" (His own position not immediately revealed since he does not know B's position.)
Self-exploratory	B.	"Well, I think I'd say the plans were inoffensive."
Aggressive control	B.	(Irritated because he did not receive a clear answer.) "But what did you think of it?"
Control and adaptation	B.	"I don't expect anything to come of it."
Control	A.	"But this is the first time we've had a promise of help from that committee."
Adaptation	B.	"Yes, I know."
Control	A.	"I think that is significant. We have been trying to get them behind us ever since I've been here."
Adaptation and Control	B.	"Yes, I think that's very good. But I don't think their plan will work."

Adaptation	A. "Oh, I'm not sure of the program."
Cooperative	B. "When are you and I going to be able to get together on the finances?"
Cooperative	A. "What about Friday at 3:00?"
Self-exploratory	B. "Well, now let's see . . ."

We need to be extraordinarily sensitive both to the effect of our own words and to the intent of the words we have just received in order that the explorations and the thrust and parry of speech *control, cooperation,* and *adaptation* may produce resolutions mutually agreeable.

While for the sake of clarity it is necessary to analyze and separate the reasons why men talk, it should be clear that in any given utterance more than one of the five reasons has usually operated. In fact, we may be urged by all five motives to the utterance of a single word. It should not disturb you that some of the reasons for talking oppose others. More often than not, as we shall come to see, man's speech reveals internal confusion and conflict. It is the aim of this book to help you understand this confusion and conflict, and so to reduce it.

QUESTIONS FOR STUDY AND DISCUSSION

1. Explain in your own words why we say that speech is the chief tool of society.

2. How would you explain the way man came to develop speech?

3. What does the universal questioning of childhood tell us about the nature of man's urge to talk?

4. Why is it that the more a creature knows the more restless it becomes?

5. Can you say in your own words why a basic force of human life is the information that runs through our communication?

6. Explain each of the five reasons why men talk. Give some examples of each.

7. You can listen to some people and change your mind; others say substantially the same thing and you resist them. Can you cite examples and explain the differences in their speech?

8. What do the words "ethics" and "persuasion" mean to you? When is it right to control another person? When, in your judgment, is it wrong?

9. Study the following diagram:

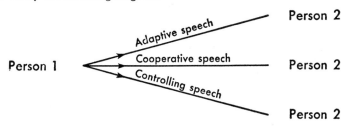

a. Using the diagram, explain the statement: When one person controls, another person submits.

b. Show how the diagram relates to the nature of democracy; the nature of dictatorship.

NOTE TO INSTRUCTOR AND STUDENTS

It is recommended that for most assignments during the first semester, students speak in the order in which they volunteer. At the close of a talk, as a student silently debates whether he should be next, he is living the situation in which he learns to initiate his own speech. If he is always last or nearly so, he must sense the indecision and procrastination which explain his lack of voice in the social world. Democratic responsibility can be learned only through the practice of self-government.

Most people will talk when their name is called. The question is: will they when they are not called upon? If not, they are learning to take the submissive role, to follow a leader. Many people do not speak up, but leave meetings declaring what ought to have been said and done. They are the ones who are always going to say something just after the present speaker finishes. But when that moment comes they grow tense with indecision, shift about, then feel a wonderful sense of relief when somebody else takes the floor. The very release from tension is reward enough to form the habit.

SUGGESTIONS AND ASSIGNMENTS

1. In the interest of developing community in the speech class, our first need is to get acquainted. To this end let each person introduce another to the class. It is suggested that this be done on a chain basis: that *One* introduce *Two* and *Two* introduce *Three*, etc. If *One* and *Two* in-

troduce each other, this sets up a "tit for tat" relationship, in which the second speaker feels compelled to match what the first did for him. If each speaker introduces himself, this directs too much attention to the self in an assignment whose purpose is to reach out to others and bring strangers into a cohesive group.

Each person should meet those next to him in the chain for informal conversation — preferably over a cup of coffee or a coke. First acquaintance involves such common data as name, home town, size of family, father's work, high school activities, interests and hobbies, work experience, courses, occupational plans, travel if any, unique experiences, ideas, and convictions.

In giving your introduction, you need not make the person you present seem larger or smaller than his biographical data justify. Just tell the facts. It is not your business to be clever or to present yourself in a good light. Above all remember you are focusing attention upon another person. What you say will make him feel at ease or uncomfortable. If you cause him discomfort even in "horse-play," your audience will resent you. You are an instrument for community. Any uneasiness you create is opposed to the welding of a group.

2. Take notes on a conversation; then while your notes are fresh, transcribe them in full and label each statement as in the conversation on page 13. Remember that statements often have more than one purpose. Write several interesting excerpts on the board and tell why you label each statement as you do. Shorthand will be helpful in this assignment but is not necessary.

3. The above device may be used for a panel discussion. Write a conversation on the board, and with several fellow students discuss the social purpose of each statement. You may also evaluate the skills with which certain statements are made.

4. Go to the front of the room, as if you are to speak, and look over your audience. This simple action orients you physically to the room and the class. Stand there until you feel collected and have a clear mental picture of your audience. This mental photograph will be useful in preparing future speeches. It emphasizes the importance of having an audience in mind as you prepare a talk (see page 50).

5. Give a three to five minute talk on "Why I Am Taking Speech." The reasons you came to the course, and what, now that you are in it, you hope to get out of the work, are interesting. Such a speech has many communicative values, too. In preparing you will do some self-exploratory talking to improve your understanding of your relations to your speech course. In addition, your classmates will be helped by knowing why you have joined the community and what you expect it to do for you. Finally,

your instructor can always organize his course more effectively in your interest if he knows what you expect.

6. Give a three to five minute talk on the topic, "What My Past Speech Experience Has Done for Me." What purposes for communicating (self exploration, social exploration, control, cooperation, or adaptation) have been strengthened by your experience? Have you been weakened in any way by your past experience? If so, how? What satisfaction have you gained in speaking?

7. Give a short speech on the topic, "A Meaningful Experience in My Life." Select an experience that impressed you, and tell what happened and the attitudes the experience left with you. How do these attitudes control you in other situations?

Such a talk is, first, self-exploration. It tells you how you came to have a value which directs you, and it suggests the way people grow to be unique personalities. At the same time this speech brings about the understanding that comes of social exploration. You as the speaker are not only exploring the capacity of the audience to accept your personal experiences and impressions, but the audience is learning the degree to which you trust yourself with them.

8. Give a persuasive speech; that is, try to convince your audience of something important to you, or try to get them to do something — to vote, buy, or give. Have your audience tell you in a discussion or by notes what influence you have had on them.

9. An informative speech permits an excellent study of speech purpose. Give a talk in which your purpose is to inform your audience on a topic of interest to you. Do not try to influence; give the facts. Let whatever influence develops evolve from the facts. Ask your audience to classify the speech according to the five purposes of speaking, as given in this chapter.

As a noted old professor once expressed it, "I seldom know what I am going to say until I hear myself saying it."

Wendell Johnson

2

The Speech Echo

YOU CANNOT LEARN to speak in college. You did that many years ago. But presumably your speech, which is now automatic, is not entirely to your liking. Either it does not match your idea of good speech, or it creates a response from others that you do not like, or both. The changes you now can make will constitute a relearning process, a rediscovery of the conditions that produce speech growth. Let us see how the human being learns to talk.

How We Learn to Talk

Experiment with Sounds. The infant's first speech is the birth cry, an uncritical response to a cold and alien world. For the first month or so his cries are all alike, reactions of the whole body to whatever stimulates it — sharp pins, hunger, wet diapers, uncomfortable position. About the beginning of the second month, the child begins to give different cries, and his mother soon learns to tell when he is hungry and when he has the colic. Shortly thereafter he begins to babble, to perform a sort of vocal play. Life is pretty much centered in and near the mouth in that early period, for the most impressive and exciting experience is eating. Between times the child makes all those mouth shapes he has learned in feeding, he rolls his tongue around, and at the same time he produces vocal sounds. He constructs at random all the sounds of our conventionalized language and many more. He is, indeed, a creative little genius.

About the beginning of the second half of the first year a very remarkable thing happens. The first step in the possibility of controlling speech — and life — takes place. The child hears himself! At this moment he for the first time receives the echo of his own speech. He likes it, and so he makes another sound, and another. The echo of some of these is probably more pleasing than others, and

18

so, as it dies away, he tries to bring them back, sometimes successfully. The difference between the echo and the unsuccessful efforts
to reproduce the desired sound stimulates new trials, with echo as
the guide. When success comes, the child "freezes" the motions that
produce the sound, and performs them again and again until they
are fixed, at least for the time being.

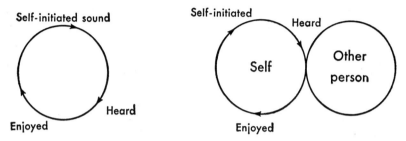

But we do not live alone, and the voices of others soon become
echoes too. By the ninth or tenth month the child begins to recognize not only that some sounds come from others, but that he can
repeat them. So now he makes a sound, hears it, likes it, repeats it;
hears a sound from others, likes it, and repeats it. Sometimes he
responds to himself, sometimes to his mother. In this way he begins
to open himself to the whole world of other people.

At about the same time the child begins reacting to both his own
sounds and those of others, he also sees the action of these other
creatures. He notes, unconsciously, how tense they are at the time
their sounds enter his echo system. He notes how fast they move,
and the expressions on their faces. He senses that the sounds range
from soft to loud, pleasant to harsh, slow to fast, and that certain
sound complexes accompany specific body sets and movements. Does
this seem too much of a task for a baby? Even the dog relaxes and
wags his tail when we drop our tension and speak to him in a low soft
voice. But the essential thing to notice here is that sight cues are
distinctive to communication with others — the child "sees" others
talk; he does not "see" himself.

Meaning and Structure.   At about the end of his first year he
starts the long process of associating meaning with the sounds he
utters. The process of thinking, like that of walking or talking, is so
much with us, so automatic, that it is almost beyond our analytical

The mind does not hold thoughts
in separate bins. . . .

grasp. It is enough here to understand that the essential feature of spoken language is that the speaker focuses his attention upon the *associations* and *connections* of the things he speaks about. Hence language has structure. We do not communicate by saying "boy, ball, house, throw, tree," because the mind of the speaker does not hold these items in separate bins. We say, "The boy threw the ball into that tree beside the house," because we fasten in the memory a picture, a set of relations between things that have been brought together by time and place. Intelligible speech is organized into sentences and paragraphs, units that communicate the pictures in the mind. The structure of language reflects the relationships in the mind and thus in the external world as the mind comprehends it.

Several important facts of learning in general and of speech in particular must be clearly understood if we are going to change our speech:

1. The first step in learning is random, uninhibited, non-corrected activity.

2. An echo of this activity, via the ears, is the first *corrective* approach to speech.

3. The ears are also used to gain information from others.

4. The eyes are the speaker's essential guide to his effect on the listener.

*. . . Language reflects the relationships we see
in the world about us.*

5. Repeated speech becomes fixed and habitual.

6. Fixed speech is automatically controlled.

7. The echo, guide, or "feedback" in language development is the "awareness" of structure or relationships among things seen, heard, tasted, and touched.

Echo or Feedback

The significance of these facts from the history of original speech learning can perhaps best be understood in terms of the new science of *cybernetics*. The word cybernetics is from a Greek word meaning "the steersman," and refers to the instrument that gives a machine the ability to control its own behavior. The science of cybernetics deals with the study of messages which exert control in mechanisms and men, and with the information involved in control.

The thermostat of the heating plant in a modern home, the self-steering mechanism of the ocean liner, the automatic chemical plant, the mechanical brain, the automatic gun pointer, radar, and sonar are examples of machines that "adjust and make judgments." The human body also functions through a system of internal controls. Body temperature, the rhythm of breathing, and the beat of the heart fluctuate within a delicate range dictated by the controls of the body. We sit, stand, lean, stoop, twist, and turn, and maintain balance under the control of the delicate mechanism of the inner ear. As we walk, a series of messages, signals of relative pressure on the bottoms of the feet, shoot to the brain and back to the muscles in such a pattern as to give rhythm to the action. We start to tap the ash from a cigarette, and a flow of messages guided by the eyes keeps us constantly aware of the difference between the intended act and the present state of its completion. A pin pricks us, and our controls against injury cause us to react. On a higher level, we "decide" and "act." If the act is distinctively human, perhaps we speak. In speech we think a word which transmits messages to countless muscles that form sounds. Our ears and the sensations within the mouth tell us whether we have achieved the word. If we have not, we correct and try again. All the functions of living from vegetating to meditating are directed by interlaced patterns of self-control. Whether in a machine like a heating plant or in a man, the essential element in this self-control is what the engineer calls "feedback." Feedback is a part of the energy of the machine that returns to the source with a corrective message.

Feedback is the scanning of behavior for success or failure in order to determine how to modify future behavior.[1] It tells the heating plant when to shut off. It keeps the automatic pilot on course. It makes you adjust your walk when you step on a pebble. It tells you when you have mispronounced a word, spoken too loudly, or insulted your listener.

If in speaking you say, "Now my second point is . . . " and you *see* several of your listeners move about as if casting their eyes back over their memories, this message signals the need for correcting yourself so as to pick up these listeners once again. This sense of difference between the actual effect and the intended effect is feedback.

The terms "feedback," "echo," "reflection," "reaction," or "monitor" all refer to the same process, and we shall use them interchangeably. Choose the one that speaks to you. The point is that a self-adjusting mechanism, whether man or radar, works toward its purpose by a flow of messages that inform it of its progress. This is feedback. Upset it, and behavior goes berserk; destroy it, and the machine or organism is helpless.

[1] Norbert Wiener, *The Human Use of Human Beings,* Boston, Houghton Mifflin Co., 1950, p. 69.

Feedback is Multiple. The human being does not have a single feedback circuit that controls all his behavior. He is too complex for that. He has a multiplicity of circuits, a combination of which come into play for each act. Even the elementary act of walking involves circuits that control balance, a sense of direction, recognition of obstacles in the path, and awareness of the relative position of the legs. The synchronization of all the circuits that organize life from the heartbeat to the search for the meaning of creation is a cooperative control beyond understanding. But the principles are clear and of the first importance in all learning.

Each Act Has a Monitor Circuit. There seems to be a dominant circuit in each human act which monitors, or "oversees" and echoes back to the brain, the play-by-play movement. If you reach out to turn off a light switch the act involves the senses of movement and touch, but is controlled by sight, which feeds back the extent to which the act has been accomplished. Close your eyes during the act, or better yet, before you begin reaching for the switch, and you lose control. You have cut out the *corrective* circuit. In much the same fashion, you are guided in the production of habitual speech by the contacts in your mouth; you know whether you have said "flipped" or "tripped," even when a thousand other voices drown yours in the roar of shouting at a basketball game. Should you have trouble with the word "statistics," you raise the *self-hearing* circuit to dominance. When you are immersed in thought, you become aware of the closeness or distance between two ideas. At such a moment, the circuits that control sound production, actions, and audience-study are subordinated. All behavior is dominated by a monitor circuit which guides, governs, and stabilizes other circuits involved in the act.

Speech Circuits

The principal circuits active in speech are those of sight, sound, movement (kinesthetic), touch, and the intellectual circuits. Each of these is dominant at one stage or another in learning. From our analysis of the child's earliest steps in speaking, it is apparent that hearing is most active when we are first learning self-purpose. Sight directs behavior when we begin to understand the listener. The associational circuits of the brain regulate thinking. Good speech comes when we are able to raise to dominance the circuit needed for the particular job at hand.

Transfer of Monitor Circuit as Habit Takes Over. The control of our speech purely by hearing is soon replaced by concentration on verbal symbols. When this takes place, the control of sound production is transferred to the tactual and kinesthetic sensations of the tongue, teeth, lips, and so on. Up to the age of three or four, the reaction of a child hearing his own voice on a recording machine is merely to repeat what he has heard. Older children and adults, who have ceased hearing themselves, react with amazement at the sound of their own voices, as if hearing them for the first time. Apparently self-hearing tends to die out as we learn to listen to others and to develop the manipulation of meanings.[2]

The sight monitor, which we use in studying our listeners, cannot give way to other circuits. In conversation, of course, we depend as much or more upon the inflections and quality of our conversant's voice as on a study of his tensions and mannerisms. But when we speak in public, we are limited to what we can see, for the audience is silent — at least most of the time. Much of our difficulty and stress in public speaking arises from the fact that we have come to depend upon the monitor system of conversation, which cannot function when listeners do not "talk back." The absence of their response leaves us at a loss.

Another such transfer can get us into even more serious trouble. Ordinarily the monitor of ideas, of what we say, is our intellect and the whole body of our knowledge. But with certain words (symbols) which become habitual, we transfer control to the symbol-memory-habit circuit. Thus we say, "Hello, nice weather," "Goodbye, remember me to the family," without focusing very sharply on the facts or thoughts being symbolized. All of us thus drift into speech in which we pay little attention to the meaning of what we say and hear. What are your real reasons for wanting that new Cadillac? What caused you to be attracted to that movie title? What do you mean when you say "democracy"? If in an argument you come out with "The majority

---

[2] This is not the whole of the story. Adults are more discriminating than children, and therefore more readily differentiate between their recorded speech and the speech they normally hear, which is in part transmitted through the bones and muscles of the head.

always rules," do you really mean that it does or should? Or are you merely reacting out of habit with a stock phrase you haven't really thought through as it applies to the particular argument? It is very easy to react with words rather than with thoughts. The further we drift into a world of words, the more we have given over our original idea monitor and come under the control of a habitual response to symbols.

In short, as we gain experience in speaking and form well-established habits, we tend to short-circuit the original echo systems and transfer control to a secondary circuit. This happens with hearing, in the production of sounds; with sight, in our observation of those we speak with; and even in the formulation and expression of ideas — and it is good if the habit is good, but bad if the habit is not.

Re-establishing the Original Monitor. In speaking, we have to examine and perhaps to change our reactions to self, to listeners, and to ideas. If these responses are all right as they are, we are indeed fortunate. If one or more is not what we want, we need to utilize aids that will establish the feedback necessary for proper correction.

Perhaps in the process of your earliest learning your relations to yourself were such as to produce a satisfying adjustment to situations. If so, you have no reasons to alter the system by which your performance is fed back to you. But if you cannot be sure of yourself in the speech situation, you need to bring your self-hearing back into dominance once again, until you hear the way you talk and correct it to your liking. In like fashion, if you figure out your audience and feel secure in your relation to it, you should continue to see it as you do. But if you cannot see your audience, if in some way it is a threat to you, or if you cannot be sure what those faces and postures mean, then you need to reactivate your sight feedback in order to observe people more accurately. If your language says what you want it to say and does not convey "noise" to others, it too should stay as it is. But if you play with words, or fail to know when you have translated a thought into symbols that convey it adequately, you need to increase your feedback to symbols.

The whole process of learning speech at the college level, then, is a matter of re-creating the conditions that stimulate the feedback for the correction you need to make.

Procedure for Relearning

Target-Set.　We can learn how to develop our speech by exploring further the parallel between machines and men. As we said earlier, the machine operates within the scheme of a built-in objective. The automatic steering mechanism of the ship holds the craft to a given course. The automatic gunpointer trips off a burst of fire on or near the target. The machine's "awareness" of its error corrects and keeps it to its task. A peculiar function of the human machine is that it is designed to talk to its neighbor. As we do this, under the influence of our environment, we develop a master pattern, a standard of good speech, against which we match our efforts. Our goal in speech is to reach this standard, to hit the target. When we do, we receive a satisfying feedback from the response of the listener.

Your first job in speech training, then, is to find what kind of gauge or standard you have and to see how well it matches what the audience considers good speech. Students often reveal a vague sense of this need by the strict form they try to copy in their first speeches. It is not uncommon for them to begin "Professor Jones, fellow classmates, and my friends . . . " and to end, "Thank you." As they get a better feeling of what the audience wants, they adjust the gauge. Their speech takes on a better sense of direction. This sense of direction may be described as *target-set.*

Scanning.　The first movements of all machines toward finding their "target" are gross movements, and the more freely the machine is permitted to oscillate in its initial search, the more likely it is to cancel out its errors and come to focus upon its objective. Unconsciously this principle is taken into account by most coaches in training an athlete. The novice is given a tennis racket to handle, to swing, and to get "the feel of," before he is taught to play the game. The amateur rifleman will handle the gun and move it around to bring the kinesthetic feedback into dominance before he tries to aim. Then as he trains his eye along the sights he will note the tendency of the barrel to oscillate around the target. If he is wise he will not grow tense but will let the oscillations die out. In like fashion, at first, the baby cries and babbles at random. So relaxedly does he reach the point when he trains upon a given sound that the first scanning efforts are not noticed by the parents. He actually achieves the ability to repeat his own sounds before his mother recognizes that he has been working toward that goal. The essential attributes of the scanning stage in learning, then, are *gross error* and *loose muscular coordination*.

Most students beginning a speech course are aware that their condition is the very opposite. They are very tense; they have too much feedback, too much correction. This over-correction causes oscillation, vibration, indecisive action, so that their efforts to do the job right do not correct errors but reinforce them. The speech machinery is out of control. Chapter 19, "Fear and Confidence," is designed to help meet this problem.

Searching.   Babbling, free expression of what motivates in the speech situation, is of value in destroying inhibition, excessive feedback. Soon the speaker must, out of his babbling, find targets that he wants to concentrate on. He must then re-train himself to see, without fear, the difference between the standard of communication he has been used to and his new goals, much as the marksman's eye notes the difference between the wobbling aim and the target on which he wishes to bring the gun to bear.

In the speech situation the target search is governed by the speaker's sense of the difference between his speech and his standard as monitored by self-hearing, what he sees in the reactions of his audience as he proceeds, and how the ideas seem to progress in order and vividness. A variety of devices, to be discussed at points where they apply, are helpful in establishing these monitors. As the speaker searches for the target he will lessen the freedom of his scanning, shorten the oscillation period, and narrow the margin of error.

Locating the Objective.   By adjusting the "feedback" relationships, the speaker eventually locates his objective. With the automatic gun, the projectile hits its target; in speech, self, others, and idea are brought into proper focus. The idea monitor should probably dominate. This means that the values of the speaker have coincided with the values of the listener. Indeed, the standard of good speech is that target location where both speaker and audience are satisfied. To speak well, then, is not to stand alert, project your *d's*, start this way, and end that way. Good speech cannot fix any standard except satisfaction for both speaker and listener. Any formula beyond this produces artificial speech, and that means death to communication.

Though the eventual target in speech is a satisfying speaker-audience relationship, *to attain this end one must concentrate upon sub-goals, sub-targets.* One may want to be heard better, to avoid stumbling, to think of the right thing to say at the right time, to speak so as not to be laughed at, to please the audience, to know when to quit. The surest way to hit a target is to set one within view. This students often fail to do in speech preparation. They shoot for *good speech*, a vague target at the far-off horizon where earth meets sky. Doing this, there is no direction to preparation. Since the target is out of sight, the speaker would not know if he did hit it.

But even when a specific target has been located, the speaker is only part of the way along in the learning process. The chances are that he will find the target briefly and lose it again, just as the automatic gun sweeps across a target, hits it, and passes beyond.

Fixing the Target.   In other words, once a speech goal is located, it needs to be fixed. The first step in this process is recognition, an echo of the fact that you have hit this sub-target. At the beginning of the year you may have to depend upon your audience and your instructor to feed you the information about how well you have achieved your goal. But the sooner you learn to know from your own evaluation when you have hit the bull's eye, the sooner you become an effective and responsible speaker. Throughout the course, in both preparation and class work, you should set a specific sub-goal and evaluate your effort immediately after speaking. As you may have already discovered, speech produces a tremendously impelling echo or feedback. The accuracy of the echo is all-important. Do you know when you have achieved your purpose? When you fail, do you sense the difference between your performance and your intent?

When you miss, you will often make the remarkable discovery that you did so *because the aim of the assignment was not your real aim.* For instance, Myrna did a wonderful job in an impromptu speech. She was poised, she experienced the emotions appropriate to her talk, and she interacted with the audience better than she had ever done before. What was her post mortem? "I still stumble over words," she said, focusing on a perfectionistic standard she has been trying for weeks to meet. Even though Myrna was successful, she did not know it. *She had to be told;* because her attention was elsewhere, she had no feedback to help her fix and repeat her achievement. But the feedback she did receive is of the utmost significance. It indicates that something has to be done with her standard of fluency: she must

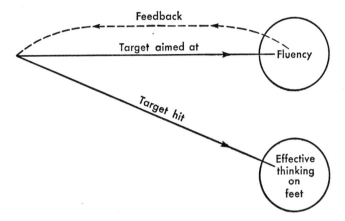

lower it, thereby reshaping her total picture, putting important needs in important places, so that she may receive satisfaction when she does a job well.

Once you have located an objective, speech development depends to a great extent upon fixing the circuits, developing the right habits. This means that you must get a sense of satisfaction when you are successful. You must learn to analyze your echo and put it accurately into words. You then have the anticipatory set necessary to repeat the performance again and again until the right responses become *automatic*.

Stabilizing. In the course of months most students learn to fix on the target in the classroom situation to which they are accustomed. But if the chairs in the rooms are rearranged, and a new audience is brought in, the student who has not learned to stablize the essential circuits, and at the same time to adjust those needed for a new situation, is "thrown for a loss." When he gets a new audience, for instance, he must reactivate his sight feedback to a conscious search for audience reaction. "I am interpreted as cool and unfriendly," may be his evaluation. He must now consciously monitor himself, bring his self-hearing to focus. Then he can adjust his attitude, muscle tone, and voice. He smiles, perhaps thinks of a bit of related humor, walks up closer. His audience warms up to him. Having adjusted to his audience, he begins to open the hearing and seeing circuits as simultaneously he closes the circuit on content, for a more critical echo to the word. When he reaches a point of balance where the idea flows with satisfaction to himself and to his audience, a sort of overall master monitor of awareness to self, others, and speech content comes into dominance and he proceeds toward the originally anticipated target.

This step, adjustment to changing conditions, while maintaining the purpose of the speech, may seem at this point in your speaking almost unattainable. Indeed, this is a description of "good speech." But the ability to remain stable in unstable conditions will develop in due time as you work out the preceding steps.

Continuous Echo to Speech Development

Start a diary of the reactions you experience after you speak. After each speech set down the major echoes you have (1) to your performance; (2) to your audience; and (3) to the development of your topic. From this evaluation, pick out the one immediate objective you most desire to attain. Prepare for your next speech with this in mind. Keep up this self-analysis throughout the year. It will let you know when and how you are searching, when you hit a target, when to concentrate on repetition, when to select a new goal, when to try developing skill in a new situation.

Learning is the process of determining clearly what goals we want to attain, trying to achieve our goals, comparing our performance with our goals, and trying again. Feedback (comparison of achievement with aim) is the means of learning. The challenge in relearning is to re-establish the feedback that guided the original learning of the act.

Three speech circuits are of utmost importance: those which monitor the self, the audience, and the idea. The ultimate goal of speech is to adjust to the audience. This means studying the audience (the target) so as to know how it receives. To reach the audience better may require a change in self. We must then hear ourselves, and hearing ourselves, try to change. In the course of change we go from scanning to searching, locating, fixing, and finally to stabilizing our new-found behavior.

QUESTIONS FOR STUDY AND DISCUSSION

1. Explain the steps a baby goes through in learning to talk.

2. How does the baby's hearing of himself affect his personality? (This is a hard question, but if you can answer it you will see much of the trouble human beings have in figuring themselves out.)

3. What are some of the things you read in the actions of others as you talk with them?

4. How does the structure of the sentence show that thinking involves seeing relations among things?

5. What is meant by "echo" or "feedback"?

6. Can you give an example of the way a changing echo monitors an act?

7. How can you explain habit in terms of echo?

8. This question is the key to the chapter: What is meant by re-establishing the echo of original learning?

9. Explain the following steps in learning a speech skill and give examples: target-set, scanning, searching, locating, fixing, stabilizing.

SUGGESTIONS AND ASSIGNMENTS

1. Alone in your room, practice babbling to sensitize yourself to the wide range of sounds a baby makes before he is imprisoned by the conventional sounds of our language. You will note as you proceed that you can regain the ability to make sounds that do not occur in English. Notice how much easier it is to say tongue twisters after having babbled a couple of minutes. Why?

2. Record your voice on tape or wire. Listen to it over and over again. As you do, you will reawaken self-hearing. At first you will hear only the quality. Then you may note the rhythm of your sentences, then the way you say particular words and sounds. If you listen long enough you can hear all the clicking and hissing sounds that you have forgotten to hear. This is best done by turning the tone control to high pitch.

3. Record a few memorized lines or read a short excerpt. Play this back and say the words as you listen. You will at first note a great difference. Keep doing this until the two merge. When they do, you are coming to hear yourself as you talk.

4. Practice a talk in an echoing room or with public address equipment. Start altering pitch, timing, and volume to find the point where the echo seems to reinforce, rather than irritate, you. What is the effect on the clarity of your mind? Do you feel a sense of self-cohesion and force?

If you are using public address equipment move back and forth from the microphone. What effect has this on you? Note the distance to the microphone you like best.

If public address equipment is not available for practice, try cupping your hand like a shell behind one ear. If the above technique disturbs you, causes you to have trouble, try speaking with cotton in your ears. What effect has this? Can you explain how "cupping" and cotton alter your hearing feedback?

5. Look in a mirror as you practice a speech. What happens to you? Do you like hearing yourself talk better than seeing yourself talk? Can you explain why or why not? Write a paper telling your instructor what you discovered in hearing and seeing yourself talk.

6. Take part in a panel discussion before the class explaining and comparing your echoes to hearing and seeing yourself with those reported by your fellow panel members.

7. Give a three minute talk on a memorable experience. In preparation look at the passing array of pictures in your mind. Search for language that translates these pictures into words which your audience will translate back into pictures.

a. After you have finished, tell the audience the major impression, the echo, you are now experiencing.

b. Have a member of the audience tell what part of your talk is still echoing in his mind. What value is there in doing this?

If people around you are spiteful and callous, and will not hear you, fall down before them and beg their forgiveness; for in truth you are to blame for their not wanting to hear you.

Fyodor Dostoyevsky

3

Responding to the Audience

SPEECH IS INTENDED for listeners. A most important task, then, is to find out about them. Most beginning speakers feel at sea; they do not know, psychologically, where the audience "is" in respect to their own position. Lacking direction, they imagine a host of vague requirements for effective speech. "I need to act intelligent, say something interesting, organize it well, put it in good language, speak fluently and with good diction, stand in good posture, be tactful, clear, effective. . . . " But what is good diction, good posture, good language? These thoughts flit through the student's mind as he prepares a speech. He tries to anticipate the demands an audience makes of a speaker, but he is not quite sure what they are. This chapter gives a general picture of the freedom and limitations of the speech situation, and suggests some techniques that will condition you to a proper relationship with your audience.

INTERNAL ADJUSTMENTS

Minimum Essentials for a Sense of Direction

1. *Putting Yourself in the Listener's Place.* The first thing to remember in order to see your audience and yourself realistically is that in the speech class you are talking to a group of people who are very much like yourself. They are not a group of scientists, a congregation of criminals, or an assemblage of kindergarten children. It will help you immeasurably during the first weeks of the term if you can drop any preconceived notions about your audience except this: that it is a group of people of the same age, with the same basic interests, and the same motives as yourself. Can you imagine the audience as a lot of "yourselves"? This is the basis of the faith which makes it possible to reach out and touch with talk.

The test of this faith is the ability to see and study the individuals who make up the group. Each time you prepare a talk, say to yourself first, "This talk is to be guided by my listeners." This constant reminder will give you an anticipatory set for speaking with the people for whom your speech is designed.

2. *Remembering That Listeners Are Kind.*   Second, remember that your listeners are sympathetic. How do you feel when you sit in the audience, listening to somebody like yourself talk? Do you want to laugh and injure him when he is in trouble? Do you want to discredit him when he does well? The chances are that you suffer when he suffers, triumph when he triumphs, become interested when he shows interest, and angry when he shows anger. Listeners, by the very fact that they are listening, accept momentarily the submissive role. To be submissive is to be kind.

It follows that you will not be rejected unless you reject the audience. It will do what you make it do. If you are friendly to it, it will be friendly in return. If you are indifferent to it, it will be indifferent to you. If you fight it, it will fight back. *If it laughs at you — horror of horrors — it does so because you are tense, giving the members of the audience a need for release from tension.*

All this is true of the audience in general. If somebody does laugh in order to feel superior, that is because he is less secure than the majority and needs to exploit the situation in order to compensate. There may be such a person in any class; your barometer is the response of the audience as a whole. The essential point to remember is that your audience is all right. Once you are thoroughly convinced that it is, you can begin to focus on the supremely important job of learning to listen as you speak — of *hearing yourself* so well in the speech situation that you can adjust to those whom you are asking to receive you. Directed by this attitude, you need not fear being offensive or being offended.

3. *Choosing a Topic.*   We shall have a good deal to say later about choosing a topic, and only one thing need be said at the moment. If you conceive of your audience as yourself in many forms, the choice of a topic is easy. Choose something that is interesting to you. What stays in your memory? What experience keeps returning with thrill, sadness, awe, or peace? If it stays with you, it can prob-

ably be made interesting and important to your listeners. A lake scene, the dog you had when you were a youngster, Christmas at home, the campus from your window, a military parade, a face that tells a story, the picture over the mantel, how to set traps, how to build a boat, how to make a stenciled placemat, how to use water colors, how to mix paints, how to improve human relations, the problem of discrimination, college athletics or politics, business opportunities — any topic that really interests you has a potential interest for your audience.

4. Discussing the Topic. The important question is not what topic to discuss but how to treat it. While the whole course in speech is wrapped around this problem, the most significant thing you can learn about treatment is to gain (and this is what this chapter is really about) the ability to see your thoughts as they will be seen by the listener. On the screen of memory, you are riding a train. You can see from the window the rush of the trees on the side of the hill. Unexpectedly you take the curve. You re-live the sense of freedom as your eyes sweep the valley. But your listener wasn't there. What can you say that will let him share the experience?

Perhaps the topic is the need for world government. Not all of your audience will agree with you. Their experiences are different, they magnify evidence that you discount. Do you understand the way they see your topic? The secret of making a speech interesting and acceptable is to see the difference between your own knowledge, memories, ideas, and opinions, and those of your listeners. To sense the significance of this point, note the ease with which you listen to one class speech and the energy demanded of you to get meaning from another. The topic may be the same, the organization and the delivery equally good. But one speech may penetrate your consciousness and the other pass over your head. So far as you can determine, the difference is one of language. Beneath that, however, the difference is in the speaker's sharpness in appraising the mental state of the listener. While there are many things to learn, this is the focal point in speech improvement.

Let us bring in a student to help us out. The following is an excerpt from a freshman speech. Anna is bright, but she has only a vague sense of her audience. Obviously she had a deep appreciation of the woman about whom she spoke, but only the delivery communicated this.

> If I were free to choose any personality in the world, I think I would choose to become Bell Carson. Mrs. Carson is only about four feet ten, but this height does not stop her from having a tremendous personality. Mrs. Carson has a very good education, but she does not boast of it. Instead she makes it her goal to have everyone like her and feel at ease in her presence. Mrs. Carson never becomes angry and just seems never to find fault in anything or anyone. If ever you have a chance to meet Mrs. Carson, I hope you will take the opportunity, because I'm sure you will find her just as wonderful as I have. . . .

Undoubtedly, each of these rather general statements aroused vivid memories for the speaker, so that her own response to her speech was one of real pleasure. But she was not communicating these memories; she conveyed only the fact that she possessed them. Essentially, she was talking to herself.

Jan, another girl in the same class, gave a speech entitled "The Hills of Home." One cannot read the following excerpt without becoming acquainted with Jan and feeling something of what a day spent at Jan's home was like for her.

> Driving north from Lawson, the first large farm you see is home. A little dirt road leads east up a hill, and there nestled among the maples and elms is the big white house. Beyond the house are the dairy barn, granary, tool sheds, and other buildings. To most people, it is just another farm, but to me it is home — where I find security, happiness, peace and the feeling of being needed.
>
> To the west the ground rolls down a valley and up the hill to a tall row of pine trees. Their dark green coolness in the summer and their crisp green in the winter, and the way the wind whispers and howls through their branches all fade into a picture that only seeing and hearing can complete. A little stream bubbles down the valley and on south to the creek. Looking north you can see the next farm about a mile away. To the northeast you can see the great white oak trees of the woodlot which is the highest elevation in our county. Then to the east the earth suddenly sinks to the fertile, black, tillable marsh land. Its black dirt contrasts against the green and brown of the crops and the blue of the sky. And then, on to the east and south, the ground begins its upward elevation, and for miles you can distinguish the different heights of trees; then they become misty and fade into space. . . .

Jan has the skill of describing her memories vividly enough to convey them to her audience. Seeing the difference between the content of her own mind and that of her listener, she has the basic set for communication. And how can this be achieved? If, throughout preparation and delivery of a speech, one keeps asking himself "And how meaningful is this to others?" he cannot go far wrong.

5. *Talking Normally.*   Students tend to feel that when they make a speech they are in a peculiarly formal situation and have to be something quite different from their normal selves. At first they are inclined to walk solemnly to the front of the room and begin, "Fellow classmates, it is indeed a pleasure to introduce to you . . . " This stiff, formal language sets up a high censorship on what is said and holds the audience at a distance.

There is every reason to be informal. Americans are essentially casual and extroverted; they like direct warm talk. As a speaker you cannot get your emotions and all the variations of your thinking into ceremonious expression. Nor is your everyday language, the language in which you are most skilled, forced and formal. Everything points to the wisdom of using your best everyday speech. It is disturbing to compare the awkward, dull phrasing and the colorless delivery of the classroom with the alert and vibrant expression of students in the halls. The thought in speeches should be more purposeful than the chatter between classes, but never at the price of boredom.

6. *Adapting As You Speak.*   No matter how well you have prepared, your audience will alter the language and the course of your speech. If it does not, you have the wrong set. Your target is the audience, not your prepared speech. Yet students are distressed to find that the speech situation affects the speech. "I prepared it very well. Then when I got up there it seemed to change." This is a common complaint, even after successful speeches.

We are not arguing for poor preparation, but for preparation modified by what happens during the speech. Anticipating change, you are not so likely to resist the inevitable. Indeed, the more you resist it, the more energy will be drained from the task of adjustment, the skillful maneuvering of yourself and your subject in response to the reactions of your audience. Search your audience and let the returning information modify the speech you have prepared.

7. *Accepting Your Voice.* Under the tension of their first talks, students often seem unable to speak in their normal voices. They also hear themselves more than they usually do. For both reasons they are frightened and driven to escape a study of the experience. While hearing is the key to change, the change cannot be in the right direction if the hearing is a shock. So you should be prepared to hear a strange voice when you first speak; this anticipation will help you accept it, evaluate it, and adjust it to your needs.

How to Stand

The audience requires a minimum of formal rules and regulations. Some students find it difficult to accept this fact; however, the study of a group of public speakers such as Winston Churchill, Carl Sandburg, Adlai Stevenson, President Eisenhower, and a host of others who might be mentioned indicates that the only rule which runs through their speech is that they marshal all their forces to the end of holding attention. Or consider those who use speech effectively in private situations: the salesman, the personnel manager, the counselor, the psychiatrist, the ambassador, the mediator. They follow no rules of action. Yet the learner wants a starting place, and he has a right to it. For this reason we suggest the following pattern for speech when you are standing:

Feet. The placement of the feet should depend on what is natural for the individual. Stand so as to permit grace and easy movement. Desirable foot positions can best be determined if you shift your weight to the balls of your feet and imagine you are about to step out onto the dance floor. With this posture, the position of the feet will take care of itself.

Knees. For relaxed alertness, your knees should be slightly bent. This gives a springy, agile, and assured character to your movements. Under tension, with the knees "locked," action is likely to be awkward, jerky, and trembling. With such a muscle set you cannot feel integrated and responsive. A slight bending of the knees gives the postural set you are looking for.

Hips and Trunk. Bending slightly forward at the hips helps to put the weight forward onto the balls of the feet. This posture calls into play muscles in the back which hold the body erect, and frees the muscles of the ribs and abdomen for proper breathing. Whereas normal breathing averages fourteen to seventeen inhalations per minute, speech slows this rate and usually increases the depth of the breath. Even under the most favorable emotional conditions, the very act of speaking is a challenge to the breathing mechanism. If you lean back on your heels while speaking, you put a third burden upon the muscles already taxed by speech.

Head and Shoulders. The late Franklin Roosevelt seemed to lunge into each phrase with head and shoulders. The unsure speaker tends to hold his head and shoulders tense and motionless. Muscles involved in forming sounds are directly related to all the other skeletal muscles, particularly those of the head and shoulders. The more the whole physical being goes to work on an idea, the more accurate is the diction and the more enlivened the speech.

Arm and Hand Movement. Obviously the more graceful and full-sweeping a speaker's movements are, the more expressive are his arms and hands. To achieve spontaneous and generous arm action, one of the more important considerations is the position of the elbows in relation to the trunk. Lack of assurance tends to bring the elbows close to the body. As a result, one gestures choppily from the elbow, as if the arms grew out of the body at the elbow instead of the shoulder. It is well to practice gesturing before a mirror. Hold your arms out and drop them slowly, searching for the point at which you feel the least muscle tension. This approximates the elbow position for graceful and energetic gestures. Once this position has been determined, gestures should be practiced. Practice daily until you get a feeling of grace and coordination. You will gradually transfer this "postural set" to the speech situation.

How to Sit

In discussion, of course, you are seated. While you will not then feel so vulnerable, your audience still wants you relaxed so that it can relax, yet it feels insulted if you sprawl. Search for a comfortable position, perhaps inclined slightly forward. Rhythmical breathing is important in speech whether you stand or sit.

Fluency and Action

In learning to pay attention to the audience you may find that your speech becomes choppy or even blocked. You may have so much to pay attention to that your language tangles and your tongue stumbles. When this happens you need to give yourself to rhythmical, smooth, and free action. If you feel the urge to move, sway, or walk about, and experiment shows that such action improves your command of thought and language, then you should move freely.

The free action of your hands and arms will be particularly helpful. It is possible that man talked with his hands before he resorted to words. His rise from a dark past is in large measure the story of what he has learned to do with his hands. Hands have a unique role in thinking.

Watch a resourceful speaker in trouble, when he is aware that he needs to find more pointed language. His hands will start wandering, flexing, and grasping. As his thoughts take form, his body rises, an expression of wonder replaces one of stress, his hands and arms make rhythmic movements. Try it when you are practicing your speech in private. Let your hands help you. Do not command them, let them work as they will; and when you need help in the real speech situation, call upon your hands.

EXTERNAL STIMULI TO ADJUSTMENT

The above suggestions will help your internal adjustments to the audience. What can you do to influence the external situation that will work to the same end? The answer varies according to your present attitudes. Your relationship to the audience depends on the amount of feedback you receive from your listeners. If you are painfully over-conscious of them, you cannot attend properly to speech communication. If you are indifferent to them, you may not sense the need for fine adjustment to their needs. Let us see what can be done to achieve a balance between these extremes.

Corrective Feedback From the Audience

Some persons are so constituted that their speech focuses naturally on the listener, as it should. Their interpersonal feedback is strong enough to tell them how their listeners are reacting, but not so strong as to blot out their original purpose. This balance can come about from three completely different motivations. Some people, who tend to be dominant, watch and adjust in order to control the listener. Others, who seek to gain recognition by pleasing, search for a way to become acceptable. A third group, halfway between these two, want to find the way in which they can cooperate with the listener on an even footing. The unmistakable clue to all these adjustments is the vocal quality and muscular set that lets the listener know he is being talked *with*, not *at*, *to*, or *past*. While the cooperative adjustment is the ideal one, aggressive and pleasing attitudes also make direct contact with the audience. The feedback which the sensitive speaker gets from the audience is an accurate reflection of how the hearers react to him, and he can therefore adjust as necessary.

Low Feedback From the Audience

But not all persons are fortunate enough to be in such close contact with their audience. Some tend to be independent and indifferent, and feel little need to make an impact on their listeners. Such people are at a disadvantage because the listeners in turn make little impact on them. An aloof speaker gives the impression that he is broadcasting in all directions, but to no one in particular.

If you are this kind of speaker, and you really want to talk better, you need to search more energetically for your target. Here are some things you can do to increase your awareness of the audience.

1. Turn on all the lights in the room, making it as bright as possible.
2. Get close to the audience. Walk up to the first row of chairs. Do not stand behind the desk.
3. Ask the listeners to slump and close their eyes when you become dull, to stare at you passively when you are only fairly interesting, and to concentrate on you when you are effective.
4. If the above signals do not stimulate you to search for a better adjustment to the audience, have one person, preferably the instructor, sit in the audience at the controls of a playback with the record of a masking noise.[1] When you are talking to your audience, he will fade out the noise. When you are talking to yourself, he will increase the volume of the noise until your decreased self-hearing causes you to adjust and search for the audience. The audience must be instructed not to react to the noise. If they do, they throw interference into your interpersonal circuit at the same time that you are trying to improve it.

[1] Any noise that interferes with communication is a masking noise. Pencil tapping will do, but a recording of noise is better, for it can be controlled more effectively.

The good speaker gets over to his audience, and they to him. The lines of communication are strong in both directions.

This may sound like harsh treatment. But the person who can benefit from this stimulation will not find it too distressing. He may even welcome the challenge.

Excessive Feedback From the Audience

Most students in beginning speech classes have the opposite difficulty. They suffer from excessive audience feedback; that is, they are too keenly aware of the audience. This awareness so fills their consciousness that they are unable to focus on their own ideas and so fail to think and speak coherently. Sensing the immediate source of all this stimulation the speaker revolts and cuts out the interpersonal circuit in an effort to gain equilibrium. Many students who respond this way do not see the audience at all. Some see it as a group, but do not distinguish individuals. Some see one or two faces, while the rest blur. Perhaps you have had the experience of shifting your attention to individual reactions and having that stimulation "jam your circuits." A few experiences of this kind and you fall into the defensive habit of looking at your notes, out the window — or even at the audience, but without seeing it.

The speaker who cares little about his audience usually gets the response he deserves.

When this happens the task is to find the conditions that permit self-hearing and other inner processes to operate normally at the same time that the attempt to make communicative contact with the audience is going on.

Here are some techniques you may experiment with until you find out what will help you tolerate that blinding reflection from the audience.

1. You may darken the room to whatever level of illumination seems comfortable. Classrooms are not equipped with rheostats, but you may put out the lights and pull the shades. This condition makes you feel more secure and allows you to maintain contact with your audience.

2. It is usually well also to move up to the first row of chairs.

3. Have the audience assume relaxed positions. This not only lessens your feeling of being challenged, but feeds back to you the message of relaxation.

4. Watch the audience as others speak. See if you can determine from postures and facial reactions what various ones are thinking.

5. After you have made several speeches in this manner, tell the audience what you remember of its behavior. You may have noted how much

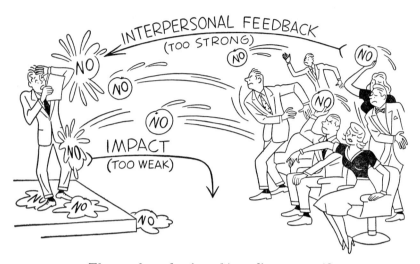

The speaker who fears his audience magnifies every re-
sponse. They affect him powerfully, and his message suffers.

restlessness there was (and at what point in the speech), who seemed to be pulling for you, who was difficult to interpret, who made you work hard for approval. Anticipating this exercise and actually performing it increases your capacity to tolerate audience responses and to adjust to them. This ability may carry over into your preparation for the next speech. A check of your interpretation against actual audience reactions is valuable verification.

Even more important, after each speech during the period when you are learning to adjust to listeners, you will profit by determining (1) how well you think you focused on your target as compared to your previous effort; (2) how the instructor and audience feel you related yourself to them as compared to your previous performances. It is with these reactions after speaking that you build a more and more accurate concept of the audience set. Don't resist the audience evaluation. They may be "wrong," but the improvement of communication begins with changes in the sender, not the receiver.

You have probably had the experience of walking down a corridor, turning a corner, and unexpectedly bumping into someone coming the other way. This "shocking" experience, "overshooting the target," results from a failure of the anticipatory set. You have also had the happier experience of hearing approaching footsteps around the corner and adjusting accordingly.

Much of your future speech growth depends upon "hearing" the audience reactions while you are "walking down the corridor." This refined skill comes as you learn to anticipate audience behavior. The first step in learning to predict your audience is to listen and to understand their evaluations after you have spoken.

Fixed Error

The above suggestions are directed to the student who finds the audience overpowering. They will be most helpful to the person whose interpersonal feedback is so great that he is relatively unstable. His very instability means that he will change, that he will respond to the pressures brought to bear upon him. In his random behavior he will occasionally bring the target into view; he may well hope to stabilize on it eventually.

In every speech class, however, there are several students whose audience feedback is excessive but who are yet stable. These students are quite composed, do a fair job, but do not improve. There are at least two reasons why they do not. Either they feel that the content of their speech is the target and therefore do not let the audience interfere, or they look alternately and rhythmically from their notes to their audience, suggesting that the feedback of each necessitates the need to go to the other.

Whatever the cause, those who find it necessary to concentrate on something besides the proper target need some kind of "shock" stimulation. The instructor may try the following techniques. When the speaker's attitude suggests an earnest effort to reach the audience, he will be permitted to proceed. When he talks to himself, to his notes, or to the wall, the instructor will start a masking noise, at first softly, then more loudly until it actually distresses the speaker, or he shows signs of trying to change. This procedure may be repeated each time the speaker drifts back into the pattern that excludes the audience.

Obviously, this experience is unstabilizing. But that is precisely what is needed: the particular pattern of stability needs to be broken up. If the noise is distracting enough and persists long enough, the speaker will search for and find the audience. The satisfaction of achievement, and the escape from the distracting noise, will then give the echo needed to direct further improvement.

Transfer From External Cues to Self-Control

As soon as such a speaker begins to talk rather directly with the audience, he should try to sustain the audience set without external support. The day he tries this he needs to be very well prepared. If the anticipating echo is strong enough, he will maintain the target set. If he loses it, he should return to the conditions that induce the proper response. This fluctuation from external aid to full self-control will, in the end, bring about the desired transfer.

Once stability is achieved, it should be followed by a speech to test it under disturbing conditions. The chairs may be rearranged, a visitor or two may be added to the audience, the instructor may stroll across the room, a couple of students may whisper. The speaker should have some voice in what the disturbance is to be, and should attempt only those situations within the range he can handle. This last step is for the future.

For the moment your concern is to get acquainted with the behavior of an audience. Your speech will improve as you learn (1) how to listen to the audience as it evaluates you after you speak, (2) how to think of your audience as you prepare a speech, and (3) how to read an audience as you speak. Most people learn to respond to an audience in these steps and in this order.

QUESTIONS FOR STUDY AND DISCUSSION

1. What is the ultimate purpose of speech?
2. Who sets the standards in the speech situation?
3. What are some values in thinking of the listener as yourself?
4. Are audiences kind? Explain.
5. How should you go about choosing a topic?
6. How does feedback apply to the problem of subject treatment?
7. What are some helpful rules for standing? For sitting?
8. How do differing degrees of interpersonal feedback affect speech?
9. What techniques can be used to change the interpersonal feedback?

SUGGESTIONS AND ASSIGNMENTS

1. Give a two or three minute talk to the class on any topic of interest to you. Ask the class to evaluate it in the following ways:

a. Did they like listening to you?
b. What did they find good in your talk?
c. What did they find fault with?
d. What did you say that carried a clear picture to them?
e. What did you say that might just as well have been left unsaid?

Tell the audience what disturbed you about yourself and see if they think you should change in that regard. Tell the audience what you saw in them that disturbed you. Begin thinking about what you are going to do to eliminate this difficulty.

2. Practice every day talking a speech idea to a mirror. This will condition you to the experience of having eyes upon you when you are trying to think and speak. If you can tolerate your own, you can others'.

3. When listening, watch other listeners. Jot down the things you read in their actions. Note the attitudes and beliefs revealed and the cues that lead you to each conclusion.

4. From the above observations prepare a short talk explaining what mannerisms, actions, and postures of his listeners the speaker uses to guide him.

5. For daily practice in learning how to read a listener, give your speeches to a friend. Arrange a set of signals whereby he may inform you when you are commanding his attention. As you become adept in responding to signals, try anticipating them by little cues of behavior. When you have learned to anticipate, have your friend listen while you signal him how you think your speech is being accepted. After the talk, check with him for verification.

You may expect some difficulty at first in learning to adapt to the use of such signals.

6. Arrange an informal social affair with class members. A picnic, luncheon, or any get-together, especially where you eat, gives the class a special bond and spirit. This may produce the faith in your audience that permits you to use your speech skills more freely.

7. Explain a simple process — how to make something, how to solve a puzzle or play a game. As you proceed, let the hearer interrupt at any time you are not clear. To make yourself understood is to improve your target-set. Note the difference in the way you talk, the language you use, and the clarity of your ideas when you make yourself understood.

We learn by doing.

John Dewey

4

Hints for First Speeches

ALTHOUGH MOST of your speaking is done in private or informal situations, such as conversations, discussions, and interviews, it is important to develop your skills in public performance for three reasons. First, there is no clear line of demarcation between private and public speech. If you are introduced at a party to a roomful of people, the tension you feel at becoming the center of attention is no different from the stress you experience in speaking to an audience. Second, if you fear those occasions when you are introduced to large groups or are asked to speak to groups, the recognition of that inadequacy lessens your confidence in all situations. You look upon yourself as limited in speech skills. So long as you feel this way, an undefined fear, destructive to natural skills, runs through all your speech. Finally, for most people, the public speech is the most distressing speech situation. If you run away from it, flight seems to prove your incompetence. If you try, and blunder or fail to live up to your hopes, this "failure" gives you proof of your limitations. So while public speaking is the least common form of speech for most of us, proficiency in it gives us added freedom and confidence in all social situations. The following suggestions will help you improve your public speech and therefore all your speech.

It is valuable to accept every invitation to speak publicly, for in the end you learn by doing. You will do well, however, not to expect too much of yourself at first, and to welcome unimportant occasions for speaking.

The Value of an Early Start

Begin to prepare for speeches, whether they are to be made in class or out, as soon as you learn of the assignment. It is wise to have at least a week's time to plan, and longer if possible. A speech needs growing time. Whenever an idea comes to you, jot it down. It makes

48

little difference whether at first glance it seems to fit in with other notes or not. The purpose of making such notes is to have a complete record of the ideas that have come to you during the "brewing" period. You can then select from a richer store.

How Much Material Is "Enough"?

You should gather far more material than you can possibly use. A little experimenting will be necessary in order to learn what is much and what is little. A well-prepared speech should not exhaust everything you know about a subject. When you stretch your knowledge to the limit, the strain undermines your confidence. If you cannot possibly say all you know, you gain security from wealth. Moreover, you will get a better reception, for an audience can usually tell when you have said everything you know. A speech which exhausts the speaker's knowledge will almost certainly be superficial, and it will seldom accurately reflect the most important things to be said. It is impossible for any of us, during a hasty period of preparation, to hit upon the most significant things to be said about a topic. It is only as we learn more and more that we can reassess what impressed us at the beginning and put it in proper relation to more important things that often emerge later. Has this not been much of the process of your education? Richness of knowledge and interpretation comes slowly and only with thought. The average student is inclined to feel that he has wasted his time if he gets something he cannot use. He thinks he has been inefficient and has done something he will get no credit for. Actually, what he knows and does *not* say enriches what he does say. A rich store of material is the basis of power and flexibility in speech.

Selecting Material

Three or four days before you are to speak, look over your ideas and select those that seem to fit into one speech. Arrange them in the order that looks most logical. The process of organizing is discussed in Chapter 8; at this point, we are interested in the initial steps of effective preparation.

Practicing the Speech

As a next step, find a room similar to the one you are to speak in, if possible. If not, go to your own room where you can be alone, *stand* at one end of the room, with your outline, and imagine that you are speaking to an audience. Two points are extremely important. First, once you start do not stop to correct yourself. To practice correction is to make a habit of what would be an error in the speech situation. If you stumble or have difficulty in getting from one point to another, plow through just as you will have to do when making the speech. Memory is continuity, and the best assurance of continuity in the speech situation is to practice the speech as a whole. After you have concluded, you may go back to the troublesome spots, find the trouble, and make some notes that will help you the next time through.

The second point is that it is important to overcome the sense of strangeness at talking when alone. Most students find the experience embarrassing. It seems to them unnatural and silly, and is therefore inhibiting. Indeed, at first, talking to oneself arouses a more than usual awareness of self, so that each movement and each inflection of the voice is disturbingly brought to attention. This is distressing because it takes one's mind off the content of his speech. All too often, having found this to be so, the student falls into the "more natural" activity of just sitting and thinking through the speech. But this decision is a bad one. Silent speech, or thought, is fleeting and incomplete. For ourselves a single word may arouse a whole chain of associations, while the same word said aloud may communicate nothing to another. When one tries to express the same idea aloud he discovers he must construct a sentence and find a correct word for each link in the chain. His ears, which are always feeding back to him his progress when he is in conversation with others, now tell him whether he is communicating anything even though he is speaking alone. Moreover, hearing oneself — an experience always associated with speech — helps to conjure up an audience. If you will persist during these first few trials in which self-consciousness is so devastating, you will find that hearing yourself talk will eventually excite your imagination. Once the audience "comes," the self-consciousness ceases. The imagined audience will react to your words and you will know rather well how your speech is progressing and when the preparation is complete. Students complain all too often that "I had it all prepared before I came to class, but when I got up there I couldn't get the ideas out. . . . And some of them acted sort of funny when I talked about my second point. That got me worried and threw me off. . . ." These statements reflect the need for a "trial run."

Speak to your imagined audience as many times as needed to gain a sense of assurance. Three or four times may be enough. Perhaps it will be a dozen. You will generally find that it does not pay to go over a speech more than two or three times at any given practice period. Never try to memorize a speech; rather, learn to welcome new phrases and words. You need not even mind if the organization changes somewhat. To be able to carry through the spontaneous development of your ideas is not only the greatest boost to self-confidence, but the best assurance of fresh and vital speech.

Preparing Key Statements

If you have trouble getting started in these rehearsals, in moving from one point to another, or in finding a conclusion that seems appropriate, write out satisfactory opening, closing, or transitional sentences. The attention of the audience is generally at its highest as the speech begins. Capitalize on this fact and get a good start. Moreover, the speaker's tension is usually greatest then, so that a well-chosen sentence or two at the beginning helps you over the worst. The audience is most likely to drift away from you when you are moving into a new idea. Therefore transitions must be clear and interesting. Finally, the conclusion is important. It will usually be a short summary, leaving with the audience the most significant impression, the core idea of the speech. In addition, if you finish with dispatch and decision, this last impression upon yourself gives you the confidence that makes the next speech easier. Students tend to overlook the preparation of a conclusion. A common closing begins with a glance at the instructor, followed by a puzzled look, and ends with the fade-away phrase, "I guess that's all."

Establishing the Rate

Practice being deliberate at the beginning of a speech. Perhaps no more common criticism is made of beginning speech students by other members of the class than, "He talked too fast." It should be understood that there is no "right" rate of speaking. The rate should vary with the temperament of the speaker and the emotions of the speech. But the fact that students so often criticize each other on this point indicates that the listeners feel hurried and perhaps robbed of a richness in communication they might have experienced had the rate been slower. To hurry in speech is to be chased by fear, and fear thrives on our efforts to escape it. Being chased, moreover, upsets three important parts of the speech process: thinking, movement, and breathing. No mind can organize efficiently if it is being rushed. Movement that is hurried is hard to coordinate. And we all know the discomfort of trying to talk while out of breath.

Yet we cannot speak well if our attention is centered on the rate at which we are talking. Anything that directs our attention away from what we are saying and its acceptance by the audience inhibits us. There is a way out of the maze, however. It is by learning to start right. You will find it best to walk deliberately to the platform, take your place at the speaker's stand, adjust your papers and any other materials you have with you, look over the audience, take two or three good deep breaths, and then begin to talk. Stop after a sentence or two and breathe deeply again. By consciously setting a pace at the outset that resists fright, you are less likely to fall into a race with fear.

This procedure must be practiced, not as you speak in class, but in your preparation beforehand. Take a seat at one end of the room, rise and walk slowly to the other end, carrying your notes and other materials. Then go through the other steps mentioned above. In the real speaking situation, a listener's second is a speaker's minute — or in some cases, eternity! You are not likely to start in a composed and collected fashion if you do not learn in practice, where there is no fear to confuse you, to judge the time element and to get the feeling of the right start.

Beginning and Ending

As a separate item in your preparation, practice beginning and ending the speech. This actually is a matter of combining your practice of key statements and rate. After you have planned the beginning and ending and have practiced walking to the front of the room, deliberately setting the stage for your speech, you are ready to put the two together. After the first few sentences, pause and pass to your concluding remarks, pause again, and walk to your seat.

Taking the Best Position Before the Audience

The physical relationship between the speaker and his audience has much to do with his mastery of the situation. The objective of your early speeches is not to learn a standard of behavior which might be called "proper." Rather, you should become thoroughly familiar with typical speech situations so that you develop such faith in yourself and the audience that you may in time adopt a form more generally approved. It is most important to get rid of the sense of *vulnerability* that many students feel when they step into the spotlight. Hence even in your initial speeches you should stand before the group, for reciting from a seat in the audience is hardly adequate training. With people to the back and sides of you, who cannot be seen, you can scarcely become oriented to the target. There are many ways in which a person may face an audience. At the beginning you should experiment to find the one that gives you the greatest assurance. The following physical arrangements are therefore recommended for beginning speeches:

a. If the chairs in the classroom are arranged in a circle, you may stay at your place and be in full view and be able to see all members of the audience. This is the most informal arrangement we can devise, which is not to say that it will be the most comfortable for every student. If one is to remain seated and talk he will find it an advantage to lean slightly forward. This gives him the maximum control over his breathing.

b. You may sit in a chair at a desk in front of the class with the chairs arranged in rows, in the usual audience fashion. This is more formal than the preceding arrangement, but still lets the speaker capitalize on the security of "being a smaller target." The introverted person is likely to find this more comfortable than sitting in the circle. The added distance from people may allow him, when under pressure, to feel more collected and in better control of the situation.

c. You may stand, "out in the open" before the class with no "props," or behind a desk, table, or lectern. If fear causes you to develop considerable nervous energy, you will have the urge to move around, or to find a relaxing posture. As Sarett and Foster say, it may be "helpful to lean on the speaker's stand. Such a posture lacks dignity and is slovenly, but it does help relax many muscles. Later, with increasing assurance, you should abandon reliance on the speaker's stand." [1]

d. If there is a raised platform or a stage at the front of the room, you may speak from that, though it is unlikely that you will want to do this in the early weeks of the course. Apparently a platform gives

[1] *Basic Principles of Speech,* Boston, Houghton Mifflin Co., 1946, p. 62.

mixed feelings. The speaker recognizes that the position lends power, but finds it difficult to identify this power with himself. Instead it serves to remind him of his own humble abilities.

A student should check with his instructor if it is not clear what speaking positions are to be used in a given assignment. He should practice accordingly in his preparation.

Mannerisms and "Negative Practice"

Some of our less desirable mannerisms come about without our being aware of them. If in the course of your speech training these are revealed to you in such a fashion that you do not fear them, yet desire to eliminate them, intentional practice raises them to the conscious level. Eventually, the muscular responses tripping off the sequence that leads to the undesired action or statement cues you to what is happening, and you lead into another choice of action. For instance, Ron spoke impetuously, and most of his ideas were tied together with "Oh, I don't know . . ." or "what I mean is. . . ." Doubtless there was fear behind these phrases, perhaps the fear that he was not making himself clear. At first he was unaware of the tiresome repetition. But when he practiced using these expressions as often as he could, both in daily ten-minute sessions at home and in class, he was able to recognize the muscle movements propelling him into the habit. First he came to know when he had just used one of these phrases; he got a delayed-action report. Later he learned to sense when he was about to say one of the phrases. At this point he was in a position to control the use of the comment; the habit was broken. Negative practice, therefore, is valuable in raising an unconscious act to the level of consciousness at which you can do something about it.

Meaningful Activity

Plan meaningful activity to replace random movement. We have indicated the need to commit consciously the errors that habit would have us commit. While this is a good first step, it is destructive, as the term "negative practice" indicates. But one can gradually learn how to put this energy into constructive movement related to speech. In the public speaking situation, the student may arrange his notes during those tempestuous early moments. Or he may adjust the position of the speaker's stand. If his talk can be highlighted with diagrams, sketches, charts, or pictures, the wise speaker will use them.

He may use a model, draw a sketch, or put some important figures on the blackboard. He may arrange to have a short distance between the stand and the blackboard and work between his notes and the board. If the action is too complicated it may be confusing. But if you *plan your movements as you act out the speech in practice*, it will not be. Be sure that in practice you have, or imagine you have, a blackboard or whatever it is you are to work with. Not to do so is to invite self-consciousness in the performance, which in the end is to lose confidence in the techniques for improvement.

Work versus Worry

One of the common faults of preparation is to substitute worry for work. It is easy to worry so much that each actual approach to preparation is emotional and ineffective. As is explained in Chapter 19, the anticipation of a feared experience arouses the fear. As a result, so much energy is dissipated in cursing the instructor, the assignment, the pressure of other duties, and one's own inadequacy, that little is left to do the job. When this happens, one is blindly following the urge to avoid the pain aroused by taking preparatory steps toward the feared situation. Such avoidance gives the student the illusion that he has worked hard on the assignment, while all he has actually done is build up his anxiety. As a result he not only wastes his preparation time but gets "worked up" and thereby impairs his mental efficiency. He comes to the hour of speech unable to concentrate. His nerves are on edge and his behavior in the speech situation is random, disorganized, and frustrating both to himself and to his audience.

The following topics suggest talks that may be helpful in shifting from me-ness to we-ness, for they deal with strong feelings and interests. A topic that stirs your interest arouses the only force that can overcome the tendency to fret as you prepare.

1. My Favorite Author
2. A Fascinating Invention
3. The Place I Worked Last Summer
4. A Summer as a Deck Hand
5. New York City
6. Jets
7. The Fun of Fishing

   8. On the Trail of a Deer
   9. A Summer Counselor
  10. What I Expect to Get Out of College
  11. My Record Collection
  12. What a Waitress Learns About People
  13. Two Years in the Army
  14. My Hobby
  15. I'll Never Forget
  16. A Different Kind of Person
  17. It Wasn't Funny
  18. How the Other Half Live
  19. Strange Customs
  20. The Greatest Problem of Our Day
  21. What I Learned on Our Senior Trip
  22. How It Feels to Be in an Auto Accident
  23. The Best Buy on the Market
  24. The Life of a Caddie
  25. Working in a Factory

Evaluation

After a speech which you have carefully prepared, have your audience pick out the strongest and weakest parts of your speech. This should indicate to you where your preparation is poor and where it is good. In the next speech try to remedy your most obvious weakness.

Pay particular attention to the subsequent chapters that deal with your greatest needs as they are shown by these evaluations.

Preparation for Impromptu Speeches

We have been discussing preparation for the speech of which you have some advance warning. What of the occasion at a dinner, a committee meeting, or a conference, when out of a clear sky you are asked to say something? The impromptu situation sharpens fear, for it makes a sudden raid upon your resources. You can, however, devise daily practice that develops the skill to meet that test. Gather a list of subjects that you know something about, but upon which you have not spoken. Go to one end of your room, choose a topic at random from your list, and talk for two or three minutes. Try this for two or three subjects in each practice session. After any effort in which you have done worse or better than usual, evaluate what you have said to determine the cause. Then give the speech again, correcting weaknesses or reinforcing strengths in accordance with your evaluation. Keep a list of the points made in these evaluations. Look them over before you practice again. The development of this skill may be tested by occasional impromptu speeches in class.

Following is a suggested list of topics for impromptu speech practice:

1. An Industry in My Home Town
2. Women in Industry
3. The Redwoods
4. The Sierra Nevadas
5. Military Training
6. My Favorite Sport
7. My Favorite Food
8. My First Job
9. Our President
10. If I Were President
11. A Famous Person I Have Met
12. A Game I Shall Not Forget
13. My Favorite Television Program
14. An Unlucky Experience
15. The Best Movie I Have Ever Seen
16. Why I Like Living in the City
17. What I Plan to Do Next Summer
18. My Favorite High School Teacher
19. Something (or Someone) I Would Like to **Be**
20. Home Town
21. Summer Vacations
22. My Family
23. Chapel Services
24. A Saturday Night
25. Television versus Radio
26. Our Basketball Team
27. The Kids in Our Neighborhood

28. Why I Came to College
29. College Social Events
30. My Favorite Magazine
31. Summer Sports
32. A Lonely Place
33. A Strange Coincidence
34. My Favorite Course
35. A Trip
36. Close to Death
37. A Dream
38. A Beautiful Sight
39. Dorm Life
40. My Ambition
41. A Description of My Home
42. College Compared to High School
43. What Baseball Gives to the United States
44. Playing Golf (Tennis, Basketball, etc.)
45. Me and the Army (Navy, etc.)
46. Hunting With a Camera
47. My Most Amusing Speech Experience
48. What Shall We Do About Communism in America?
49. What About Violence on Radio and TV?
50. Hobbies
51. What I'd Do With a Million Dollars
52. Political Spellbinders
53. Persons Who Love the Limelight
54. The Most Effective Speaker I Have Ever Heard
55. My Nomination for Public Bore Number 1
56. What Are the Earmarks of a Good Book?
57. A Truly Great Athlete
58. What Constitutes a Gentleman?
59. The Life of the Party
60. A Hypocrite
61. A Quaint Character in Our Country
62. A Man in Whom I Have Great Faith
63. An Able Interpreter of Literature

64. My Favorite Actor
65. Today's Big News Story
66. A Great Naval Officer
67. A Great Sermon I Heard
68. The Scrooge of Our Town
69. What Constitutes a Lady?
70. A Man Victorious Even in Defeat
71. The Greatest Virtue
72. My Favorite Composer
73. How Speakers Betray Themselves
74. A Man Is a Part of Everything He Sees
75. A Graduate of the University of Hard Knocks
76. What the World Expects of a College Man
77. Jesus as a Speaker
78. What Things in Life Are Worth Fighting For?
79. What Youth Can Do to Prevent War
80. False Social Standards
81. Every Man Is Entitled to a Job
82. If Christ Were to Return Today
83. The Worship of the God Mammon
84. The Problem of the American Negro
85. A Great Military Leader
86. Do Fraternities Justify Their Existence?
87. What is a "Good" Fraternity?
88. The Rights of Minorities
89. The Kind of World I Love
90. No Man is Whipped Until He Admits It

QUESTIONS FOR STUDY AND DISCUSSION

1. Why is public speaking an important skill to learn, even if you have little intention of becoming a public speaker?

2. What are the steps in speech preparation?

3. Why is it important to collect more material than you can use for your speech?

4. Why is it important, in practicing a speech, to say it aloud rather than think it silently to yourself?

5. If you are going to write out parts of the speech, which should they be? Why?

6. What is the importance of beginning slowly?

7. What four physical relationships can be established for the speech situation?

8. Describe a technique for eliminating undesirable mannerisms.

9. How can you learn to replace random activity with meaningful activity?

10. Discuss the process of daily practice in impromptu speaking. What is the value in learning impromptu speech?

Faced with sudden and capricious changes in his environment, man has methods at his disposal, if he will but use them, to combat such threats effectively.

John R. Kirk

5

Meeting the Situation

"I THOUGHT I had improved until I spoke at the Political Science Club. I was just as bad as ever. I was scared. My organization wasn't any good. I don't know. I might just as well not have taken the course." One of the most serious disappointments a student can have, after taking a speech course, is to meet a new or different situation some months later and find that some mistakes he made as a novice are still clamoring to make their presence known.

There are two things to remember about this experience. First, you are very likely to have it. It is practically impossible to reduce fear and increase skills so much in a single year that you will not suffer under the pressure of new situations. Indeed, it takes years of experience as a successful speaker to gain even a reasonable assurance against the hazards of new situations. Merely to keep this thought in mind will have its favorable effects. Being forewarned, if you should have a bad experience you will have steeled yourself against the blow; you will understand also that speech training is not magic and does not replace sound preparation.

The second thing to remember is that in your speech training you need the experience of meeting many kinds of situations — and increasingly difficult ones — after you have attained some skill. To learn many different skills under adverse but not impossible conditions is the hard road but the only road to speech improvement. The wise course is to accept this "hardening up" process as you would welcome the challenge of a game. You are both wise and courageous if you do not object to speaking under difficult conditions. You may not do as well as you might otherwise, but so long as you have mastery of the situation, you are becoming more and more flexible.

UNSTABILIZING INFLUENCES

The first step in achieving this flexibility is to have the pressure of the situation fluctuate quickly between the easy and difficult several times during the same speech. When you are ready to subject yourself to this stretching experience, you should plan to make a prepared or an impromptu speech, whichever is the easier for you. You should also choose the most comfortable physical relation to your audience — before or behind the desk, with or without a lectern. The first time or two the situation is intentionally made difficult, you should be told what kind of novelty you are going to face. For instance, you may know that books are going to be dropped on the floor, or that two students will break out in laughter at some point in your speech. Later you should speak several times when you know disturbing influences are going to be introduced, but do not know what they will be. Finally, you may profit from having the totally unexpected happen.

Four Reactions to Interruption

When the unstabilizing influence is brought to bear, you may be thrown off your course. Obviously your task is to try not to let this happen. There are four ways of reacting to such situations, any one of which is acceptable, according to the circumstances. One adjustment is simply to ignore the interruption or distressing stimulation, to close your mind to it. This is particularly effective if your recognition of the disturbance will be embarrassing to a member of the audience. For instance, if a listener is seized by a coughing spell (whether by instruction or by accident) he is probably better ignored. A second response is to stop and wait until the interruption is over. Perhaps there is a loud knock, the door opens, and one of the instructors walks in asking for Luella MacDonald, who is wanted on the phone. It is scarcely polite to go on talking — and probably futile, for all eyes follow the lovely Luella as she makes her departure. A third adjustment is to maintain your purpose and hold the attention of the audience despite the distraction. The furnace blower comes on, passing students stop outside the classroom door to talk a few minutes, a truck grinds up the hill. If the annoyance is of some duration perhaps you can speak louder and overcome it. The fourth and final adjustment is to incorporate the disturbance into your remarks. An apt answer to the tape recorder that just squealed will bring the startled audience back to you. A bit of imagination suggests that combinations of these adjustments are possible.

Many disturbances are unplanned and unexpected, and they may last too long or be too distracting for you to combat successfully. If so the best you can do is wrestle manfully against defeat. In learning to overcome manufactured interruptions, it is best to have two or three in a speech, so that you may receive the conditioning that comes from moving back and forth between conditions of pressure and security. Your instructor will not permit one of these difficult moments to come at the end of your speech; you always need a strong finish if you are to associate mastery with experience.

As soon as you have finished speaking, evaluate your technique for handling the disturbances. Tell the class how skillfully you think you were able to adjust. Check your judgments with the comments of your listeners. If your speech was recorded, listen to it after class, and compare it with the evaluation you made immediately after speaking. Write down what you think you have learned about yourself in this situation. Select a particular objective for your next experience. In practicing speeches you should have your roommate create annoyances, so long as they are within the range you can cope with.

Fluctuating Annoyances

For home and the classroom situation, the following "unstabilizers" are useful.

1. A stranger walks in after you have started, sits down, gets up and leaves a minute later.
2. One listener reacts unpredictably. He laughs unexpectedly, opens a newspaper and starts reading, or leans forward in exaggerated interest. Such interruptions frequently happen, as any experienced public speaker can verify.
3. As you speak, walk to the back of the room, stay there and speak for a minute. Cease talking as you come forward, continue as you turn about at the speaker's stand.
4. Walk behind a screen that has been set beside the speaker's stand. Continue your speech for a minute before you step out in view again.
5. Use a microphone for one minute of your speech.
6. Have the audience laugh in ridicule two or three times, first at your signal, later at the signal of an appointed listener.

7. Have two or three listeners fall to whispering periodically, first at your signal, later at the signal of a member of the audience.

8. Instruct the audience to begin gathering books and to lean forward as if about to leave. (What instructor has not faced this? Student watches are never accurate!)

9. A student goes for a drink and returns a minute later. (You should speak at a convention!)

10. Walk back and forth in the aisle for a minute of your speech.

11. Pass out papers as you speak.

12. Ask a student sitting by the window to open it. Continue your speech as he does so.

13. Give a speech of demonstration, using your models or other material periodically throughout the speech.

14. Put on and take off your topcoat as you speak.

15. Read two or three well-chosen quotations that fit into your speech.

These are a few of many contrivances that may be used. Perhaps the more they approximate real situations the better, but the important thing is that they keep changing and that they be difficult yet not so difficult that you cannot master them.

Constant Annoyances

As a beginning device and for much of the course, the kind of interruptions described above give better practice than constant annoyances, for they permit several recoveries in rapid succession. The sense of difference in your body set between moments of security and pressure sensitizes you to the posture you assume to meet stress. Yet there is value in adjusting to constant annoyance, for it too is a kind we often have to face. But this kind of challenge should not be faced until you have become accustomed to the "stretching techniques" above. Until you learn how to recover, a bad situation may be overwhelming and may teach you to fear new speech situations rather than adjust to them.

When you are ready, the following more extended stress situations are suggested.

1. Give before another class a speech which your classmates considered well done. Immediately thereafter write down the differences between your *impressions* and *reactions* in the two situations. How did your

speech change in the second? Why? Hand ın this paper; it may help your instructor devise assignments for your special needs.

2. Speak to your class in a different classroom. Evaluate the effects immediately thereafter. Compare your reactions with those of your classmates.
3. Stand on a bench or a chair and give an announcement or a speech. Compare your impressions and behavior with those of your audience.
4. Speak from the stage of an auditorium. Evaluate as above.
5. Have two students whisper throughout your speech.
6. Speak from a carefully prepared manuscript. Tell your listeners to become restless and scrape their feet when you fail to hold their interest.
7. Speak in clothes you do not normally wear to class. They should be better or worse than the usual ones, since either kind will have a disquieting influence. If you are particularly sensitive to your appearance, try better and poorer clothes in consecutive speeches.

MEETING VICTORY AND DEFEAT

Whether we like it or not, western culture places the highest value upon the victory of one man or group over another. As a result, most of us have a delirious love of success and a shocking fear of defeat. Unless we learn to meet both sucess and failure, we are vulnerable.

It is possible to give a good speech and to be unstabilized by the victory, upset by the applause, incapable of accepting the praise with poise. This is the lowest price which victory may cost. Those who yearn too much and too long for the glory of success in speech, or in anything else, grow to be victory addicts, and live in misery except during those hours when they are under the influence of winning. Actors, athletes, politicians, and speakers must guard against these needs. The pleasure of experiencing success should always be mixed with humility and a recognition that the fates are whimsical.

Nor are the effects of defeat entirely helpful. It is even possible to improve and to do our best job in a speech in which we suffer the humiliation of rejection by the audience. The tragedy is that failure in the eyes of men so often fixes our own eyes on failure. We then stumble further into error, making mistakes below the usual level of our skills.

There is nothing to be gained by deploring these facts. But there is much to be learned by understanding the problem and training ourselves so that we may grow in victory and in defeat.

188923

Victory

Following are some victorious experiences which you may practice adjusting to, through role-playing:

1. Have one of your classmates introduce you with considerable praise in your next speech.
2. Give a speech, playing the role of the main speaker at a banquet.
3. One of your classmates will nominate you for the presidency of the class. Make a short acceptance speech.
4. A classmate may present you with a plaque for having been selected as the best speaker of the class. Make a short acceptance speech.
5. One of your classmates presents you with a school "letter" before the student body in assembly, or at a dinner. Make an appropriate response.
6. A student shakes your hand and welcomes you into the fraternity. Make a proper response.

These assignments should be recorded and studied carefully later. The evaluations of the class, of course, are valuable. If possible, it is extremely helpful to have a motion picture of these to study.

Such assignments can be easily subverted. If you make a joke of the role, you are evading and you learn nothing.

Defeat

The following are defeats that teach you how to adjust to humiliation:

1. Try to persuade the class to a belief or action which from the outset you know they will not accept. You have a dual duty here, to be as earnest as possible and yet detached enough to accept rejection without being hurt.
2. The next time you feel the urge to complain about a grade or a purchase, register your dissatisfaction even though you feel your chances of success are small.
3. When you have an unintentional speech failure, whether in talking with a classmate or in giving a speech, search out a similar situation as soon as possible.[1]
4. List a number of situations in which it would be difficult to accept failure. You hate to be turned down when you ask for a job, or a date. You find it embarrassing to be criticized for giving a wrong answer in class. It makes you uncomfortable to have a speech criticized. Intention-

[1] See pages 394–395 for a discussion of the value of "negative practice."

ally perform these tasks poorly enough to evoke an unfavorable response. Before you try such a situation, play the role of failure with a roommate.

These are probably the most difficult assignments you can perform. But if you can meet such defeats with equanimity, you will gain a freedom and courage you probably did not know existed. The truly adventurous personalities are those who can walk into the jaws of rejection with a laugh.

Sometimes we pay a high price for mistakes, but we can make no mistake so great as to follow a path directed by the fear of blundering, for achievement is built, in part, on the correction of error. It is tragic that our culture punishes so heavily for error, but it does. In so doing it seldom stops errors, though it does stop people. To reach your potential you must learn to live in an emotional field in which you are not paralyzed by the urges of victory and defeat. To learn this is to become free, free to guide yourself.

The Need For Practice

Time will permit you only a limited number of these experiences in the classroom. Therefore while you are working on assignments with unstabilizing influences, you should practice meeting similar situations outside of class each day. In class and out, invent original situations of your own, but before each speech tell the class what novelty you tried in practice. This exchange of ideas will help your classmates manufacture original techniques for their practice sessions.

Your instructor may choose to introduce unstabilizing assignments each time he thinks you have learned to fix a desirable aspect of your speech. For instance, when your tensions have habitually lowered, he may raise and lower the pressures in a speech to teach you to stretch your power to maintain easy control. Or after you have learned to produce a well-organized speech, he may upset the situation to test, and even overpower, your ability to maintain equilibrium. You should be able both to meet the applause accorded a well-organized speech and to face a situation so difficult that it teaches you how to handle yourself when your organization goes awry.

You will tend to resist and resent anything which, at the moment, subtracts from your skills, but, as suggested earlier, these assignments are necessary if your speech course is going to help you meet new situations.

QUESTIONS FOR STUDY AND DISCUSSION

1. What is the purpose of giving you pressure situations?

2. What are the four ways in which you may favorably adjust to a disturbing influence?

3. As a teaching technique, why does this book favor the situation that fluctuates between stress and ease?

4. What is the value of learning to speak in situations of persistent stress?

5. What are the values of meeting actual victory and defeat?

Part Two

Speech and Thinking

———

Mind and Message

So FAR WE HAVE focused mainly on the relation of the speaker to his audience, for good speech grows out of an honest wish to make contact and to communicate. But good speech communicates *something*, and it is time we turned our attention to the nature of this message.

The message of speech is the embodiment of thought. It may be considered the ammunition we use in trying to hit the target of effective communication. Communication usually brings people together, and destroys them only when misused. Nevertheless there is value in drawing an analogy between speech and ammunition. For we do direct our speech at each other, no matter how mercifully.

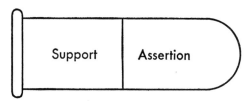

The ammunition of speech is molded in the speaker's thought. His assertion is a projectile powered by support, and the shell is language. We shall be concerned with all these matters in the next four chapters. Let us begin by considering the basic nature of the ammunition which is the material of thought and speech.

ASSERTION AND SUPPORT

The essentials of a thought are an assertion and the reasons for it.

"This is a nice day." — assertion or conclusion (projectile)
"Why?"
"The sun's out, the air's clear, the temperature is 72." — reasons, evidence, or support (powder)

71

Sometimes the ammunition can be just an assertion. "It's a nice day." "America's foreign policy is changing." "The best buy is Fordillac." Such statements may be like bombs, the projectile and the powder exploding in all directions out of themselves.

But disciplined thinking involves more than a series of unguided mental explosions. It takes on direction, which means that power is assembled behind an assertion. To supply this power, the mind must be inhibited enough to ask "why" or "how." Somebody has said that the difference between the impulsive and the disciplined mind can be expressed in the following two responses to a colorful picture.

"Oh, how lovely!"
"What is it?"

The first is a bomb of reaction governed by the senses and the emotions. The second restrains itself, asking a reason beyond immediate gratification. Thinking which just happens is quite different from thinking which withholds judgment until the evidence is examined.

It should be clear, then, that the units of disciplined thought — and speech — are assertion and support, conclusion and evidence, projectile and powder.

Assertion and support — conclusion and evidence — are not separate things like tables and chairs. Disciplined thought is in motion and has direction; it moves from evidence to conclusion, and its course is guided by the nature of the evidence. Moreover, a statement which may be a conclusion in one thought sequence may become the evidence for a new conclusion in another. For these terms express relationships, not absolutes — just as one point on a map (say Pittsburgh) may be east in relation to a second (Chicago) but west in relation to a third (New York). Note in the following chain of statements how the relations change. In each the support is in italics.

> The dangers of a disease must be weighed against the dangers of the cure *because the ill effects of the cure may be the greater.*
> *The dangers of the disease must be weighed against the dangers of the cure.* For this reason we do not dare act hastily in this case.
> The ill effects of the cure may be greater than the disease, *for the drug in the medicine is hard on the heart.*

In each of these statements the support is the reason for the assertion. It is the powder which propels the projectile. A sentence may contain support, assertion, or both, and the support may precede or follow the assertion. You can easily tell which is which because the support gives the reasons for the assertion.

Description

In all but the simplest speech, support and assertion are amplified by what we may call description. Either by definitions or by word pictures, we fill in the background around the main terms of our statements to make them fully understandable, vivid, and memorable. Notice how the italicized phrases amplify the central thought and complete the meaning.

The grid *in a vacuum tube* regulates the flow *of electrical energy.*

The stripped statement, "The grid regulates the flow," would be quite obscure.

English is *the most widely spoken* language *in the world.*

Again the bare statement, "English is language," has almost no meaning.

The descriptive parts of our language, which modify, amend, and shape our main statements, make communications full and accurate. If support and assertion are properly related and adequately described, the ammunition of speech is good.

Creative Thinking: From Support to Assertion

Creative thinking is the process of moving from the known to the unknown. "It's Friday evening. No classes tomorrow. My allowance came today. [Flash!] Tonight's a good night to take in a show." The first three "knowns," because of their harmonious relationship, lead to and become support for an assertion, a new known — which in turn might become the support for a new assertion, which . . . and so on. This is creative thinking.

Speaking: From Assertion to Support

While our thinking must move from the known to the unknown, our speech generally operates in the opposite direction, beginning with the assertion. Thus when the idea of going to a movie "dawns" on you, you are very likely to say to your studious roommate:

"Hey, fellow, let's go to a show."
"What's on?" asks your friend.
"I don't know. Come on, let's go."
"Why?"
"Well, it's Friday, isn't it? I've got money. Come on."

Here the support comes last. Often indeed, it is expressed only when the assertion is challenged.

Sometimes for dramatic effect, or when we suspect a listener will oppose our views, we give the evidence first and build up to the assertion. But in ordinary discourse, where the essential need is clarity, the reverse is the rule. Why? Because the assertion-support sequence gives headlights to our speech. It enables the listener to follow us more easily, for we tell him where we want to take him when we start.

How We Reach Conclusions

Reaching a conclusion that fits the evidence — a projectile that fits the powder — is the trickiest operation in human thought. Consider the process that led you to be a college student. How did you make the decision? Following are some of the reasons we often hear:

I was interested in the high school studies that lead to college.
I was too young to go to work.
I didn't know what I wanted to do.
Everybody should get as much education as he can.
Nobody can take an education away from you.
It is difficult to get a good job without a college education.
My parents wanted me to go.
I want to be a lawyer, and law requires a college education.
I want the prestige of being a college graduate.
I wanted the experience of college social life.
I just wanted to know more.
All my friends were going.

No matter what combination of these or other reasons led you to believe you should go to college, it is important to recognize that your mind made a "because" bridge from reason to decision. There is no way in the world for you to know whether you will be interested in college *because* you were interested in high school, whether you will profit from college *because* you were too young to work, whether college is right for you *because* you did not know what else to do. It is the nature of human thought that we gamble with reality when we assert a belief. Two or more things associate favorably or unfavorably in the mind. The uniting force is expressed in the word *because* or its equivalent.

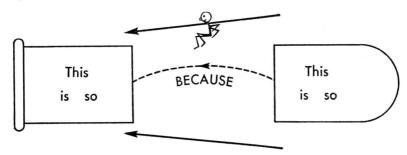

For this reason two or more people can agree on the support for a conclusion and still arrive at different conclusions.

1. We should attack nation X
2. We should send a strong note to nation X
3. We should take the problem of nation X to the UN
4. We should compliment nation X

because Nation X has taken an aggressive move.

Because the same evidence can lead to a variety of conclusions, all of us need to appraise carefully the assertions we make and hear. *To test, we must forget the assertion for a moment and ask, "What does the evidence say?"*

Relationships That Make Us Say "Because"

There are two kinds of relationships that lead us to join two statements with *because*.

1. Association in Time or Place. If two or more things happen at the same time or place, thus coming to your attention at the same time, you are likely to associate them. The association may lead to a true conclusion or to a false one. Suppose you are on your way to a football game. As you approach the stadium you notice an exceptional number of cars. You conclude the game is drawing a larger crowd than usual. You hurry, push, and make yourself generally unpleasant, only to find the stadium partially filled. Later you learn there were two conferences on the campus that afternoon. Many cars *near* the stadium *at* game time caused you to make a faulty "leap."

Again, suppose you see a policeman, two stopped cars, and an approaching ambulance. So you conclude — "Look, there's been an accident." But the ambulance goes by, a man walks out of a nearby house, and gets into one of the cars. The policeman gives the driver of the other car a ticket and walks to his motorcycle. As the driver of the second car at the scene of the "accident" departs, he grumbles "And for going 30 miles an hour!"

In both these cases the mental leaps were wrong. But they might just as easily have been right. There is no logic to insure the wisdom of the leap. The only protection is the weight of evidence. The more support for a leap, the more likely it is to be correct. In the first example above, had people been getting out of the cars and walking toward the stadium, and had there been unusually long lines at the ticket windows, we would have had additional, even though not conclusive, evidence for anticipating crowded stands.

2. *Association by Sequence.*   If one thing follows another we are likely to consider it the effect of the other. John had pneumonia and died. We would say, and generally with accuracy, that John died *because* of pneumonia. But he *could* have had a heart failure, committed suicide, or been poisoned by a jealous wife. Perhaps, even, the truth of the matter is that in a high fever he threw himself out of bed and broke his neck.

There are four possible errors in relating sequential occurrences, that is, in asserting cause-to-effect relationships in such cases.

a. No Relationship May Exist.   An accidental time relationship can be easily misinterpreted as causal, even though no such connection

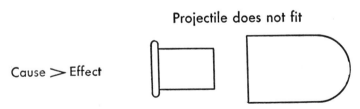

Projectile does not fit

Cause $>$ Effect

exists. The black cat and the four-leafed clover have yet to be proved as causes of bad or good luck. The watched pot boils as quickly as any other, and there is no evidence that Friday the thirteenth brings more misfortune than any other day. The stock market crash of 1929 occurred under a Republican administration, and in the following election, a Democratic President was elected by an overwhelming majority. But the economic situation was so complex that there was no justification for people to assume, as many did, that the Republicans had "caused" the crash and the depression. Conversely, during the New Deal period, it was common for opponents of the program to argue that various government regulations were strangling free enterprise. Yet there is every evidence that free enterprise and individual initiative were undiminished during the thirties and since. It is never safe to assume that because one event precedes another, the first is cause and the second result.

b. *Additional Causes May Exist.* Two or more causes operating at the same time to produce a given effect must all be taken into account if the causal leap is to be justified. It is common for people to com-

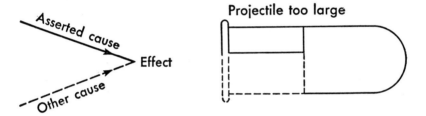

plain that successful sons of wealthy and influential men would not themselves hold responsible positions if it were not for their fathers' help.

> "What's he got that I haven't?"
> "A father who's President of the Inland Boat Company."
> "Aha!"

No one doubts the value of a wealthy father. But heredity and environment together explain most of what we are, and in this case these factors operate in the same direction as "pull."

Let us see how this kind of reasoning operates in formal speech.

> America should attack Russia and have this thing over with. Russia has the "A" and "H" bombs. Her eventual goal is world domination. We had better attack before she has the armament advantage.

Most of us would reason that the support here is not big enough for the assertion. In the language of logic, we would say the conclusion is a hasty generalization.

c. *Additional Effects May Exist.*   Our leap to a conclusion may be bad because we fail to recognize that the same cause may be followed

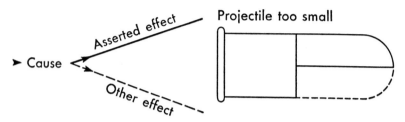

by more than one effect, either in harmony with or opposed to the one we have discovered. Thus foreign aid may eliminate starvation, but it may also produce resentment. When a person takes penicillin he expects to be rid of his infection. He may, however, be in bed for several weeks with penicillin poisoning — and no trace of the original infection. Dependable thinking takes into account the additional possible effects as well as the predicted effect.

d. *Counter Causes May Exist.*   Finally, we sometimes make the error of expecting a given effect which fails to develop because we

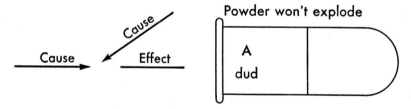

overlooked opposing causal forces. Because of the complex operation of causes, two people may be exposed to a disease and one will contract it while the other will not. Or two boys may come from the same home, and one will become an engineer and the other a lawyer. Intelligence, achievement, and aptitude tests may predict that a given student cannot do passable college work. Yet he may do well because he wants so badly to be a chemist that he is willing to pay the price in hard work. World policy makers, after World War I, stripped Germany of her colonial empire, arguing that a nation without natural resources cannot wage war. They did not foresee the future of Germany's foreign trade and the synthetic production of oil and rubber, which made it possible for Germany to revive her economic and military strength and so to fight again even without essential strategic materials drawn directly from natural sources.

All leaps in human thinking from support to assertion result from (1) association in time and place or (2) the sequence of events. The leaps may or may not be justified. Checking against the support is the only test.

How We Get Support

We get all our support for what we say, if we trace it back far enough, from what we or somebody else observed or thinks he observed. With eyes, ears, and other sense organs, all of us have been receiving impressions since birth. All our stored-up experiences, what others have written or told us, and the things we see at the moment we speak, constitute the support we offer for assertions.

Your speech instructor — indeed all your professors — are concerned that you develop as much skill as possible in first-hand observation. As you well know, the more ears and mouths a statement passes into and out of, the less likely it is to be accurate. Each of us puts his own errors into a message. We forget parts of it and create new ones to fill the gaps, or we simply misinterpret. It follows that the closer you are to the original observation, the more likely you are to be accurate.

But do not for a moment assume that your observations are always accurate and dependable — though the more you are aware that you might be wrong, the more likely you are to be right.

Causes for Error in Observation

There are two main reasons why we do not always see things as they are. The first is sensory error; we do not always hear and see what we think we do. A fire whistle turns out to be a tea kettle in the kitchen. A big fish (all too often) turns out to be a large black stone. The object here is a close-up of the business end of a pencil. Would you have guessed it?

The second reason concerns motive: we tend to see what we want to see. Somebody has said we see things, not as *they* are, but as *we* are.

The psychologist J. F. Dashiell [1] has expressed the idea in the formula $Pr = H \times A$. We perceive (Pr) in accordance with our habits and attitudes. Rumor illustrates the power of human motives to create out of nothing support for conviction. This is especially true in times of war. In World War II the writer was the Communication Officer of an ammunition ship. Such a position meant that no information came to the ship that did not pass through his hands. However, he received a great deal more exciting information from the men aboard than from more authentic sources. "I understand we are leaving Friday with a single escort for Manus. I'm sure glad, never been across the Equator. I guess we're going to take a load of six-inch shells and small stuff." Or it might be Iwo Jima, or Okinawa, or the Philippines. The more dejected the crew, the more pessimistic the rumors. When they could stand the pain no longer, a burst of hopeful "evidence" would re-direct the conversation. Deep beneath all their stories was the question: is our number up? No one dared put it in words, but the urge to ask it found acceptable release in rumor.

Lest the student dismiss the above illustration with the feeling that this is a problem of unusual circumstances, he should remind himself that it is also rare for the two drivers in a traffic accident to report exactly the same "facts."

Recently the writer drew a line on the blackboard in one of his classes and asked the students to estimate its length. As is usual in such an experiment, they tended to underestimate. The line was 29 inches long. Estimates ranged from 18 to 30, but only one of them exceeded the actual length of the line. After the class was told that the estimates were low, 27 dots were placed on the board, and this time the estimates ran from 25 to 50. All but three were over 27, and the average was 40. The information concerning the tendency to underestimate did not improve observation. Rather, it aroused the motive to estimate higher than the senses reported. Motive was more powerful than eyes in the very task of seeing.

It is little wonder that Republicans see most good in Republicans, and Democrats in Democrats; that laborers see labor's side, and capitalists see the side of management. We see as our training and our interests direct, even when we think we see the truth, the whole truth, and nothing but the truth. In short, the observations on which our speech is based are no better than our driving wants and desires.

[1] *Fundamentals of Objective Psychology*, Boston, Houghton Mifflin Co., 1928, p. 396.

How to Check Observations

This universal human failing should not lead to cynicism or despair, any more than should the knowledge that few of us grow to be seven feet tall. But we do need to recognize our limitation and do what we can to correct for it. The following are techniques for checking observations before we speak (or accept, as a listener), and surely before we take issue with our neighbor.

1. What is the Observer's Purpose? Whether the observer is ourself or someone else, we need to isolate the purpose for which he has made his observations. In other words, purpose gives us prejudice. A student who does good daily work and writes a poor examination tends to see daily work as the important feature in learning. Conversely, the student who writes a good final examination is likely to consider this the all-important fact of his course. The English teacher finds it hard to evaluate a scientific paper apart from its style. The science teacher, if the paper is clear, may be oblivious to its style. Most of us note what time it is when we look at a watch; a designer may see the style of the case; a watch repairman looks for the name of the make. It naturally follows that the more the speaker can dissociate his personal interests from his purpose, and the more curious he is to know the facts pertinent to his topic, the more dependable his observations will be.

2. How Much Background Has the Observer in the Area in Which He is Reporting? A botanist generally sees more, and more accurately, on a walk through the woods than does a businessman. Conversely, the businessman more readily grasps the details of a contract or the implications of a balance sheet.

3. Was the Observer in a Position to Observe Accurately? Sense organs have their limitations. Regardless of a man's background and equipment, if he is not in a position of advantage, his so-called facts are subject to greater error. A dirty car looks clean at a distance. A view of a person's profile may not reveal emotions seen from a full-face view. Those in the back row may say the commencement speaker read his speech; those in the front row say he spoke from notes. A student who was charged with cheating was looking for an eraser. For a hundred and fifty years people have been complaining that the President spends most of his time vacationing; presidential press secretaries report staggering daily schedules. Most of us tend to evaluate our observations without due consideration for the advantage or disadvantage of our position of observation.

4. Did We Interpret the Reporter Correctly? When the data of our speech are borrowed from the observations of others, this question always arises. It is of particular concern, for obviously a great share of what we say comes from others. Did we hear as the sender intended? To understand the full implications of this question, consider how accurately others grasp your meanings. How often are your conversations, speeches, classroom discussions, and examinations misinterpreted?

5. Is the Report Clear? Is the report sharp and vivid, or is it confused? Clarity of reporting is no final proof of validity, but it is a healthier sign than fuzziness. Do you evaluate the clarity of the reports you hear? Do you evaluate the clarity of your own reports?

6. Is the Report Complete and Detailed? Sketchiness is suspect. The fullness and specificity of a report is in its favor, though there is no standard of absolute completeness.

7. Is There More than One Observer? Often the best check on facts is to compare the reports of different observers. All other things being equal, if ten people report one set of observations and one person a different set, wisdom suggests the acceptance of the former.

8. Is the Observation Internally Consistent? In a speech on crowded dormitory conditions, it was stated that three boys were assigned to most apartments designed for two. The speaker advocated the conversion of a second building, pointing out that tiers of bunks and lockers could be installed to accommodate 100 boys. His listeners rejected the solution because the "better" living he described sounded worse than the condition to be remedied. If an observer does not know when he is reporting pertinent facts, we cannot trust his ability to see the pertinent facts.

Kinds of Support for Assertion

Support for an argument ranges from specific detail taken in by the eyes or ears to an evaluation of something supposedly seen. It is helpful to go a step further and divide all support into two categories: *fact* and *opinion*.

What Is a Fact?

A fact is something which is known to be true, or to have happened. The thermometer reveals the temperature. If the thermometer is accurate and we have read it correctly, we may say that "the temperature on my back porch this morning was 18 above zero." This is a statement of fact. We discover for ourselves, or get from others, a great many facts of this order. Too much sun blisters the skin. Columbus discovered America in 1492. The formula for the circumference of a circle is $2 \pi r$.

Opinion differs from fact in this important way: it is what someone thinks, not what is objectively verifiable for all. When it is 18° above zero the man from Florida may say, "This is sure enough cold." The man from Hudson Bay may say, "Very mild, indeed!" Both statements are opinions.

While the evidence of fact is subject to errors of perception, the evidence of opinion is not only subject to those errors but also to the infinitely more complex differences that arise from evaluation. It follows then that when fact is available, it is vastly preferable to opinion.

The distinction between fact and opinion gives us another tool by which to check ourselves against error. Unfortunately the distinction is not always clear-cut. Examine the following statements:

> Reading, writing, and arithmetic are not taught as effectively as they were fifty years ago.
> The present economy is unsound.

Are these facts or opinions? Can we say? It is probably wiser to conceive of fact and opinion as labels for the ends of a continuum which has no sharp dividing line in the middle.

Fact	Opinion

Facts and opinions both require observation and interpretation. Fact involves more of the former, opinion more of the latter. Facts are *more* directly related to sense perception than opinions are, so that what we see, hear, smell, taste, touch, and finally what we are "sure" of, constitutes the data which we call facts. When we cite examples, illustrations, statistics, laws, and principles, we are using facts. But as we move from concrete examples to principles, we move toward opinion, bringing in more and more generalization and judgment.

Kinds of Facts

Examples and Illustrations. An example is a single instance, sample, or specimen of a class or type. You may be explaining that modern art emphasizes straight lines, and support your assertion by showing an example of modern art which does so. The more obviously typical the example, the better. The more examples, within the listener's ability to pay attention, the better.

Sometimes examples are used as illustration rather than as proof. A speaker explaining the income tax may say:

> Many people have more deducted from their salaries than the total of their tax; that is, they have a return coming at the end of the year. For instance, the average deduction for a $5000 income is $750, but the tax is more likely to be $600, so that the man in this situation will receive a check for $150 at the end of the tax year.

Here the income tax process is made clear by an illustration.

Statistics. Statistics are numerical facts. As suggested above, time puts a limit on the number of separate examples that may be cited. But examples can be collected into a statistical tabulation. In the talk on modern art, the showing of one painting may be followed by the observation that of twenty-five modern paintings examined, twenty-three showed a dominance of the straight line. Statistics are readily available on a wide variety of subjects. Here are a few:

> Fifty-five per cent of the votes in the last national election were cast for the Republican ticket.
>
> Two out of every three persons on the face of the globe are non-whites.
>
> The national debt is reaching the three hundred billion mark; that is, roughly $2000 for every man, woman, and child in America.

Statistics in speeches are usually most easily grasped if rounded off. If they are larger than are usually meaningful, they should be related to some meaningful unit, as were the national debt figures above.

Laws and Principles. A law is a generalized fact. Newton observed, as many had done before him, that all unsupported objects drop to the earth. But unlike most of us, he proceeded to investigate the factors that determine the speed of the fall, and formulated the law of universal gravitation — that all objects attract each other in proportion to their masses. Most people today accept the principle of gravity as a fact, though a generalized one.

Here are some other generalized statements:

> Most people will fight if attacked.
> Starving men will follow the ideology that insures food.
> The urge to learn is a part of childhood.

These statements, and many like them, are laws or principles based on collections of facts, very much like statistics, but not expressed in numerical form.

Generalized facts court the danger of over-generalization. We hear that the Chinese are philosophical, that Americans are money mad, that athletes are dumb, that professors are absent-minded, and that college students are lazy. In guarding against the sweeping statement, it is dangerous, however, to accept the notion that citations of specific examples, page numbers, and names in themselves guarantee the truth of an assertion. Many factually indefensible assertions pass muster by support of specific details that either have no bearing or are not true. The statistic is doubly dangerous, for it is a generalized fact that usually passes as a specific one. But the point is: a fact is not tested by its specificity or generality — rather, by its accuracy.

What Is Opinion?

An opinion is an evaluation:

> It is cold.
> He is not very bright.
> Education is not taking into account the basic needs of students.
> Our social salvation can come only through science.

These statements, alone as they stand here, are unsupported evaluations — opinions. They are worthy of consideration only if they have arisen out of a careful evaluation of facts. At the best they have gone through the dangerous process of observation and the mental leap by which they came into existence. Yet opinion constitutes a great deal of the support for our assertions, and in many cases it must, as we shall see.

Kinds of Opinion

As we move from our own opinions to the use of authority, analogies, and assumptions, we have to depend more and more on internal

leaps and associations. Therefore with each step away from what we
know at first hand, the problem of handling material becomes more
difficult and the dangers of error increase. A glance at four kinds of
opinion will show why.

1. *One's Own Opinion.* The opinions closest to the speaker's experience are of course his own. Unfortunately, we live so closely with
our own opinions that we sometimes fail to distinguish them from
facts or do not take the trouble to verify them by a check against the
facts. Failing to make this fundamental distinction, we sometimes
create towering structures of thought in which one opinion rests in-
securely on another without a solid foundation of fact. For example:

> We need another fraternity on campus. The present three cannot
> grow larger, for their houses are filled to capacity. These fraternities
> are not much interested in extending their membership beyond the
> numbers that they can house and work with effectively. This is ap-
> parent by the fact that, while the student body has doubled in the past
> five years, fraternity men have increased only by 20 per cent. You
> know as well as I do the competition to get bids has become more
> difficult every year. I am sure that there are enough men among the
> independents who wish to join, to launch a new and a large new fra-
> ternity.

There is only one solid fact in this paragraph, the statement comparing enrollments and fraternity membership over the past five years.
Most of the content is opinion heaped on opinion, all stemming from
the speaker. Any one of these opinions could be challenged, and only
if he presents enough fact to support them will the speaker stand
much chance of convincing an alert audience.

2. *Authority.* We are all authors of opinion. When that author-
ship gains prestige, the person is called an authority. As speakers we
add prestige to our own assertions by citing authorities who reason in
the same fashion as we do. The speaker quoted above might have
continued with the following argument:

> I have talked with Professor Jones and Professor Smith, both of
> whom have spent many years in fraternity work. Both have said that
> another fraternity is needed on our campus. Even Mr. Kards, the
> traveling secretary for Kappa Theta, says that most colleges of our size,
> and even smaller ones, have two or three more fraternities than we
> have.

The tests of authority are two. Is the so-called authority in a position to know the facts about which he forms his opinion? Is the authority known to give sound and impartial judgments?

Very often it is necessary for all of us to depend upon authority. We may not have the background, knowledge, or time to examine the facts. We rightfully depend upon the shoe clerk to tell us which of two pairs will give the more service. We cannot determine for ourselves how big a national defense budget is needed, whether there is waste in government, how far it is to the moon, or what is the second law of thermodynamics. Intelligent reliance on authority is necessary to mature thinking, but it is selective, not blind.

3. *Analogy.* An analogy is a comparison between two objects, circumstances, or ideas which are strikingly similar in one or more ways but different in others. When facts are known, analogy is useful to illustrate and clarify:

> The heart is like a pump; it forces blood through the body as a pump forces water through a pressure system.

But often the very use of comparison implies opinion — the belief that the comparison is sound. And it is easy to use an analogy as a springboard for assertions and conclusions. As soon as an analogy becomes the basis for an argument or a prediction, it becomes open to question:

> You can't mix labor in management problems. Oil and water don't mix.

Actually, this analogy is simply a figure of speech. It helps the listener visualize what the speaker has in mind, but it is description, not dependable reasoning.

Often an analogy tries to establish parallels between situations which, the speaker *thinks*, follow the same laws. Political speakers sometimes argue much like this:

> We cannot afford to soften our policy toward the aggressor. To do so is to insure world conflict. The events leading up to both World Wars stand as incontrovertible evidence that nations bent on conquest exploit the good faith and good will of nations that search for a basis of cooperation and mutual agreement.

Or:

> Socialized medicine would give America bad medicine. England's medical bill increased and her services decreased with the coming of government-controlled medicine.

Such analogical reasoning is not to be flatly condemned. When we try to predict the future, we have to depend on comparison with similar events in the past. But it is important to understand such evidence for what it is, reasoned opinion, not proof. Circumstances preceding World Wars I and II may have been similar enough to those the speaker has in mind to form a dependable basis for judgment, or they may not. Conditions in England and America may be similar enough to support a prediction on socialized medicine, or they may not. These parallels are not factual evidence for what would happen. The only way we could accurately test socialized medicine in America would be to try it out.

Since all knowledge of the future is based on knowledge of the past and thus partakes of analogy, we need to observe carefully the most significant forces in the situations being compared. Are they substantially the same? The more the two pictures look alike in every important way, the safer is the leap that since "A" produced "B" in case number one, "X," which is very much like "A," will produce "B" in case number two.

4. Assumptions. An assumption is a supposition, conjecture, or hypothesis. It is an assertion that does not claim to rest on proof.

> This world was created.
> Democracy is the best form of government.
> Life has a purpose.
> Love is the highest ideal.
> Capitalism produces the best economy.

These are assumptions and must remain so until we gain additional facts, if we ever do. At the end of every trail taken by the human mind, we look into the darkening jungle and see suggestions of a pathway, a pathway very much like the one we have been traveling. We have no other recourse at this point than to say, "So far as I can see, this is the way it is."

Assume we must, when we run out of facts, but we should not assume when facts are available. Equally important, the mature person does not insist that his assumptions are based on fact; he recognizes them for what they are, and treats them accordingly.

THE KINDS OF SUPPORT AND THE AUDIENCE

We have been considering kinds of support quite independently of the circumstances under which a speaker may use them. The speaker soon learns, however, that what one audience will "swallow whole," another may accept only with qualifications, and a third may reject entirely. The wise speaker judges his audience — their disposition toward him and his subject — as well as he can ahead of time, and varies the kind of supporting evidence accordingly.

The Audience in Agreement

So far as support is concerned, the easiest audience to deal with is the one that agrees with your assertion. Listeners who agree with you are not going to be critical of your leaps from assertion to support. They are not "suspicious"; they are following you for the pleasure of seeing their own ideas mirrored. Your greatest danger is that you may not identify yourself closely enough with such an audience. We-ness dominates successful talk among those who agree.

People enjoy agreeing with each other, not only at teas, parties, and bull sessions, but also at conventions, fraternal meetings, and church services. Following is a typical example of the more formal type of speech which makes use of this principle.

> Democracy is not dying.
> We know it because we have seen it revive — and grow.
> We know it cannot die — because it is built on the unhampered initiative of individual men and women joined together in a common enterprise — an enterprise undertaken and carried through by the free expression of a free majority.
> We know it because democracy alone, of all the forms of government, enlists the full force of men's enlightened will.
> We know it because democracy alone has constructed an unlimited civilization capable of infinite progress in the improvement of human life.
> We know it because, if we look below the surface, we sense it still spreading on every continent — for it is the most humane, the most advanced, and in the end the most unconquerable of all forms of human society.[2]

[2] From President Franklin D. Roosevelt's Third Inaugural Address, Jan. 20, 1941.

Here is assertion supported by assertion. The speaker, Franklin D. Roosevelt, was not trying to prove anything. He knew his audience believed in the strength of democracy. He was simply telling the nation that he thought as it thought.

The Indifferent Audience

The indifferent audience, on the other hand, needs to be stimulated. Speech for the indifference audience can well afford to capitalize upon "we" techniques, but its great need is to arouse and awaken the listener. Above all, the speech needs to be vital, vivid, fast moving, alive.

Consider the following story by Ernie Pyle.

LIMIES HAVE GUTS

We drove into the tiny town of LaDetinais, a sweet old stone village. . . . As we stood there talking in the lonely field, a soldier in coveralls ran up breathlessly and almost shouted: "Hey, there's a man alive in one of those planes across the road! He's been trapped there for days." . . .

We ran to the wrecked British plane, lying there upside down, and dropped on our hands and knees and peeked through a tiny hole in the side. A man lay on his back in the small space of the upside-down cockpit. He turned his eyes toward me when I peeked in, and he said in a typical British manner of offhand friendliness, "Oh, hello."

"Are you all right?" I asked, stupidly.

He answered, "Yes, quite, now that you chaps are here."

I asked him how long he had been trapped in the wrecked plane. He told me. And I said, out loud, "Good God!" For, wounded and trapped, he had been lying there for eight days!

His left leg was broken and punctured by an ack-ack burst. His back was terribly burned by raw gasoline. . . . He was in agony, yet in his correct Oxford accent he even apologized for taking up our time to get him out. The American soldiers of our rescue party cussed with open admiration. . . . One of them said, "God, but these Limies have guts!" It took us almost an hour. We don't know whether he will live or not, but he has a chance. . . .

When they finally laid him tenderly onto the canvas litter and straightened his left leg, you could see the tendons relax and his facial muscles subside, and he gave a long half-groan, half-sigh of relief. And that was the one sound of human weakness uttered by that man of great courage in his hour of liberation.[3]

[3] From *Brave Men* by Ernie Pyle. Copyright, 1944, by Henry Holt and Company, Inc. Reprinted by permission of the publishers. Pp. 452–455.

If you go straight to human experience of any consequence, even the indifferent listener will come to life.

The speech classroom gives you a particularly good opportunity to develop skill in dealing with indifference. From hour to hour your audience has moved from one listening situation to another. Explanations, facts, and descriptions have bombarded them for weeks. In the speech class the same thing happens, except that here they are asked to change from subject to subject as one speaker follows another. Listening fatigue sets in.

It is possible to analyze the kinds of stimuli that capture lagging attention. But such analysis does little to help you know when you yourself have developed something that arrests the roving minds of your audience. There are, however, two ways of finding out. One is to study the content that captures *you* as a listener. Why do you remember Mary's speech clearly but forget even what Jerry's topic was? Part of the answer rests in the inherent interest of the topic to you. More important, the content of the remembered speech arouses your imagination, feelings, or thought.

Analyze the impressions left with you at the end of an hour of listening. Was it language, was it the suspense of a story, fast action, clarity of explanation, or the impressiveness of a thought? Whatever it was — and this is basic — it was something that touched off your feelings. You became happy, sad, depressed, excited, angry, thoughtful. In some way you responded sensually, physically, as well as intellectually.

This leads us to the second approach to sharpening the skill of gaining the listener's ear. You must pour into your speech the thoughts, explanations, stories, and descriptions that aroused you. Why did Ernie Pyle command such a widespread audience? He was a *sensitive* man and he was *willing* to put on paper the experiences that touched him deeply. *Sensitivity* and *willingness*. These are essentials to successful communication, whether written or spoken. To be sensitive is to have a feedback to the messages that come your way, whether from books, conversations, lectures, people, or the soil under your feet. Many of the assignments in this book are designed to help you hear the echoes of your experience. You must also be willing to tell what counts with you, if you are to be interesting. Much of your attention in a speech course is directed to the techniques for lifting your faith in the worthwhileness of what happens within you. The key to capturing an indifferent listener is to be *willing* to talk about the things you are *sensitive* to.

You will gain unforgettable satisfaction and learn a profoundly important lesson the day your audience become as children, really listening.

The Uninitiated Audience

When your audience is unfamiliar with your topic, your essential concern is to make the central assertion not only exciting but very clear. Analogies and illustrations are your best explosives.

> . . . and the whole multitude stood on the shore.
> And he spake many things unto them in parables, saying Behold, a sower went forth to sow;
> And when he sowed, some *seeds* fell by the wayside, and the fowls came and devoured them up:
> Some fell upon stony places; where they had not much earth: and forthwith they sprung up, because they had no deepness of earth:
> And when the sun was up, they were scorched; and because they had no root, they withered away.
> And some fell among thorns; and the thorns sprung up, And choked them:
> But other fell into good ground, and brought forth fruit, some a hundredfold, some sixtyfold, some thirtyfold.
> Who hath ears to hear, let him hear.[4]

How do you explain a way of life to the unlettered multitude? How do you explain the movement of the earth to children? How do you explain the principle of radio, television, or the airplane to your speech class? The speaker who deals with an audience unacquainted with his subject can often draw a comparison within the range of their experience. Through this door he may enter.

The Neutral Audience

The *uninitiated* audience doesn't know. The *neutral* audience hasn't made up its mind. The neutral audience is open-minded, and the open mind calls for facts and carefully reasoned opinion. The neutral audience is not likely to respond to we-ness or to stimulation. Like the uninitiated it wants clarity; but more, it wants information. Let us look at part of a highly informative speech on the most pressing problem of our time.

4 Matthew 13:2–9.

It will be said, of course, that if nations will not collaborate in an alliance or debating society like the United Nations, they cannot be expected to come together or stay together in a world state. The American States could not or would not collaborate under the Articles of Confederation before 1787, but they did come together, and, with the exception of one period, they stayed together under the Constitution.

It may be admitted that there were ties which united them which do not unite the nations today. On the other hand, we should not forget that many differences deeply divided the American States, so much so that, three months before the Constitutional Convention, Madison wrote that "he trembled for the issue."

Mr. Hooker has lately shown in the magazine *Common Cause* how serious the divisions among the States in the Confederation were. Virginia had twelve times as many people as Delaware, Georgia claimed a hundred times as many square miles as Rhode Island. There were so many Germans in Pennsylvania that Franklin feared they might make German the language of the State. It was impossible to get along in some sections in New York without knowing Dutch. The trip from Boston to New York, which now takes less than an hour, took four days to a week along the finest road, or longer than it takes now to go around the world.

Gouverneur Morris thought that a federal tax was impossible because of the extent of the country; and one member of the Convention asked, "How can it be supposed that this vast country, including the western territory, will, one hundred and fifty years hence, remain one nation?"

When Washington took charge of the armies surrounding Boston, he wrote that the New Englanders were an exceedingly dirty and nasty people. On the other hand, Ephraim Paine, of Vermont, complained that the southern members of Congress regarded themselves as a superior order of animals. Tithes were levied by New York, Pennsylvania, and Maryland on the goods of other States; and New Jersey taxed the New York lighthouse on Sandy Hook. New York, New Hampshire, and Massachusetts quarreled about Vermont, and Pennsylvanians battled Virginians on the Upper Ohio. It is no wonder that, when the Constitution was completed by the Convention, the principal attack upon it was that it was utopian — a visionary project, an indigestible panacea. . . .[5]

Carefully selected information impresses the neutral mind.

[5] Robert Maynard Hutchins, "The Third Year of the Atomic Age: What Should We Do now?" Reprinted by permission from the University of Chicago Round Table Pamphlet, August 24, 1947, Number 492, pp. 9–10.

The Critical Audience

The emphasis on fact comes into sharp relief in preparing for the audience that is either skeptical or openly hostile to your central assertion. It is important to search for dependable data, and for as much fact as possible that they will agree with. Marshal at the beginning the material that will not be challenged. The sooner you can establish some common ground, the more time you have to develop more common ground. Fact and tact are for the critical audience.

This audience will test every piece of evidence to see whether it is true. In this speech fact is of first importance and examples are particularly telling. Your listeners will be alert to your faulty leaps. They will see the motives that blind your vision. They may even impute to you motives you do not have. You know how easy it is to doubt the sincerity of those you do not agree with. You will have to be particularly careful to make your claims conservative. This means qualifying carefully and asserting in accordance with the strictest self-criticism.

Since dealing with a critical audience is a particularly precarious undertaking, your personal defenses will want to rise. If this happens it is fatal to persuasion, for two reasons. First, your suspicion of the audience will raise its suspicion, and thus increase your problem. Second, you are almost sure to show some hostility, and hostility will not persuade.

A good way to train yourself to correct for this natural tendency in dealing with those who do not agree with you is to try purposefully to persuade a person you know you cannot convince. To do this you must get a proper attitude toward your target and check your inclination to try too hard. It is always easier to act as you desire if you plan your behavior.

1. You must assume the attitude that your listener has the right to his position and that he may be correct. Do not say this at the outset; to admit lack of hope gives the listener every reason to reject you. Express your respect for the opposing belief only if, in the course of the discussion, it is clear that your listener fears your aggression.

2. Enter the battle expecting to be defeated. Do not state this view either, but consider it dignified to be defeated so long as you retain your poise. Indeed, defeat is not hard to accept if you are ready for it. (See Chapter 5, pages 65–67.)

These two attitudes are necessary to successful persuasion with a hostile audience. If the listener feels that he is not being pressed, he may explore with you. If you show him, by not fearing defeat, that you see no shame in it, he is going to be more willing to let you see him play the defeated role, which he must play if he says, "I believe you are right. I never saw it quite that way before."

Consider the tone of this passage from Booker T. Washington's "lecture" to the white race:

> If you want to know how to solve the race problem, place your hands upon your heart and then, with a prayer to God, ask Him how you, today, were you placed in the position that the black man occupies, how you would desire the white man to treat you, and whenever you have answered that question in the sight of God and man, this problem in a large degree will have been solved.[6]

The hostile audience is not to be forced. It can be persuaded only by the speaker who sets up the conditions in which it may persuade itself.

A study of speech content begins with an analysis of the way we think. A complete, mature thought is composed of two parts, assertion and support, which are bridged by a "leap." The "leap" expresses a cause-to-effect relationship, which may or may not be valid. It is important to distinguish between support which is soundly based on fact and that which is itself opinion or mere prejudice. It is also important to distinguish among the kinds of facts and opinions that go to make up the support for our conclusions. Finally, an audience will react differently to different kinds of material, depending on the state of its knowledge and its disposition toward the speaker and his views. Therefore the speaker should learn to use supporting arguments that appeal to his audience, which may be favorably disposed, indifferent, uninitiated, neutral, or critical.

QUESTIONS FOR STUDY AND DISCUSSION

1. What are the two essential parts of speech ammunition?
2. Describe disciplined thinking.
3. Choose a sentence at random and underline the descriptive parts of it.

[6] From "Address at the Jamestown Exposition," August 3, 1907.

4. What is the purpose of description?

5. What is meant by the "leap" or "because" in thinking?

6. What are the two bases for causal reasoning?

7. What are the four tests of causal relationships?

8. In the end, from what source do we get our support? Explain.

9. What are two common errors of observation? Explain and illustrate each.

10. What are the ways of checking observations?

11. What are the two kinds of support? Give an example of each.

12. What are the kinds of facts? What are the kinds of opinions? Give an example of each.

SUGGESTIONS AND ASSIGNMENTS

1. *a.* In the paragraph below, which sentence is the central assertion?

b. Which sentence describes the central assertion? Which is supporting material? Is the support fact or opinion? What kind of fact or opinion is it?

The deadly facts of war compel nations, for simple self-preservation, to make stern choices. It does not make sense, for instance, to say, "I believe in the defense of all the Western Hemisphere," and in the next breath to say, "I will not fight for that defense until the enemy has landed on our shores." And if we believe in the independence and integrity of the Americas, we must be willing to fight to defend them just as much as we would to fight for the safety of our own homes.[7]

2. *a.* There are three separate assertions in the following paragraph. Underline the sentences that state them.

b. Part of the paragraph is an assertion followed by support. Mark off this part with parentheses. What is the nature of that support? Is it legitimate support? Why or why not? With what kind of audience would this paragraph be effective?

Never before has a giant empire been shattered and overthrown in a shorter period than Soviet Russia now! This could only happen with such success through the unheard-of, unique bravery and self-sacrifice of our German armed forces, which endured inconceivable hardships. Words cannot express all that the German arms accomplished here. We can only bow our heads most humbly before our heroes. I have already said in Berlin that whether we use our armored troops, our Pioneers, our ar-

[7] President Franklin D. Roosevelt's broadcast, Washington, D.C., May 27, 1941, White House news release.

tillery, our communication troops, our fliers, our dive-bombers, our pursuit or scout-planes, or our navy, — no matter whom we choose, in the end we always reach the same conclusion: the crown belongs to the German infantryman, the German rifleman. He marched endless distances over boggy paths, through morass, through swamp; he marched under the burning sun, over the endless fields of the Ukraine, in rain, snow, and frost, and conquered one bunker after another. Together with his comrades, the Storm-Pioneers, he tears through front after front. It is truly a heroic saga that he is weaving himself here.[8]

3. Write seven sentences, one to illustrate each of the seven kinds of support: example, statistics, law or principle, your own opinion, authority, analogy, and assumption.

4. Choose an assertion that you firmly believe and support it as well as you can. Then read to the class your support, but not your assertion. Ask the class to decide what the support asserts or "proves." Do most of the students agree with your unread assertion, or do most of them feel the support argues more effectively some other point? Correct your support so that the audience considers your assertion legitimate.

5. Take a belief which is very real to you and support it with one paragraph you think will be effective. Read the assertion to your class and ask the students to tell you the support they would consider effective. Then read your support to them to see how closely you and the audience agree on what is effective.

6. Select a common topic of discussion and conversation. It may be a question of national policy, education, college sports, fraternities, morality, etc. Phrase your major assertion both ways, for instance: "I believe (do not believe) that labor unions should have the right to strike." Ask two or three students to give their reasons for their position on the topic. Ask two or three laborers, two or three businessmen. Evaluate your evidence. What kind of support seems to be most effective with each of the three groups? How would you change your speech if you were to talk to each of the three groups? Make a report to your class of your findings. Have the class evaluate your conclusions.

7. Take a topic on which you do not agree with the majority of the class. Determine this fact by ballot before you start working on the speech. Then gather the best evidence you can for your position. Give the speech, and take another poll of opinion to see what influence you have had.

Have the members of the class state at the bottom of the ballot (1) why they did, or did not, change their opinions, (2) how they were af-

[8] Adolf Hitler, Speech to the Old Guard of His Party, Munich, November 8, 1941. From *Voices of History*, New York, Franklin Watts, Inc., 1942. Edited by Franklin Watts, translated by Mischa Meller, pp. 491–492.

fected by the manner in which you talked. This same procedure, of course, can be carried on when your audience is generally neutral or in agreement with you.

8. Your experience in this study of ammunition will bring you to see that one of our most common errors arises from the inability to recognize irrelevant support (page 76). To sharpen both yourself and your listeners in this ability, select two assertions and support each with good evidence. Then change one of the assertions just enough so that it no longer evolves from its evidence. Give this assertion and support along with the logically sound assertion and support in a short speech to the class. See if the class can recognize which assertion is well supported.

9. A perhaps equally common fault is to accept the description of an assertion as support. As above, select two assertions that you believe. Support one well and merely describe the second more fully. Give this material in the form of a talk to the class and see if they can pick out the well-supported assertion.

10. Select an editorial for evaluation. Underline the supporting material. (1) Determine what kind of support most of it is. Write a paragraph in explanation. (2) Determine how well the support bears out the main assertion. Write a paragraph on this point.

Actual knowledge is one thing; always imperfect and incomplete; but the spirit of knowledge is quite another, always insatiable. . . .

Cassina J. Keyser

7

Subject and Substance

Two ACTIVITIES that always go together in speech are the choice of a topic and the search for something to say about it. The two processes are inseparable, for we tend to talk about things we know, and our learning clusters around subjects that have already attracted our attention and aroused our interest.

CHOOSING A SUBJECT

Under the right circumstances, any subject can be a good one to talk about; and conversely, under the wrong circumstances, any subject can be a bad one. What makes the difference? Essentially, three things: the speaker, the listener, and the occasion.

For the Speaker

Obviously, no one can speak well on a subject which is of no interest to himself, or one about which he is ignorant. Probably the last person in the world to discuss the fine points of gussets, darts, and hemlines would be the captain of the football team. The chances are he couldn't care less about such matters, and he probably wouldn't know basting from bombazine anyway. Likewise, it is improbable that the campus beauty queen would know much about the technicalities of frequency modulation, or that she would be brimming with eagerness to talk on the subject. Good speech grows out of interest and knowledge, for only with something to communicate and the honest desire to do so can the speaker "touch" his audience in any real way.

For the Audience

But speech is a two-way process, and the listener also should be considered. Most of your classmates are not willing or able to follow a technical discourse on the intricacies of strict musical counterpoint,

99

The thoughtful speaker considers his listener
— and the occasion!

or the similarities and differences between the mystical doctrines of Plotinus and Dionysius the Areopagite. A good subject therefore overlaps the worlds of both speaker and listener. This is not to say that you should never talk on a subject which your listeners do not already know something about. While the speaker cannot — or at least should not — talk out of an empty magazine, the listener may be strongly motivated by his relative ignorance of your topic. Indeed, in the public speaking situation, and to a lesser degree in social speech as well, the listener expects to receive something and has a right to do so. Unless he does, there is little to keep his interest alive, and in spite of the best intention to listen, he will soon find his attention slipping away — and so, unhappily, will the speaker.

For the Occasion

Finally, the subject should be accepted, rejected, or modified in accordance with the occasion. Your professors talk less formally and more personally in conference or on the campus than in class. You would not entertain a sick friend with stories of illness and calamity. You can speak intimately to your roommate as you could not to a stranger; and you can say things to your roommate privately that you would not say in class. The professor who discourses on cosmic radiation at a class picnic will pretty quickly make himself unpopular; but he may be equally discredited if he spends the class hour on recollections of his own college days. There is an eternal fitness in all things, and subjects for conversation, speeches, and discussion are no exception.

EXPLORING YOURSELF

One of the more tragic questions often put to teachers of speech is, "Where can I get a subject?" It signals that the student is not aware of what is happening to himself. His life is too automatic. Here he is, a magnificent and complex organism, unique in possessing the most sensitive communication system in the animal kingdom. He has come to walk the paths of earth for a short space, searching for the meaning of his experience. Half unconsciously he gains a sense of achievement, dignity, and worth at those moments when the world takes on new meanings, when he feels he can better see the shape of life, when he feels he has penetrated the past and the future. This is the human adventure, and he has been permitted a part at one of its more dramatic moments. How can he possibly lack things to talk about?

In the past hundred and fifty years the pace of social change has risen to a tempo never known before. In earlier times transportation was slow and communication poor. In little more than a century have come the telegraph and the telephone, power printing, the automobile and the airplane, electric light, radio, movies and television. The world has been thrown topsy-turvy by these changes. The skills of grandfather are now interesting hobbies. Within one lifetime there have been two world wars, the possibility of world government, and the terrible actuality of the hydrogen bomb. Ideas, religion, politics, ignorance, and knowledge have created problems the earth has never seen. It is your lot and luck to live at this point in the drama.

You are a college student preparing yourself for a responsible part in life. If you can learn to become sensitive, first, to the messages that your environment directs at you, and second, to the effect of those messages upon yourself, you have the priceless and basic skill for find-

ing topics to speak about. And here in speech class, as you listen to
yourself and receive the evaluation of your classmates and your instructor, you will mature into the roles necessary to function effectively
in your day. You can teach yourself to be thoughtful by taking yourself aside for a few minutes each day and asking, "What new impressions came to me today?" "What did they do to me?" "What old
impressions were driven home again, and what did that reinforcement
do to me?" In this process lies the secret of maturing, and the germ
of many a good speech.

> . . . How could I have known that my life was to be changed that morn-
> ing? I sat in the same seat, the same room, and listened, it seemed less
> intently than usual. I cannot remember what Mr. Martin was saying
> except that he was discussing a character in the novel we had just
> read. He talked as if he might have in mind a well-known friend. "He
> must have been terribly hurt," said the instructor. "I cannot bring
> myself to condemn him. I only suffer to know he did this violence to
> himself. Who was responsible? Who of us is ever responsible. . . ." I
> was shocked; I had never questioned rightness and responsibility. But
> I could hear, for my teacher did not say it as if he knew. The unre-
> hearsed, unaggressive manner of a thoughtful man branded my memory.
> Since that day I have not been able in my quiet moments to make a
> man responsible. Every time I become too insistent and hear myself
> declaiming the right, I also see and hear the rightness of a man who
> need not pass judgment.

This quotation from a student speech illustrates the way we grow
and the way ideas and attitudes fall upon fertile soil if our minds are
alert. For different listeners, the same teacher's remarks could have
led to entirely different but related topics, such as "How the Law
Treats Responsibility," "What is the Religion Needed Today?" "How
to Become Responsible," "Judge Not Lest Ye Be Judged," "The Power
of a Teacher," "The Danger of Going to College," "The Most Impressive Experience of My Life," "We Are Our Memories," and so on
almost *ad infinitum*. The essential point is that the search for topics
is vastly simplified for the person who is aware of what is happening
to him.

When a student cannot find or decide on a topic, the instructor
usually suggests a conference to get at the difficulty. And from this it
almost always develops that the student has had experiences that are

unique and interesting, but has simply not recognized them as potential speech material which would interest others.

Alice insisted that she had nothing, *nothing* to say that would hold the class's interest. Her father owns a lodge in the extreme north country where the family is snow-bound in winter, where firs and birches dominate the landscape, where the closest neighbor is ten miles away on a dirt road. With a little encouragement, she came to see that this unique setting could be a springboard for a speech, and she was able to give the class a humorous and exciting account of a way of living foreign to their experience.

Jerry almost shouted in his efforts to convince the instructor that he had nothing to talk about. A little calm conversation, however, brought out the fact that he was an avid "radio ham." Later, in a series of speeches, he told of the skills and knowledge necessary to get a license, the kind and cost of equipment, the number of amateurs in the world, what frequencies were allotted them. He told of the friends around the world with whom he talked daily, what he had learned of different parts of the world. He spoke of emergencies and tragedies in which he had taken a part, and of the ham in Texas who, it turned out, was the husband of a former girl friend.

Our lives are all colored and shaped by impressions, interests, irritations, joys, sorrows, doubts. These we talk about every day. If we talk and have anybody who listens to us, we have the materials for speeches. As we choose and explore topics, we are forced to become more alert to our experiences and their meanings.

Classification of Topics

Subjects can be selected more easily if you divide your world into areas of experience, and explore the various areas for topics to discuss. Here is a convenient classification.

1. Your Own Reactions. We all feel strongly about certain experiences we have had. These experiences and feelings can become a valuable source of things to talk about. Your listeners see much the same world you do, but your speech gives them the only way they can see it through your eyes. Besides — and this is extremely important — if you make your feelings meaningful to others, it will be because you bring them to life for yourself. The profit to the listener can be great. It will be even greater for yourself.

2. Learning Through Impressions. Your life in class and what you learn through books does something important to you. The more you put these experiences into words, the more you see how well you are acquiring the information — and more important, the attitudes — which college has to offer. One girl, an occupational therapist, learns how well she can demonstrate the making of fiber place-mats, and how to interest her future patients in making them. An electronics student tries to reduce the fundamentals of radio to the level of exposition which "even the girls" can understand. It is amazing how one's faith in himself and his subject increases as he finds the techniques of bringing others into the world of his interests. The physical education major stirs the imaginations of students not particularly interested in his speciality by telling the history of field games, which once were the skills of survival. A major in mathematics describes the uses of geometry among the Egyptians in building temples and "predicting" the floods of the Nile. Any course you take and any book you read can lead to a speech. Even the most specialized topic has facets which can interest the general listener.

3. Jobs. Many of you have or have had a job. What have been your experiences as camp counselor or clerk, waitress or chemist, factory hand or cement construction worker? What was unique about the company you worked for? What did you learn about life from those who worked beside you? What did you learn of human relations, the attitudes of workers and businessmen? One student, who spent his summers as a reporter on a newspaper in a small city, gave a series of speeches on what he had seen on the police beat, at the city hall, and in the mines near town. He didn't talk at all about himself, but he gave the class many valuable insights into aspects of life they had never known.

4. Reading and Listening. All that you read and hear is a source of material for speeches in class. If you learn to ask what in all this may interest others, you will be amazed by the number of provocative ideas that come to your attention. Popular magazine articles and current popular books, especially, can be a fertile source of subject matter. Even though they tend to oversimplify, they do discuss the ideas with which people are concerned. That is one reason why so many people gravitate to them. Since this kind of writing has the target-set of the millions, if an idea you find there strikes you, it is likely to interest your audience.

The same thing may be said of radio and television listening. Can you enjoy it and still stay sufficiently detached to be ever aware that this daily chatter on the airways expresses the dominant feelings and motives of a nation? Here is the living pulse of America. You need not become entirely a part of it. Indeed, if you do, you cannot evaluate it. Yet not to listen is to fail in understanding the world you live in, which of course means losing your target-set. You can listen and still remain detached. Indeed, it's more fun if you do, for you can then evaluate and assess even as you listen and perhaps enjoy. And you can talk about mass entertainment with the additional interest of one who has *thought* about it, not just responded to it passively. What are the *silent premises*, the silent principles, the silent gods, that shape the stories on radio and television in the soap opera, the western, the situational play, the life drama, the crime story, the variety show, the music, the news report? Whatever holds the attention of large numbers of people expresses the dominant urges of the listeners. What are these urges? In the answers to these and similar questions are the topics for many speeches.

One girl, who chose to study soap opera for two weeks, listened to two serials each day and went to the library to read critical appraisals of the type. She then gave a fascinating speech, which brought to light some of the principles that govern the construction and content of the soap opera. Romance, she said, is a religion in this country. Women over thirty-five need to feel that they are still young and desirable, and they like to see life as a series of romantic crises. But most listeners to soap operas are not very discriminating, so the characters are usually passionately good or unbelievably bad. And the listeners are conventional and naïve, so the good always wins out in the end. Moreover, many women find their lives humdrum, so they are subtly made to feel that there is significant drama happening in the most prosaic events of daily living. All this is given a sense of profound intensity by low, rich, serious voices, and appropriate "mood music."

It is by no means recommended that you remain on the popular level for your reading and listening. But here are found the universals of your day, and you should at least know what they are in order to find the common point of departure for communication with all persons who share the American background. Many people quickly move beyond the stereotypes of popular movies, radio, and television. But we are all exposed to them, and they are therefore a powerful undercurrent in all our lives.

KNOWLEDGE OF THE SUBJECT

Quite often, when a student is aroused to look at a topic that interests him, he gives up with, "But I found I really didn't know enough about the subject to say more than a few sentences." Or it may be, "I found I didn't know what to think on the subject. I just don't know enough about it." These are very good signs. They are not the basis for giving up. Indeed, though you should of course deal with topics that interest you, it is sometimes a healthy thing if you know little about them at the start. Preparation for speeches on such topics will help you build up knowledge around your own doubts and questions. One of the great dangers in college is that you may conceive of education as the process of learning only what your professors tell you to learn. While it is well to know that those who have gone ahead can direct you into areas about which you should be informed, you can become nothing in your own right merely by absorbing what you have been told to study. Achievement comes as you learn to steer a course dictated by your own urges, and the most persistent cry of the self is for proof of its resourcefulness. This you cannot have if you permit your world to be created by other people. To live fully is to follow your own inclinations and to blaze your own trails.

Moreover, learning more about a topic for speech teaches you the basic skills of tapping the environment around you. You will learn where information is and how to get it. It is a mistake to think of your speech class as a place to say only what you knew when you first came to it. What are some of the sources of information on topics that interest you?

Interviews

Students often develop the notion that study is reading in the library. To a point, it is; but it is also considerably more. Volumes of fact are being enacted by people daily. A wise student will search for those who are authorities and ask them questions. Perhaps the greatest value of information gleaned by interview with a "reliable source" is that it seems so much more real, so much more a part of life and events, than if it came from a book or a magazine. You will note that the speech which is supported by data from interviews is usually enthusiastic and confident.

When you interview, be alert to the fact that you are using a man's time. Make appointments in advance. Have your questions well prepared. Have your own pencil and paper available for notes. And be as brief as possible, yet get all the information you will later need.

Letters

It is not always possible to see the man who has the information you want. A letter may do the job, and there is something authentic in the quality of a speech that is supported by information gathered by such efforts.

Make these letters clear, pointed, and courteous. There is always a note of appreciation and thanks implied when you furnish a self-addressed envelope.

The Library

Many students stay away from the library because it seems a labyrinth. It is. But the student who is too timid to learn to use it is at a crippling disadvantage in much of his college work. Many of the things he must read simply can't be found anywhere else. He should remember that no one knows everything about a library and that librarians are there to help. Ask questions.

There are a few general techniques for getting information from various kinds of printed matter in the library:

1. Newspapers. In the periodical room of your library is a selection of daily newspapers. Here is your most up-to-date printed information about current problems and events. Do you note any differences in coverage, policy, or slant between newspapers? From a selected few, can you tell by the general make-up the quality of the paper? Examine the *New York Times* and the *Christian Science Monitor*. These two newspapers command universal respect. What do these papers have that is different from the ordinary? Read some of the leading news stories and editorials in one or both of these papers and compare them with those on the same subjects in your home town paper. What do you learn? This may suggest a good idea for a speech — with evidence to support it.

2. Magazines and Journals. The periodical room also contains current magazines and older issues in bound volumes. You should browse through at least the current issues to get a view of the classes of magazines and the subjects they cover. The following will help you know where to go for various types of information. Magazines like *Collier's,*

The Saturday Evening Post, and *The American* represent a type that
deals with popular attitudes and ideas. Most college libraries will not
have them. *Time, Newsweek, United States News,* and *The Reporter*
are magazines that summarize and interpret the news each week. A
study of the tables of contents will show the classifications of the news
which each stresses. There is a host of magazines, for the most part
monthly, which deal with the popular concerns of the day in a more
extended and thoughtful manner. Among these are *Harper's, The At-
lantic Monthly, The Nation, Fortune,* and *The New Republic.* You
should note in these, though the articles are signed and written by
others than the editorial staff, that the staff selects articles according to
its own bias. There is also a large number of professional journals, in
almost every field of academic interest from agriculture to philosophy.
In speech alone there are *The Quarterly Journal of Speech, Speech
Monographs, The Speech Teacher,* and others equally good. Suggestive of the general variety are such titles as *The Political Science Review, Annals of the American Academy of Political and Social Science,
Journal of Applied Psychology, American Historical Review.* Most if
not all professional organizations have their journals, and your college
library subscribes to a number of them.

If you are interested in federal affairs, *The Congressional Record* is a
valuable source. Since Congressmen can have anything of their own
bias inserted in the *Record,* whether or not it concerns the actual daily
proceedings, you will note editorials, excerpts from daily papers,
speeches, anything a Congressman feels is of persuasive value. In a
sense the *Record* is as much a reflection of the ideas of the most aggressive members of Congress as it is an account of legislative proceedings.

3. *Biography.* If you want facts about people, there are several excellent sources, notably *Who's Who* (for England), *Who's Who in
America, Who's Who in Education, Current Biography, Twentieth-
Century Authors, American Men of Science, The Dictionary of National Biography,* and *The Dictionary of American Biography.*

4. *Statistical Data.* If your speech calls for statistics, there are many
sources, including *The World Almanac* and the *Information Please
Almanac,* both of which are annual compilations of facts and figures on
a wide variety of subjects. The *Statistical Abstracts of the United
States* is one of the more comprehensive and authoritative sources of
information concerning American business and financial affairs.

5. *Encyclopedias*. Encylopedias are a good source for broad general background and history on a wide variety of topics. *The Encyclopaedia Britannica* is especially valuable for cultural, literary, and philosophical topics. *The Encyclopedia Americana* serves much the same function, except that it is generally considered more adequate for scientific subjects.

For special areas there are such works as *The Encyclopedia of Social Sciences, Encyclopedia of Religion and Ethics, Dictionary of Political Economy, Dictionary of Philosophy and Psychology,* and *Cyclopedia of Education.*

Using The Library

1. *Periodical Literature. The Readers' Guide to Periodical Literature* is a monthly listing of almost all magazine and journal articles of general interest. Entries are by subject, title of article and author. You can thus start with the subject, at first, and later check on specific authors and articles you find out about as you read.

The Public Affairs Information Service lists periodicals and also cites books, documents, and pamphlets. The listing concerns only public affairs, but public affairs is an extremely broad classification.

2. *Books.* Just as the periodical guides tell you what has been written in current publications, the card catalogue of your library lists the books it contains. Listings are alphabetical, by author, title, and subject. To see whether a particular book is available, look under the name of the author or the title of the book. To find what books the library has on your topic, look up the general subject matter areas which might apply. Thus if you are interested in medieval clothing you might look under Middle Ages, Clothing, Armor, Chivalry, and any other topics you think might be fruitful.

Reading for Information

Many college students have difficulty in gathering material for speeches, or for any other purpose, because they do not have a sense of perspective in their reading. If such a student finds ten articles on his topic, he may do one of three things. (1) He may select two or three, though he is more likely to stop with one, and put the others aside. (2) He may start reading with the vague notion of plowing through all ten articles. When his reading time is up, he pulls together whatever he has and forms it into a speech. (3) Or he may skim through the articles quickly, eliminate those that seem least valuable, then read the remainder for comprehension.

The last is the way to do the job. It surveys the entire project at the outset, establishes a pace and plan of work, and lets the student feel master of the situation as he proceeds. The student who works this way can do a good deal of skimming, that is, skipping along rapidly, reading the topic sentences and perhaps final sentences of paragraphs, noting the subdivisions of an article or chapter, and its plan. Often one can tell simply by noting the organization whether the author is looking at the subject from such a point of view as to add to one's knowledge.

This does not mean that all good reading is fast reading. *Indeed good reading is a conversation with the author, and you need to listen rather carefully to a man who has something to say; it requires time for you to answer him.* By talking back you comprehend, fix material in mind, and often add something of your own. Good reading is two-way communication. It ought to be a thoughtful experience. Skimming the irrelevant leaves you time to concentrate on the important points. The essential skill is to get an overall picture of your material before you begin to deal with it.

Taking Notes

As you read you are impressed by ideas and support for ideas. When you are struck by a statement, put a light check in the margin. Then when you have finished the article or book, leaf through it again, stopping to reread the points you checked. Is the idea still important, or on second look are you less impressed? If you respond favorably again, note the information on a card. This double check before you make a note saves wasted effort and keeps you from cluttering your mind and speech with facts and ideas which in the end you will — or should — throw away.

Do not take reading notes in a notebook. The organization of a speech usually requires the actual assembling of notes into appropriate stacks by topics, and reading never follows such an order. If you take notes on sheets of paper, do not write on both sides. It is best to use cards, either 3×5 or 4×6 inches. If you write very large, you had better use the larger size.

There are a number of ways of organizing your data on the cards. The essentials are the subject, source, and either a direct quotation

or your own statement of the author's idea. The following is one
system for handling the information.

Subject

> *Democracy in America*
>
> "The idea of democracy was not im-
> ported into America by the first
> colonists who came here. On the
> contrary, the first immigrants
> were opposed to the rule of the
> majority, and they had very
> imperfect ideas of 'democratic'
> justice."
>
> Harold D. Lasswell, *Democracy Through Public Opinion*, Menasha,
> Wisconsin, George Banta Publishing Co.,
> 1941, page 2.

Content

Source

Or if you choose to put the subject matter in your own words the card
might appear as follows:

Subject

> *Democracy in America*
>
> Lasswell explains that the idea of
> democracy has developed in America,
> that the first immigrants were even
> opposed to majority rule and did
> not really understand democratic
> justice as we see it today.
>
> Harold D. Lasswell, *Democracy Through Public Opinion*, Menasha, Wisconsin,
> George Banta Publishing Co., 1941,
> page 2.

Content

Source

In phrasing the subject, it is important to state the content exactly. The heading should accurately label the content of the note.

So far as the content is concerned, the prime question is, of course, do you want it? Can you use it? If the answer is yes, then your problem is purely mechanical. Copy direct quotations with careful concern for details, and be sure to place them within quotation marks. If you paraphrase, think through your note and state the idea or information accurately.

The source material includes the name of the author, the title of the book, the city of publication, the publisher, the date (year) of publication, and the page numbers. If your material comes from a magazine or journal, you have two further items of information, the title of the article and more detail on the date of publication:

(Source)
    David Olmstead, "Two Korean Villages: Culture Contact at the 38th Parallel," *Human Organization*, 1951, 10(3), 33–66.

The title of the article precedes that of the periodical and is in quotation marks. That of the magazine or newspaper is underlined. The data also include year, volume and number — 10(3) — and pages.

This source material is often valuable if you decide to investigate the topic further. A card file is almost indispensable to the person who wishes to develop a store of knowledge. But you will often find that the source of information has a more immediate value, and can effectively be cited as an authority, particularly on crucial points. Audiences tend to give credit to those who demonstrate that they know where they get their information.

Looking Toward Organization

While you are gathering information, you need to evolve some ideas about how you are going to organize your speech. If you are working toward a speech concerning democracy in America you will have read about its history, its weaknesses, and its strengths. If this three-point organization of your knowledge seems to come out of your research, before you consider your reading completed, you should divide your cards into three stacks corresponding to this plan. Then read through each group of notes. Do you have adequate material in each of the three groups? Perhaps you need further reading, interviewing, or thought on one of the divisions. If you do not have time for this, can you drop the weakest point and still have a unified talk? Perhaps you have enough material for just the history of democratic thought in America from 1787 to 1860. Would just this part of your original plan meet the needs of the speech situation? Such decisions must grow out of three determinants: your interest, your audience's interest, and the occasion. Out of all this comes a controlling statement that holds it all together. This is the core of your speech, your central purpose.

QUESTIONS FOR STUDY AND DISCUSSION

1. What are the three determinants of a good subject?

2. Why are topics which require self-exploration of value beyond satisfying the requirements for a class assignment?

3. What is wrong with a person who can not find topics to talk about?

4. Why is it desirable to select topics of interest but about which you can, at the outset, say little?

5. Can you go to the library and search for material on the subject you want? What are the uses of an encyclopedia, *The Readers' Guide*, the card catalogue, a statistical almanac, *Who's Who?*

6. What are the values of skimming and slow reading?

7. Can you draw up a note card? What items go into the citation of sources?

SUGGESTIONS AND ASSIGNMENTS

1. List three topics that you think would be especially interesting to each of the following groups: your speech class, a parent-teachers' meeting, a service club luncheon, a young peoples' church meeting, a fraternity or sorority dinner. If you do not know how to select for a given group, interview appropriate people.

Read your topics to the class. Have them vote on the group for which you have been most skillful in selecting topics. How do you account for their selection?

2. List five topics that you would most like to talk on. Make enough copies for the class. Hand them out and ask your classmates to rank them from most to least interesting. Have them "X" any topic they would not want to listen to.

3. Select a topic that interests both yourself and your class (see 2, above) and gather information. Keep a record of each step you went through in pre-

paring. Hand to your instructor, after you speak, this outline of steps you went through, along with the note cards you used.

Have the class evaluate your speech for strength and weakness in material. In order to do this, at the beginning of your speech have the students write down the main points. At the end of the speech have them mark each point as strong, passable, or weak in support. Collect these papers. Add up the "strong," "passable," and "weak" scores for each point. Can you understand the class reactions? Do they check with your own appraisal? If not, see your instructor. Discuss the matter with your classmates.

4. Prepare a speech in which the major support depends upon information gathered from interviews and letters. How do you react to the satisfaction you receive from this speech as compared to previous speeches? Is the difference due to subject matter or the process of gathering material? How did the class seem to react to this speech?

Necessarily, you state your case, and you prove
it. We cannot state a case and omit to prove it, or
prove a case without first stating it; one who
proves must have something to prove, and one
who advances a statement does so for the purpose
of proving it.

Aristotle

8

Purpose and Pattern

THE HUMAN MIND cries for patterns. We understand only as details
unite into form. Compare the following two versions of the same
passage from a student speech.

(1)

George Bernard Shaw was born in Dublin, Ireland. He was a great
man. His mother was talented in the arts. She sang and was exception-
ally musical. When she married Shaw's father, he was many years her
senior, and he drank heavily. Shaw's *Major Barbara* is probably a revolt to his unhappy childhood. It has been said that Shaw's mother
married his father to escape a nagging aunt. They were not a happy
couple and fought quite a bit. This could have given Shaw the mean
streak that so often comes to light in his writings.

(2)

To understand Shaw's writings, and his *Major Barbara* in particular,
is to know his background. He was born in Dublin, Ireland, of an unfortunate marriage. His mother loved the arts, was musically talented,
and sang especially well. She married to escape a nagging aunt, and
the man she escaped to was a heavy drinker, many years her senior.
Life in the Shaw household was unhappy at its best and tempestuous
at the worst. This was the home into which George Bernard Shaw was
born.

These passages deal with the same data, but the first has no dis-
cernible order, while the second states a point and phrases sentences to
develop it clearly.

THE PURPOSE

In Chapter 6 we pointed out that the general architecture of speech is assertion followed by support. The first decisive step toward design comes with the statement of purpose, the central assertion, which gradually evolves as we read, take notes, and think about our topic. During the remainder of the preparation this becomes a constant feedback for directing and evaluating the development. We cannot overstress the principle that the pattern of speech depends first upon clearly perceiving a central idea. Organization then keeps the central idea in focus. If this were not true, nearly any organization would be as good as any other.

Stating the Purpose

A satisfactory statement of purpose involves a good deal more than merely announcing the topic. Thus the sentence "I wish to discuss American democracy" names the subject, but gives no clue to what the speaker plans to say about it. "Discuss" in this sentence can mean almost anything. Following are four sharp and helpful purpose statements on this same topic. Consider the difference in the scope of the needed support as we make "minor" changes from one version to the next.

I would like to point out that the practice of democracy in America is significantly below the ideal to which we subscribe.
I would like to point out the way in which we have come by our democratic practices in America.
I would like to point out the ideals of American democracy.
I would like to point out the fundamental principles of democratic practices in America.

The above are varying combinations of, additions to, and deletions from the first statement. In no two is the purpose the same and no two imply the same support. Support for the first statement consists of a contrast between ideal and actual behavior. The second promises an explanation of the education and attitudes of our founding fathers, as well as a history of events and arguments that hammered out our basic laws. Third, to talk on the "ideals of American democracy" is to search the Declaration of Independence, the Constitution, and many speeches, essays, and articles. The last statement directs the mind to an evaluation of the practice of democracy in America. All four statements stem out of the same subject, but the design and content of the respective speeches must be distinctly different.

The Purpose and the Audience

Once the speaker has phrased for himself the main purpose of his speech, he is ready to begin casting about for ways of organizing his material to carry out that purpose. In doing so he must constantly keep in mind the probable attitude of his audience toward him and his subject, for success with an audience that has one bias may require wholly different techniques of presentation from success with an audience with different convictions or prejudices. It is good, therefore, to begin by first assessing the audience and phrasing the statement of purpose with due thought for the attitude of the listeners toward your position.

The Audience in Agreement. For the audience that agrees with your position and feelings, the problem is easy. The need is to stir their "we" feelings. Probably the best guide is a sensitivity to the language which best expresses your own emotions. Assume that you are constructively critical of democratic practice in America. You find fault, but in the interest of improving the system. Which of the following statements best serves your purpose?

We must work for more democratic practices in America.
Some so-called democratic practices in America imperil the nation.
The practice of democracy in America is not the ideal we talk about.
It seems to me that the practice of democracy in America is significantly below the ideal to which we subscribe.

The first statement stresses "we-ness," the feeling of community. The second is critical and emotional. The third is critical but unemotional. The last is cautious. For the audience favorably disposed to your speech the first is the most desirable statement. It joins hands with the audience and therefore best serves the speaker-audience needs.

The Indifferent Audience. The indifferent audience lacks "we-ness," and anything that can be done to create this feeling is desirable. But more important than this, if the audience lacks interest, is the problem of gaining attention. Of the four purpose statements above, the second is probably best calculated to arouse interest. The phrase "imperil the nation" is a strong alert against danger.

Though statements tinged with alarm or urgency can be powerfully effective, they should be used with care. Simply because of their power, their use implies responsibility. Unfortunately, they are the standard weapon of advertisers, politicians, writers of "scare" headlines, and news commentators, whose success depends on commanding our attention. Such people often seek to electrify us, not because we are indifferent to social needs, but because they are anxious lest we be indifferent to themselves. For the indifferent audience the purpose must be cradled in excitement; the question is, how valid is the purpose for which we arouse drowsy listeners?

The Uninitiated Audience. The first need of the uninitiated is clarity. Since our four purpose statements are probably equally clear, the speaker who is to face such an audience will then concentrate on the clarity of his presentation. He will take pains that terms are defined and concepts explained and illustrated simply and thoroughly enough so that there can be no danger of misunderstanding. If he has occasion to discuss subversion, the doctrine of "clear and present danger," or guilt by association, he will make sure his audience knows what he means. Of course, it is not likely that the topic of subversion would raise many such problems in most college speech classes. But a speech on electronics which talks about impedance or frequency modulation would find one listener who understands these terms to ten who do not.

The Neutral Audience. A number of studies in audience behavior indicate that the neutral audience is most responsive to fact and to clear reasoning. The central statement, quite obviously then, should be framed with this knowledge in mind. Of our four statements, the one with the strongest informational slant is the third, "The practice of democracy in America is not the ideal we talk about." The sentence suggests matter-of-fact analysis, and is cast in a mood attractive to those who want to balance and weigh.

The Critical Audience. Doubt is the beginning of good thinking. The audience that is suspicious or downright critical of your conclusion is going to check every statement you make. It is important, then, to frame your purpose in language that suggests caution and consideration. "It seems to me that the practice of democracy in America is significantly below the ideal to which we subscribe." Care, temperance, and doubt are written into the purpose with "it seems to me" and "significantly below." To put the purpose this way tells the audience you are aware that differences in position exist, that you appreciate and respect the opposite stand. The listener is inclined to lower his guard if you show that you do not hurt those who disagree with you.

Not only does the statement lower defenses by suggesting self-criticism and responsibility, but it searches for common ground. The clause "to which we subscribe" takes care to minimize difference and to establish common purpose. If you seem much like your listener, the threat of your "peculiarity" is lessened.

A warning is again in order. Caution and qualification can be overstressed. Our purpose statement carries distinct overtones which will have their effect on the listener's responses, but the purpose of the speech is still to convince. The purpose is not clouded by the urge for good will, as in the following, "I may be wrong, but I wonder if we in America don't fall below the democratic ideal sometimes." In this statement the outstanding purpose is "I don't want to offend."

Moreover, if additional statements of personal attitude seem desirable, they should follow the clarification of purpose. To suggest self-doubts before you state your purpose is to prepare the audience to dismiss your intention even before you begin. Get your idea out in an appropriate statement first, then clarify your attitudes if necessary.

It is extremely important in the building of a speech to get a clear, *exact* statement of purpose. The guiding question thereafter is: what effect do you want to have on the target? The sooner you can clarify your purpose the better. Put it down on paper and occasionally throughout the preparation evaluate what you are doing by checking against it. Keep your purpose and what you say in harmony.

Placement of the Purpose Statement

While it is obvious that the speaker cannot choose and arrange material without a clear purpose in mind, it is not so obvious just when the purpose should be revealed to the audience. As a general rule it should come right after the speaker's introductory remarks.[1] As suggested earlier, the usual structure of speech is assertion followed by support. At least for the sake of clarity, the central purpose, the most embracing assertion of the speech, should come early in the speech. The listener understands the meaning of each point you develop if he knows to what purpose you speak.

[1] The next chapter explores this problem more fully. See pages 154–155.

PATTERNS OF ORGANIZATION

Determining the Main Points

Once the purpose has been clarified, the next move is to bring up the smaller guns, one at a time. The central purpose is, let us say, "I would like to point out that the American practice of democracy is considerably below the ideal to which we subscribe." This statement implies a discussion which is inherently a comparison. It establishes two main areas to explore, democratic ideals and democratic practice. Having decided this we then ask, which topic comes first, the ideals or the practice? Again the purpose statement is the guide. Placing the discussion of democratic practice first would suggest that we want to appraise the ideals that follow in the light of the practice already described. But that is not our purpose. The ideals should be discussed first, because the purpose statement suggests that we want to evaluate practice against the yardstick of ideals.

Invariably, a good outline grows organically out of the purpose statement. It follows that we need techniques with which to examine the central idea.

Five Kinds of Organization

Most speeches fall into one of five general patterns. In order to follow the one best suited to your ideas, as soon as your central idea is clearly stated, you should ask yourself the following questions to see which kind of treatment best fits your purpose.

1. Do I want to make a comparison?
2. Do I want to tell what I think are the important facts on the subject?
3. Do I want to tell how something happened?

                                    or

Do I want to tell how to do something?

4. Do I want the listener to see a picture?
5. Do I want to tell how to solve a problem?

1. Comparison. From the preceding discussion it should be clear that any topic which implies an *evaluation*, a *judgment*, as the central purpose, will have two parts, the standard and the thing being measured. Usually it will be logical to place the standard first, as in our speech on the differences between democratic ideals and democratic practices. It is conceivable, however, that the purpose statement could assume knowledge of present conditions and stress only the standard. Some famous books, including Plato's *Republic*, Thomas More's *Utopia*, and Edward Bellamy's *Looking Backward*, all of which portray ideal societies, are written on this plan. Conversely, a classic satire, Swift's *A Modest Proposal*, assumes the standard and concentrates on present evils. In general, however, a comparison or judgment is most easily handled by stating the standard first, as a basis for measuring things as they are against the way you think they should be.

2. *Telling the Facts.* A purpose statement which implies presentation of the facts about a subject calls for what is sometimes called a *topical* outline. It breaks up the subject into smaller topics. If the subject is teaching, and the central idea is: "I want to tell you about the teaching profession," the topics might be as follows:

1. Educational requirements
2. The social status of teachers
3. Salaries
4. Opportunities for service.
5. The future

This is a simple kind of speech to organize, since it usually does not require that some topics be presented before others can be understood.

If there is any question in your mind about the most effective order of subtopics, you have a time-honored rule to fall back upon. Get a good strong point out first, and hold an equally good one for the end. Put the less interesting points between.

The topical is a good outline when the sole purpose is to give information. It is easy to work with because it permits as many subpoints as your time and knowledge allow. But the topical speech is weak in analysis, and therefore tends to be less interesting than the speech which demands a logical development of point upon point. In short, the topical speech, like a series of one-act plays, lacks sustained dramatic suspense. Notice the way an audience shifts about when the speaker says, "Now the third thing I want to talk about. . . ."

The topical outline is misused when the speaker implies a comparison. Its use then shows that the speaker has not forced himself to state clearly and to justify the standards upon which he is going to measure the conditions, behavior, person, or thing under observation. Because the topical order is the loosest, it is the easiest, and therefore the most commonly used.

3. *"How" Speeches.* A story, or a history, naturally falls into the order in which events took place, and organization requires only memory and selection of materials. In like fashion if you explain a process — how to make a boat, how to operate a tape recorder, how to make a dress — the natural order is the order of steps in the process. In a speech in which you logically put the parts together by "First . . . second . . . next . . . then . . . ," your choice of outline is and should be the chronological. It is then important to see that each step is presented clearly and in the right order.

4. *Description.* If you tell about your house, a mountain scene, an airplane design, a new-style factory building, you need (1) to give an overall picture first, (2) to develop each significant part, (3) to relate each part, in turn, with others, (4) and to use visual nouns and active verbs as much as possible.

Few speeches are exclusively descriptive, but many are partly so, and in that part can follow this pattern or some variation of it.

5. *Solving a Problem.* When you are tempted to put your title in the form of a question (What Should We Do About the National Debt?), or when you are suggesting a new policy, or a change in something, you will find that the *logical* order is best. This consists of four parts: (1) present conditions, (2) cause, (3) solution, and (4) effect. To explain a solution of a problem requires, first, a description of the condition that needs to be changed. It automatically follows that something should be done. If the action is desirable, it is so because it meets the *cause* of the trouble. In other words, problem-solving implies (1) a sick patient, (2) a cause for the illness, (3) a cure, (4) the effect of the cure.

Let us apply the principles to a case:

I want to explain why I think we ought to buy a new fraternity house.

Present   A. Present house is not adequate.
Conditions   1. Too small.
                    2. In bad condition.
                    3. Poorly situated.
Cause   B. Students do not want to live here.
                    Therefore we do not have sufficient income to expand and maintain the house.

Solution	C. Buy a new house.
	1. Larger.
	2. In better condition.
	3. Better situated.
Effect	D. Will get more residents.
	1. How many expected.
	2. Size of income.
	3. Total effect on fraternity welfare.

In experimenting with various kinds of speeches, you will find that above all others the problem-solving speech most challenges your thinking powers. Can you pick out the causes of the difficulty you are trying to correct? Can you make it clear why your solution will eliminate the cause and thereby correct the condition about which you speak? If you can say "yes" to these two questions while you are preparing your speech, you can probably handle such a subject effectively.

The Right Order for Your Subject

To help you associate a central idea with the proper order, let us take a subject and formulate as many different purposes as we have kinds of outlines. The subject may be the Indians of North America. The kind of outline is labeled at the left margin for each of the purpose statements. You may cover this with your hand, read the purpose statement, and determine which outline is called for. Then outline the idea, as best you can from your present information, and compare yours with the outline in the book.

Comparison
(I want to make a comparison.)

(Purpose)
I want to talk about the mature philosophy of the Indian tribes of North America.

(Outline)
A. The nature of a mature philosophy.
  1. It must show insight into social purpose.
  2. It must fit the physical environment.
B. How Indian philosophy showed maturity.
  1. Indians believed in teaching the child how to be secure in a world of insecurity.
  2. They had a deep respect for nature.

Topical
(I want to tell
what has come
to my atten-
tion on the
subject.)

(Purpose)
I would like to tell you some interesting facts about
the Indians of North America.

(Outline)
A. Where the Indians came from.
B. Family relationships among Indians.
C. The educational system in Indian tribes.
D. The general nature of Indian religion.
E. Indian arts

Chronological
(I want to tell
how something
happened.)

(Purpose)
I want to give a brief history of the Indians of North
America.

(Outline)
A. The first traces of Indian life in America.
   1. The time.
   2. Where the Indians came from.
B. How they spread over the continent.
C. How three sections developed three different cultures.
   1. The southwest.
   2. The southeast.
   3. The northeast.
D. What happened in each section as the white man
   moved west.

Descriptive
(I want you to
see a picture.)

(Purpose)
Let me describe an Indian village.

(Outline)
A. The overall organization of a village.
B. The chief's home.
C. An average home.
D. The governmental organization.

Logical
(I want to tell
how to solve a
problem.)

(Purpose)
I believe the federal government should begin a large-
scale program to help the Indians make their reservations into model communities.

(Outline)
A. The conditions of reservation life.
B. The reasons for these deplorable conditions.
   1. Poor land and climate.
   2. Poor tools.
   3. Lack of money.
C. A proposed program.
   1. Reservations should be irrigated and made fertile.
   2. Develop the present medical program.
   3. Give Indians more voice in planning improvements.
D. The results that may be expected.
   1. Description of expected reservation life.
   2. Raise the self-worth of Indians.
   3. Repay an old debt.
   4. Create more respect for America abroad.

The central idea must be clearly framed before an outline can be constructed. One of these five kinds of order, or some variation of it, will lead you to successful organization of a speech on any topic. The one you choose will depend on the general purpose at which the central idea is aimed.

SUPPORT FOR MAIN POINTS

The further we go in organizing a speech, the smaller the caliber of ammunition to which we turn our attention. We started with (1) the central idea, which is the broadcast statement in a speech. We followed with (2) the main points of the outline. The next step (3) is to amplify each main point with our most specific support, facts and opinions. Let us go back to the first of the five outlines just discussed and see how the third step works.

An Example

The first point in the outline was, "The nature of a mature philosophy." Here you would probably want to define maturity. This would be support by opinion. If your definition is taken from a dictionary, or any other source than your own reasoning, you are citing the opinion of authority. You might want to quote a passage from *The Mature Mind* by Harry Overstreet. You can give some examples of individuals or nations that you think measure up to greatness in belief and action — the compassion of Lincoln even in times of stress, the intellectual depth of the Athenians, the firm resolves of Britain under a rain of bombs. These are the kinds of facts and opinions that can be used to clarify your standard of human greatness, the capacity to achieve a worthy ideal.

The next step is to show the kinds of behavior in which the Indians measured up to your standard. One may be, "Indians believed in teaching the child how to be secure in a world of insecurity." You might tell a story (illustration) of the manner in which the Indian taught his child poise. You could tell some of the tribal rituals that are designed for this purpose. It may help to describe the way an average Indian adult behaved in moments of stress and emergency. You could cite authorities who have described Indian behavior. By example, illustrations, and authority you support the point.

Again, if there is any question about the order of material, get most of your effective ammunition out first, but hold some for last. A strong beginning and a strong finish is a good rule.

Forms of Support

It is easier to put material together into a meaningful unit if one has a sense of the various forms of content. Any statement either explains, narrates, or describes, or does several of these things. It is important to know how to do them well.

1. Explanation. To explain is to clarify, to elucidate, to "make plain." An explanation answers the question "how?" or "why?" and shows relationships, sets forth reasoning, or states and illustrates principles. An explanation can deal with anything from the rules for playing chess, or your objections to the direct primary system, to the success of Thomas Edison. This paragraph is explanation. Because explanation presents facts and gives reasons, it is the most difficult form of expression and requires the most thought and the most careful planning. The more completely an idea or a body of information is a part of our own internal processes, the more difficult it is to see that our listeners may be utterly unfamiliar with it, or may with equal justification hold contradictory ideas. Blinded by our own knowledge or beliefs, we may fail to see the target. In explanation, therefore, we must take particular care to tell our listeners what they need to know.

We must examine a chain of reasoning to be sure we are presenting every essential link. We must check every step in a process, and every item which is a foundation stone for the understanding of something else.

There are at least two valuable kinds of practice to help you explain clearly. One is to ask your listeners to jot down, as you speak, any important questions you fail to answer for them. You can study these questions later — or better still, attempt to answer them just after your talk. The nature of the questions will show how clearly you saw the target at which your explanation was aimed.

In one such assignment, a girl explained the career of Sister Elizabeth Kenny, the Australian nurse who developed a method for treating infantile paralysis. The central question at the close of her speech was, "Why did Miss Kenny give up love for nursing? How do you explain her drive?" And the common evaluation of the speech was that "It was well done, but somehow I didn't get interested in Sister Kenny. I thought I ought to, but I didn't." These reactions show that the speaker had failed to let others see the drama of Sister Kenny's life. The speaker's amazed reply was that she was carried away with the study of Sister Kenny. The speaker had to learn by answering questions the difference between what she felt and what she actually explained.

The second approach to sharpening your explanations is through choice of language. The more concrete and vivid your words, the more likely the listener is to follow your reasoning. Let us contrast excerpts from two famous authors. Both are explanations. The first, a paragraph from Emerson's *Man the Reformer*, is difficult partly because the diction is largely abstract.

The idea which now begins to agitate society has a wider scope than our daily employments, our households, and the institutions of property. We are to revise the whole of our social structure, the state, the school, religion, marriage, trade, science, and explore their foundations in our own nature; we are to see that the world not only fitted the former men but fits us, and to clear ourselves of every usage which has not its roots in our own mind. What is a man born for but to be a reformer, a remaker of what man has made; a renouncer of lies; a restorer of truth and good, imitating that great Nature which embosoms us all, and which sleeps no moment on an old past, but every hour repairs herself, yielding us every morning a new day, and with every pulsation a new life? Let him renounce everything which is not true to him, and put all his practices back on their first thoughts, and do nothing for which he has not the whole world for his reason.

See how much more concrete and vivid is the language of this paragraph from H. L. Mencken's *Notes on Democracy*, equally abstract in subject.

> The fact is that liberty, in any true sense, is a concept that lies quite beyond the reach of the inferior man's mind. He can imagine and even esteem, in his way, certain false forms of liberty — for example, the right to choose between two political mountebanks, and to yell for the more obviously dishonest — but the reality is incomprehensible to him. And no wonder, for genuine liberty demands of its votaries a quality he lacks completely, and that is courage. The man who loves it must be willing to fight for it; blood, said Jefferson, is its natural manure. More, he must be able to *endure* it — an even more arduous business. Liberty means self-reliance, it means resolution, it means enterprise, it means the capacity for doing without. The free man is one who has won a small and precarious territory from the great mob of his inferiors, and is prepared and ready to defend it and make it support him.[2]

Emerson is discussing reform, Mencken liberty, both abstract subjects. But Emerson's idea remains rather abstract; Mencken, largely through the use of simple and homely examples, and vivid words and images, of mountebanks, and blood, and men defending ground, actually makes us "see" — if not liberty, at least the difference between the false kind and the true.

By giving explanations, by sharpening the language of our explanations, and by studying the mind behind the question that a listener asks, we can improve our ability to make ourselves clear.

2. *Narration.* Narration, story, is usually much easier than explanation. Its order is guided by something other than our decision — time, the order of events. Other people live in and observe the same world, and so the communication of events is relatively easy to compose. Narratives range in length from a few words to volumes. They range from a bit of dialogue, a humorous tale, the story of a trip, or a life, to the history of the world. Often, material which is essentially explanatory is cast in narrative form. Here, for example, is the story of a changing attitude.

[2] Henry L. Mencken, *Notes on Democracy*, New York, Alfred A. Knopf, Inc., 1926, p. 44.

The first Englishman to notice an Americanism sneered at it aloofly, thus setting a fashion that many of his countrymen have been following ever since. He was one Francis Moore, a ruffian who came out to Georgia with Oglethorpe in 1735, and the word that upset him was *bluff*, in the sense of "a cliff or headland with a broad precipitous face." He did not deign to argue against it; he simply dismissed it as "barbarous," apparently assuming that all Englishmen of decent instincts would agree with him. For nearly a century they seem to have done so, and *bluff* lingered sadly below the salt. When it was printed at all in Great Britain it was set off by sanitary quotation marks, or accompanied by other hints of depreciation, as *rubberneck, hot spot* and *nerts* are accompanied today. But then, in 1830, the eminent Sir Charles Lyell used it shamelessly in the first volume of his monumental *Principles of Geology*, and from that day to this it has been a perfectly respectable if somewhat unfamiliar word in England, with a place in every dictionary.[3]

The key to good narrative in speech is the clear, yet rapid, presentation of each important step in the action. Thus the basic skill is selecting the right things to say. A sense of timing is probably the next most difficult skill involved. The pace should be not too fast but not too slow, and the good speaker has a fine appreciation of dramatic pause. There is no formula. You must practice and study your audience to find when you bore, when you excite. But a good story always has point, and the more significance it has, the more interested your audience will be.

As a beginning, to improve your narrative skills tell an anecdote, the story of a recent campus political campaign, the events of a current issue that dominates the news, an impressive experience.

On a more complex level, tell the history of an idea: the development of freedom of the press; the history of the automobile, airplane, radio, or television industry; the history of the atomic or the hydrogen bomb; of cancer, polio, or yellow fever research; the rise of Hitler; the fall of Mussolini; England's experience with socialized industry; the history of your college; or the life of a well-known member of your faculty. There is a multitude of movements and people whose stories arrest attention.

Preparation for a narrative speech should be guided by the questions, "What happened?" and "What meaning does the story have?" It is

[3] Henry L. Mencken, "The American Language." Reprinted by permission from *The Yale Review*, Volume XXV, March, 1936, p. 538. Copyright, Yale University Press.

good practice to give at least one speech which is entirely narrative in form.

3. *Description.* Description paints a picture. It appeals to the senses — to sight, hearing, touch, movement, smell, and taste. Colorful nouns, active verbs, and a minimum of adjectives make for good description. Good description focuses on the essentials of the subject — scene, action, object, or creature. Most effective descriptions in speeches are short. The mind operates at remarkably rapid speeds, while speech plods along at 125 words a minute. If the listener has completed his picture — and he needs but a few brush strokes on your part — while you are still trying to work out details, he becomes bored waiting for you. We do not like to anticipate the speaker. We want him to lead. The speaker's real aim in description is not to complete the task but to start it.

Note the language, the carefully selected details, and the completed pictures in the following.

> The voice of the Soldier was silent. His glowing body began to fade. Suddenly he was a shadow again, and the shadow, a darkness. I was alone. The wind was cold upon me, and I shivered. Then I seemed to start, and wake, as though from sleep. It was the draught from that open window in my room. I rose to shut it, and my book tumbled noisily to the floor. What was it I had been reading, as I sat down here in this chair, and looked out over the city, and thought of the Unknown Soldier far off there on the hill? Oh, yes — a book of poems! And here was the open page — and two short stanzas. I must have been pondering them, as I fell asleep:
>
>> Who goes there,
>> In the night,
>> Across the wind-swept plain?
>> *We are the ghosts of a valiant war,*
>> *A million murdered men.*
>>
>> Who goes there,
>> In the dawn,
>> Across the sun-swept plain?
>> *We are the hosts of those who swear*
>> *It shall not be again.*[4]

[4] From a sermon, "The Unknown Soldier Speaks," by John Haynes Holmes, published in *The Sensible Man's View of Religion*, New York, Harper and Brothers, 1932.

Descriptions seldom bulk large in a speech, but they are important when images are needed.

To develop your skill in describing, find what arrests your own attention in the things you want to discuss. Look out your window, listen to your favorite record, note your responses as you step out of doors on a beautiful morning. Then jot down the impression that lingers. Work it over until it captures the images and the heart of the feelings. Say it to the class for appraisal.

4. Forms of Support in Combination. As we suggested earlier, the support for even a single point usually weaves together explanation, narration, and description. All three appear, for instance, in the introductory remarks by Prime Minister Winston Churchill in his world broadcast about a historic meeting with President Roosevelt.

> I thought you would like me to tell you something about the voyage which I made across the ocean to meet our great friend, the President of the United States.
>
> Exactly where we met is a secret, but I don't think I shall be indiscreet if I go so far as to say that it was somewhere in the Atlantic. In a spacious, land-locked bay which reminded me of the west coast of Scotland, powerful American warships, protected by strong flotillas and far-ranging aircraft, awaited our arrival and, as it were, stretched out a hand to help us in.[5]

All three forms here are interwoven in fairly even balance, but the emphasis will vary with the speech. To develop a sensitivity to each of the three skills, study and practice them separately and together. Idea rather than form should be your main interest, but all skills require self-conscious practice and only gradually become dependable habits.

Having gathered your material, the first job is to construct your purpose; everything you do thereafter is in *support* of it. Next, main points need be formulated. Last, but certainly not least, come the specific facts, illustrations, and opinions, grouped according to the points they support. Facts and opinions are of three forms, and the whole structure of speech is no stronger than the explanations, stories, and descriptions you present.

[5] Speech delivered August 24, 1941. From *The War Speeches* of the Rt. Hon. Winston Churchill, Boston, Houghton Mifflin Company, 1953, Volume II, p. 59.

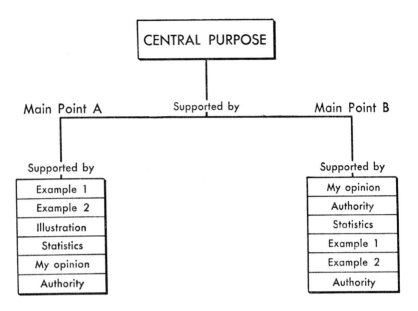

The One-Point Speech

As a device to sharpen your ability to build sound support for main points, it is well to give speeches that develop but one main point. Generally a speech, let us say on football, would have several points. The purpose statement and outline might run as follows:

Topical   (Purpose)
I should like to tell you a number of interesting facts about the great collegiate sport of football.

(Outline)
1. How widespread among colleges.
2. Cost to colleges.
3. Abuses.
4. Relation to school spirit.

Here are four points. A one-point speech would take any one of the four and develop it. If the second point is chosen, the central idea becomes: "I want to tell you about the cost of football to colleges." The speech would then tell how much it costs to operate a squad in small, medium-sized, and large schools, how much goes into equipment, facilities, traveling, scholarships, salaries for coaches and assistants. On the other side of the ledger it would explain the size of the gate receipts in small, middle-sized, and large colleges. It would explain the circumstances in which football pays for itself, and those in which it requires subsidy. The discipline of such a speech is that it organizes fact and opinion in one limited area. Anything on scholarship abuses, or how a college decided in the interest of school spirit to subsidize football, or the number of colleges that play football, is then out of order. The speech must stick to the cost of football in colleges. If you learn this technique, it is no problem to combine several well-supported one-point speeches into a speech of broader purpose.

THE LAST STEPS

Now that your speech is assembled, whether it is a one-point speech or one of many points, give attention to ways of beginning and ending it.

The Introduction

The introduction should lead the audience to your central idea. It should be prepared with three purposes in mind: (1) to capture attention, (2) to make the audience like you, and (3) to create interest in the subject. Notice how clearly and quickly the late Supreme Court Justice Robert Jackson achieved these purposes in the introduction to his speech, "Why a College Education?" given to an audience of college administrators.

> Perhaps you have heard about the college executives who were discussing what they wanted to do after retirement age. One hoped to run a prison or school of correction, so the alumni would never come back to visit. Another chose to manage an orphan asylum so he would not be plagued with advice from parents.
>
> I cannot afflict you with the views of a college alumnus, for I never attended college. The reasons have long ceased to be important, and the results are too painfully apparent.
>
> I once knew a really great lawyer who liked to discuss his most perplexing cases with laymen. He considered that professionals always stood in need of the correction sometimes found in what he called "the reactions of the untutored mind." Notwithstanding the courteous terms of Father Sheehy's invitation to me, I had no difficulty in recognizing that he wanted you to hear, in reference to your own specialized educational problems, the "reactions of an untutored mind." He has assumed that, since our son has just entered college, I must have given

the educational problem consideration. I can serve no useful purpose here except by a frankness which is intended to be helpful, and in no case to be unkindly.[6]

The first sentence commands attention because it is directed to one of the chief concerns of the audience. Both the language and the humor are attractive. As the speaker proceeds he assumes honest, fair, and mature attitudes. He seems comfortable with himself and others. Finally, he indicates the subject he is going to talk about. His central purpose is not stated, for that belongs to the body of the speech.

The Conclusion

The conclusion gives a speech the finishing touch. It will often restate, or at least re-stress, the central idea, in new and striking language. William Trufant Foster concludes a speech "Should Students Study?" with this forceful restatement of his main point.

> The undergraduate who is eager to excel in his life-work and who is brave enough to face the facts will take down that sign from the walls of his room, "Do not let your studies interfere with your college education," and replace it with this one: "Do not let your college life interfere with your life's ambition." The boy without ambition will take for his motto, "Let well enough alone," oblivious to the fact that boys who are content to "let well enough alone" never do "well enough." [7]

The striking phrase that goes to the heart of the speech idea is the key to a good conclusion.

Introductions are important and students seem to know it; conclusions are equally important and students seem not to know it. They do not have trouble with the skills involved, once they see the difference between a finished and an unfinished speech. To check yourself, study the conclusions of the speeches given in class in the next few days. Ask for an appraisal of your own conclusions.

[6] Lew Sarett and William Trufant Foster, *Modern Speeches on Basic Issues*, Boston, Houghton Mifflin Company, 1939, p. 58. Reprinted by permission from *Vital Speeches*.

[7] Lew Sarett and William Trufant Foster, *Modern Speeches on Basic Issues*, Boston, Houghton Mifflin Company, 1939, p. 75. Reprinted by permission of Mrs. Faith Foster Lee.

LANGUAGE

In the end, the ammunition of speech is language. In the last three chapters we have been discussing techniques for bringing the mind to grips with the problems involved in producing effective language. If you have an interesting topic, possess the necessary information, have formulated a specific purpose, and have seen the organizational route to achieving it, language will come. Intense discipline designed to the end of striking your target is the source of words. Perhaps a few standards for spoken language may help.

The Sound of Speech

We all love musical speech. A *flow* of sounds and phrases is pleasant to hear, and is one of the most effective tools for holding attention. But what makes for pleasantness? Instant intelligibility is important. This means sentences that are direct, to the point, efficient. Compare the two sentences below and note how much pleasanter is your reaction to the second:

> The listener is inclined to raise his guard when a speaker sets out to attack and to change his convictions; the good speaker lowers the listener's guard.

> We are inclined to lower our guard when a speaker shows he does not want to hurt us if we disagree.

The first statement is longer than the second, and because the words and phrases are "bigger," is harder to take in. The easier language is to understand, the pleasanter it is to listen to.

Pleasant language has movement. It sweeps us along and focuses our attention on meaning. Consider the following:

> It may be said of Washington that for the most part people were loved by him.

Unnecessary words and indirect attack clutter and slow down what is intended to say:

> Washington loved most people.

The essence of life is action, in language as in man.

Pleasant language flows, or, if you like, it has rhythm. Compare the following two sentences:

Eighty-seven years ago our ancestors created here a new country, in liberty and equality.

Fourscore and seven years ago our fathers brought forth upon this continent a new nation, conceived in liberty, and dedicated to the proposition that all men are created equal.

The two sentences say approximately the same thing, but the first is choppy while the words of Lincoln flow.

Pleasantness comes partly from consistency of vocabulary level. Note the difference:

The gentlemen *kicked out* President Cleveland's proposal.

The gentlemen *rejected* President Cleveland's proposal.

A speaker who uses jarringly inconsistent phrases tends, moreover, to change his manner and attitude as his language shifts, and this adds to the discomfort of his listeners.

Efficiency, movement, rhythm, and consistency are but a few of the elements of pleasant language, but they are important ones. How is pleasant language attained? Here are some practical suggestions.

Reading and listening to direct communicative language gives your memory linguistic patterns. To speak or write immediately thereafter helps you apply them. Putting your speeches on tape and listening to them several days later helps you sense the difference between your good and your poor language. Writing a speech, laying it aside, and reading it back days later sharpens your feedback. Writing and rewriting, arranging and rearranging, while arduous, is probably the most effective way to polish language. It is particularly helpful for the beginnings and endings of speeches.

A good start gives you the set for producing language of character. A bad start gives the set for feeble or fumbling language. To end well is to establish a feeling for language — and at a crucial moment, the moment of lowered anxiety. To finish the job awkwardly is to fix the habit of awkwardness.

Chapter 4 emphasized the value of saying your speeches many times aloud to yourself. This is probably the most effective way to learn smooth and pleasant language. Having no one present sharpens your feedback to your own language. If you do not like it, this is not the signal to close your mouth, but to open your ears. How can you say it so you can not only stand it, but actually like it?

Variety in Vocabulary and Sentence Structure. The same words said over and over in the same sentence pattern become monotonous and awkward. Variety in language requires a knowledge of synonyms. It also requires a mixture of long and short sentences, and a variety in kinds of sentences. Too many that begin with "I" or "and" are deadening. Again, speaking, writing, and comparing set up the feedback for search in variety.

Repetition of Ideas and Sounds. Repetition is the most primitive form of emphasis, as is suggested by the baby's first words: mamma, papa, dada, baby, go-go, ba-ba. This suggests, first, that the surest way to make your central idea dominate is to state it occasionally. That is precisely what happens if you summarize each main point of a speech as you complete the point. Second, a rhetorical effect may be produced by alliteration, the repetition of initial sounds in key words: the dank, dark tarn; stem to stern; nefarious nonsense. Alliteration can have a strong effect on the listener. Repetition of ideas and sounds is most appropriate when you see signs of anxiety or bewilderment on the faces of your audience.

Familiar and Simple Words

One of the common and foolish fears of students in speech classes is that they do not have a "good enough vocabulary." If you know your subject, you have all the vocabulary you need; for you cannot grasp the subject until you are familiar with the words it uses. The real problem in language is to see that your words are familiar to your audience. This means that to insure yourself against the differences in background and knowledge among your listeners, you should in general use simple words. Moreover, simple words have power, regardless of the sophistication of your listeners. Take any idea and express it in both big and little words, and the plain, short expression will usually have more drive.

> I desire to announce a proposal of considerable magnitude.
>
> I want to talk about a far-reaching plan.

The only people who "desire to announce" are those who do not strongly wish to communicate directly, but wish, rather, to hide in formal cloaks. For these few, language should wear tails and stiff collars.

Why do students deplore their poor vocabularies? Because when they read at the college level, they often find it hard to handle the ideas and the language involved. This is a real handicap, for no matter what we may say for or against your own use of *big* words, the fact remains that as a reader you are constantly meeting *new* ones, many of which happen to be big. It is hoped that you will go on learning new words, throughout your college years and after. The point is to know when to use them. Except in speeches on specialized subjects, most of the ideas you will express can be put in reasonably direct and simple words. Big or strange words have no value simply because they are big or strange. But simplicity has a power and a dignity which every good speaker knows.

Pronouns

The more *you, we, our,* and *I* get into your speech the better. *We* and *our,* particularly, strengthen the sense of community. All we have said about the target-set of good speech should point this up.

The Rhetorical Question

As Professor Andrew Weaver says, the question mark is a grappling hook by which we may take hold of the listener's mind. It forces attention and demands an answer. Like most tools, of course, the question may be misused. (1) Be careful not to use it after you have explained something which is very obvious.

> We in America believe in the rights of the individual. We believe in the democratic process. We believe in the freedom of speech. We believe in these things, do we not?

Here the answer is so obvious that the question is merely embarrassing or annoying. (2) Do not use rhetorical questions aggressively. You make your listener squirm when you bear down on him with questions you do not intend him to answer, even silently, except in the way you dictate.

> If we believe in these things, we should act as if we believe in them, shouldn't we? Now I ask you, isn't this true?

The question is a tool for collecting and focusing thought, and therefore may best be used at a transitional point, a place where you want the audience to exert additional energy.

Now we have the money, the location, and the plans. What is our next step?

As distinct from the question whose answer is self-evident or already clear, this kind honestly leads forward.

A few guiding rules in language usage, a *technique* for assembling speech ammunition, and plenty of ammunition, are the most important things to remember in speech composition.

Practice

Having constructed your speech, practice it aloud according to the outline. By listening to it, you will sense where it moves along comfortably. If there are places where it does not, or where it sounds shallow and ineffective, restudy these parts for corrections and additions to the outline or language. Say it over until it sounds right. At this point you have your speech prepared.

QUESTIONS FOR STUDY AND DISCUSSION

1. What are the three basic steps in preparing an outline?
2. What is the controlling element in the selection of a kind of order?
3. What are the five kinds of order? Describe the use of each.
4. At what point in your speech preparation should the introduction and conclusion be developed? What are the essentials of each?
5. What are the three forms of support? Give an illustration of each.
6. What are the guiding rules in the use of language in speech?

SUGGESTIONS AND ASSIGNMENTS

1. Select a topic and formulate five purpose statements, each of which suggests a different kind of order. See if your classmates agree.

2. Formulate two purpose statements on the same subject which are very close, yet which you think call for different kinds of support. Describe the support needed for each and tell what order will best suit. Write this out and give it to another student for evaluation. Hand in your material and his evaluation.

3. Prepare and give a three to five minute one-point speech. Write the speech out to check your discipline. Let the class judge whether you confine your remarks to the one point. Be prepared to defend or eliminate any remarks that listeners say belong to another point.

4. Give three one-minute speeches, each using exclusively one of the three kinds of support. If you can make the three on one topic, so much the better. Biography permits this: describe a person, tell something of his history, and explain his personality.

5. Give a speech in which you weave explanation, narration, and description together. Have the class determine which predominated. Have them evaluate the balance among the three. Where might you have explained, narrated, or described more or less fully?

6. Prepare a ten to fifteen minute speech, going through the following steps:

    a. Select a topic.

    b. Write the purpose statement.

    c. Outline the speech, for both main points and supporting data.

    d. Practice the speech.

    e. Write an introduction and a conclusion.

    f. Give the speech, first giving the instructor a copy of the outline and a full statement of introduction and conclusion.

    g. Have one third of the class write and hand to you after you finish a statement of what they think your major purpose was. Have another third evaluate your introduction and conclusion. Have the last third (1) outline your speech as you proceed and (2) write an evaluation of the evidence after you finish.

    h. Study the evaluations of: (1) introduction and conclusion, (2) clarity of central purpose, (3) clarity of outline, and weight of evidence.

    i. Give a second speech, following the same procedure, paying particular attention to the point on which evaluation suggested you were strongest. See if evaluation indicates further improvement.

    j. Give a third speech, following the same procedure, paying particular attention this time to the point on which evaluations of the first speech indicate you are weakest. See if the evaluations after this speech suggest improvement.

EVALUATION FORM FOR LISTENERS

INTRODUCTION AND CONCLUSION

Speaker _____

Listener _____

1. Comments on introduction:
2. Attention power:

(✓ a point between 1 and 10)
(10 is best)

1 2 3 4 5 6 7 8 9 10

3. Attitudes established:

1 2 3 4 5 6 7 8 9 10

4. Subject brought to focus:

1 2 3 4 5 6 7 8 9 10

. . . .

1. Comments on conclusion:
2. How well it fit the speech:

1 2 3 4 5 6 7 8 9 10

3. Effectiveness of language:

1 2 3 4 5 6 7 8 9 10

. . . .

THE CENTRAL IDEA

Speaker _____

Listener _____

1. A statement of the central idea as I understood it:

THE OUTLINE

Speaker _____

Listener _____

1. As I heard it:
2. How well supported:

1 2 3 4 5 6 7 8 9 10

When the aim is to rouse from indifference, to inspire or to stimulate lagging enthusiasms and faiths, persuasion is a process vitalizing old desires, purposes, or ideals.

When the aim is to secure the acceptance of new beliefs or courses of action, persuasion is a process of substituting new desires, purposes or ideals for old ones.[1]

William Norwood Brigance

9

Persuasion

EXCEPT WHEN we talk exclusively to ourselves — and this we rarely do — speech, or any other form of communication, is designed to affect another person in some way or other. Even so simple a statement as "That's a pretty dress!" "Two plus two are four," or "Look, it's stopped raining," changes the emotional state, information, or behavior of someone else, however slightly. The speaker may deny his effort to influence, or may be unaware of it. Worse, he may not sense the effect his words are having. Speech that seeks a listener is intended to influence, and, in a broad sense, to persuade. For persuasion is defined as "the intricate science of *influencing* human behavior."[2] The effectiveness of persuasion rests on our "knowledge of the relevant bases of human behavior." Thus the key to persuasion is an understanding of the broad range of influences to which man is susceptible and a selection of those particular influences to which a given listener or audience will favorably respond. Man responds to the smile and the clenched fist, to the melodious and the strident voice, to information and emotion, to fact and to opinion, to truth and to fancy. In the completely amoral sense the tools of persuasion are all things that influence man.

Perhaps because the most obvious efforts to influence us are put

[1] William Norwood Brigance, *Speech Composition*, Second Edition, New York, Appleton-Century-Crofts, Inc., 1953, p. 139.
[2] Winston L. Brembeck and William S. Howell, *Persuasion*, New York, Prentice-Hall, Inc., 1952, Preface.

into dynamic and energetic form — as in much of the advertising, salesmanship, preaching, and campaigning that we hear — we may tend to think of persuasion as necessarily emotional and forceful, but when the "disk jockey" announces "And the time now is exactly 7:52," the student who thought it was 7:30 will alter his behavior. Some of the most effective persuasion in modern society is carried on by the psychiatrist, who simply helps his conversant say for himself things that may alter his whole life. The words "powerful" and "gentle" do not divide speech into persuasion and non-persuasion, but label kinds of persuasion.

For reasons we shall understand better when we study the nature of aggression (Chapter 21), we tend to use the more energetic forms of persuasion when we speak about convictions based on shaky evidence — when we are not sure, but would like to be. Persuasion thus may be unwisely identified with the speech of controversy. But it has been found that a discussion group tends to gravitate toward the position held by the best informed person in the group, that discussion shifts opinion more than debate, that education affects attitudes, beliefs, and thinking ability. Persuasion is not something peculiar to controversial issues, and speech generated by controversy tends to strengthen convictions rather than to change them.[3] This does not argue that informative speech is better or worse persuasion than the speech charged with feeling and judgment.[4] It explains that both are persuasion and suggests that they are effective or ineffective according to the situation and the needs of the audience.

Varieties of Persuasion

The scope of persuasion may be understood more fully by examining the following statements from a listener's point of view. The order in both classifications is from most to least commanding.

[3] See the following for a full development of these findings: Karl F. Robinson, "An Experimental Study of the Effects of Group Discussion Upon the Social Attitudes of College Students," *Speech Monographs,* Vol. VIII, 1941, pp. 34–57; William A. D. Millson, "Audience Reaction to Symposium," *The Quarterly Journal of Speech,* February, 1935, pp. 43–53; Howard S. Woodward, "Measurement and Analysis of Audience Opinion," February, 1928, pp. 94–111; Edward M. Glaser, "An Experiment in The Development of Critical Thinking," New York, Teachers College, Columbia University, 1941; William E. Utterback, "The Influence of Conference on Group Opinion," *The Quarterly Journal of Speech,* October, 1950, pp. 365–370.

[4] Franklin H. Knower, "A Study of the Effect of Oral Argument on Changes of Attitude," *Journal of Social Psychology* (1935), VI, pp. 315–347.

*Directive
Persuasion*

1. If you are late again, I shall take appropriate measures.
2. Don't say that!
3. I shall expect you at two.
4. The record proves that recent legislation is opposed to the best interests of the farmer.
5. The Civil War stimulated industrialization in America.

*Suggestive
Persuasion*

1. Are you going to take the job?
2. What do you think we ought to do about labor legislation?
3. You'll make an "A" if you work hard for the rest of the semester.
4. You'd make a good doctor.
5. I'm going to study for that exam.

Several observations should be made about the persuasive qualities of these statements. The first and most apparent distinction is that the "directive" statements are intended to give the listener no choice, whereas the "suggestive" statements give him varying degrees of freedom. Second, the most powerful persuasion man can devise threatens the listener if he does not comply. "If you are late again, I shall take appropriate measures." The threat is the most aggressive tool of linguistic persuasion. Any action beyond the threat is the persuasion of force, and perhaps of violence. In contrast, the more suggestive the persuasion, the more it resorts to information and appeal rather than penalty. The "weakest" persuasion illustrated above is the statement, "I'm going to study for that exam." By personal example, as implied in the statement, the persuader "forces" his listener to appraise his own choice of action, or at the very least invites the listener to approve of the speaker. The third distinction to be noted among the statements above is that some of them are intended to direct the behavior of the listener, while others are intended to direct his beliefs and attitudes. Moreover, both kinds of statements may be commanding or suggestive. "I shall expect you at two," and "The Civil War stimulated industrialization in America" leave the listener little choice; but the first tries to control his behavior; the second, his mind. "Are you going to take the job?" and "You'd make a good doctor," do give the listener a choice. The first is designed to elicit immediate commitment and action. The second, at least for the moment, is satisfied to make the listener think.

One other distinction among the statements should be made. The control of one's behavior does not necessarily mean a control of his mind. "If you are late again, I shall take appropriate measures" is a statement that may alter the receiver's behavior. He may still want to be late, may still have little regard for promptness. "I'll expect you at two," may bring the listener to an appointment he believes is a waste of time. Other refinements could be made, but the essential point is that all these varieties of speech are persuasive in purpose, for their purpose is to influence the listener in some fashion.

PERSUASION AND THE AUDIENCE

Though speech is persuasive in intent, it does not follow that all speech is persuasive in effect. But it does happen that all speech has an effect, whether the intended one or not. "I think he is right," "I think he's dead wrong," "I don't understand what he means," "I never listen to him any more." All speech has its effect, but the effect often differs from listener to listener. The success or failure of persuasion hinges on the attitudes and beliefs — the desires, purposes, and ideals — of the listener. The more independent and dominant a listener is, the more likely he is to resist forceful persuasion. The more confident he is about what he wants to do and believe, the less likely he is to respond favorably to forceful persuasion. When the listener accepts the speaker as an authority, he is willing to accept directive persuasion.

Effective persuasion is always geared to the motives of the audience. When the audience is one person the speaker, if he is to be effective, must understand, appreciate, and respect that person. In like fashion, the persuasive public speaker understands people as they behave in groups. Sarett and Foster define persuasion as "the art of adapting oneself and one's ideas to the basic nature of an audience." [5]

The Nature of an Audience

What is the nature of an audience? An audience is a group of people attending the same communication, who, because they are in a group hold themselves less responsible for their respective decisions than they do in private. Let one person applaud and all are likely to

[5] Lew Sarett and William Trufant Foster, *Basic Principles of Speech*, Boston, Houghton Mifflin Company, 1946, p. 487.

applaud; let a few whisper and the rest will tend to shift about and pay less attention; let several "boo" and others are likely to join the chorus. Because of the tendency of an audience to reinforce the responses of its members, college students are often surprised at the ease with which they trip off laughter in the speech situation.

Not every person will join the group in any common response, but when we talk about the audience we must talk about the *common* response. Moreover, those of the audience who set off a given response do so because they represent an attitude held by most members of the group. The atypical person, whether he applauds, whispers, shouts, or goes to sleep, does not change the more common attitudes already present, but arouses and intensifies them. The Communist heckler will not turn a Republican rally into an audience of hecklers — rather he will organize the group against himself. An audience has a personality to which the individual members tend to defer. Most people want to belong to the group and will, within limits, shift to the temperament, attitudes, and beliefs of the majority.

Audience Demands

For these reasons persuasion in the public speaking situation can be much more forceful and aggressive than the members of the group would accept in person-to-person relationships. You will note in your speech class that both instructor and students rate the dynamic, assured, authoritative, and commanding speaker higher than the person of opposite traits. However, the public speaker can usurp too much power and thereby initiate a revolt against himself. This does not alter the fact that a certain degree of dictatorial behavior is expected of public speakers.

While the usual shift in the speech development of students is in the direction of aggressive persuasion, students must learn that the power of the speaker in part belongs to the role that his audience bestows upon him. Effective high school and college debaters often have to be penalized in private arguments before they learn that the role of public debate and that of private debate are two different things. The teacher, minister, counselor, salesman, parent, and friend all play the game of persuasion in different fashions because the audience of each puts different demands and limitations upon the speaker.

Kinds of Audiences

A crowd is a group of people who have no special group reason for being together. Its members have no common purpose. People on the streets, at the fair, at the railroad station, constitute crowds. It would be hard to classify most crowds and say how they would respond to a given message.

People who assemble in an audience are somewhat more predictable because they do have an urge or a need to listen to a given communication. They have something in common, even if it is nothing more than common interest in a topic. Usually, however, the community of desires, purposes, and ideals goes beyond interest in the topic. Audiences assemble as Democrats, Republicans, teachers, lawyers, doctors, executives, students, parents. In some way because of the identity of their past experiences and their hopes for the future, people meet as audiences with a relatively common set of beliefs and attitudes toward the subject of discussion. We may analyze the kinds of audiences in order to gain a sharper understanding of the way a speaker must adjust himself and his language to his audience.

The Audience in Agreement. The content of the speech for the average audience in agreement can well afford to be emotional and "propagandistic." [6] The more intelligent the audience, the more subtle the emotional appeals should be. If the agreeing audience is highly intelligent, the speaker will improve his cause if he presents arguments both for and against his position. For the agreeing audience of average intelligence, it is better to stay with the evidence that furthers your cause.[7] In other words, the average audience favorably disposed toward the speaker is submissive. It looks upon the speaker as an authority. He can use commanding statements and is expected to do so. A student gave a speech on cancer in which he warned his audience of the danger and threatened them with the likely consequence if they didn't follow his suggestions. The audience fully agreed with him on the danger of the disease and did not object to his forceful persuasion. The speech was rated one of the best of the year.

[6] Paul F. Lazarsfeld, Bernard Berelson, and Hazel Gaudet, *The Peoples' Choice*, New York, Duell, Sloan and Pearce, Inc., 1944, Preface, and Chapter IX.

[7] Carl I. Hovland, Arthur A. Lumsdaine, and Fred D. Sheffield, *Experiments on Mass Communication*, Princeton, Princeton University Press, 1949, p. 225.

In other connections we have noted that the audience in agreement is susceptible to the play on "we-ness." Mix "we-ness" and commanding persuasion and you have the character of the benevolent dictator. A speaker may play god with the audience that agrees with him so long as he remembers to remain *their* god.

The Indifferent Audience. The indifferent audience cannot be commanded. It must be appealed to. It must be aroused out of its indifference. You may have had a teacher who was not aware of this. Being distressed by class apathy and indifference he may have followed one of three ineffective courses. (1) He may have retained "we-ness" and attempted to persuade by concentrating on the danger of not learning the material. (2) Or perhaps he dropped the "we-ness," and attacked the class for not wanting to learn. (3) He may have attacked and threatened. Of the three, the last is most likely to get action, but the persuasion is not likely to affect the mind, at least not in the way intended.

Persuasion of the indifferent mind must as a rule help the mind to replace indifference with enthusiasm. The indifferent audience has closed its ears; it has withdrawn from the speaker. It needs shock treatment — but of the right sort. Any kind of resistance to audience apathy, as suggested above, is likely to arouse the justification and fixation of apathy. The speaker must close the distance and break through the barriers that have been raised against stimulation.

Sometimes he can do this at the beginning of his speech. One student noticed the general weariness of the audience in a round of speeches, and when the time came for his own speech his accurate diagnosis of the situation made it possible for him to arouse their interest. He had gathered material on mercy killing, which he opposed. But instead of giving the information in the usual straightfoward fashion, he began by taking an extreme position on the opposite side. With a straight face, he vigorously advocated the legal destruction of all permanently institutionalized people — of the blind, the deaf, and the crippled, and of all people the third time they were admitted to a hospital. He pointed out how such a program would reduce taxes, how it would eliminate the shortage of doctors.

His audience sat bolt upright. When several seemed about ready to take the platform themselves, he unmasked his real viewpoint with the statement, "But now isn't this fantastic picture simply an exaggeration of a position that is scarcely more defensible?" With his audience alert, he then explored the topic in a more reasonable fashion. The introduction is of the most vital concern to the speaker when he must deal with an indifferent audience. But elsewhere, as at the beginning, the same principle holds: the indifferent audience needs intensely stimulating content and delivery.

Audience participation is particularly valuable when the listeners are indifferent. Ballots to fill out, questions and answers, any fitting activity that the speaker can design for the audience will aid his purposes.

The Uninitiated Audience. When the audience is uninitiated, as we said in Chapters 6 and 8, the challenge for the speaker is to help them understand. When his listeners know little or nothing about his topic, he need have no concern about their preconceived attitudes. They do not present a fixed position that offers resistance to his message, for they have no position. They are strangers to his topic. Yet because they have no emotions on the topic, they are not likely to be moved by emotional appeal. If people are ignorant of a topic and are willing to listen, it is because they want information. The speaker's problem is to ascertain the intellectual level of the audience, their past experiences, the way his subject is related to their lives. The uninitiated audience has little or no data to start with, perhaps no clear sense of the relationships among the parts of the idea involved, and no conclusions. The approach must then be extremely elementary, and must make sure that each step in the development is carefully related to the whole. High on the list of specific items for special attention are the following: (1) a clear statement of the purpose early in the body of the speech, (2) careful definitions of important terms, (3) a larger than usual number of transitions, and (4) frequent summaries. The uninitiated audience needs a careful application of the principles of organization discussed in the preceding chapter.

Note in the following passages the techniques Dr. Alvin M. Weinberg used in explaining to an intelligent lay audience the problems of producing atomic power.

> . . . I should like to summarize these scientific facts about nuclear fission which explain . . . Why nuclear reactors are hard to build. . . .
> It is simplest, in reëxplaining nuclear energy, to compare a nuclear

fire with an ordinary chemical fire — or if you will, a nuclear reactor with a coal furnace. . . . When a piece of coal burns in air, electrons of carbon and electrons from oxygen undergo rearrangements which cause the release of heat, light, and products of combustion. . . .

I have already mentioned that when an ordinary chemical fire burns it gives off heat, light, and products of combustion. . . . It is instructive to compare the chemical fire and the nuclear fire with respect to each of these characteristics; and to indicate which kind of energy is more convenient in each of these respects.

1. *Heat.* With respect to heat, nuclear fire at first sight wins hands down. Everybody is familiar by now with the fact that one pound of U^{235} has as much heat energy as 1260 tons of coal. As columnist Sam Grafton once said, there is enough atomic energy in a battleship to drive a toothpick twice around the world, or something. But while nuclear fuel wins by a walk as far as its *compactness* as a heat source is concerned, it does not do so well as far as the temperature at which its heat is easily and practically available. . . .

2. *Light.* Chemical burning is accompanied by light. If the fire is hot enough, it may give off ultraviolet light which might hurt one's eyes. Nuclear burning also gives off light but nuclear light has far shorter wave lengths than chemical light; it manifests itself as x-rays or even gamma rays which, in the large doses given off by a nuclear reactor, are deadly. For this reason a high-powered nuclear reactor must be shielded by heavy concrete walls which add to the bulkiness and to the expense of a nuclear reactor.

3. *Combustion products.* A coal furnace produces ashes and smoke, both of which are nuisances which however can be dealt with rather easily. A nuclear reactor produces ashes too — the so-called fission products — but these are enormously radioactive, and disposal of this waste is a problem of major magnitude.[8]

Note the orderliness of the presentation, the clarification by means of comparison, the care with which the speaker related the various parts of the idea. This is the kind of speech that makes for effective persuasion with the uninitiated audience.

In the above illustration the persuasion is completely removed from the area of controversy. There is no argument whether a nuclear furnace should or should not be more difficult to build than an ordi-

[8] "Nuclear Energy Development and Military Technology," a speech delivered at the annual Institute of Public Affairs of the University of Virginia, Charlottesville, July 17, 1950. From *The Age of Danger*, New York, Random House, Inc., 1952, pp. 322–323. Reprinted by permission of the author.

nary coal furnace. What if the speaker had met his assignment with an evangelical attitude? He might have emphasized the frustration scientists meet in trying to combat the perverse atom, or how little people appreciate the persistence of the man in the laboratory. But had he done so he would have wrongly evaluated the needs of the situation. And this is precisely what people so often do when speaking to the uninitiated about a topic that arouses strong feeling more easily than this one does.

A father spoke often and at length about the great danger of fire, but his four-year-old son persisted in playing with matches. Finally the father said, "Son, you do not understand what you might do to yourself and the rest of us. I don't want to do what I am going to do, but you must know how it feels to be burned. . . . " The burn was slight, but the boy played with no more matches.

The moral? Do not tell the uninitiated about the great tragedy of war; tell him war stories, or show him some authentic pictures. Don't exhort against the dangers of alcohol; present case histories, or testimonials. Don't generalize in a speech to your class about how slums contribute to delinquency. Go to the slums and describe what you saw. Of course there is room for conclusions, reasoning, and appeal in a speech to the uninitiated, but the emphasis should be on information. Bring your audience as close as possible to actual experience. Clarity, simplicity, facts, and description are the tools most likely to bring the uninitiated audience to see as you do.

The Neutral Audience. People who are neutral on a subject are impressed by conflicting arguments and evidence. They have not formed any fixed conclusions. The conclusions of the neutral audience are any one, or a combination, of the following: (1) "I do not have enough information on this subject to know what position to take," (2) "I do not know that there is enough information available on this issue for anyone to form a valid conclusion," and (3) "I do not think events have moved far enough to justify a decision on this issue." When students say they do not know what occupation to enter, when people say they have not made up their minds whom to vote for, they meet the speech on such a topic with an open mind. Such people are generally very intelligent. They indicate a need for adequate evidence and a keen awareness that evidence on issues, controversial or otherwise, comes gradually as time and events choose to reveal it. They have learned that the pleasure of hasty action is overbalanced by the pain of leisurely repentance. In a sense, thinking is the act of restraining oneself from impulsive action. That is one reason why it is so painful. Observing and weighing is hard for thoughtless people. They want answers as soon as the questions are asked. The neutral audience is intelligent enough to wait and weigh.

One qualification needs to be made about this appraisal of the neutral mind. There is considerable difference between studying a question and being indecisive. Some people are neutral because they are too weak to assume the responsibility of a decision. These are the parasites of neutrality. Persuasion designed for such people is less focused on the topic than on their psychological deficiencies. Fortunately, in the group situation the speaker usually need not divert his energies to strengthening the courage of the weak. When the neutral audience, to which such people attach themselves, comes to the act of decision, they will accept the choice of the majority and escape the need of deciding for themselves.

The nature of the truly neutral mind indicates that persuasion which will be effective must explore the evidence thoroughly. Organization is important, but mainly because the good mind does not respect disorganization. The neutral mind does not need to have interpretations spelled out letter by letter. Indeed, reasoning that is too close and confining may create resistance. The neutral person wants the truth, the whole truth, and nothing but the truth, and truth usually rests in the quantity and quality of the evidence.

This should not suggest that the neutral mind is difficult to deal with. Indeed a number of studies reveal that the greatest changes produced by speech are made by neutral persons. To be neutral is to be interested and susceptible to change. The neutral listener is interested in the topic or he would not have been alert to so many messages from so many different sources. Professor John Dietrich found that it is the interested person who is most influenced by a speech.[9]

The Critical Audience. The neutral mind is critical, but critical of its own processes as well as others'. When we speak of the *critical audience*, we mean the audience that opposes the beliefs and conclu-

---

[9] "The Relative Effectiveness of Two Modes of Radio Delivery in Influencing Attitudes," *Speech Monographs,* No. 1, Vol. XIII, 1946, pp. 58–65.

sions of the speaker. The critical audience has made up its mind in some way different from the speaker. The speaker faces a potential battle, and yet he must not fight, unless he wants either to lose or to control only by threats. If he chooses the latter course, he must recognize that threats may control action but will not persuade the mind, particularly the critical mind.[10]

Nor can the speaker afford to be superior to the critical listener. Thus Allied propaganda directed to the German soldier during World War II was based on the argument that "he was being crushed by Allied superiority of material, rather than out-fought man for man." [11] We have said that the indifferent audience offers perhaps the greatest challenge to the speaker because it has closed its ears. To speak and not to get attention is maddening, like living in the world of the dead. Even the most biased politician is more distressed by those who will not vote than the most vocal and active opposition. The critical audience at least offers attention, and very good attention.

But the critical audience presents the speaker with a formidable problem. Professor James Winans has defined persuasion as the "process of inducing others to give fair, favorable, and undivided attention to propositions." [12] The critical audience is likely to offer undivided attention; and according to Herz, to every detail. The challenge is to make this attention fair and favorable.

But, as we have said, changes in the thinking of listeners cannot be enforced. The speaker must change himself if he would remove the barriers against himself. Those who think differently from us are foreigners to our minds; and it is natural, if not healthy, to be suspicious of those whose minds speak another language. Yet the speaker cannot gain admittance for his ideas until he himself has been admitted to this alien and hostile territory.

The technique of persuading a hostile audience, then, is basically that of removing the hostility. The speaker must make every effort to join the audience. Since it is difference of opinion that separates him from his listeners, he must take the greatest care, first in his introduction and later in the body of his speech, to concentrate on the points on which he agrees with the audience. He must begin as if he

[10] Martin F. Herz, "Some Psychological Lessons from Leaflet Propaganda in World War II," *Public Opinion Quarterly*, No. 3, Vol. 13, 1949, pp. 471–486.
[11] *Ibid.*, p. 480.
[12] James A. Winans, *Public Speaking*, New York, The Century Company, 1917, p. 247.

were speaking to an audience favorably disposed to his central purpose. This, in essence, is what is meant by changing himself as a means of changing the audience.

Interestingly, the critical mind, at all intellectual levels, is more convinced by persuasion if the speaker presents both sides of the question.[13] It does no good to act if there is but one answer or to ignore opposing arguments. Apparently the critical person gains faith and can hear the argument of a man who can face the issue squarely and compare views.

In the last chapter we advocated placing the purpose statement early in the speech. This is logical and for most audiences it is desirable. But to begin by stirring up disagreement in an audience which holds different views is to fail in persuasion. To speak effectively to a critical audience calls for an organization that (1) establishes all the common ground that is logically possible, (2) forms the purpose statement in harmony with the common ground, and (3) supports the purpose statement with evidence that is as agreeable as possible to the audience. The whole technique is that of being no more different from the audience than honesty requires and making that difference as inoffensive as possible.

Some people even advocate withholding the purpose statement until late in the speech when dealing with a critical audience. Professor William Norwood Brigance has called this approach the "this-or-nothing" order, in reference to the fact that the speaker builds from common ground to the purpose statement, so that the audience is faced with accepting the conclusion or rejecting all the common ground which they have accepted as he proceeded.[14]

But as Professor Brigance explains, the dangers of trying to keep your purpose a secret are great. Audiences know a speaker has a purpose. The failure to state it arouses the question "Why?" It requires the subtlest of techniques to lead a mind without telling it where you intend to take it. What's worse, when the audience is finally told, it may reject the "this-or-nothing" gambit, and may accept the common ground while refusing your conclusion, choosing an alternative one instead. For as pointed out in Chapter 6, there is no law that

[13] Carl I. Hovland, Arthur A. Lumsdaine, and Fred Sheffield, *Experiments on Mass Communication,* Princeton, Princeton University Press, 1949, pp. 224–225.
[14] *Speech Composition,* Second Edition, New York, Appleton-Century-Crofts, Inc., 1953, pp. 102–109.

requires two minds to accept the same conclusion because they accept the same evidence. Or, if the listener has little intellectual pride, he may even say, "O.K., if it's 'this-or-nothing,' I'll take nothing."

Probably in the long run the wiser plan is to let your purpose "slip out" fairly early in your speech, but to make no issue of it until all possible common ground has been explored.

Norman Thomas, the perennial Socialist candidate for the Presidency, was a master of dealing with the critical audience, and most of his audiences were critical. Everybody knew his purpose: the gradual replacement of private ownership of industry in America with public ownership. He never hid it. But his case was always built on the common ground of Christian morality and democratic principles. On his sixty-fifth birthday he was honored at a dinner sponsored by several thousand Democrats and Republicans. While he had not attained his objectives, he had built a lasting respect among even those who most bitterly opposed his views. It is difficult to see how he could have been more persuasive, considering the unpopularity of his aims.

If persuasion is the process of gaining "fair, favorable, and undivided attention," the speaker's task, especially when he is opposed, is to give his audience "fair, favorable, and undivided attention."

PURPOSE, ORGANIZATION, AND PERSUASION
Purpose

The preceding discussion suggests what we have all learned from common experience: that the goals of persuasion should be *reasonable*. The speaker cannot always expect complete victory, and unless he can properly appraise the distance he may go, he is doomed to failure. Moreover, half a loaf is better than none. The purpose of a speech should be appraised in terms of the degree of control the audience will permit.

Studies of audience reaction suggest that listening to a speech, which is a "unidirectional" performance, does not have as long-lasting an effect as listening to a discussion, which is "bidirectional." Many experiments show that people who shift their position on a subject as the result of listening to a speech tend to revert to their original position after several weeks. William S. Howell did not find this to be true in the case of discussion. After five weeks, re-testing revealed that the audience retained most of the changes in attitude they had

made by listening to a discussion. These observations are not conclusive, but they strongly suggest that the listener who is offered freedom
makes a more profound change than the one who is directed.[15]

Organization

These findings would seem to have some interesting implications
concerning speech organization. They suggest that the more closely-
knit the organization, the more a speech blots out creative delibera-
tion in the listener. He must follow the speaker's line of reasoning
and accept or reject it. Conversely, if the speaker's thoughts move
without fully expressed transition, the listener is less likely to follow
him with full understanding, and more likely to get ideas of his
own. Obviously, actual disunity will make the listener give up and
shift his attention away from the speech. But if the leaps are coher-
ent and the listener can follow in his own way, he will be sufficiently
unstabilized to make new associations, to see the topic from points
of view he has not before considered, perhaps the ones the speaker
would desire.

This suggests that the choice between close and loose organization
depends upon (1) the speaker's purpose and (2) the listener's orientation to the subject. If you want to give your listener very precise instructions on how to vote, tour Europe, or play chess, the tighter the
organization the better. If you want him to think things out for himself, as is often the teacher's purpose, a skip, a leap, and a pause will
often do it. If the listener is willing to accept your message, you can
afford to lead him by the hand. If he is likely to resist you, it is
futile to lead him so closely. A few well-chosen but loosely directed
remarks will not frighten him away and may attract him to look at
the subject just a little differently. That is often as far as you can go
for the time, but you will have planted a seed which may grow of itself.

Note the difference in the effect of the organization in the two following selections.

> Before we examine some of the most significant trends in modern
> literature, let us agree on a definition of terms. I take it that a trend
> means a sustained movement in a given direction, a prevailing tendency
> or inclination. The characteristics of one book, therefore, do not con-
> stitute a literary trend. A trend is established only by the reappearance
> of certain characteristics over a considerable period of time.

[15] Winston L. Brembeck and William S. Howell, *Persuasion*, New York, Prentice-Hall, Inc., 1952, pp. 419–420.

The word "modern" has no well-defined limits. Its limitation depends upon the thing it modifies. For instance, when we speak of modern civilization we mean civilization beginning with the Renaissance approximately five hundred years ago. But when we speak of "modern warfare," or "modern medicine," or "modern education" we limit our period to the time between World War I and the present. For the purpose of this discussion, therefore, modern literature means literature produced since 1918.[16]

This passage directs your mind; you cannot escape the speaker. Each sentence picks up the thought, carries it further, and you must go with it. Not so the following:

And yet, owing to the central and preponderant position of the United States in our common Western community, we in my country, Great Britain, and the rest of us in all the other countries of the Western world or countries that are even remotely associated with the Western world, follow your politics, I think, with greater interest and with greater anxiety nowadays than we follow our own local politics.

Why this interest in American politics outside the United States? It is because we have all come to realize that American politics have become a matter of life and death for us. We have not votes, but, though we cannot vote for the President of the United States, he is the most important executive official that we possess. We have no voice in who is to be Secretary of State, but he is the most important diplomatic officer that we possess. You did not ask for it; we did not ask for it; but that is the situation, and I do not quite see how that can last as between peoples who are all accustomed to democratic processes of self-government, and who prize this heritage of self-government almost as highly as they prize life itself.[17]

Toynbee's discussion is just as well organized as Ford's, but he leaves more opportunity for the receiver's response. He makes you see the topic from a different angle than is your custom, and he does not tell you what you ought to see — but he does make some subtle suggestions.

Albert Einstein gives even greater freedom to the listener's mind in the conclusion to a speech entitled "Peace in the Atomic Era."

[16] Nick Aaron Ford, "Trends in Modern Literature," *Vital Speeches*, Vol. XIII, January 15, 1947, p. 217. Reprinted by permission.

[17] Arnold Toynbee, "The Fulcrum of Western Civilization," a lecture delivered at Stanford University in the fall of 1950. From *The Age of Danger*, New York, Random House, Inc., 1952, p. 78. Reprinted by permission of the author.

In the last analysis, every kind of peaceful cooperation among men is primarily based on mutual trust and only secondly on institutions such as courts of justice and police. This holds for nations as well as for individuals. And the basis of trust is loyal give and take.

What about international control? Well, it may be of secondary use as a police measure. But it may be wise not to overestimate its importance. The times of prohibition come to mind and give one pause.[18]

The speaker leaves big gaps between his sentences. You must think to follow him, and in a sense you do not follow him, but lead yourself, for he does not say specifically what you are to believe. Organization needs to be tight or loose, depending upon the kind of listening the speaker wants and can induce.

Speech is intended to influence — even salutations and social conversations. What is good persuasion in one situation may be ineffective in another. Effective persuasion depends upon the speaker's awareness of what the audience expects of him and his ability to understand their attitudes, beliefs, ideals, and purposes. The more profound the difference between the beliefs of the speaker and of his audience, the less persuasive the speaker should expect to be. He should recognize that his persuasiveness is inextricably bound up with the way he phrases his purpose statement and the way he organizes his speech.

There is no easy or pat formula for persuasion. The best assurance of success is a deep sympathy for mankind and a thorough understanding of the motives of human beings, particularly those of your audience.

QUESTIONS FOR STUDY AND DISCUSSION

1. Explain the statement, "All speech is intended to be persuasive." Select a number of comments at random and explain how each is intended to affect the listener.

2. Explain the basic problems involved in dealing with each of the five kinds of audiences.

[18] "Peace in the Atomic Era," reprinted by permission from *Vital Speeches*, March 1, 1950, p. 302.

3. What special considerations should be given the speech for each of the five kinds of audiences?

4. What kinds of audiences need closely-knit organization? What kinds need loosely-knit organization?

SUGGESTIONS AND ASSIGNMENTS

1. With your speech class in mind, write five purpose statements, preferably on the same subject, one for each of the five kinds of audience. Check with the class to determine the accuracy of your choices.

2. Assume your class is any one of the five kinds of audience and prepare a five minute speech with the special consideration that that audience should receive. See if the class can determine from your treatment which of the five kinds of audience the speech was designed for.

Part Three

Some Speech
Situations

———

10

Listening

OF THE FOUR COMMUNICATION skills, reading, writing, speaking, and listening, most of us spend almost as much time listening as we do on the other three skills combined. Thus as measured in time — the most precious possession of life — listening is the most important of the communication skills.

It is equally significant from another point of view. The members of a home, school, occupational group, state, or nation tend to be more alike than members of different homes, schools, occupations, states, and nations. Listening teaches us our language, attitudes, beliefs, and manners. Listening makes us what we are.

This does not mean that our listening is necessarily efficient. How well do we understand even our best friends? Breathes there a teacher who arouses the same set of ideas in all his students? How often do two people interpret a speech, movie, or news broadcast in identical fashion? Perhaps the implication of these questions is not quite fair. The nature of language itself is partly to blame. Words convey different impressions to different people, and arouse different chains of association and thought patterns, because we all have different experiences and different responses to our experiences. Indeed, it would be another world, and perhaps a duller one, if everyone had precisely the same response to stimuli. It is only in transmitting information that uniform response is essential. What freedom do we prize when we demand that people listen alike? It is suggested that, as you read this chapter, you think out for yourself the values and dangers of two kinds of listening — listening independently, and listening as the speaker would have you hear. To get a better grasp of the listening process, let us consider the various ways in which the mind receives incoming messages.

*Everybody likes to hear things that put him in
a better position, or enlarge his world.*

HOW WE RECEIVE MESSAGES

Whether we are conscious or unconscious of the effects of messages
upon us, there are six ways in which we act upon them. The difference
in our response depends upon the way a message affects our self-image
and the mental world in which that image exists.

1. Reinforcement: Acceptance

We readily accept the message that reinforces our position. It is
usually easy to accept the statement that flatters.

> "I like your new hat."
> "That was a good speech you made."
> "I have a high regard for college students."

The message that reinforces our purposes is equally acceptable.

> "It looks like good weather for your vacation."
> "There's a big demand for people in your field."

These and similar messages are easy to hear. They give us security, for
they reinforce the self-picture. They make us feel much as we do after
invigorating exercise. Our self-image is clear, vivid, and intact.

2. Broadened Horizons: Acceptance

We tend to accept the message that adds to our present picture.
Unless we are extremely rigid and inflexible, we tend to accept messages when they leave our world unchallenged and add to it. Most of

us enjoy the freedom of "having our horizons pushed back," especially if the message comes in such a way as to let us feel that we made the change ourselves.

> "Judging from your work in the last debate practice, I think you are ready to go into a contest."
>
> "What you say about the post-Civil War years is important. You can apply that same reasoning to the present period."
>
> "Since you are a college student, you may be interested to know what various social and occupational groups have found to be the values of a college education."

When we receive such messages, something is added to our life. They give us a greater sense of significance and enlarge our world.

3. Threats to Security: Rationalization

We tend to rationalize impressive messages that threaten our security. None of us like to accept messages that (1) belittle us or (2) tear our world apart. Yet a message that seems to speak the truth cannot be dismissed. What are we likely to do? There is a remarkable word in the language that allows us to remain as we are and yet accept, as we must, that which contradicts our picture. The word is that little conjunction *but*. In answer to the disturbing message we say, "I know I shouldn't have lost my temper, *but* I do not see how . . . " "I see what you mean, *but* the fact still remains . . . " As is always true when we rationalize, we become partitive — we are divided against ourselves — and we try to hold our self-image and our world together with verbal maneuvers.

"But" — the little word that often holds a rationalized world together.

1.   2.   3.   4.

Some painful messages cannot be ignored; so we
accept them finally — and change accordingly.

4. Threats to Security: Resistance, then Change

Though we may at first resist, we may finally accept an impressive message by changing either our views or our behavior. This is dynamic learning. It is, of course, painful, because it involves changing either our self-image or our picture of the world. It is fortunate that we resist change at least to some extent, for not all messages which seem to demand change should be accepted. We can learn and accept what is bad or untrue just as well as what is helpful. Only fools believe everything they hear.

Yet maturing is a matter of changing, changing selectively. Good learning is the product of a feedback that operates in such a way that (1) we are not too rigid to change, (2) we do not oscillate between change and rigidity, and (3) we do not change with the wind. Is it too contradictory to say we want *unstable stability*, a central purpose that holds the self-image intact and yet flexible? The whole practice of democratic education is designed to this end, that you may (1) gain faith to act on your own decisions, realizing that you could be wrong; and (2) recognize that there are many ways to solve a problem. This is flexible stability.

We cannot learn unless we change, yet change must leave us intact. A threat to security so great, therefore, that it threatens destruction must be differently acted upon.

When a message does violence to ourselves or our world, we arm ourselves against it.

5. Threats of Destruction: Resistance

When a message would destroy us or tear our world apart, we have no other recourse than to reject what is so foreign that if it makes sense, we do not. The moment we feel that we are faced with this terrible choice, all listening stops. Consider the effect of the following messages:

> "The religion you profess is one of the stupidest faiths I have ever heard of."
> "This democracy of yours is a big fraud."

These are words of destruction. They are effective only with those who are already so dissatisfied with themselves that they want to destroy themselves and their world. But since most of us have no such wish, we reject messages of this kind.

6. Refusal to Listen

Finally, a message may be so uninteresting to us that we simply refuse to hear it. We can adopt the posture of listening, and yet hear nothing. When this happens we have so much to say back to some message, other than the one being sent, that we do not hear. The message to which we are attending may be one we received a sentence or so before, or it may be the remembrance of something in the past, even totally unrelated to the present topic. The speaker may be discussing the law of supply and demand, which reminds a listener of his high school history class. Then his mind may leap to his home and family. . . . You know the boy at meetings who comes up with a wonderful idea ten minutes after the group has discussed it. These people speak, become silent while another takes the floor, but rather than listen go on talking to themselves.

We can seem to be listening without hearing a thing.

All these are the maneuvers of the receiving mind. While they have rich implications for the student speaker, they should also indicate that listening is not passive response, that the entire responsibility for influence does not rest with the speaker, that the speaker cannot change the mind that does not want to change. Listening is an active experience. Success or failure in communication is shared by the receiver. Let us now turn our attention to some specific factors that contribute to the way the mind chooses to deal with a given message.

DETERMINANTS OF LISTENING

Motivation

The way we deal with a message is shaped a good deal by the motives that impel us at the time we are listening. This means that we must prepare to listen just as we prepare ourselves for success in any activity. If we are tired, worried, immersed in decisions just made or to be made, or attracted to the girl across the room, we cannot hear well. We must reject messages because our motives focus our attention on an unrelated set of messages. Some students come to class habitually late and spend the first few minutes preparing themselves for the activity of the hour. Some go to lectures only because they have to, and the fact that their presence is enforced tends to become a motive for not listening. The only motive that facilitates listening is interest, the urge to hear. Any shift of attitude that makes us consider the experience of listening valuable will improve our listening beyond measure.

Attitude Toward the Subject

A second and closely related factor determining the way we listen is the attitude we bring to the subject under discussion. We may hear what is said, but we truly listen only to what we want to hear. This is one of the basic reasons why people interpret the same message differently. We are all prejudiced by our past experiences. The more anxiety associated with that prejudice, the less objectively we listen. It requires the ultimate in self-confidence to try to hear why the speaker believes as he does when his conclusion differs from ours.

It is interesting to note, in the evaluation of class speeches, how some critics are driven to cite the points upon which they disagree with the speaker, almost as if they were not free of the possible influence until they have cast it out verbally. To guard against your own prejudice in your next evaluation of a speaker, in class or elsewhere, try restating what the speaker has said, rather than what you want to answer. If you cannot give an accurate report of his argument, you have not permitted yourself to listen.

Attitude Toward the Speaker

The third determinant of listening is our attitude toward the speaker. If we like him we are much more likely to find that he makes good sense than if we do not. For then we not only understand what he says, but fill in where he is weak. Conversely, when we dislike the speaker, we tend to blot out or distort reception of his best evidence and move to the attack.

Both our code and our logic tell us not to reject messages simply because we dislike the speaker, though there is reason to doubt the speech of a person whom we distrust on good evidence. When, however, we reject an argument because we dislike the speaker, we will seldom admit the real reason even to ourselves. We rationalize our rejection by picking little flaws here and there in the language, content, and style of the speaking. Picayune criticism is a signal that our dislike of the speaker has closed our ears.

Again, when we choose to evaluate the speech of a person we dislike, we should first try to reproduce faithfully what he said. If we can do this, we are in a reasonable frame of mind to appraise it.

Focus of Attention

Finally, listening is shaped by our focus. Sometimes we tend to concentrate on content; at other times, on style. Ideally, it is best if our thinking is influenced purely by our appraisal of what is said. But the fact is that most of us are highly responsive to style. Students sent to college assemblies for listening assignments quite often respond to content in accordance with their appraisal of the speaker as a speaker. His language, voice, posture, and mannerisms seem to guide their hearing of conclusions and evidence, probably because these factors measured by the eye and ear are so much easier to deal with than the more difficult matters of logic, accuracy of statement, soundness of judgment and knowledge.

This tendency to judge by superficialities is a threat to critical listening. Again the test is whether you can give a faithful report of the main points and supporting data used in a speech. This is the test of whether you are adequately prepared to evaluate.

Here a qualification needs to be added. In the interest of learning the techniques and standards of effective speech, it is desirable that you study the language, voice, posture, and mannerisms of speakers — but not merely to be impressed by them; rather, for the purpose of learning to speak more effectively. But our concern at this point is with the improvement of your listening to what is being said.

TWO KINDS OF LISTENING

In a sense good listening comes of the capacity to see through the eyes of the speaker, to live his life as he speaks, just as good speaking comes of the capacity to adjust and live in part the experience of the listener. You may adjust to the speaker for one of two reasons: (1) to appreciate fully and for its own sake the evidence which the speaker is presenting, or (2) to use his evidence as the basis for stirring your own mental processes. That is, you may set yourself to listen in one of two ways: submissively, or creatively.

Submissive Listening

In learning to function in our culture, you have been impressed with the need to absorb facts, beliefs, attitudes, and opinions that are common to our society and to the profession in which you hope to function. The educational system, in large measure, is designed to place you at the receiving end and to test your ability to "take in." What is basic to reception?

The Central Idea. The key to accurate listening is to learn how to pick out the central idea of an assignment, a lecture, or a set of instructions. The mind is so constructed that meaning is a constellation in which facts and opinions are planets circumscribing a sun, a central idea.[1] The various parts of a discussion then maintain their relationships by the centripetal attraction of the core of the meaning structure, the central idea, for the planetary facts and opinions. And the difference between a person who merely learns an unrelated mass of facts and one who understands is the difference in ability to perceive through the data the central idea about which they revolve. Thus all good submissive listening begins with searching out the "big idea."

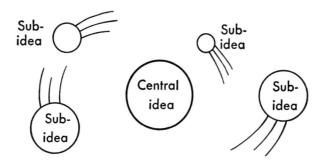

This done, the job is then to place the rest of the data in their positions in the system. It obviously follows that, if you happen to mistake a minor idea in a speech for the main one, or if you grasp the main idea inaccurately or incompletely, the whole meaning you derive is distorted.

Improving Reception. Like any skill, listening improves with practice. As a college student you have plenty of opportunity for this. Make it a point in listening to lectures to search consciously for the main idea. A good lecturer usually states his purpose at the beginning, but it is too much to expect that all lecturers will do so, or that

[1] This is really another way of saying that any whole message is made up of assertions and support.

all lectures need follow exactly the same plan. The important point is for the listener to extract from the discourse that statement which best covers all the major emphases — or if, as often happens, there is no such single statement, to formulate one for himself.

If you can get the main point at the beginning, so much the better. Write it down. It will help you recognize the chief supporting points more readily as they are made. Should the speaker say, "It is my purpose this morning to point out that the national tax structure is unsound," you may write, "What are the evidences that the national tax structure is unsound?" — or simply, "National tax structure unsound." If the central purpose of the speech is not clear to you at the outset, write down in as few words as possible the important points you identify as the lecture proceeds. When the speaker says, "Now the second important reason is . . . " or when his manner of speaking becomes more emphatic than usual, you are receiving what in a textbook would be a heading or a subheading. Write this down.

If you have not ferreted out the main idea by the end of the lecture period, look over the main points in your notebook as soon as possible thereafter, and formulate a statement that unites all the points. Write this down.

As an evaluative feedback, check your main points and your subdivisions with other students. If you find agreement, your listening is probably pretty accurate. If you do not agree discuss the matter to see if you can find out why other students received a different impression. If this daily practice does not gradually bring you closer to the listening of others, see your speech or English instructor for special aid in this problem.

Should your difficulty be unique to one course, see the instructor in that course. Ask him for a conference. This will often be of help to him as well as to you. College professors need a constant echo from their students to keep them alert to you, the target. When you talk to a professor about your problems of listening, you will find it helpful to have with you your notes on one or two of his recent lectures.

Reading does not involve quite the same skills as listening, but you can gain in some of the skills common to both if you will outline some reading every day while you are concentrating on improving your listening skills. Every extended communication, regardless of the form or medium, has a central idea and related parts, and you need practice in manipulating these things.

The above techniques are designed to test and improve your capacity to see the order, emphases, and aim of a communication. Of perhaps equal importance is your ability to retain what you have heard. This may be tested and developed by writing all you can remember of a classroom speech or a lecture immediately after its completion, or a day or a week later. If the whole class performs the assignment, a comparison of papers gives each member a more vivid picture of his strengths and limitations in accuracy and completeness. A discussion of personal differences in memory reveals much about the factors of listening. Persistent practice of this kind improves the listening set and the memory.

Listening to Criticism. One of the most difficult exercises in submissive listening is accepting criticism, and particularly criticism of our speech. Speech is the skin of the self. Unless we have a great deal of security, we are compulsively driven to defend ourselves, no matter how delicately or skillfully the criticism is offered. "Yes, I know, but. . . . " "I had to study for a history exam last night." "But that isn't what I wanted to do in this speech." "But I said that!" When these responses come, the critic might just as well cease operations.

The question is not one of right or wrong, good or bad. If we want to speak better we must listen to evaluations. We cannot grade ourselves independently of the reactions of the audience. The areas they disapprove of are the areas where we should seek change, provided that we want to communicate. If the audience demands changes which we refuse to make, we have the right to refuse; but our refusal is not in the interest of improving our speech, at least with that particular audience.

If you can stand it, do not argue back when your speech is criticized in class. Hear each critic out, and then restate what he has said. You'll be amazed how quickly this will improve your speaking. You'll improve because you have permitted yourself to see the difference between your aim and your mark.

Creative Listening

Concentrating on an accurate grasp of what others say, in order to repeat it when the appropriate time comes, is the kind of listening which receives major emphasis in most lecture courses, for the dominating purpose of tests and examinations is to see whether you "know" what you have read and heard. As we have seen, such listening has its values and uses. The trouble is that students sometimes learn to be too absorbent — or, more accurately, come to feel that uncritical memorizing is the only aim of listening. One girl listened to a half-hour speech intended to stir her to think and react on a number of related topics. Her speech which followed turned out to be a remarkably full restatement of what she had heard. She not only remembered all the main points in perfect order, but also much of the detail. She was hypnotized by the impression she had received, but she had no reaction of her own to offer. This girl had a good mind, but she was too submissive for her best development.

In contrast, here is the comment of a mature man about a book he had just read: "I don't know when I've read such a good book. It sure started my wheels spinning. Actually I don't agree with his analysis, but he got me talking back. That's the only reason I read. I use reading to stir my own processes, when the machine runs down."

This man is well educated. He can afford to use the communication of others as a stimulus for his own processes and powers. Most students cannot go this far as yet. But the greater danger lies in not going far enough in "talking back" to the communications one receives.

Almost everyone has to some degree had the experience of reacting in his own personal way to what he hears. If you have had the thrill of "giving birth to an idea" you know what this means. It is well, for the sake of keeping our egos under control, to recognize that these creative bursts are not entirely ours. Our past unites with a message from without, and the offspring which we so lovingly call ours is, like all children, born of two parents. However, an idea does not have to be ours alone or unique in the world to be the product of creative-listening — which in essence simply means "thinking back" at the speaker. The test in which you are asked to interpret a phrase, to explain the implications of a quotation, a law, or a principle, is designed to stir you to think, to talk back.

For the sake of this kind of listening, it is well in lectures to take only essential notes. While you write you are practically incapable of thinking about the message being sent. You need to be free of the guided pencil to say to yourself, "That reminds me of a similar idea . . . Oh, yes, I've heard of that before . . . I don't know whether it is as inclusive as you make it . . . I don't believe I understand that . . . Where are your facts? . . . I can think of some to the contrary . . . Oh, that gives me a new idea . . . I must read on that subject . . . Strange how so many things that once I thought unrelated fit together . . . What kind of experiences and impressions cause a person to talk that way? . . . Maybe this explains that question that keeps returning . . . " These are the twists and turns of a mind listening creatively. Write the gist of your answering for future meditation and exploration.

Improving Creative Listening. Silent speech is creative, but it can be extremely vague and formless. To see if your critical thinking is clear and productive, you need to speak or write your reactions. As one technique, you may listen to a lecture and then note down, say, five related topics which come to mind. The more exciting and significant they are, the more productive is your listening. An evaluation of your results by other students and by the instructor gives you an objective feedback on your skill.

Another technique is to listen to a speech, movie, drama, set of directions — any spoken communication — and formulate a short speech on a *significant idea* which it suggests to you. What is significant? Whatever seems significant to you. Having given the speech, you need the evaluation of the class and the instructor to check you against the standards of others. By seeing what other students bring forth, and by noting what your class at large considers significant, you gain the knowledge necessary for changes in your future listening.

A third technique is to listen to the statement of a problem. What should be the next move of the United States in dealing with "foreign power X"? What are the ways of getting your work done if you live in a dormitory? What should the class do about the slump it has fallen into in recent weeks? If one member in a group project should give a talk on a problem, discussing the situation and the causes of it, the rest of you may think in terms of possible solutions. Put down on paper all the possible solutions that occur to you. Look these over and evaluate them. Read your solutions, indicating the one that seems best to you. Others may offer theirs and thereby evaluate yours.

Still a fourth technique is to listen to a short, well-prepared informative speech over a public address system in which the instructor irreg-

ularly raises and lowers the volume. This will disturb your listening
set and cause you to see the ideas in the discussion, and others related to them, in a new and different fashion. When the speech is
over, write down immediately as many ideas as were suggested to you
by the speech. Compare these with your usual reactions to a speech.
What, if any, difference do you note?

A final technique is to compare the ideas you write down when
listening to a fluent, well-organized speech, and when listening to a
non-fluent, relatively disorganized speech. The latter makes you expand your listening comprehension span, and you will make leaps
you do not for the former.

Critical Listening

Within the realm of creative listening is a special kind which may
be called "critical" listening. When we listen critically, the same inner
speech goes on as with any creative listening, but the purpose is
different. In "pure" creative listening we use the incoming message
as a stimulus to set our own exploratory and expressive processes to
work. When listening critically we answer, but we answer defensively.
We are guarding ourselves against the logical and emotional weaknesses of the speaker, that we may not accept illusions and delusions.

A boy gave a speech defending the entertainment level of radio
and television. His speech ran something as follows:

> I don't understand the attack on radio and television entertainment.
> A person ought to be allowed to listen to what he wants. It's nobody's
> business if it's high or low. If we like it, that's reason enough. And
> we do like it. You don't suppose for one minute that Colgate, Geritol,
> and Bardahl, and all the rest would spend millions putting on programs
> that people do not want. They give us what we want so we'll be there
> to listen to their advertising.
>
> Besides, look at all the newscasters we have on the air. Radio and
> television keep us up on what's going on. . . .

The class criticized the speech on three counts. (1) That people
should be allowed to listen to what they please is beside the point; the
question is, is the program level high or low? (2) That people listen
is beside the point. If they are going to listen, they have to listen to
what is offered. Besides, even if the public did play a decisive role in
the choice of programs, the question remains: is the level high or low?
(3) News programs are not entertainment, and are irrelevant to the

speech. This is critical listening, and it is a creative experience. In this case the criticism was a little rough on the speaker, but such evaluations are not harmful, so long as they are not exploited — used as a release for the critic's need to hurt someone.

But critical listening is more than merely pointing out weaknesses. It means doubting and questioning, which may or may not lead to modification or rejection of the speaker's position. Another student gave a speech explaining the success of a developmental reading program. He had statistics which showed that, as a result of taking the course, freshmen could double their reading rate and improve their comprehension level by 20 per cent. One listener, in the question period, asked "How much does a freshman improve in the year if he doesn't take the course? I'm not sure I know whether your figures show the results of the course, natural growth, or both." This listener was not primarily pointing out a weakness in what the speaker said. He was doubting, and he was exercising the skill of critical listening at its best, as indicated by his intelligent question.

The source of critical listening is critical thinking, and this was the burden of Chapter 6. If you do not listen with discrimination, make that chapter your bible.

The Signal to Inner Speech

Creative listening is the skill to respond thoughtfully to what is happening to yourself as you receive a message. How can you sharpen this signal? One way is to (1) take any experience that has impressed you, (2) describe it, and then (3) tell what the experience did to you. How do you see and act differently, having had this impression? Here is an illustration of one student's response to a moving experience.

On Easter morning at dawn I sat with thousands of other people in the Hollywood Bowl. This multitude of people had gathered for the sunrise services held in the bowl annually. The choir broke forth into song as the first rays of the bright sun broke over the surrounding hills. This wondrous sight and sound bore down on me with great magnitude and touched me deeply with emotion. As the services continued their reverent solemnness, my mind went blank to the events around me, dwelling only on the naked beauty of the sun rising in the east. At that moment I felt there could never be another time when I'd be so close to God.

As the service ended and the sun rose above the hills, the spell was broken. Yet, in a way, that spell has never been broken, for by closing my eyes, I can recapture the scene with all its soul-lifting power. And so even today, thirteen years later, I am able to relive the awe-inspiring moment of an experience I shall never forget.

Even better, can you anticipate an impressive experience and "hear," as you pass through it, what it "says" and what you "say" back to it? This is what a freshman girl did who gave the following talk:

Last weekend, after five weeks of college life, I went home. I'd like to tell you about it.

I had not planned to go until Thanksgiving, because I live so far away. But when I was offered a ride I couldn't help jumping at the chance. The thought of seeing my family, along with the newly acquired member, "Bargain" (a puppy whose family tree dare not be traced), was too exciting. I couldn't resist.

While we were on the way I tried to remember how the street I live on looks, and our house and my family. I had the strangest feeling that everything was going to be distant, as though I were a visitor seeing it all for the first time. You would think I had been away five years.

As we drove through Detroit the lights were so bright they hurt my eyes. I've lived in Detroit all my life, but it had never looked so industrial. Quite a contrast to quiet little Kalamazoo.

The song says "the longest mile is the last mile home," and I believe it. When we reached the last mile, I began getting butterflies in my stomach, like a little girl waiting for her first dance. I wanted to put my foot on the accelerator and push it to the floor. Then, as though I had closed my eyes for a second, we were in front of my house, and my mother and father were running toward the car. Mother was crying and Dad was holding the new puppy. The car pulled away and the three of us walked into the house.

I don't think that my house ever looked so good to me.

My family was still the same too, still there when I need them.

It was I who was different. I had broken away from depending on my parents. Now that I knew home was still there, I was ready to go back to school.

Consistent practice like this will place this girl at the helm of her own life. What greater freedom can she have?

We are all impressed, every day, by the significance of some idea, fact, or experience, and the sum total of these impressions guides our reactions and our behavior in every new experience. The question is:

are you the slave to the messages that come your way, or have you developed an echo that allows you to hear, select, and reject? Creative listening is talking in response to incoming messages. The skill is improved and sharpened by talking aloud. The real difference between creative and submissive listening is whether or not you phrase to yourself the effect upon you of what has commanded your attention.

QUESTIONS FOR STUDY AND DISCUSSION

1. What are the six ways we react to messages? What are the values in knowing these kinds of reaction?

2. What factors determine what we hear?

3. What is meant by submissive listening? What are its values, its dangers?

4. What is the value of searching for the central idea when listening? How can you discover it when it is not clearly stated?

5. How can you learn to improve your submissive listening?

6. What is creative listening? What are its values?

7. How can you improve your creative listening?

8. Why is it valuable to write and speak your impressions and reactions?

SUGGESTIONS AND ASSIGNMENTS

For Submissive Listening

1. Take down the central idea and outline of the speeches given in class. Compare your version with those of two other students and make a short report to the class on places where you agree and disagree.

2. Attend (with your class) a campus lecture and outline the speech. From the outline construct a statement that covers the main points. Compare this statement with the main idea you think was intended. If they are different, why? Did the speaker emphasize ideas that did not fit his main purpose or did you outline poorly? Report the facts and your judgment to the class.

3. Examine your lecture notes (for every course) after each class. Write down the central idea of each lecture. Is this statement the purpose of the lecture? Check your statements occasionally with the lecturer.

4. Listen with your classmates to a speech. Either immediately, or at a given time thereafter, write out the speech as fully as you can. Check the paper for accuracy and completeness against the papers of others.

For Creative Listening

5. Listen to a speech in class. Immediately afterwards write other main points that might have been included, and list topics related to the central idea. Compare these with those of several other students. Can you see how their main points and topics are related? If so you have expanded your view.

6. Draw up a speech on one of the related topics that you thought of which seems particularly interesting to you. For instance, one of the speeches you listened to may have been on the problem of parking on your campus. That may have raised a question as to increased property values with the growth of your campus, or the cost of turning a part of your campus into a parking lot, or the objections of the Administration to adding another parking lot. Any one or all of these ideas might be investigated and made into a speech. Following through your own creative listening may suggest to you the possibilities of listening more independently. Again have the students and instructor evaluate your product.

7. Take any problem you have heard discussed and set down as many solutions as you can think of. To return to the parking problem on your campus, how many solutions can you see? For instance: (1) more efficient use of present lots, (2) purchase of additional land, (3) alteration of city parking regulations on nearby streets, (4) parking meters on the campus, (5) elimination of student cars on campus that are not needed, etc. Investigate the proposals, pointing out the evidence for and against each. Defend the solution you think best. Have the students evaluate your thinking.

8. Be alert to an experience that impresses you either favorably or unfavorably. Describe it and your reactions to it. Write this up and hand it in. A daily diary of impressions and reactions is an excellent device for improving your listening.

9. Choose a topic and a classmate who is interested in the same topic. Prepare some ideas on the subject and meet with your friend to discuss it. Record your discussion. When you have a five minute section in which you both were interested and involved, stop and play this back several times, seeing if each of you can label the ways you handled the messages of the other. From analysis you may see which of the six ways of receiving messages was used most often; more important, which kinds were most used by each of you. The person who accepted the most was obviously the more submissive. Was it language or ideas that caused the one to be the more dominant?

Play back a section to the class and analyze it. Out of such analyses you gain a better understanding of the target-set that is effective, of the self-hearing that produces self-change.

10. Give a speech which you have prepared well and have a student record it, altering the volume with the interest, loudest when you are most interesting. Study the recording and see if you can determine why your sending varied with the receiver as it did.

It is not sufficiently considered that men require more often to be reminded than to be informed.

Dr. Johnson

11

Conversation

To CONVERSE WELL is to commune with another person. To exchange, uncensored, the thoughts aroused as we take turns in speaking and listening is the closest, most direct, and most informal of all ways that human beings communicate with each other. What can we learn of this experience so close to the core of living?

A student of speech secretly recorded the conversation at social gatherings for several months in order to determine the motives and patterns it revealed. He concluded that most people talked pretty much for the sake of talking. Sometime when you are in a contemplative mood, you may check this finding. Just listen to people around you. Perhaps one student has just heard the baseball scores:

"The Giants won 4 to 3."

"They won yesterday too, didn't they?"

"Yeh, looks like Chicago's dropping out of the picture again."

"I was down at Chicago yesterday. Gee, it was hot!"

"What'd you go for?"

"Oh, Bob wanted me to go with him. He had to see his father about something."

"Drive?"

"Yeh, I took my car."

"How come you didn't take Bob's?"

"The darn thing's on the fritz again. I wouldn't have one of those crates."

"That reminds me, I've got to pick up Phyllis at 3:30. How about going with me?"

"Okay! She working again today?"

A study of this typical fragment of talk indicates that the course of most conversation is directed by free association. It is subject to the same random currents of influence as the individual's stream of consciousness. One topic suggests another, seemingly almost by accident, except that in conversation the process is social; that is, it incorporates the associated ideas of two or more people. In contrast, discussion (see Chapter 12) is the effort of a group to solve a problem, to work toward a specific answer. Discussion therefore has a specific goal. But in conversation we generally do not care especially where we go. We wander and explore whatever is mutually agreeable. We dabble with a subject until it wearies us, until some aspect of it opens new avenues of interest, or until some more alluring topic rises from the mind of one of the speakers.

Values of Conversation

In spite of its seeming absence of direction, the values of conversation are profound. It is conversation that teaches us how to relate ourselves to other people. As we listen and throw out comments, we receive satisfaction or dissatisfaction, reward or punishment. By comparing the techniques of success with those of failure, we adjust and try new kinds of behavior.

Since conversation is so free, it is the most creative of our speech experiences. Ideas may not often be tracked very far, but new paths are started. Indeed it will usually prove frustrating and futile to try to follow through an idea that has just been aroused.

Some writers suggest that good conversation deals only with "knowledge" and "ideas." Others gravitate toward the position that conversation is a social grace, involving adjustment to the group, attractive and clever response. Both views contain elements of truth, and yet in important ways are beside the point. They emphasize the need to meet the level of the group you happen to be cast into — merely in order to make a good impression. Naturally, everyone wants to make a good impression, but if the sole purpose of your conversation is "to get ahead" or "make a hit," this is a perversion that prevents sincerity, relaxation, and real enjoyment in many conversational situations.

To converse is to commune, and demands some degree of real interest in the other person, the subject, or both. Good conversation is life at its best, and at its best a vital interest between people is its motive and its spark. This kind of conversation takes place when you are with those you enjoy the most and fear the least. It cannot be forced or even prepared for, except as your whole life is a preparation for the moment when you fall in with people of like interest. Ordinarily, conversation has no end beyond mutual exploration and enjoyment. Good conversation can be on football or philosophy, girls or gambling, boys or bicycles. Any subject is suitable if there is a genuine exchange. You don't work at it, or assign it standards; when you really wish to communicate, the rest will take care of itself.

Motives — Good and Bad

As we pointed out in Chapter 1, the human being uses his speech to probe into his own life. Early in life we say whatever comes to mind, soon to be hush-hushed by our parents. As life proceeds, speech becomes a matter of selecting, according to the social penalties which threaten, the thoughts that seem most acceptable out of all those that flit across the mind. Rejected thoughts pile up, and at times marshal themselves to demand expression. At such moments we are confused. Most of us in such situations find a great need to soliloquize. We must reverse the balance of power within ourselves, and a jumble of speech follows, conflicting and disorganized.

Self-Exploration. Take a simple example. You have come to college to get an education, and of course the grades you receive and the reactions of your instructors serve as an occasional reflection of your progress. Meanwhile you are in constant communication with students. All those interests unrelated to grades demand time and energy — dates, athletics, bull sessions, campus politics, and social affairs. Unexpectedly you get a *D* on a test, and this brings to sharp focus your underlying purposes. Before you run to your books, however, speech must turn the tide of your behavior. You fall into step with a friend as you leave class.

> "Gee, I studied for that exam too. Cut all my classes the day before. What stupid questions! Look at the way he graded. Took off for every little thing. I was sure I'd get a C. Did you notice Joe drew a *B?* Holy cow, if he can get a B, I'm good for an A. I don't get it. I suppose I should have enough sense not to ask questions in class. . . ."

All this is a sort of compromise. It admits concern for getting through school, but does not admit responsibility. Yet underneath there is a haunting feeling that some change must be made.

While you are talking, your roommate is reacting, and you are guided by his response. If he counters that you didn't study soon enough, you go into a more exhaustive self-justification. If he agrees that the professor is a "sad character," you may take off from this revelation into a vivid description of professors in general, and this one in particular. If your friend says that he had to study pretty hard to get a C and that he made some pretty bad mistakes he hopes not to make again, you make the swing. "Yeh. Well, I guess I'll have to hit the books."

Your experience here is self-exploration, for you are confused and are looking for a clear picture. The need for speech which helps to clarify the problem will be necessary until a solution comes into view, and the more distressed you are, the more you will depend upon an audience to direct you to the heart of the problem.

Understanding Others. Just as self-exploration leads to insight, so talk with others leads to "outsight," the understanding of others. As we suggested earlier, the most interesting element in the environment is other people. We explore each other's attitudes, experiences reactions to us, and the world at large through conversation. The game seldom grows stale, for the "inconsistency" of human reaction is the basis for perpetual surprise.

Release. Or conversation may be used to release pent-up emotions. This usually takes the form of complaint — about the weather, the government, the next-door neighbor, the food, anything that happens to come under observation. When we feel bad, everything seems out of order, and we may rid ourselves of this frustration and hate by turning to argument. The first person to contradict us may expect a headlong attack. It is doubtful whether the listener derives any value from such conversation — except for the insight it gives him into the nature of the speaker — but for the speaker it is at least temporarily helpful. Emotional festering is not conducive to mental health, and verbal washing is the best of cleansers. The way to improve conversation is not to restrain bitter talk, but to alter the attitudes and conditions that give birth to the need for complaint.

Exhibitionism. Sometimes conversation which sounds exploratory degenerates into little more than "showing off." On the surface, speech may purport to be self-exploration, while actually the conversationalist is revealing his internal reactions not for examination, but for the pleasure of parade. Symptoms of the motive are intonation, pauses that suggest the anticipation of effects, the satisfied smile at the ends of phrases or sentences. Communication drops into the background and the participants rush forth to display their cleverness at sketching self-portraits.

Competition. In our culture, there is a great danger of conceiving of all situations competitively. Some people feel slighted if they do not get to talk more than the rest. More, longer, and louder all too often go together.[1] The competitive spirit gets into story-telling too. You have no doubt met the kind of person who suffers until he is assured his story topped the rest.

Exploitation. Talk unites people. The exploiter uses the resulting cohesion as the basis for self-advancement. The college student falls to talking with Joe, having met his beautiful sister. The businessman joins clubs and entertains people who can advance his personal aims and ambitions. There is something revolting about conversation whose only motive is exploitation. When personal interest coincides with the urge for companionship, most of us are not distressed. This is a dependent world, and all of us must work and play within the structures of the groups we know.

Conversation and Information

Conversation is used to exchange information. It would be a mistake, however, to assume that men often talk primarily for this purpose. Information is objective and of itself is not a common motive.

> "Say, there's a good movie at the State!"
> "What problems do you want us to work on tomorrow?"
> "I went hunting last week."
> "Did you see that article in last night's paper about the cost of living?"
> "Little Betty Jones has the measles."

Any one of these remarks may blossom into a lengthy conversation, but each is inspired by a complex of urges to speak. Knowledge is power, power that we may wish to share with another or exert over another, or power which we may use to gain more power. The motives to converse will always be found within the self and its relation to

---

[1] It does not necessarily follow that the person who dominates a scene is aggressive. Perhaps the others want him to lead, especially if he has an idea or an experience they want to share.

other selves, and information is only the currency of these transactions.

Requisites for Good Conversation

Zest. The beginning of good conversation is a buoyant spirit. Life is exhilarating. Speech bubbles over because it is difficult to restrain. In good conversation the present moment is supreme. Jobs undone, bills unpaid, tomorrow's classes, are of no concern. Zest is the beginning, and satisfaction is the end. Perhaps the most important condition for good conversation is expressed in the vague utterance, "This is it." "It" is discovering purpose fulfilled, release from yearning.

Interest in Others. A second condition needed for good conversation is a genuine interest in your conversants. You cannot force this, either. Nor is there any moral obligation involved. If, with you, the very act of breathing is good, you are so related to yourself and the world that others are important. It is just the way of nature that enthusiasm for life brings others within our vision. As Robert Louis Stevenson says, there are only three topics of conversation: "you, the person with whom you speak, and other people in the world." All other things are but properties on the stage.

Sympathy. Perhaps no quality of good conversation is so evident as sympathy. According to *The American College Dictionary*, sympathy is the "relation between persons whereby the condition of one induces a responsive condition in another." In a sense sympathy is not a cause but a description of the situation where barriers are low or non-existent. What, then, are the conditions that favor sympathy?

Mutual Respect. We can talk openly only to the person for whom we have respect. We feel confident that he will not laugh at what he sees within us, nor use our revelations against us. We then do not need to censor the stream of thought, and our friend keeps lifting our half-conscious reactions to vocal expression. Perhaps the core of respect is confidence in the appreciation and values of the other person.

Social Sensitivity. Closely related to respect is social sensitivity. This is essentially the ability to see the structure of human relations and to read the reactions of others. The sensitive person knows, particularly, when those around him are bored, unhappy, worried, immersed in thought, afraid, constrained. He sees the self-images that direct others. He knows that the same quip makes one man laugh and another feel hurt. He has perhaps unconsciously cultivated the language of testing another's inclinations, so that invitations and requests do not create stress and embarrassment. The result is that we are comfortable with the person who is socially sensitive.

Common Interests. No man can understand another except to the degree that he is like the other. Sympathy is based on community of reaction. We cannot talk to the man of foreign tongue. We cannot talk much better to a man who speaks our own language but has different meanings for words from our meanings. We cannot share words unless we and our listeners interpret them in the same or nearly the same way. In a sense, a man talks with nobody save himself. We carry on conversation with others because they take a part in our personal drama, they "speak our language." To say "I understand you" is to say "That part of you sounds like a part of me."

Self-Confidence. A final factor that "induces a responsive condition in another" is our own self-confidence. Respect, social sensitivity, and common interest do not break down barriers unless we trust ourselves. The person who fears himself may be a receiver, but he cannot be a sender. It is common psychological knowledge that when we fear, when we cannot accept ourselves, we cannot share with others.

Understanding Ourselves. In general, we carry on good conversations only as we understand and are willing to express ourselves. What else have we to talk about that is any more interesting? People are not primarily interested in our ability to report the news, the world we have seen and heard. If so, we might each better carry a sound-equipped movie camera and show each other the film we have taken during the day. In this way each of us could experience the travels of others without being misinformed by their prejudices. When we want news, we go to the papers or the radio, not to our friends — unless it is easier.

We go to our friends to find out about them. Max says Mary gave him a bad time when he asked for a date. Why are you interested in Max's interpretation? You want to find out what happened to him, of course. But more important, you want to know it from him. With any other source, even direct observation, you as a person have not "been dealt in." You do not become a part of the conversation until Max interprets the incident for you. What you really want to know is how he took it. The more adequately Max can talk out his experience, the more interesting he is to you.

Did you ever converse with a person who upon returning from a trip could say only:

> "It was wonderful; you should take that trip."
> "What did you see?"
> "Everything. Boy! It was wonderful."

We want to see the journey through his eyes. If he can tell us little of his reactions, except that he was there, he does not understand himself and can be of little conversational value to us.

Humor. Good conversation is generally shot through with humor. This does not necessarily involve skillful story-telling or even wit. These things of course have their place, but humor is more persuasive. It means seeing ideas and people, particularly ourselves, in new and surprising ways. It is philosophy in action, the inclination to regard "an annoyance in the very stroke of it as another man shall regard it when the annoyance is long past." Charles S. Brooks, who so well describes humor in these words, goes on to tell of a friend with whom he camped in the Canadian woods.

> I do not recall that he said many comic things and at the bottom he was serious as the best of humorists are. But in him there was a kind of joy and exhaltation which lasted throughout the day. If the duffle was piled too high and fell about his ears, if the dinner was burned or the tent blew down in a driving storm at night, he met these mishaps as though they were the very things he had come north to get, as though without them the trip would have lacked its spice. . . . A ————— laughed at the very moment of disaster as another man will laugh later in an easy chair.[2]

When people laugh, anxiety is dead, the barriers are down, and they can converse. Humor is a close ally to comradeship.

Patterns of Conversation

Conversation has structure, as does any social organization. There are three relatively distinct patterns which you may have noted.

[2] Charles S. Brooks, *Chimney-Pot Papers*, New Haven, Connecticut, Yale University Press, 1919, p. 133.

Soliloquy or Monologue. Some people converse as if they were
giving a public speech. They take over the transmitting function and
relegate others to the role of listeners. People who converse in this
fashion are immersed either in self-exploration or in exhibition. The
good monologist is an effective self-dramatist. He stages himself in a
one-man play, taking in turn the roles of the various "little people"
within him. If successful, he is an energetic and commanding story-
teller.

Reactive Conversation. For every monologist there must be at
least one good listener. Such a listener is not impassive, and the skill
with which he plays his role has much to do with the flourish of his
partner. He does not say much, but he is a good analyst. He interprets the speech as it gushes out, and he reacts (with a number of
techniques to be discussed shortly) in such a way as to tap and direct
the flow. If the monologist is the actor and the dramatist, the skillful listener is stage manager, scene designer, and prompter, as well as
audience.

The monologist usually recognizes these qualities and searches out
persons who have them in order to lift him to his conversational best.
Monologist and listener esteem each other, each holding the other
in a certain awe, each seeing in the other a less developed part of
himself. It is probably the experience of seeing oneself in new and interesting ways as revealed by the other person that cements individuals
into society.

Mutual Interaction. Equal sharing of the roles of speaker and
listener probably yields the richest conversation, at least the most
democratic. This happens when each person acts as a fuse for explosions of thought in the other. John Buchan, novelist and one-time
Prime Minister of Canada, thus describes one of England's Prime
Ministers:

> One key to the understanding of Arthur Balfour was his conversation.
> Unhesitatingly I should put him down as the best talker I have ever
> known, one whose talk wasn't brilliant monologue or a string of epi-
> grams, but a communal effort which quickened and elevated the whole
> discussion and brought out the best of other people.[3]

[3] *Pilgrim's Way*, Boston, Houghton Mifflin Company, 1940, p. 155. Reprinted
by permission of the Tweedsmuir Trustees and Messrs. Hodder and Stoughton,
London, England, publishers of the English edition, *Memory Hold the Door.*

In contrast is the talker who habitually blocks his partner — as Fred Allen put it, the person who "always carries a spare subject to introduce into other people's conversations." [4]

Techniques of Conversation

Conversation is such a natural and familiar experience that it is easy to overlook the fact that it has techniques, like any other activity. Here are some of them.

Non-Possessiveness. One good way to establish desirable relations with others is to give credit where credit is due. "As you were saying. . . . I don't believe I have heard it put that way before. . . . Boy, you can say that again. . . . Where did you say you heard this? . . . Tell me where I can find out more about that. . . . That's an exciting idea you have there. . . . "

Conversely, the way to grind conversations to a stop is to assume that every contribution is your own. "As I was saying. . . . " "Don't you think I am right? . . . " "I wish people could get this idea. . . . " Good conversation gives others a fair share of credit and esteem.

Parallel Talk. By parallel talk we mean the technique of signaling *reception* and *acceptance* of what the other person says. You do not have to know very much on the subject or be talkative to carry on parallel conversation. You run alongside the person carrying the ball, keeping him aware that you are there. While surely you must not reject his thought processes, perhaps you excite the best in him if your responses are neutral, for this very neutrality, while reassuring, encourages the exercise of his finest powers.

Interpretation. There are essentially two ways of carrying on parallel talk. The first is to interpret the conversant, to restate in different words what he has said. If your statement is clear and accurate, it is satisfying to him. You will often see his face light up. It is as if a part of himself has come to life and spoken.

Interpretation may recognize the content of a remark or may comment on the motives of the speaker. Let us take an example of each.

"I was sitting there, I guess an hour, when all of a sudden I got a strike. Man, he must have been a big one! I began hauling him in.

4 *The Reader's Digest*, June, 1941, p. 85.

I was too excited. I got in a hurry. He broke water twice in rapid succession, then he was gone, snapped the leader."

"Takes a pretty big one to snap a leader."

Such a comment reacts to the facts of the situation and gives satisfaction to the conversant because it acknowledges reception. Contrast the following response which is less to the facts than to the speaker's feelings:

"That's an awful moment, when the fun suddenly stops."

This understanding comment shares the inward world of the speaker and indicates a kindred spirit.

Notice the difference in the two interpretive responses to the following remark:

"He knows I like him, but I don't want to marry him. It's no fun going with a fellow who is always acting disappointed because you don't feel different than you do."

"He probably thinks if he hangs around you'll change your mind."

This rejoinder signals reception by commenting on the structure of the relationship being discussed. Here is a different response:

"You're caught in a situation where you find his company both pleasant and painful."

This time the comment recognizes the first speaker's conflicting motives. Conversation that leads to deep friendship is built on this kind of understanding. Only sincere interest allows a listener to hear the purposes and feelings of his companion.

If you are at ease with your companion, such understanding responses from him will endear him to you. If you are defensive with him, they may irritate you for they show that he is too close for your comfort.

Restatement. Besides interpretation, a second way of carrying forward parallel talk is by vivid restatement. The speaker whose ideas are rephrased by his conversant feels not only that he was received clearly, and even appreciated, but that his comment may have more vitality or importance than he had supposed. Perhaps he recognizes that the contribution is not his own, or perhaps he does not. In any case he feels that his remark has been responsible for exciting his companion, and this is deeply satisfying. Notice the response to the following:

> "I don't see how we are going to be popular on the campus so long as we take our stand on issues purely on the basis of how much we can hurt the Delta Theta's."
> "What you are saying is we won't regain leadership until we begin standing for something again."
> "That's it. That's exactly it."

The Probe. A good deal is often done to advance conversation by the person who suggests that exploration is not complete. "I don't believe I understand. . . . Tell me more about that angle. . . . There is probably a good deal more to the story. . . . I keep wondering why. . . ."

The voice of cogitation and neutrality lends greatest effect to such statements. If, when you probe, you assume the attitude "I am not sure why. . . . " your voice will carry no sting, and will urge the speaker to seek further in an area that has already proved interesting to him — and to you.

The Incomplete Phrase. A great deal is done to direct conversation by unfinished statements. "Yes, I suppose . . . Well . . . Humm . . . But . . . If you remember . . . They can't all . . . What about . . . ? You don't mean . . . ?"

But flat contradiction seldom stimulates productive talk, except when both speakers conceive of conversation as argument. The uncompleted statement may be used to veer the conversation, as you see it, to a more desirable course, without bringing in the destructive attitudes established by direct block.

As you have probably noted, the directive incomplete remark is most useful when your companion is in full swing. That is, you must use the incomplete statement as a partial interrupter. You touch him just hard enough to turn him, whereas if you bring him to a halt he will turn against you: "What do I mean? I've been telling you what I mean. . . . "

Stumbling Statements. Closely related as a stimulus to thoughtful talk is the partially confused comment. Too much fluency invites superficiality. If the conversation is too glib for the desired depth, a

bit of thoughtful search says inoffensively, "Stop, look, and listen."
For instance:

> "Talk about stupid! There we were trying to get the prof to shut
> off the breeze and let us out, and she kept saying. 'I don't think it's
> wise to print criticism of our country in college texts!' Who cares?"
> "Yes, I suppose so . . . but . . . I keep wondering . . . I know democ-
> racy can't work unless you know what's going on . . . but . . . maybe
> she's . . . how . . . where do you draw the line?"

The chances are your friend will think twice before he comes up
with the answer.

Structure. Perhaps the structure of a conversation is the total effect
of all the more specific responses we have mentioned, but it merits a
second look. Each person, by his responses, helps to shape the conversation. If you accept the statements of your companion, he is encouraged to go further in the direction already chosen. If you object,
deflect, react to his emotions, suggest a new area to talk about,
stumble and examine, your responses help determine the subject,
the depth of the discussion, the attitudes expressed, and the time to
be spent. Other persons in the conversation exert their influence in
the same ways.

Some people involve themselves personally in what they say; they are
warm, and mix their emotions generously into their talk. Others hold
conversation at arm's length, responding only to the intellectual content
of what is said. You can know such people for years and still feel
you scarcely know them at all. Still others contend with their com-
panions; a topic of conversation is the arena for a tussle.

With one person we may habitually tangle, with another we adopt a
poker face, and with a third we commune. Or we may talk openly
with a person on the subject of baseball, but struggle with him on
politics or avoid the topic completely. All conversations have structure, built by the interactive effect of the personalities and the subjects
involved.

Situation Analysis. This is a pedantic term for "small talk." But
the idea, if not the term, has its value, for small talk or social chatter
grows out of the common and obvious news or gossip of the moment.

"Warm day. . . . Nice dress you have on. . . . The Giants won
again. . . Two cars locked bumpers down at the corner. . . . Hope

this weather lasts through the week. . . . The Joneses left on their vacation this morning. . . . My, our gas bill was high this month. . . . Did you know John took Mary to the movies last evening?. . . . "

Any one of these comments may send people off into an extended exchange. The effortless observation of common events is not to be discredited. We cannot always be searching our souls or unveiling the secrets of the universe. We have a right to relax and let the social urge take over.

He is a hard man to live with who does not occasionally notice that his neighbor's grass is doing better of late.

QUESTIONS FOR STUDY AND DISCUSSION

1. For what purposes do we use conversation? What are its more desirable uses?

2. Explain the three patterns of conversation.

3. What are the prerequisites of good conversation? Explain sympathy and those attitudes that induce it.

4. What is the value to conversation of understanding oneself?
What is the value of humor?

5. What do we mean by the techniques of conversation? Explain them.

SUGGESTIONS AND ASSIGNMENTS

1. Give a short talk on one of the best conversationalists you have known. Analyze his abilities in terms of this chapter.

2. Record a conversation and study it. Write a few sentences of it on the board and analyze it for the techniques that:

   a. Kept it going.
   b. Redirected it.
   c. Raised or lowered its level.
   d. Stopped it.
   e. Turned it into an argument.

3. Record a conversation. Study it and select statements that illustrate various uses of conversation. Discuss these briefly.

4. Start a conversation with your roommate in order to experiment with several techniques. Report the results to the class.

5. If you feel that you are an inadequate conversationalist, observe your small talk for a week. How well do you adjust to inconsequential subjects aroused by the immediate situation? Report these observations to the class.

6. If you feel that you do not take an active enough part in conversation, experiment for a week with the techniques of:

    a. Parallel talk.
    b. Incomplete phrases.
    c. Stumbling statements.

Note particularly how you bring out and direct the other speaker. Respond to his feelings and note what this does to him. Keep a diary of this information. Combine the most interesting experiences into a short talk.

7. If you feel that you irritate others when you indulge in monologue, practice for a week: (1) consciously giving possession of ideas to your conversants, and (2) using the "probe." Keep a record of the results and make a short report to the class.

8. Observe for a week the way your conversations are structured differently as you talk with different people. From your observations, make a short talk.

9. Keep an inventory of all your conversations for two days to determine what you use conversations for. Give a speech explaining the motives that dominate you. Give examples.

We agreed that all questions coming up were to be considered as being brought up by the group as a whole rather than by any member. If a member had an objection to any point, it was regarded as something that troubled the group as a whole.[1]

Norman Cousins and Thomas K. Finletter

12

Discussion

DISCUSSION IS CONVERSATION with a specific subject and a central purpose. Whereas ordinary social conversation may touch upon a dozen subjects in as many minutes, discussion sticks to one subject, and tries to bring out various points of view about it with the aim of coming at the truth.

The most productive discussion comes from groups of three to eight. When the time for talk is short and the need for action great, a smaller number is desirable. When the need to explore all points of view is of utmost importance, a larger number is better. If the group exceeds seven or eight, it tends to get out of hand. First, so many points of view are suggested, and so few can be followed up, that central ideas do not come to focus. Second, with larger groups, the situation begins to approximate that of public speaking. The dominant members then take over and the rest listen.

The Values of Discussion

From a social point of view, discussion is a technique by which a group, as a group, clarifies its thinking and determines its action. In essence, therefore, discussion is a primary tool of the democratic process. It is opposed to the notion that one person ought to direct society, and it springs out of the belief that the best action comes from the free flow of thought and speech. In short, the faith in discussion is the faith that in the free exchange of ideas, the good ones usually prevail.

[1] From "A Beginning for Sanity," *The Saturday Review of Literature*, June 15, 1946, p. 9.

From the point of view of the individual, discussion is a means of becoming better informed on the thinking of others and a way to solve problems by pooling information and opinion. Both for participants and for listeners, there is no better way (except perhaps conversation) to keep the mind flexible and creative than the experience of listening to the unorganized messages of a group of people trying to work through a topic. The gaps in thought that must exist as the topic passes from speaker to speaker force the listening mind to make leaps, twists, and turns as a single speech does not. As the discussion is handed from one speaker to another, the very changes in voice, vocabulary, body-set and belief, exercise the mind as no other external speech stimulus can. None of us live in the world alone, and the most influential part of our environment is other people. Discussion keeps us acquainted with people, helping us maintain our target-set in a world where other people change just as we do.

ATTITUDES OF GOOD DISCUSSION

The Open Mind

It should be made clear that the most important attitude for fruitful discussion is an open mind. Ideally, discussants are flexible. Naturally, they know what they think. But they should not have made up their minds irrevocably, and they should be willing to give consideration to every new opinion expressed. People who flatly refuse to consider new messages cannot properly discuss. Unwillingness to consider other people's views may come from the determination to get one's own way regardless of the cost to others. Often, however, rigidity is a sign of fear, revealing itself in the need to argue and overpower. The worst enemy of real discussion is the compulsion to win the blue ribbon.

Participants who are determined to get their own way are prepared to argue, but not to discuss. It is not suggested that argument should be ruled out of human speech. That is neither possible nor altogether desirable. But we ought to see a clear distinction between argument and discussion. We confuse ourselves when we insist that we are using one tool when actually we are using another. We also confuse others and disappoint or disillusion them. "I tried to discuss the matter with him, but the first thing I knew he got mad. There's no use trying to solve problems by discussion." The fact is that people do not get angry when the atmosphere is one of seeking. They do get upset when a message is forced upon them against their will, or when others are not willing at least to consider their views.

Should we then, not recognize differences of opinion in discussion? Of course we should; but we should explore them with a view to finding the best answer to our problem, not with the urge to make one side prevail at any cost. If two or more people disagree, it is time for each to state the best evidence he has for his position. When all sides have been expressed, and carefully weighed, the discussion is over. It has fulfilled its basic function when it succeeds in reviewing the facts and attitudes of the discussants.

If the purpose of a discussion is to find common understanding and often common action, differences of opinion should be expressed always in the hope that, in the end, the urge for common agreement will be greater than the urge to differ. For instance, the members of the homecoming committee may express a variety of attitudes on the question whether to have floats in the torchlight parade. When other details have been arranged to mutual satisfaction, it may be clear that floats are not wanted. If so, a possible argument has been avoided. If, on the other hand, the differences prove strong enough to make agreement impossible, the only wise move is for the leader to summarize the differences clearly and ask for an investigation of possible compromises and alternatives. Perhaps half as many floats, or dormitory exhibits in place of floats, will be agreeable to all. Discussion is by its nature an exploratory process. Struggle and dispute are destructive to the attitude required for successful exploration by a group.

If discussion is to be helpful in seeking solutions to problems, it must not, therefore, be allowed to degenerate into dispute. The Quakers are extremely alert to this underlying fact. Since they believe only in unanimous decision, they adjourn when they disagree, saving the technique of discussion for times when their minds are ready to use it. We have said (1) that the open mind is a necessary condition for group exploration, and (2) that the open mind belongs to the person who is sufficiently secure to adjust to group interests. The Quaker philosophy reasons that if you can't keep your mind open, it is wise to keep your mouth closed.

Another school of thought holds that conflict is lessened, and at best eliminated, by frank confession of feelings on the matter in question. In this view, most of our beliefs are the expression of emotional attitudes toward ourselves and others. It reasons that the basic aim of discussion is to discover better human relations. The key to this point of view is the belief that people can hear the messages of the other man and can change beliefs as they express, and thereby get rid of, the emotions that resist change. To put it very simply, if you don't like Joe you tell him so, and tell him why. If you think Sally's argument is foolish, you tell her so, and tell her why. If you think the topic is stupid, you say so. This should not be taken to imply that "getting things off your chest" is the goal, but rather that the goal of the discussion cannot be brought into focus until the emotional blocks are out of the way.

Certainly it is true that if you are going to discuss your feelings at a point of conflict, it is better to be honest and tell what you feel. If you are motivated by anger and decide to speak but to hide your feelings, your attention is split and your reasoning may suffer. You will be in danger of fastening upon some trivial point and trying to make it the issue. Others will see what is happening to you, for conflict has a way of sharpening the perceptions of the listener. The result of this kind of concealment, even though it is directed by "good manners," is poor analysis and sustained suspicion. The open mind is not very well acquainted with this kind of etiquette.

Ill feeling and prejudice cloud the mind, and honest speech is cleansing. Yet it is not wise to burden the discussion of problems with emotional "excess baggage," Freedom from this kind of impediment comes through ever-increasing knowledge of ourselves, and this is achieved in large measure by private study. The later chapters of this book are designed to give you the knowledge and techniques for hearing yourself as others hear you. This, in the end, is the key to the open mind.

Knowledge and Judgment

No less important to good discussion is the attitude that a valuable exchange implies something worth exchanging. Collected ignorance, whether from open or closed minds, adds up no faster than zeros. Words are never really empty, but they have been known to carry a light load. The awful truth is that most people are so amazed when they achieve a lively and fluent discussion that they feel they have attained the ultimate. They are often so excited by the mere act of speech that they become oblivious to the value of what is being said.

Vague generalities based on feeling, and "facts" that are not facts then gain uncritical acceptance.

A study of the ability of college students to recognize good and poor evidence showed a consistent ability to discriminate between fine distinctions which several professors who validated the test felt were too exacting.[2] But the test was not made under the conditions of discussion. "Good" and "bad" evidence was furnished, and the students' job was to evaluate it while free from the need to respond to other discussants. In discussion — or any kind of speech for that matter — an additional skill is required, the ability to know when you are prepared to evaluate evidence and form conclusions. In short, the characteristic weakness in the thinking of college students (and others) is not inability to separate the wheat from the chaff, but a tendency to begin the threshing process before the grain has been gathered.

The test mentioned gives us a clue to the reason why students (and, we repeat, other people) make this error. The most common failure in the selection of adequate support is the attraction to assertion. In assertive reasoning the support *is* the conclusion, stated in different words.

> "Why do you say we should cut our armament expenditures?"
> "We're just spending too much, that's all."

It's as simple as that. That's the conclusion, and the conclusion is based on the "fact" that that's the way it is. The reasoning is motivated by the satisfaction received from completing a task with certainty. Self-satisfaction is misinterpreted as a signal that the facts are in.

The tendency to talk when we have little to talk about is the problem of the closed mind again. But the influential attitude in this case is not prejudice or ill-feeling; it is the failure to be intellectually critical, to respect evidence and reality, to admit the cold uncompromising facts of the world outside the human skin.

A group of students were discussing American defense:

A. *Time* magazine last week stated that no strategist has figured a defense against an attack by planes carrying H-bombs. Teller's bomb can wipe out a city. The evidence suggests there is no defense by military might.

---

[2] Charles T. Brown, "An Experimental Diagnosis of Thinking on Controversial Issues," *Speech Monographs*, November 1950, pp. 370–377. Each conclusion in the test was supported by five statements which the student ranked. Well supported statements "won first place."

We must turn to international law. I string along with Norman
Cousins.

B. But international government means America and Russia and all the
rest will have to give up their sovereignty. They just won't do this. I
admit the dangers, but I string along with our present universal military training program.

A. We don't have universal military training. . . .

B. What do you mean? Where do you think all the fellows are going who
leave college, on a Sunday school picnic? Didn't you ever hear of the
draft? You will, Buddy.

A. The draft and U.M.T. are two different things. Besides that's not my
point. The point is . . .

Here the discussion slips off the problem because the second
speaker does not know enough to speak to the point.

When you discuss, your professor has relinquished his authority
in the interest of your own self-government. If he criticizes you because you are not informed, you tend to stop talking. Discussion
dies. If, in the interest of a free flow of imaginative exploration, your
instructor does not criticize poor preparation, discussion may not die,
but should. Windy talk tends to discredit discussion and fosters misunderstanding of its value. Self-government implies responsibility.
Self-government is freedom, but freedom cannot live in ignorance.
Good discussion, in other words, requires information.

COMMON FORMS OF DISCUSSION

The Roundtable

The "purest" form of discussion is the roundtable. Here a group
gathers, preferably in a circle, so that each may easily hear and see
the others. There is probably no objective support for the following
statement, but it seems to be true that the "table" in the roundtable
discussion should be taken figuratively. Any physical barrier between
people is a symbol of separation. The typical roundtable arrangement
looks like this:

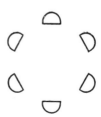

The roundtable is a "pure" type of discussion because, in its strictest sense, it allows a group to meet for no other purpose than to exchange ideas. Social exploration, within the confines of a single topic, is the beginning and the end of its existence.

In making the physical arrangements for a roundtable discussion, or for that matter for any of the other forms, it is wise not to place people who tend to oppose each other in opposite physical positions, but side by side.

The Committee

The committee is much like the roundtable. As a form, its "purity" rests in the fact that it, too, is private discourse; that is, the committee does not exist to perform before an audience. The committee differs from the roundtable in that it is usually designed to "report out" a solution to a problem. A fraternity committee, for instance, may be appointed to make arrangements for a dance. Such a group cannot fulfill its purpose merely by an exchange of information, attitudes, and possible solutions. It must go beyond these to eliminate, select, report, and possibly to carry out a course of action.

It should be clear that leadership and organization are more powerful in the committee than in the roundtable.

The Panel

The most informal type of discussion that takes place before an audience is the panel, the purpose of which is to present a variety of points of view for public consideration. The number of participants ordinarily ranges from four to six. If the panel is composed of experts on the subject, they may go into discussion with little or no preparation. When the members are amateurs in discussion and new to the subject, they need to prepare individually and together for their performance. Almost always a "warm up" period just before "going on" gives a vitality, assurance, and movement to the discussion.

Because the panel is a performance, it is probably unrealistic to think of it as an exploratory group, except in so far as it explores the subject before it meets the actual audience. When panel members come to the platform, they know what they, as individuals, will stand for, just as any public speaker does. In the actual presentation the exploratory phase of public discussion shifts from the participants to the listeners.

The seating arrangement should allow the members of the panel to see each other easily, and to be in full view of the audience. Of the two arrangements below, the first is more formal and is necessary if the audience is large. In an ordinary classroom of thirty people or less, the second arrangement is obviously more desirable. Anything that

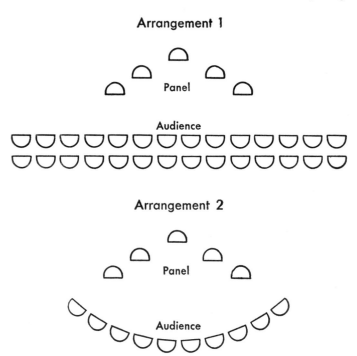

suggests informality encourages the spirit of free discussion. If the audience is very large, the panel should be seated on a raised platform or a stage.

The Colloquy

Sometimes a group may desire to retain the informality of the panel and yet be able to call upon expert knowledge when the give-and-take of ideas suggests the need. Hence they may turn to the colloquy, a form which brings in one or more experts to serve as a sort of "human library" to supplement what the panel group can contribute.

The idea of the colloquy is good, but the practice is sometimes dangerous. It is good because the expert can often provide facts or informal judgments at a crucial moment. But panel members some-times tend to shrink from the task of thinking for themselves, or of revealing ignorance before superior knowledge, and so resort to asking questions. Often the expert, stimulated by the attention on himself, takes possession of the subject, and the focus of discussion moves from the panel to the "encyclopedia."

Room arrangement can help safeguard against this. The expert may be placed to one side so that he is not in the direct crossfire among

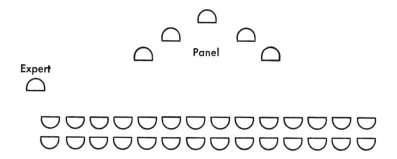

members of the panel or between the panel and the audience. It is fatal to place him directly across from the panel, unless it is intended that he control the situation.

The Symposium

In modern usage, a "symposium" is a group of speakers, usually three or four, each of whom prepares and delivers a speech. The in-terchange of ideas here occurs almost entirely in the minds of the listeners, who can see how different speakers consider the same sub-ject. The great value of the prepared speech in a discussion is that a considerable amount of data can be organized for comprehension. If the audience is new to the subject, or the subject is extremely com-plex, the speeches help to construct a picture for the listener. The symposium is most valuable when the chief need of the audience is for information. The symposium should not be used when the au-dience is well informed on the subject.

In a symposium, the subject may be divided among speakers in either of two ways. Each may discuss the whole question from his own point of view. Or, each may confine his remarks to a particular phase of the topic; thus one may give the history of the problem, another may discuss the severity of the problem and its causes, and a third may present possible solutions.

The Lecture Forum

At the fringe of discussion is the lecture forum. Here the element of discussion is that the audience, at the close of a formal speech, is alloted a period of time to ask questions or make comments, usually the former. The lecture is the most efficient form for transmitting information by speech. It therefore permits the least exploration on the part of the listeners.

The Forum

Whenever the audience takes part in the discussion by means of questions or comments, the result is a forum. It may be a panel forum, an expert-panel forum, a symposium, or a lecture forum. In order to safeguard against the disruption of the program by the audience, the forum — the period for questions or discussion — is held at the end.

TECHNIQUES OF DISCUSSION

Phrasing the Topic

The topic should be stated in such a way as to suggest the purpose of the investigation. The best way to insure this result is to phrase the subject as a question, for the question implies the search for an answer. If the topic is mercy killing, it may be stated, "What Are the Facts Concerning Mercy Killing?" or "What Should Be Our Attitude Toward Mercy Killing?" If the topic is elementary education, the question may be "What Are We Educating For?" or "How Well Are We Educating Our Children?"

It is probably unwise to phrase the question in such a way that it may be answered "yes" or "no." "Should We Adopt a Mercy Killing Law?" or "Is the American Child Being Well Educated?" Such questions do not call for exploration but for the defense of a position. They tend to close the mind to facts other than those in support of one answer, and to direct the mind to the search for ammunition to support a predetermined conclusion.

Kinds of Questions

Examination of a number of questions soon suggests that they fall into two classes, divided by the ticking of the clock. They are questions about the past, and questions about the future. The problems of the past have been solved, one way or another, but we are not always sure how. The past therefore raises questions of fact and interpretation. In questions about the future the focus is implied in the general question, "What shall we do?" The future presents us with problem-solving questions. Knowing which kind of question is up for discussion is helpful in choosing an outline and in selecting material.

Outlining a Discussion Topic

Let us look over a series of discussion topics and see if we can find some techniques for directing the discussion to its end purpose.

Kind of Question	*Statement of Question*
Question of Fact	What is our foreign policy?
Question of Policy	What should our foreign policy be?
Question of Fact	What has this class achieved?
Question of Policy	What shall be the goals of this class?
Question of Fact	What is our defense policy?
Question of Policy	What should our defense policy be?

Questions of fact call for (1) knowledge of facts plus (2) an interpretation of these facts. Again, to answer the question, "What are the hopes for world government?" we need, first, a description of the behavior of most of the leading nations and of what their leaders say. Second, we need to determine how this behavior and speech does or does not direct these nations toward world government.

The policy questions ask what to do about something. To solve a problem we need to go through several steps. (See Chapter 8, pages 122 and 123, for additional explanation.)

1. A description of the problem, a statement of the symptoms of the trouble, comes first. To apply the theory more easily, conceive of yourself (in the discussion group) as examining a sick patient and describing his behavior.

2. Having described the problem, search for the causes of the illness. This is difficult, but you need to be highly skeptical of your solution if you are not clear as to the causes. It is the accuracy or the inaccuracy of the analysis of causes that determines the validity of the choice of action. Is nation X bent on world conquest, determined that her ideology shall dominate the world, or trying to secure herself

against future enemies? All three are possible causes of international stress. The person who understands the causes of nation X's behavior is most likely to propose a realistic solution.

3. Propose various solutions for the problem.

4. Reason through how well each solution seems to meet the causes without creating new problems.

5. Determine which solution should be adopted.

6. Decide what steps should be taken, and by whom, to put the solution into action.

You may have noted that this is a variation of the philosopher John Dewey's five steps in thinking through a problem. Step four is an addition. Students tend to overlook the task of trying to determine how well a proposal meets causes, and therefore how well it solves the problem. They become so immersed in the details of the plan that they mistake them for proof of the plan's workability. There is no final proof of a proposal except to try it, but the degree to which we have evaluated proposals against causes before acting is the degree to which we have replaced trial and error with thought.

The above outline for solving problems is merely suggestive. Any particular question must be carefully examined before you can see how to apply this scheme. Consider, for example, the question "How High Should Taxes Go?" What is the problem? One may be tempted to say "high taxes." But this is not quite accurate. High taxes are the symptom of more fundamental matters, the size of the government debt, and its twin, the operating budget. First, then, we must find the minimum needs of the government. Second, we must determine the causes of the needs, and establish the degree to which each of these causes (military, civil service, interest on the national debt, public welfare, etc.) is justifiable. We should then decide what we think is the absolute minimum budget. This is the gauge of how high taxes should go. *The key to making the problem-solving outline work is to be accurate in describing the nature of your problem.* There are errors that may be made thereafter, but a clear beginning is likely to direct the steps to come.

Questions, then, are of two kinds: (1) they call for fact and interpretation, or (2) they formulate a problem to be solved.

Skills and Duties of Discussion Leaders

Guidance. Since by nature discussion is a democratic process, the leader ideally accepts democratic (self-accepting) attitudes.[3] This is indeed a broad definition of his function, but there is no formula to offer. The group has a topic; it is the leader's task to aid the group in exploring it as fully as possible. He must be dominant enough to keep the other members operating with him, and yet not so dominating as to enslave them. The leader is not the boss of the group; he is its conscience. He helps it see where it is going; he does not tell it where it must go. Otherwise, why have discussion? Lincoln said that the power of the leader in a democracy is to help the people attain what they want.

Planning. Sometime before the discussion, the leader should call the group together to set down a program of work. Assuming that the discussants have a purpose which has made them into a group, they need to (1) frame a question that involves their subject or purpose, (2) discover what knowledge is already possessed by the group, (3) decide what additional knowledge is needed, (4) determine who is going to be responsible for various areas of information, (5) decide on a form of discussion, (6) develop an outline that covers the information to be drawn out in the discussion. It is the leader's business to gain the cooperation of his group in this preliminary work.

Seating Arrangement. The leader is also responsible for a proper seating arrangement.

Introducing the Members. He needs to introduce all members of his group if they are not known to each other or to the audience. (Unless the situation is formal, it is desirable to use first names.)

Stating Topic and Procedure. When the discussion begins, the leader should introduce the topic and state the procedure and the outline to be followed.

Starting the Discussion. If the discussion is to be roundtable or a panel, the leader needs to establish an atmosphere for free and easy talk. An excellent way to do this is to describe an incident, a case, or an example that illustrates a part of the first point. Rather than say, "Would somebody begin by describing the pres-

[3] See Chapter 20.

ent parking situation," or "John, will you begin by . . . ," it is better for the leader to start in some such way as follows: "As some of you delightfully remember, because he had to hunt twenty minutes for a parking space, Professor Bookcase did not meet his one o'clock class yesterday. A friend of mine who works in Allington could not get his car out of the lot behind Spaulding Hall last Monday at 3:00. He was an hour late for work and is still trying to make his boss understand. I am wondering whether these are unusual cases." Bringing the minds of his discussants to the data of the initial point by some such introductory remarks will usually arouse them to volunteer their own knowledge and thinking on the situation.

Steering the Discussion. Once the group begins to function, the leader keeps close watch on the development of the point under discussion. So long as the group is bringing out valuable information, he should be reluctant to interfere. He may study the audience to evaluate the interest aroused. When it is clear that the significant information has been brought out, or that the discussion has wandered to the verge of confusion, the leader should *summarize quickly what has been said on the point under consideration.* He does not pass judgment on the contributions. He summarizes. He may then suggest the next item in the outline. "Perhaps we might look into the situation for some causes . . ."

Giving Everyone a Chance. In the course of the give-and-take, he sees that everybody has equal opportunity to speak. If one or two persons tend to have more skill than others in maintaining the floor, he interrupts, at a pause or the end of a sentence, and invites comment from the person who has been trying to get a word in.

Summarizing. He summarizes at the close of the discussion — *very briefly.*

Serving as Moderator. He is the moderator for the forum period, if there is to be one. That is, he keeps order and determines who is to speak and for how long.

All this may seem like a great deal of responsibility for the discussion leader. But if you study the foregoing, you will see that his task is fundamentally a matter of recognizing the essential needs along the pathway of discussion.

Skills and Duties of Discussants

As the leader of a discussion has certain well-defined responsibilities, so has the participant. They can be summarized briefly.

Information. A good participant makes it his business to be well informed, and to listen to himself in order to be sure that he is not talking to overcome the guilt feelings aroused by ignorance.

Admitting Errors. A good discussant is willing to admit errors in his thinking and the limitations of his knowledge.

Drawing in Others. One's own information is obviously an important contribution, but skill in drawing others into the discussion is equally important, and more difficult to develop. Parallel talk, the incomplete phrase, stumbling statements, and the probe — explained in the preceding chapter — are techniques that weave individuals into a spirited and unified group. A good discussant helps others talk

Being at Ease. A good discussant is comfortable with himself. He does not use the discussion as a place to exhibit himself, to air his complaints, to search for prestige, or to gain personal power over another person, either present or absent. All this is a big order and rather a negative one. To put it more positively, a good discussant thinks straight, and one's thinking is about as straight as his motives permit.

Being a Good Listener. A good discussant is a good listener. He evaluates all contributions in the light of the point under discussion and speaks when some of his information sheds light on what has just been said. He does not spend his listening time marshaling information for the next time he gets a chance to talk.

Interrupting at Pauses. A good discussant interrupts only at pauses.

Refusing to Argue. A good discussant states his information and attitudes almost disinterestedly when they differ from those of other speakers. He refuses to argue so long as the group exists in the name of discussion. He is sensitive to the fact that discussion is social exploration.

Evaluating a Discussion

The value of any process is determined by measuring the beginning and end products. It was suggested above that in preparation the group catalogue its present information in order to assess the areas in which further study was needed. This first discussion may be recorded. Recording the final discussion gives the difference to be evaluated. Differences fall into several categories which may be looked at in the light of the following questions:

1. How much was learned?
2. How much did each person learn?
3. What happened to the status of agreement in the process?
4. How far was the question answered by the discussion?
5. How much did the organization of the ideas improve?

These questions can be answered on a ten-point scale by each participant, or by an observer, immediately after listening to both recordings.

A similar approach may be used to assess the value of the discussion to listeners. Each listener may write a paper on the question both before and after the discussion. These papers may be evaluated by the writer, another student, or an evaluating group. Listeners may then recommend to the discussants objectives that both individual members and the group as a whole should work toward in their next discussion. The group should compare its own evaluation with those of the listeners and set down objectives in order to steer preparation in the next effort.

Discussion is the exploration of a specific subject by a group of people. It is the process by which decisions are arrived at democratically. Good discussion required the "open mind" and adequate information. The discussion technique may be used by a group to solve its own problems, as a committee does, or it may be used to explore a topic before an audience. A discussion investigates a question of fact or a question of policy. There are probably no skills more difficult to acquire than those of the good participant and the good discussion leader, for the great problems of society always seem to involve man's choice of force by the individual against decision by group discussion.

QUESTIONS FOR STUDY AND DISCUSSION

1. What are the two purposes of discussion?

2. What two attitudes does good discussion emphasize?

3. What are the more common forms of discussion? What are the values of each?

4. What are some important facts to be considered in phrasing a question for discussion?

5. What are the two kinds of discussion topics and the typical outline for handling each kind?

6. List the essential skills and duties of a discussion leader, of a discussant.

7. Explain ways of evaluating discussion.

SUGGESTIONS AND ASSIGNMENTS

1. Phrase and outline three discussion questions. Give these to two classmates for evaluation. Let each attach a sheet with criticisms. Attach a final sheet on which you evaluate their criticisms. Turn in all papers to your instructor.

2. Meet with several members of your class and prepare for a class discussion. Choose a topic, frame the question, select a chairman, carry on a preliminary discussion to determine your present knowledge and the needed information. Record this preliminary session. Assign research, choose a discussion form, formulate an outline, arrange the room, and carry on the discussion. Record the discussion. Write a report evaluating the group skills in handling each step. Have several student listeners in the class write papers on the question both before and after your discussion. Evaluate these and the two recordings. Write a statement setting forth the outstanding need of (1) yourself and (2) the group.

3. Go through the same steps for a second discussion on a new topic, first agreeing with your group on the objectives you as an individual, and the group as a whole, should concentrate on.

Once a man takes sides, he begins to see a little less of the world.

Heywood Broun

13

Argument: Verbal Warfare

IF DISCUSSION is group exploration, its opposite may be called "verbal warfare." This kind of speech springs from the urge for personal superiority. It is born when one person tries to destroy the thinking of another and substitute his own. When it arouses anger and hatred it turns against society.

Verbal war breaks out when men want to begin talk with the end result of their own thinking. They do not then want to think together, beginning with observation and working toward a conclusion that emerges from observations of the group. They want to impose their own views at any cost.

WHY MEN ARGUE

There are a great many reasons why men argue. Sometimes arguments arise because people fail to understand each other, and sometimes because they understand each other perfectly but represent clashing interests. Whatever its reason, argument is exhausting and unproductive — unless it is resolved by compromise, when it ceases to be argument and becomes discussion.

Misunderstanding

Most frequently, men argue when they do not understand each other, and there are three main reasons why this happens. First, we do not all respond to the same details when we observe the same thing. You can easily find evidence of this fact by noting the difference in the observations made on your speech by various members of your class. Or have three of your classmates look at a picture and describe it, and you will probably find that each focuses on a different cluster of details (see Chapter 6).

A second reason for misunderstanding is that we do not all reach the same conclusions even when we do look at the same details. Stu-

214

dents discussing the football team may agree that the blocking and passing are good and that the running and tackling are poor. But one may blame the coach, and another the material. The difference is a matter of judgment.

A third cause of misunderstanding is words. Two people may use the same words to represent entirely different concepts. "Democracy" denotes different things to different people. It may mean kindly dictatorship, action by majority rule, that everybody has a chance to talk, or that we are against the Russians. Equally disrupting is the use of different words for the same concept. It may go like this:

> "Jones is just a politician."
> "Politician! He's a crook."
> "Well, what's the difference?"
> "There's a lot of difference."
> "What?"
> "Well, not everybody in politics is a crook, is he?"
> "No, who said so?"
> "You."
> "I did not."
> "You said there was no difference between a crook and a politician."
> "But that doesn't mean everybody in politics is a crook."
> "Aw nuts!"
> "Just because a man's in politics doesn't mean he has to be a politician."
> "Well, how can a man be in politics and not be a politician?"
> "He can be a statesman, can't he?"

Two hours later they agree that Jones has misused his office and that neither would vote for him again.

Men misunderstand each other when they do not see the same details, when they do not reach the same conclusion from a group of details, or when they do not use words to express the same meaning. As a result they become hurt or angry, and strike back.

Frustration

Men also argue because they are frustrated. Somebody has said that if you want to understand why a man misuses you, find out who he was talking to just before he met you. This is a world in which each of us is restrained by all the other people around us, by the tyranny of the clock, and by our own standards. We can take just so much pressure before we have to "let off steam." If we are with people when this happens, it all too frequently takes the form of an attack on them. Who has not in retrospect seen that he argued because he was irritated?

Argument relieves men of tension and frustration. When irritated, they find it helpful to release the tension in some way acceptable to their standards. They may beat a tree with a club (as is done in one culture), or run until they grow tired, or scream at the family, or complain about the weather. Either by physical exertion or by talk they get rid of their internal stress.

Certainty

But not all arguments arise from misunderstanding or from personal, psychological stress. Men also argue when they are very sure of themselves and when they understand each other all too well, but have opposing information and views, and feel that further consideration is wasted time. When people meet, each with the thought, "Let's do it my way," argument is sure to follow. For each has passed beyond the point of looking into the problem. He is ready to act in accordance with what he has seen and concluded, and he has closed his mind to further thinking. In this state, a man is distressed by messages which suggest that there is more information to consider. Psychologically he is like a man waiting for the whistle at five o'clock, impatient to get home and angry if he is told he has to work overtime. When purpose calls for action, it is painful to reconsider.

Partisan Loyalty

Men also throw words at each other when they have partisan loyalties. Labor and management dispute because one wants higher wages and the other does not. The United Nations is an arena because most delegates come to it with the purpose of taking back prizes to their respective nations. They therefore tend to think of world problems not in terms of the general welfare but of solutions that favor the nation to which they owe allegiance. In like fashion the United States Congress becomes a ring where state and party loyalties are pitted against each other. Democrats want to work for Democrats, Protestants for Protestants, women for women, and the Elks for the Elks. By definition, a partisan is one who sees only the part. He wants a solution that fits his part as if it were the whole. Verbal war, if not "hot war," is inevitable so long as interacting people cling to clashing allegiances. A senator has a social right to think as a citizen of his state when he is solving a local problem. He must think as a citizen of the nation when he turns his attention to a national problem — unless he has already decided that he wants to fight.

Entertainment
Verbal war is excited by the fact that it entertains people. Instructors employ argument knowing that it will maintain attention. Radio and television networks search for combatants to "discuss" issues "in the public interest." Questions in public forums are phrased in such a way that we can scarcely avoid taking sides: "Should Tariffs be Lowered?" "Should the Public Schools Teach Religion?"

The Urge for Victory
Verbal warfare sets up a situation in which a person may win over his neighbor. When a man is motivated, at all costs, to get that raise, remain in the public eye, or beat his opponent at the polls, he knows that his victory means another's defeat, and he welcomes the tools of struggle (or deception). He is not looking for common ground, he does not want to discuss, he does not want to compromise. That would mean self-change, change of plans, sacrifice of what he wants to gain. In answer to a proposal for scaling down armaments, the late Russian diplomat Mr. Vishinsky made the infamous reply, "I could hardly sleep all last night. I could not sleep because I kept laughing."

The only message that stops the cry for victory is superior power. The more factual and the less emotional that message, the more it is likely to have its restraining effect. If at all possible, let the would-be-conqueror *see* the power; don't merely tell him about it. Indeed, under such circumstances extended talk is harmful; an aggressor knows that protest means uncertainty or weakness. Only when the aggressor is willing to compromise is it time to discuss. Tensions can be lowered by talk only when conflict is caused by misunderstanding, irritation, closed minds, partisan blindness, or ignorance. These are the problems to which this chapter speaks. Conflict that springs from the urge to conquer must ultimately be solved by other means.

WHAT ARGUMENT WILL NOT DO
Change Convictions
As suggested above, argument seldom changes the minds of those who oppose each other. We are not less driven to preserve our be-

liefs than we are our lives. Indeed, history is rich with the stories of men who have died for their beliefs. And no one changes beliefs except the man who owns them. He may be aided, but he cannot be forced.

The only way we can get a person to agree with us by argument is to threaten him. We can then force him to be silent or to say what he does not believe. The threat in argument can take a thousand forms. Fear of a caustic tongue, derisive laughter, a word in the ear of a third person, grades, exposure, can exercise restraint as potent as the threat of physical harm. Argument by threat may successfully control action, but it cannot persuade the mind.

Improve Cooperation

Moreover, argument will not bring about cooperative action. Professor Irving J. Lee points out that of two hundred groups he studied, he saw a group exchanging ideas in an exciting and productive fashion only sixteen times. He found that on these rare occasions the leader had effortless patience and revealed a deep faith in his group's ability to solve the problem. Among participants in these sixteen groups he noted two characteristics. The first concerned the manner of speech. Members felt they had something important to say and they wanted to say it. They spoke with force, firm gestures, and a rush. The second characteristic was an attitude of "reasonable" conviction. They looked upon their own beliefs as something to be prized, the product of their past, something that was alive and changing. They listened and evaluated the experiences of others. They looked upon them as the source of exciting new knowledge that would help change their own views. Such was the speech and listening of the groups that achieved the most. In the groups that achieved little, the attitude was one of man against man and conviction against conviction.

Just as internal conflict gnaws at the life of an individual, so conflict affects the performance of a group.

CONDITIONS OF ARGUMENT

It is almost self-evident that it takes at least two to have an argument, yet the persons involved in one seldom recognize this truth, perhaps because it is almost impossible to avoid the conviction that it was the verbal attack of the other person that started the thing: "Anything I did was only to protect myself." It is hard to imagine that we may have started the war in the act of listening. Yet, if we do not interpret the meaning of the speaker as he intended it, we may be just as guilty of bloodshed as he. It then does little good to counter with, "But that was what you *said*." For even if we are right, we are wrong; it is what the speaker meant that counts, and it is the listener's job as well as the speaker's to see that the message is correctly received and interpreted.

THE TECHNIQUES OF VERBAL WARFARE

The purpose of all warfare is to stop the advance of the enemy. In argument the blocking device is the contradiction. "Stop! Your influence is bad. I shall talk. Listen, and I shall correct the error in you." Notice in the following excerpt how the student who is speaking builds toward a flat assertion that his view is wholly right:

In a class in education recently, the old question of separation of church and state was taking quite a beating. Many thought that religion should be taught in the schools. The opponents of such a policy based their opposition on the phrase "church and state shall forever be separate." There could be no solution, of course, and recognizing this, I did not contribute to the discussion. However, the arguments of the "separatists" sounded to me to be basically unreal, in that they conceived of our country to be separated, *in toto*, from *religion*, which is a long way from being separated from The Church, or a church. Finally, when silence on my part seemed unbearable, I spoke as follows.

"I consider it unreal to base an argument on the premise that our national government, or its people, can separate any single phase of their life, or existence, from religion. Every founding document, every subsequent document or organization within our national entity has been founded upon the Judo-Christian code of ethics and morals. Our constitution is plainly a political expression of the Sermon on the Mount. Such a nation cannot separate itself from this code, for when it does, it separates from tradition, which is the one single unifying thread throughout our history. This tradition has been based upon our religion, not as a state but as a group of individuals."

The debate ended there. I really don't know that anyone was persuaded. I was approached after class, and commended on the manner in which I spoke the *Truth*. However, I suspect the separatists only need time to rally . . .

It is easy to imagine that "the separatists" would be on guard, and would begin to muster their own arguments in opposition. And it is likely that when the topic is reopened they will listen only well enough to assemble their own ammunition against the speaker's arguments. The following are some of the common attitudes that make persuasion impossible. They indicate stages along the path from incipient to actual verbal war.

Military Maneuvers

1. I don't believe you, but I want to listen to what you have to say. (There is a possible chance of mutual agreement though there are rumors of trouble along the border. The voice is pleasant, and the body relaxed.)

2. I don't believe you, but manners insist that I let you talk. War is barbaric. Perhaps we shall not recognize we are at it if we each let the other talk. (This stage has all the outward appearances of communication. The voice is cold and formal; the body is alert, movements are deliberate.)

3. I don't believe you, but I like to hear you talk. You make me laugh. Laughing is an act of good will. How can you say I am against you? I am just laughing. Okay, get mad, maybe you won't think straight, then I'll have you. You can't pin anything on me. I'm just laughing. Can't you take a joke? (The voice is caustic, the body feigns relaxation, movement is gross and exaggerated.)

Open Warfare

4. I don't believe you, because I don't trust you. But let's keep talking. Give me one good reason for believing you. Quit kidding yourself. You know that isn't so. All right what are your *real* reasons? (The voice is high, insistent, incredulous. The body is tense and leans forward.)

5. I don't believe you, and I am going to blitz you. Every time you say anything I'll crash right in before you get a chance to answer. This'll confuse you. Good, you're stammering. Faster, louder. This is the final word. I'll leave while you're groggy. You'll doubtless be the better for this. I'm a busy man. (The voice is rough, contemptuous, and inordinately forceful. The body is dynamic, perhaps spastic, overpowering.)

6. I don't believe it; if you are right, prove it. I don't have to prove anything. The responsibility is yours. If you don't make me believe you, I win. All I have to do is keep saying "That doesn't make sense to me." (The voice is caustic, and irritating. The body is alert but not tense.)

7. I don't believe you, and I'll never give up trying to change you. Both of us can't be right, and I know I'm right. I shall carry the banner of truth to victory or death. A dedicated man must be patient. You're wrong and you've got to come to see you're wrong. (The voice is forceful and dogmatic. The body is a solid fortress.)

8. I don't believe you, and if you don't come to my terms I'll make you pay. Do you see my feverish smile? I can be cruel, but I am giving you time. You're beginning to worry what I'll do. Good, while you're attending this, your resolve will weaken. Think it over. I'm looking you in the eye. (The voice is low, smooth, deliberate, calculating and well-controlled, perhaps guttural. The body is relaxedly alert.)

Isolationism

9. I don't believe you, and I'm not going to argue with you. I know what's right and I've said what's right. Take it or leave it. (The voice is cold and self-righteous; the body alert, but not tense.)

TECHNIQUES FOR RESOLVING CONFLICT

When people are in conflict they are at the stage of solution or evaluation in their thinking, but generally they can see that only one solution is possible. The whole of the effort should be directed to ways of returning them to an examination of what it is that needs to be solved. If there is any hope for agreement, it is that considering the problem long enough and from enough points of view may bring it to look the same for different people. What are some of the techniques that turn minds back upon the problem?

Restating the Problem

"What do you mean?" "Could you give some more examples?" "Illustrate the way the thing works." "Describe the problem further." "Let's examine all the details." When either you or others are tempted to argue and yet you feel that it is important to come to an agreement, keep making these statements that turn your conversant back to stating the conditions which distress him. This will give you a picture of the problem as he sees it. Obviously there is no guarantee that you can bring yourself to see it as he does, but at least you can make a sincere effort to do so.

Just as it helps you to get your opponent to restate his views, so it helps him for you to restate and clarify yours. "May I describe the facts as I see them." "We all see differently because we live separate lives. Let me explain how my past forces me to see this thing." In this restatement, do not imply answers; give the facts on which answers may be based. Facts are examples. If the problem is the federal budget, forget for the moment — a long moment — that the budget may be looked upon as high or low. Examine it. Where does every dollar go? How does the expenditure for each item this year compare with the expenditure for the past ten years? What does each agency do? How much does it accomplish? What are the salaries in the agencies?

Answering questions like these may seem like a prodigious amount of work, and it is. It is the kind of work that goes into making a national budget. Yet without any such exploration, millions of people assert what should be done — and they "know!" We are not here passing judgment upon the wisdom of our budget. We are stressing the fact that people often disagree because they talk about solutions without even a partial examination of the facts.

Let us see how this process of focusing on a thorough examination of the problem works in a potential conflict between you and your father over your allowance. If you ask for an increase and he says "No!" you have the perfect situation for an argument. What should you do? First, you should forget your conclusion and ask your father to examine the facts. "Dad, will you look over my allowance situation with me? Last month you gave me thirty dollars. I spent five for bus fare, and that seems to be a fixed charge from month to month. My laundry was twelve. I did not go to a movie. I did not spend anything for clothes. Here's my clothes situation, etc. . . . What do you think we can do?" This is "description," not "prescription"; and if your father comes to see the problem your way, it will be because you make it as vivid to him as it is to you. Then and only then are the two of you ready to reason out a solution together.

The same kind of full statement of the facts in the problem is the major need in a speech where you feel that your position may be rejected. Do not give your audience an opportunity to take issue. Keep their attention to the facts of the case. Give them example after example of the evil that exists in the situation about which you are concerned. You may or may not thus bring listeners to the solution you think desirable, but you will probably move them to desert the position that fosters the evil.

Compromise

There are those who scorn compromise as though it were the work of the devil. "A man of character stands by his principles. The truth's the truth. We're in for trouble when we flirt with compromise." The speaker who makes such statements usually goes on to explain how people will look down on you if you don't stand by your guns, and no wonder, for compromise is appeasement, and you know where appeasement gets us.

This pattern of thought is so commonly accepted that we need to examine it. Compromise is not opposed to principle; rather, it is democracy in action. It is a principle, the principle of adjusting conflicting principles, the principle of settlement by *mutual concession*. It is opposed to the dictatorship of one man's principles. Compromise is not appeasement. It does not try to pacify the aggressive. It is an act of two or more persons with varying interests who adjust to each other in order to live together. As Samuel Johnson said, "Life cannot subsist in society but by reciprocal concessions."

Time to Consider

It takes time to reach mutual understanding. In the age of the assembly line, we have come to feel a terrible urgency about time, to feel that everything must be done as fast as possible, that spending time is almost equivalent to wasting it. Automobile and airplane, radio and telephone, victorious over the hands of the clock, are the symbols of progress. An hour or two or three spent in thrashing out an idea, in such an age, comes to seem like primitive and disorganized effort. If somebody could invent a language that said the same thing to everybody, if men could be trained so that facts took the same shape in all minds, the exchange of a few words would solve most of our problems. But this is wishful thinking. Communication, even in a speech class, indicates what invariably happens when people try to share information. An assignment is made. It may even be repeated. Some perform it according to directions. The majority do something similar. Some do not hear. Others get the wrong due date. A few forget. Some find that they do not understand when they try to carry out the assignment.

Note the problem as two men fall to arguing.

> "Freedom of speech doesn't mean the freedom to say anything you please."

"But how can you have free speech if it isn't free? Free means un-regulated."

"How about free enterprise? Isn't it regulated?"

"But we don't have free enterprise."

"You mean we have socialism?"

This is misunderstanding at its worst. Yet even the best conversation is only relatively efficient and is a variation on the game of twenty questions in which we keep probing each other, trying to pinpoint meaning. It takes time to understand. One of the greatest enemies of human understanding is the attitude that we are too busy to waste time talking.

Avoidance of Anger

It is fatal to the soundness of your conclusions to deliberate in anger. Trying to solve any problem involving two or more persons can arouse tempers. Even when you are trying to do a hard job alone — say a difficult math problem — a point is reached when you become angry with yourself. You might then better quit, temporarily, for after that point you merely dissipate energy. The same is true in human inter-action.

The Quakers, as mentioned in the previous chapter, are extremely sensitive to this human weakness. As soon as a voice becomes irritable, the "leader" calls an end to the discussion for the time. It may be years before the problem is finally solved. Most of us in Western culture seem, on the surface, to get things done quickly, but our solutions keep returning to haunt us. The Civil War is a striking example. Talk went on for twenty-five years, most of it angry, and then came four years of war. Now, almost one hundred years later, we are still solving both the economic and the sociological problems then at issue.

But what if you do not get a feedback to yourself until you hear yourself saying, "That's crazy. What's wrong with you? . . ." "You ought to know better than . . . " When this happens, you should have your blow-up; you may need it. But as soon as you can bring it under control, openly admit the irrelevancy of your behavior. "Well, let's get back to the topic. I've let off my steam. I did the conversation no good. Maybe I did myself some good. Let's see how we can get at this thing agreeably." Unfortunately, our tendency is to lose our tempers and then to justify our action, so that others must submit hands down if there is to be peace. Few people will do this except under threat, and so vindicated anger usually means an extended feud.

The Impersonal Approach

It also helps to take the "I" out of your voice and facial expression. In every discussion there are two subjects, the thing talked about and the people talking. When people want to come to mutual agreement, energies converge upon the "thing." When they disagree, the thing becomes a field on which they struggle.

A good deal can be done to keep minds on the topic simply by keeping voices and faces calm. When there is doubt whether your listener can accept your idea, express it as if you were the messenger rather than the creator of it. Occasionally you have known people who can disagree with you without causing you to bristle. Their secret is that they can do so without endangering your self-respect.

Be particularly careful at the ends of sentences. There we relax momentarily, and are most likely to let ourselves enjoy our own statements. A defensive listener will be particularly sensitive to this.

Notice Donna's humility and her concern for the feelings of her listeners in the following report of an experience in persuasion.

My freshman roommate and I were studying Saturday afternoon when, as usually happens, we began to talk about what we were reading, and to stray from that to all sorts of things. At the time I was reading philosophy, and she made the statement that she wished she could get all of her Group III requirements in philosophy so she wouldn't have to take history. She went on to assert that she thought it was silly to have to take things you don't want to.

I showered her with all the authoritative arguments I've ever heard about the value of general education, but I was getting absolutely nowhere. She simply knew how she felt and my ideas were going in one ear and out the other.

I changed my direction and began to talk more specifically about "Foundations of Western Civilization" and its values to me. Knowing that she is interested in religion, music, and science, I told her how these subjects were treated in the text we use. I told her how grateful I was personally for the things I had learned. In conclusion I mentioned a couple of interesting facts about religion which I hadn't known previously and had learned in the course, things which were new and interesting to her. I have a pretty good hunch that when the time comes she will take history without too many complaints.

I cannot give an exact sentence when my persuasion succeeded because it was a rather gradual process, but I think she was finally convinced some time while I was telling her some of the specific things I had learned.

I think I was successful partially because I changed my attitude from that of one who is right, telling one who is wrong, to that of one who has been wrong too and is changing. Another factor in my success was that I avoided the objections she held most strongly and talked more about things in which we were in basic agreement, helping her to find what she wanted and needed in history, not trying to force on her what she did not want.

When we wish to eliminate differences, we must be impersonal; we cannot afford to need a victory.

Gentleness

Cushion your remarks when your statement is obviously being opposed. Your views will gain a better hearing if first you call your conversant by name, subtly recognize his dignity, and then make a gentle remark. "John, I wonder about this point of view," or "Bill, we ought to think about this too . . . . " Such remarks cue the listener to the fact that he is going to receive some opposition. But the blow is softened and prepared for by anticipation. Perhaps he will then listen.

When people want to resolve their differences they may do so if they will forget their individual solutions and turn their attention to a careful re-examination of the problem. The more people discuss the specific details of a situation the more likely they will come to similar solutions. But if a person dares to see as those do who differ with him, he must honor the principle of compromise. Conflict between people is resolved only when they, as individuals, want to change, want to see as others do — and this takes time, patience, humility, and gentleness.

What can be done to gain the ears of the man who, regardless of how skillfully you deport yourself, insists that he is right and you are wrong? There are three courses of action open to you. You can retaliate and go into battle, give in and admit your stupidity, or depart and turn your attention to other matters. While this chapter would suggest the last, it is impossible to recommend a hard and fast rule. You must evaluate the situation and see how important the issue is. If you give each of the three possibilities hasty review as the deadlock develops, you learn the skill of making your responses fit the situation as you see it.

We have no panacea for the struggle of man against man. Beneath the logic and language of human speech must be the desire to work out solutions. The best we can do is teach a man to hear himself so that he may know what he is doing to his listener.

QUESTIONS FOR STUDY AND DISCUSSION

1. What are the reasons why men argue?
2. What things will argument not do?
3. What are the conditions needed for argument?
4. Discuss some of the techniques of verbal warfare.
5. Name and discuss the techniques for resolving conflict.

SUGGESTIONS AND ASSIGNMENTS

1. Work out a roundtable discussion with four or five members of the class in which you demonstrate the language and attitudes of conflict and of peace. Let each person exemplify both good and bad techniques. Record your discussion, and play it back to the class for their evaluation.

2. If you can take shorthand, or better yet, get a recording of a "genuine argument," analyze and label the techniques from sentence to sentence that favor and disfavor bringing the argument to a peaceful close. Play a few sentences to the class and explain what you have observed.

3. For one week, keep a record of the sentences you speak or hear that skillfully turn away opposition. With several other students in an impromptu panel, read, explain, and compare these with those brought in by other members of the panel.

4. Take part in a class debate, presenting a point of view you firmly believe in. Your purpose is to see how skillfully you meet opposition without arousing antagonism. Have the speakers and the class evaluate all speakers on this point, as well as on effectiveness in persuasion. Have two recorders in class take down sentences that they feel illustrate tact. Record the debate and study it afterwards to see how well you handled your relations with the opposition.

5. Give a speech in class in which you know that your point of view is not held by all your listeners. Your objective is to see how neutral yet how effective you can be. If you want a hard test, tell your listeners, before you begin, to "boo" you when they dislike your position. At the close of the speech, have those who oppose you ask questions. How skillfully can you answer? Have the speech, questions, and answers recorded. Study the recording after class and write a paper evaluating yourself.

Part Four

The Mechanics of
Speech

―――――

There are a thousand unnoticed openings . . .
which let a penetrating eye at once into a man's
soul: and I maintain . . . that a man . . . does
not lay down his hat in coming into a room, or
take it up in going out of it, but something
escapes, which discovers him.

Laurence Sterne

14

Visible Speech: Movement and Gesture

THE WORD "SPEECH" generally connotes spoken words, and the finest graduations of "intended" meaning in speech are transmitted by sound through words. Man, in all cultures, has refined and systematized communication through the oral symbol. Three quarters of a century ago textbooks in public speaking and elocution also developed elaborate systems of gestures, which purported to express various emotions and emphases. These gestures were diagrammed, sometimes even with dotted lines to show arm and hand motion, and students learned them by rote. Today only the deaf develop gesture into a systematic "language," and they do so of necessity.

Yet action does communicate, often more honestly, or more revealingly, than the word.

"What's wrong with you, Jim? What's bothering you?"
"Nothing, I didn't say anything."
"I know, but you act as if . . ."

And no matter how Jim may deny it, his behavior, his actions, his mannerisms express his mood or his state of mind.

In their search for a good pattern of speech, students want to know the rules of acceptable action. You gain confidence in speech as in anything else if you are sure you are not violating etiquette. Some rules were given in Chapter 3 so that you might be released from this concern at that point, and so that you might be free to direct your attention to more immediately urgent communication skills. This does not mean that action is unimportant; quite the contrary. But its significance is not in its form; rather, in what it says. Let us turn our attention to action, not in search of a formula, but for more understanding of the ways of man and his language and for the increased control which better insight can give.

Two Kinds of Action

In speech, action is comparable to that four-fifths of the iceberg concealed beneath the surface. That which one fears to say, does not think wise to say, and indeed is unaware of, is often conveyed by action. One experimenter concluded that self-revealing gestures originate in conflict situations, that is, where the person is indecisive and unsure. He also observed that people are "relatively consistent" in their responses to situations and that their unconscious actions have a close relationship to the words that are involved in the situation.[1] It is little wonder that the listener's confidence in the speaker is guided by what he sees as well as what he hears.[2] This kind of self-revealing action, directed by the impelling needs of the self, is variously called *involuntary, self-directed,* or *expressive.* But much of our individual style of action is under conscious control. *Intended* action, or gesture, while not so specific in intellectual content as words, does nevertheless reinforce the verbal intent and is part of our conscious expression. Thus selected movements are used to indicate direction, size of an object, points of emphasis, and the whole range of emotions. This is called adaptive or voluntary action, that is, action which is controlled by our purposes in talking.

Determinants of Unintended and Intended Action

The psychologist, Gordon W. Allport, has listed eleven factors that shape action.[3] Some are unintended, some intended, some both. They are as follows:

---

[1] M. H. Krout, "Autistic Gestures: An Experimental Study in Symbolic Movement," *Psychological Monographs,* 1935, No. 208; "The Social and Psychological Significance of Gestures," *Journal of Genetic Psychology,* 1935, No. 47, 385–412.

[2] The characteristics of voice are equally significant in the listener's confidence, but voice is an aspect of body and is governed by the same attitudes that govern postures and mannerisms.

[3] *Personality: A Psychological Interpretation,* New York, Henry Holt and Company, Inc., 1949, p. 468.

Unintended	1. Cultivated tradition 2. Local fashion 3. Transitory emotional states 4. Strain or fatigue
Unintended and Intended	5. Age 6. Sex 7. Body build 8. Health 9. Accidental deformation
Intended	10. Training such as speech, military experience, professional experience. 11. The use of tools such as pen, saw, gun, etc.

As is readily seen, the first four of these are unintended and involuntary. That the first two are of social or cultural rather than personal origin should not be disturbing, for there is no clear-cut distinction between the self and society. Daily communication shapes people after the patterns of the culture around them, and the culture is the common behavior of individuals. The second group of five are determinants influenced both by the will and by physical factors. Consider age, for instance. A boy and an old man walk differently because of differences in purpose and in physical maturation. The last two items are clearly expressions of purpose or of learning.

It is for the listener to determine what is involuntary and unconscious and what is intended. Thus most of us know that faces involuntarily come to bear the stamp of suffering, self-awareness, kindliness, wonderment, receptivity, anxiety, debauchery, or sadness. We learn unconsciously to separate these characteristics from the immediate intent of the speaker, though they doubtless have their effects on any conscious purpose he may have. Moreover, all wear masks sculptured by the manners of the day. Most people smile when they meet others. Ladies and gentlemen do not show anger. But as readers of action, when we note firmness of facial set and tightness of lips, what shall we say the speaker reflects? Are we seeing his present purpose, his past life, or the "etiquette" of his environment? Careful discrimination and cross-checking of observations are necessary to gain accurate insight. Some of us are better at this kind of reading than others, but all of us acquire considerable skill at it very early in our lives.

Three factors complicate the problem of reading action. One has been suggested above. Standardized behavior, the stamp of the culture, tends to mask emotions. Second, habits have a way of outliving the motives that brought them into being. Furtive movement, blushes, rhythmic swaying may continue long after early self-consciousness has passed. Third, imitation of other people's speech brings into a person's behavior mannerisms which reflect something other than his immediate state of mind. It is little wonder that we misinterpret one another.

The Unintended Revelation

At first thought it may seem odd that the body should tell what the speaker does not want to say, and even more — what he does not consciously know. But when we remember that the body is a total reactor to that which commands attention, it does not seem so strange that it should speak for the self. There is considerable evidence that the structure of the body reflects the temperament to which we were born and the muscular sets, the training of our past.[4] By little "signs of which the audience is often unaware" it learns something of the speaker's emotional stability, his attitudes toward himself, the attitudes and enthusiasm he has for his subject, and his feelings toward his listeners.[5]

Reaction to the Physical Self

One's size and build, and the way he reacts to both, are revealed to sight. Heavy people and thin ones often have defensive mannerisms, and these may be as varied as the race of men. Heavy mature women in speech classes tend to look upon the work of the class as an affront. They usually vacillate between anger and apology. At one moment they attack the assignment or the "speech class," the next, they apologize for having "nothing to say," or for being poorly prepared, even though their preparation may be quite adequate. Heavy girls of college age are very likely to become meek, and to regress to earlier behavior patterns, but they make fewer delusory explanations about their concern than do their older sisters. Thin girls and women are less

[4] G. W. Allport, *Personality, a Psychological Interpretation*, New York, Henry Holt and Company, Inc., 1949, p. 482.
[5] Lew Sarett and William Trufant Foster, *Basic Principles of Speech*, Boston, Houghton Mifflin Company, 1946, p. 30.

likely to react negatively to themselves, for our culture imposes no penalty for this quirk of nature except in its extreme form. Short women are fashionable too, but a very tall girl chastises herself and suffers considerably. Instead of becoming meek, she is more likely to become aggressive or overly generous and gracious. Big men are inclined to use their weight to aggressive advantage. But a fat college boy, while he is jolly (because he is supposed to be) often feels silly and resents nature's trick on him. One may sense a trace of "what's the use" beneath the jovial smile, particularly as the speaker walks to his seat after a speech. And if he does not prepare so well as he ought to, perhaps these attitudes toward his physical self may explain his carelessness. Men are supposed to be dominant. Since slight build may easily be interpreted as non-dominance, slender men tend to react apologetically. Short men, while there are exceptions, by and large compensate with aggressive techniques. They capitalize upon their quick reactions and take advantage of their opportunities.

Tall college men are very often either slouchy, swaying half-grown boys, or stiff, formal new-grown men. One student vividly described the social adjustments to a foot's growth in a year. His reactions to himself were in a continual state of re-education, for other people were constantly altering their relations to him. Another self-conscious, gangling boy showed considerable insight when he said, "I am always expecting the remark, 'Richard, how tall you have grown; when are you going to stop?'"

Dress

One's dress — the styles, color and pattern he chooses in his clothes — also speak for him. Very careful dress is the reflection of either a meticulous and aggressive person or one who is compensating for feelings of inadequacy. Very slovenly dress suggests defeat, rebellion, independence, or self-effacement.

As a rule, if a person wears clothes that are outstanding in color, pattern, or design, we have reason to wonder whether he is gaining all the attention he would like. While such a person may use clothes as his only device to gain attention, he is likely to reveal striking speech also. He may be very glib, sensational, sophisticated, pictorial, or "very" anything else, in either content or delivery. In addition, the person whose dress is colorful tends to wear his emotions and appreciations on his sleeve. If he is consistently extroverted, his thinking and speech tend to be relatively formless or disorganized. Conversely, the introvert, who keeps his emotions to himself, is usually conservative in dress — unless he does just the opposite and uses dress as a compensation. While not necessarily more penetrating, the thinking and speech of the introvert are likely to follow more rigid form and order.

The person whose clothes are a careful ensemble is likely to have a keen sense of unity, balance, and coherence. Some people, on the other hand, seldom dress with a pattern in mind; if a green tie is the favorite of the moment, they may wear it with whatever is at hand. Such a person, often not concerned for relationships, is likely to be distorted in his thinking. Again, the person who must fashion his entire dress around one detail, say a given hat or one style of shoe, thereby implies emotional rigidity. We say that such a person is emotional, which is another way of saying that he does not see things in perspective, in proper relationship. Dress, like manner and expression, are externals that give ready signals about the person "inside," and while such clues should be interpreted with caution, it is surprising how frequently they have significance.

The Eyes

Our eyes also reveal significant things about us. Lifting the eyebrows suggests further consideration, while a quick lowering closes the issue. Tense, partially-closed lids characterize the eyes of a man who harbors controlled hate. A quick closing and slow opening of the eyes belongs to condescension. Partial closing of the eyes and raising of the cheeks attends perplexity. It is said that Mussolini's indomitable will pervaded his action, even to the voluntary raising and slow lowering of his eyelids. No wonder he had ulcers. One investigator concluded that non-dominant men tend more than dominant ones to fix their eyes upon a conversant or on the task at hand.[6] The compulsively aggressive seem to study every movement of their conversants. We close our eyes and perhaps move the head slightly to one side when we would escape unpleasant and circulating thoughts. A person who is afraid of the impact of others tries to evade looking at his audience when he speaks. The visually-minded close their eyes, or fix them on an object when they are trying to recall. People who "remember with their ears" cock their heads. Some, apparently trying hard to

[6] Philip Eisenberg, "Expressive Movement Related to Dominance," *Archives of Psychology*, No. 211, Vol. 30, 1937.

hear, both close their eyes and cock their heads. One gets a blank expression when a new idea, a new relationship is taking form. The facial muscles fall, the mouth drops open, and the eyes grow wide. Children adopt these tensions when a story transports them into a new world. Quite inaccurately, we often call this set a "dumb expression."

The Mouth

Some investigators believe that the mouth is the most expressive of the facial features, since it is the most mobile. A feeling of scorn, a smile, a distrustful thought, anger, trembling fear, disdain, happiness, bitterness, are all readily expressed by the mouth. And when we are struggling to "keep a straight face," it is the mouth that wants to get out of control.

Facial Structure

We have discussed some of the communicative possibilities of the features of the face in isolation. But our impressions are quite often drawn from the speaker's face as a whole; and while the conclusions of the ancient study of physiognomy are often discredited, Allport, Vernon, Reiter, Brunswick, Dunlap, Blake, and Giese, among others, are inclined to believe that the relations of the facial features have significance. Such observers attach importance to the distance between the eyes, the height of the brow, the position of the nose, the length of the nose, the height of the mouth, and the size of the features. They are inclined to believe that the pattern of the features is related to intelligence, prevailing emotions, age, and energy. While nothing conclusive can be taken from the objective studies in this field, it would seem strange if the face with its concentration of nerves and voluntarily controlled muscles should not reveal the subtleties of human make-up, particularly since we think of ourselves as our faces. As Allport suggests, the intimate connection of the face with feeding, oral communication, and the reception of most of the messages from the outside world focuses the self and its expression in the face. The question is not so much whether the face communicates reliably, but whether we read its subtle signals accurately.

Posture and Walk

The proud stand tall. Those who lean forward are likely to be aggressive. Indeed, a man's walk is governed by his purpose. Wilsmann, a German psychologist, noted the following characteristics of walking: regularity, speed, length of stride, elasticity, definiteness of direction, pressure, changeableness or variability. He concluded that the rhythm of the walk comes from the union of these traits. Eisenberg, in the study previously cited, noted the following kinds of walk: even, jerky, bouncing, stiff, and erect. In addition, according to the study, non-dominant men tend to walk faster than dominant men, though this difference, for some unaccountable reason, does not hold true for women.

We have all had the experience of identifying people, when we could not see them, by the sound of their footsteps. Interestingly enough, though we seldom see ourselves walk, we identify our own gait accurately. This has been tested by taking motion-pictures of people in action, dressed in masks and long loose-fitting gowns. The ability of people to pick themselves out on the screen suggests that our walk is intimately related with our self-image.

Associated with the walk is, of course, the posture. Some people are characteristically tense, some are formal and self-conscious, some relaxed, some toneless, some weary, some naturally animated, some self-consciously animated.

Miscellaneous Mannerisms

The nervously energetic tear their nails, bite their lips, swing one leg when seated, or thrash about in their chairs. Those in conflict sigh. The extremely fearful blanch. The submissive slouch. The shy often blush. The friendly smile spontaneously. The generous nod in quick approval. We unconsciously express ourselves in a multitude of ways.

Self-Directed Action: A Summary

Of course, we do not wisely describe a personality from the observation of a single mannerism; it is, rather, the total impact that counts. Experimental study shows that a person exercises a certain similarity in the performance of unrelated tasks. For instance, a man who writes large *tends* to take long strides, to overestimate angles, to cover much space in drawing, etc.[7] In addition, judges matching handwriting, character sketches, voice recordings, and portraits agree to an extent which indicates that it is the common factors in many observations that we must depend upon if we are to read a person accurately.

[7] G. W. Allport and P. E. Vernon, *Studies in Expressive Movement*, New York, The Macmillan Company, 1933.

Intended Action

Conscious action during speech is generally called gesture. As we react to the ideas we are expressing, the movements of the arms, hands, and body which we make add meaning to our words in one or more of three ways.

1. Descriptive gestures are movements which point out shape, or physical relationships. That fish you almost caught, the kind of desk lamp you are looking for, the way paper is folded to make a stencil, call into play movements of the head, arm, and hands that are descriptive in character.

2. Emphatic gestures add emotional intensity to our ideas. Essentially they add the force of physical energy. An angry "No" is punctuated by explosive action. A deliberate but determined "No" might bring a slow wagging of the head, momentarily stopped at each end of the "wag," forcefully expelled breath, and a heavy fist upon the table.

3. Gestures also have a symbolic or suggestive aspect. Feeling tones such as submission, fear, indifference, amusement, exhilaration, distaste, approval, scorn, doubt, sadness, attend our thoughts and are carried into the gestures we make.

Timing

Since we think all over, not only in our heads, the general postural set and the response to a developing thought are revealed at the moment of expression or just before. When we are tense or self-conscious, our timing is thrown off. In these moments it is well to remember that normally action is synchronized with, or just precedes, the word. The reverse timing is ludicrous and is therefore used as a conscious technique in farce.

Forces That Mold Intended Action

1. *Sex Differences.* Our gestures are culturally shaped, and culture dictates that they be different for men and women. A man is expected to use larger and more decisive gestures than a woman; hers must be more dainty and restrained. It is unfortunate for either the man or the woman who encroaches too far upon the gesture pattern of the opposite sex.

2. *Size Differences.* Obviously the size of a person influences the general character of his gestures. A small person quite obviously uses

smaller movements. A very small or very large person needs to be particularly careful. A small man using very small gestures shrinks to the stature of a mouse. Nor does it help him to go to the opposite extreme, for he then seems grandiose, or even ridiculous. A large man using small gestures looks like an overgrown boy. On the other hand, if he uses unduly large gestures he suggests that he is trying to "throw his weight around."

In addition, a person's size alters his rate of action. A small person, by virtue of less weight and shorter limbs, tends to react more quickly than a large person. He may quite naturally compensate for his size by accentuating this speed of reaction. Fast action on the part of a large person suggests that he is bouncing around. A drama critic, in typical generosity, said of a large actor, that "The hero prepared to exit from both sides of the stage at the same time."

3. *Smoothness.* The harmony of one's nervous system and of his whole make-up is revealed in his action. Beginning students in speech usually exert considerable energy trying to gain this kind of control. While stability is to be desired, over-control (exercised to "acquire and beget a temperance that may give it smoothness") sacrifices the spontaneity so vital to conviction. Dull smoothness is satisfying only to the speaker. It is better to focus upon the target and let smoothness come with practice.

Objective Study of One's Own Action

Speech action may well be practiced before a mirror in order to gain something akin to an objective picture of your physical behavior. Motion pictures are even more helpful, for in them you study yourself while you are completely dissociated from the act of speaking. Be particularly alert to the postures and expressions you assume at the ends of sentences. At these moments of pause we tend to relax and react to our own purpose. It is then that the self-image of the speaker is most readily communicated.

A compromise between these two methods of observing yourself is easy to work out if you have a helpful colleague and a mirror. You may place a relatively large mirror half way between yourself and the person with whom you are talking, just to the side of the line of vision between yourself and him. Mirror depth will then place your reflection at the side of your listener, so that you can look at both yourself and your conversant. With a little practice you may learn to talk and react as if to two other people.

This technique is particularly helpful in detecting undesirable mannerisms and attitudes. Having "discovered" the behavior yourself, and in surroundings where neither blame nor shame arises to plague you, you are likely to respond favorably to the knowledge you thus gain.

An Attitude Toward Learning Action

Naturally, you would like your actions to speak well for you. This means that they should be spontaneous and related to your purpose. It is highly questionable whether you should try to learn a "correct" form of moving and gesturing. In the first place, there is no necessarily correct way. More important, "correct" expression masks natural inner expression. A person who learns "proper" gestures must to that extent erase his own individuality. When a personality is encrusted with action by rule, the person may be complimented for having "taken speech." A considerably more significant compliment is that he "speaks well." An even better one is, "that was an exciting point he made." Action is good when it does not come to attention, but blends into the expression of ideas. Effective speech focuses the listener's attention on what is being said. Gestures, like words, are tools. They should aid expression, not overshadow it. They should ultimately become as natural a part of your speech as your verbal rhythms and stresses.

QUESTIONS FOR STUDY AND DISCUSSION

1. What are the two kinds of action?
2. What are some of the determinants of action?
3. How does our physical self affect our reactions?
4. What things may we learn to suspect of a person by a study of his dress?
5. How do the eyes reveal us? The mouth? The posture and walk?
6. What are the three kinds of gestures? Can you illustrate each?
7. What is the rule for the timing of gestures?
8. How do sex, size, and the standard of smoothness affect gestures?
9. How can you study your own action? What would you look for in such a study?

SUGGESTIONS AND ASSIGNMENTS

1. Walk to the platform. Walk from one side of the table, desk, or speaker's stand to the other. Be seated, rise, walk back to your seat. Then say how you felt as you did these things.

2. What does each classmate's walk say about his attitudes toward himself? Toward others?

3. Turn on a television set with the sound off, particularly when there are just one or two people on the screen. Take notes of the things you think you learn about the people by watching their mannerisms, gestures, and postures. Note particularly the ends of sentences. What is the difference in the behavior of the person who seems to communicate with you and one who does not?

4. Study the gestures of a professor or one of your classmates for a week and make a report.

5. It is customary to have pantomimes in speech class. To pantomime is to communicate by action alone. Tell a story, describe a process, or imitate a well-known person on campus for a minute by pantomime. See if the class can follow you.

6. Put on a hood and imitate the responses of emotions such as fear, joy, sadness, anger, contempt, etc. After each attempt, see if the class can guess your intent. Have members of the class describe the basic characteristics of the posture and action associated with each emotion.

The voice is the echo of the soul.

Pythagoras

15

The Speaking Voice

THE CLASS was assembled for the first time. Professor Johnson called off the names on the class cards. "Mr. Andrews, Mr. Bailey, Miss Beason . . . " His voice was clear, loud, and precise, somewhat constant in pitch. Having laid down the cards, he looked out over the class.

> "This course is entitled *American Economic History*. The name of the text is written on the board. You will read the first two chapters before . . ."

Some forty minutes later the students filed out of the class. Had Professor Johnson followed, he might have heard an intensely interesting conversation.

> "Gee, I don't know whether I should have signed up for this or not."
> "Nothing but American history from the economic angle."
> "Yeh, I know, but that guy's got ice water in his veins!"
> "I know what you mean."
> "I'll bet he's a tough grader. He wouldn't give a dime to a starving man."
> "Well, that's one class you won't cut, anyway."
> "You're telling me! A test every other week, a dull term paper, and a honey of a final. And to think, yesterday, I had the old world by the tail."

The professor had made no cutting remarks, no threats, no judgments, had said nothing about the difficulty of the course, grades, examinations, term papers, or finals. But the students (sophomores, of course) knew, or thought they knew. From what source had they gathered their information? At least in part they drew their conclusions from the professor's breathing, his attack upon sounds, his pitch level, his inflectional patterns, the loudness of his voice, the sounds

243

and words stressed by pitch intensity, and duration, and by the quality of his voice. Each one of us is judged daily by these features of our speech.

What The Voice Reveals

What are a few things the voice tells? Most obviously it differentiates men and women, even though half the range of the bass and the soprano is identical. There is something at the beginning and end of male and female sounds, even of the same pitch, which distinguishes them, though at present we do not know just what the differences are.

It is quite easy to tell whether the people in the next room are children or adults, somewhat more difficult to identify young boys and girls, fairly easy to pick out the aged. Since voice uses the muscles, cartilages, and bones of the body, it is affected by physical structure. Large people tend to have bigger and deeper voices, small people the converse. However, this index can be upset by the fact that small men often try to sound big and large women often want to be dainty.

In one study, judges listened to the voices of a group of boys and picked out the leaders with remarkable accuracy, even though they did not see the lads.[1] A number of experimenters have concurred that the speaking voice reveals whether we are essentially extroverted or introverted, aggressive or submissive, dominant or non-dominant, orderly or disorganized, thrifty and restrained or reckless and impulsive, confused in our attitudes or clear and decisive. In one study persons of strong aesthetic, political, and social inclinations were distinguished by voice.[2] In another study, it was found that those with breathy or whiny voices scored low in a test of dominance and emotional stability. Those with voices of harsh or metallic quality scored high in dominance and average in emotional stability.[3]

What do you associate with a narrow, high pitch range? A great deal of volume? Clipped sounds and cold quality? Rapid badly formed speech? A lavish use of inflection? Precise diction and a weak voice? Or a slow, low drawl?

---

[1] E. D. Partridge, "Leadership Among Adolescent Boys," *Teachers College Contributions to Education*, 1934, No. 608.

[2] P. J. Fay and W. C. Middleton, "Judgments of Spranger's Personality Types from the Voices as Transmitted Over a Public Address System," *Character and Personality*, 1939, Vol. 8, pp. 144–155.

[3] W. E. Moore, "Personality Traits and Voice Quality Deficiencies," *Journal of Speech Disorders*, March, 1939, pp. 33–36.

The voice indicates other things than personality. It is a rather faithful register of the part of the country from which you come. The drawl of the South, the nasal twang of New England, the hard attack of the East, the double stress and harsh "r" of the Midwest are some of the more common sectional attributes. Social position also has a direct effect on voice. Most professional people have more precise and "cultivated" voices than the rest of the population, and for this reason are often more difficult to judge, both in personality and in geographical origin.

Why Voice Reveals the Speaker

The voice has no physical organ or organs. Each part of the body associated with the voice has a more primary, and usually a more vital, function. The breathing mechanism used in voice supplies oxygen to the blood. The nerves that control breathing are close to the core of life. The vocal cords form a muscular door to the trachea, or windpipe, which closes to permit the impounding of air in the chest cavity and to make it rigid, a condition necessary for heavy work and elimination. This door also keeps foreign particles from entering the lungs. The resonators or sound chambers (mouth, pharynx, nasal passages, etc.) have their obvious life-sustaining purposes. Nor are the tongue, teeth, lips, velum, and palate speech organs primarily. Voice uses physical structures which evolved for other functions, and very important ones. This is of great significance to us, for whatever causes a flaw or excellence in these organs, so basic to life, is of necessity reflected in the voice. Vigor, weariness, health, illness, strength, weakness and all the emotions show themselves in the voice.

THE PRINCIPLES OF SOUND

Sound Waves

The product of voice is sound. Sound is energy that travels in waves of air from a vibrating source to the ear. As a child you were perhaps delighted by the waves or vibrations that moved out in all directions, when you dropped a pebble in a quiet pool. In like fashion, when you speak you set up vibration among air molecules, and the energy which sets the air in motion travels in waves to the listening ear. These waves are alternating periods of condensation (compacting) and rarefaction (spreading out) of the air particles. The wave length is measured by the distance between two adjacent condensations of the air, and constitutes a complete *cycle* of the action through which the molecules go. Regardless of how long or short the waves are, the transmitted sound energy rides at the same speed, roughly 1100 feet

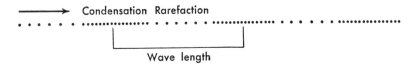

per second. The disturbed air does not move continuously at this speed; sound is not wind. The molecules of air act like relay men passing the energy along. You may have seen the impact of a railroad engine against the nearest car of a long train travel down the length of cars and back again. It was the energy or action that was transmitted. It made little difference how long or short the cars were; the impact traveled at the same speed. So it is with sound waves and the speed of sound.

Frequency

If sound moves in varying wave lengths, it is clear that the number of waves per unit of time varies. The *frequency* of sound, then, refers to the number of waves a vibrating source sets up per second. This is the element that the ear differentiates as pitch, the highness or lowness of sound. The bass voice, for instance, is low pitched; the soprano, high. We use the two words *frequency* and *pitch* to describe different aspects of the same phenomenon, for the former is the objective reality — the number of waves per second — whereas pitch is the ear's interpretation of frequency. If all other sound elements remain constant, frequency and pitch fluctuate together — the higher the frequency the higher the pitch. The human ear may be sensitive to frequencies as low as 12 to 16 and as high as 50,000, though most people cannot hear those above 20,000. From middle age on we are seldom sensitive to frequencies above 10,000 or 15,000 cycles.

The sound we call middle C, a frequency well within the range of all human voices, is approximately 256 vibrations per second. The musical standard divides sound into octaves. To raise a sound one octave is to double the frequency. It follows that C above middle C is 512; C below middle C is 128.

Overtones or Partials

Thus far we have spoken of a sound wave as if the vibration moved as a unit, setting up just one frequency. Indeed, this is possible; the tuning fork does it. Most objects, however, vibrate as a unit *and in parts*, so that the resulting sound waves are multiple. Most sounds

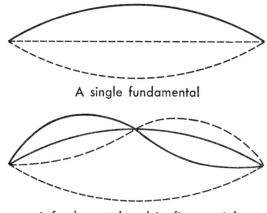

A single fundamental

A fundamental and its first partial

that we hear, then, are composed of the unit vibration (the fundamental) and the half, third, fourth, etc., partials of the fundamental, which are called the overtones. Because of resonance, which will be discussed shortly, varying combinations of these overtones are carried to the ear. It is these combinations of overtones and their varying loudness in relation to each other and the fundamental that causes us to say that the timbre or *quality* of a voice is pleasant, harsh, rich, thin, etc.[4] The flute, which resonates few overtones, is pure, thin, clear, and piercing as compared, for instance, with the clarinet. It is this compound of fundamental and partials that tells our ears which of the many musical instruments we are listening to. It is this impact that helps us identify people's voices.

Resonance

The crack of a gun is carried for some distance by the sheer force of the displaced air. But the vibrations of violin strings or the human

[4] Other factors such as sharpness of attack, pitch level, volume, rate, monotony, and clarity of articulation have their effect on our interpretation of a sound as pleasant or unpleasant.

vocal muscles do not operate with such force. Their carrying power
is increased by resonators. A resonator is either a hard surface that
reflects and directs the sound waves to the ear (as in a band shell) or
a chamber which by internal reflecting walls builds up the amplitude
of a wave length peculiar to its size. A small chamber resonates the
shorter waves (the higher frequencies) and a large chamber, the
longer waves (the lower frequencies). You have doubtless noted
that the depth of a musical instrument is closely related to its size.
Resonation is also related to the hardness of the surfaces. You may
deaden the acoustics of a room by rugs and drapes or liven it with
hard surfaces.

There are three kinds of resonance: reflected, forced, and sympathetic. As in the band shell, *reflected resonance* is the collecting of
sound energy and the directing of it to one point. Sound moves out
in all directions from its source, so that the increased volume of reflected resonance is not the result of sound reinforcement, but rather,
of the control of its direction.

A vibrating body will set into vibration a rigid but elastic body that
is in direct physical contact with it. The second vibrating body also
sets the air in motion, so that the intensity of the sound is increased.
This is called *forced resonance*. As a child you may have annoyed
your parents (when your mother served spinach) by plucking the
tines of your fork and fluctuating the volume of sound by alternately
lifting the fork handle and pressing it against the table top. The vibration of the table increased the intensity of the sound that began with
the vibration of the tines.

The third kind of resonance is *sympathetic*. As we said earlier, a
cavity will reinforce the intensity of the frequencies that "fit" its
size. You may have noticed that the tubes beneath the bars of the
marimba vary in length with the depth of the tone to be resonated;
the deeper the tone, the longer the tube. Reinforcement that comes
by the selection of the fundamental or partial peculiar to the cavity is
called sympathetic.

Amplitude, Intensity, Loudness

Have you ever sat on the beach when the water is relatively quiet
and watched the long forceless waves roll in to land? And have you,
at other times, seen waves of approximately the same length or even
shorter splash with force upon the beach? The difference in the force

is the difference in the height of the wave, in its *amplitude*. The high wave contained more water, and more power, more energy. In speaking of sound waves, we generally refer to the wave energy as the intensity of the sound. The ear interprets the amplitude or intensity as loud or soft. The inaudible voice does not put enough energy into the wave, so that it dies out before it makes sufficient impact upon the ear.

You should be able to define and describe *sound, wave length, frequency, pitch, overtone, partial, resonance* (reflected, forced, and sympathetic), *amplitude, intensity,* and *loudness* if you are to have a clear understanding of voice. All too often, students do not understand the evaluation of voice and the assignments given to correct their peculiar problems because they have a confused concept of the nature of sound. We have here presented the barest essentials, and you should study them carefully. If you do not understand them, you should raise questions with your instructor or read further in other sources.[5]

THE FOUR STEPS IN VOICE PRODUCTION

In the piano, the original source of energy is the action of a hammer striking a taut wire. In the violin, it is the displacement of the string by the bow. In wind instruments, it is air pressure that sets lips or reeds to vibrating. In voice it is the cords of the larynx (to be discussed later) which vibrate, due to the outward passage of air between them. The production of voice begins with air pressure, which brings us to the nature and problems of breathing.

Breathing

Breathing is accomplished by enlarging and diminishing the size of the thoracic cavity, and is performed by three related kinds of action. By pulling down and forward the muscles of the diaphragm which separate the abdomen and the thorax (that part of the body enclosed by the rib cage), the thorax is lengthened. In addition, the intercostals and rib elevators contract to lift the rib cage and to enlarge it both from front to back and from side to side. The scaleni muscles of the upper thorax and neck raise the top two ribs; the clavi-

[5] James H. McBurney and Ernest J. Wrage, *The Art of Good Speech,* New York, Prentice-Hall, Inc., 1953, Chapter XIX. Giles W. Gray and Claude M. Wise, *The Bases of Speech,* New York, Harper and Brothers, Revised Edition, 1946, Chapter II. Claude M. Wise, *et al., Foundations of Speech,* New York, Prentice-Hall, Inc., 1942, Chapter 7.

cal muscles (near the collar bones) lift the cage and lengthen it. Conversely, as these various muscles relax, the thorax becomes smaller in all dimensions.

The rib cage consists of twelve pairs of ribs which circumscribe the upper part of the trunk. All are attached to the backbone. The

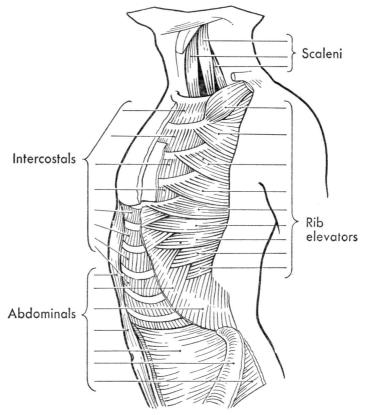

Some of the muscles of the thorax
and abdomen used in breathing.

six upper pairs are joined in front to the sternum cartilage, the breastbone. Each of the four pairs directly below is joined by cartilage to the one above. The lowest two pairs, called floating ribs, are not attached in front. While no part of the cage structure is rigid, the lower part is the more flexible in lateral or outward action.

It should be noted that breathing is not a process of drawing in or expelling air. Rather, at inhalation air rushes in because the contraction of certain muscles, previously mentioned, increases the size of the chest cavity and thus reduces internal air pressure; consequently air from the outside rushes in. We call this the *inspiration* phase

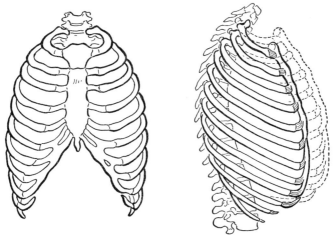

Front and side views of the human rib cage.
Dotted lines show ribs raised in inhalation.

of breathing. When contraction has reached its maximum, these mucles relax and the cavity becomes smaller. This compresses the air in the lungs and increases the internal air pressure over that outside the body. The air then rushes out the mouth and nose. This is called the *expiration* phase. Thus breathing is a matter of enlarging and decreasing the size of the air cavity, altering the internal air pressure in respect to the external.

For normal life-sustaining purposes this complete cycle, intake and outgo, occurs from fourteen to seventeen times per minute. The same time is required for each phase when one is awake and not speaking. But when we speak, the breathing rate is usually slowed down. This is compensated for by deeper breathing. The ratio of intake to outgo time also changes. We speak only on the expiration phase, and since speech is relatively continuous, we draw the air in quickly and expel it in a series of brief spurts, progressive relaxations, as we speak. The ratio of expiration time to inspiration time, in normal speech, is approximately ten to one. On the two graphs below, taking in air is represented by the upward curves; letting out air by the downward curves.

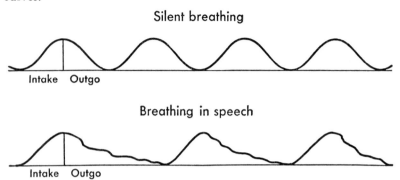

approximately ten to one. On the two graphs below, taking in air is

Kind of Breathing. The thorax may be enlarged in three ways, and each of us uses one way more than the others. We may be a diaphragmatic, a medial, or a thoracic breather. The diaphragmatic breather depends chiefly on the action of the diaphragm. The medial breather uses the muscles that expand the rib cage from back to front and side to side. The thoracic breather lifts the cage and performs most of his breathing in the upper chest. The more diaphragmatic action there is, the deeper the breathing; the more exclusively the action is thoracic, the shallower the breathing.

It would therefore at first glance appear that diaphragmatic breathing was preferable. As far as speech is concerned, however, experiment does not entirely support this view.[6] The correlation, for instance, between ratings of students by speech instructors and the kind of breathing of the speaker is low.

Supply of Air and Breath Control. But examination of the breathing graphs of good and poor speakers does reveal two important relationships between breathing and speech. First, good speech is produced by persons who have an ample supply of air to meet their phrasing needs; and second, good speech is attended by an adequate

[6] Giles Wilkenson Gray, "Regional Predominance in Respiration in Relation to Certain Aspects of Voice," *Studies in Experimental Phonetics,* Baton Rouge, Louisiana State University Press, 1936, pp. 59–78. Willard Wilson, "Breath Control: A Common Sense Summary," *Quarterly Journal of Speech,* Vol. 28, 1942, pp. 338–343.

control of the air. In any case, then, it seems wise to advocate the
development of breathing habits that produce both control and
sufficient quantities of air.

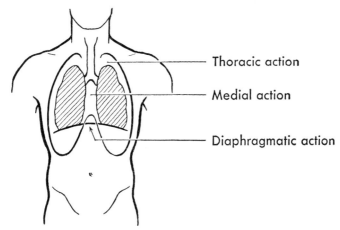

Three kinds of breathing. In each of us,
one of the three predominates.

While research does not demonstrate that diaphragmatic breathing
is essential to good speech, it does suggest obvious advantages.[7] Research indicates that 43 per cent of the total breath capacity is brought
about by diaphragmatic action. This divides the remaining 57 per
cent between the other two kinds of breathing.[8] Increased diaphragmatic action, then, appears to be the best way for the person with inadequate breath for speaking to augment his supply. Further, the
type of breathing which induces control is advisable for those who
suffer fear in the speech situation. Diaphragmatic action is natural
when one is relaxed or asleep; it seems reasonable to expect that the
breathing of the relaxed state would help reduce emotional stress. The
"sigh of relief" is more than a phrase.

Muscles of Breath Control. Breath control in speech is, in part,
produced by the muscles used to draw in air. But muscles are not

[7] E. M. Huyck and K. D. Allen, "Diaphragmatic Action of Good and Poor
Speaking Voices," *Speech Monographs*, IV, 1937, pp. 101–09.

[8] H. H. Bloomer, "A Roentgenographic Study of the Mechanics of Respiration,"
Speech Monographs, Vol. 3, 1936, pp. 118–124.

active in two directions. They do not contract and expand; they contract and relax. Thus the muscles which, in inhalation, lift and expand the rib cage and draw down the bottom of the cage, relax to
let air out. They provide a smooth supply of air for speaking when
they relax evenly, not jerkily, and at a rate that fits the phrasing of the
speech. At the same time that these various sets of muscles in the
chest and diaphragm relax, the abdominal muscles contract, thus
helping further to expel air from the lungs. Except when we scream
or shout, however, the abdominal muscles do not become extensively
engaged in voice production.[9]

According to Victor E. Negus, the vocal folds, commonly known
as the vocal cords, in the larynx or voice box, play a crucial part in
control of breath during speech.[10] Therefore, many breathing problems arise from the faulty action of these muscles. The importance
of vocal action to breath control comes into sharp relief if we compare
the quality of normal speech with that of the grunt. When we are
hit in the stomach, we give a "toneless" or dead grunt because the
vocal folds are being used passively. In other words, if the vocal folds
were not actively engaged in breath control, the normal speaking
voice would be grunt-like in quality. In creating speech sounds the air
does not *act upon* the vocal folds. Normal speech is produced by the
interaction of air pressure and the control over that pressure by the
vocal muscles. The degree to which the closure and tension of the vocal
folds resist the free escape of air is the degree to which the vocal
folds control breathing.

Phonation

The production of speech sounds is called *phonation*. In exhalation,
expelled air passes into the larynx and between two muscles, the
vocal folds, which act like a pair of combination sliding and swinging
doors (see figure). At the most open phase, the muscles may be as
much as four millimeters (a little more than an eighth of an inch)
apart. The upward movement does not exceed one-half millimeter.[11]

[9] R. H. Stetson and C. V. Hudgins, "Functions of the Breathing Movements
in the Mechanism of Speech," *Archives Néerlandaises de Phonétique Expéri-
mentale*, 1930, 5, pp. 1–30.

[10] *The Comparative Anatomy and Physiology of the Larynx*, New York, Grune
and Stratton, Inc., 1949, p. 144.

[11] Robert Curry, *The Mechanism of the Human Voice*, New York, Longmans,
Green and Company, 1940, pp. 67–68.

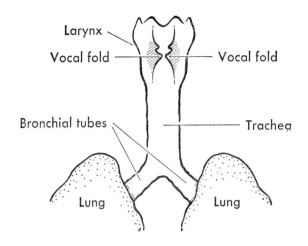

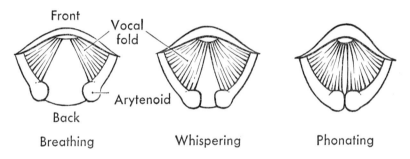

*Diagrammatic representation of the larynx
and the vocal folds. The vocal folds are shown
in three positions.*

When these two vocal folds, bands, cords, or muscles, are closed, a pressure exceeding their tension will open them and cause air to escape and thus produce sound. When the air escapes, the pressure beneath drops, and the "doors" close. In speech the pressure builds up again and again. The alternate opening and closing of the vocal folds sends up puffs of air. This process of phonation is roughly comparable to the action of blowing air through closed lips, as a child does to imitate the sound of an automobile or an outboard motor.

The two vocal muscles join the thyroid cartilage in front, just behind the protruding V point of the Adam's apple. At the back of the larynx the muscles are attached to the two ladle-shaped arytenoid cartilages, which by rotating open and close the vocal folds and help the muscles gain the varying degrees of tension needed to alter pitch, force, and quality. The opening between the muscles, produced by the rotating action of the arytenoids, is known as the glottis. In normal speech it is slightly wider in the forepart.

The average length of the vocal folds in men is nine-tenths of an inch, as contrasted to seven-tenths in women. This, coupled with the facts that the folds are thicker in men and the resonators are larger, accounts for the deeper voices of men. But for either sex, of course, the slower the vibration of the vocal folds, the lower the pitch; the faster the vibration, the higher the pitch.

Phonating Attack. The combination of breath pressure and the tension of the vocal muscles results in one of three kinds of attack, or initiation of speech sound.[12] These attacks are directly related to the emotions involved in the communication. When our emotions are relatively neutral, the resulting lack of tensions produces what is called the *soft* attack, as when we converse in ordinary tones with little need to command. Weak or gentle emotions produce an *aspirate* or breathy attack, and strong feelings or the need to control produce a *hard* attack. The speech initiated by hard attack is usually higher pitched than that of soft or aspirate attack. While these differences are not easy to describe in words, they are unmistakable to the listener, and he inevitably reacts to them whether he is aware of doing so or not.

These various types of attack are not produced solely by the tension of the vocal folds. Tension is not usually so clearly localized as that. The governing emotional states and attitudes impart laxness or tension to the whole body and therefore to the muscles of breath control, resonation, and articulation. It follows, as we shall see, that emotional orientation is communicated not only in the vocal attack, but also in the pitch level, resonation, and the sharpness and force of articulation.

Resonation

If you remove the mouthpiece from a wind instrument and blow into the mouthpiece, you produce a weak noise. The difference from

---

[12] Leopold Stein, *The Infancy of Speech and the Speech of Infancy*, London, Methuen & Company, Ltd., 1949, pp. 56–59.

the rich, full sound of the instrument is one of resonation. In like fashion, much of the quality of the human voice is determined by the chambers of the head in which the sound reverberates. A resonator, as explained in our discussion of the physics of sound, (1) amplifies sound, (2) selects and emphasizes certain frequencies, and (3) prolongs the sound.

The essential resonators in speech are the pharynx, the mouth, and the nasal passages [13] (see figure). Of these, the pharynx and mouth

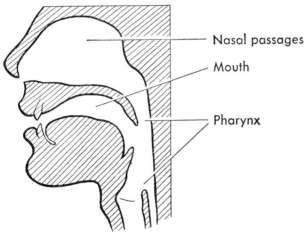

Nasal passages

Mouth

Pharynx

Resonating chambers of the nose, mouth, and throat.

are flexible and may be changed in size to accommodate a wide variety of frequencies. The nasal passages are more fixed and therefore respond to a narrower range of frequencies. They are desirably the focus in resonation only in the *m*, *n*, and *ng* sounds.

The hardness of the resonator surfaces also varies the frequencies that are transmitted. Soft surfaces absorb rather than reflect sound, particularly in the higher frequencies. Therefore high muscular tension emphasizes the higher frequencies, while low muscular tension emphasizes the lower frequencies by eliminating the higher ones. In addition to frequencies, muscular tension affects intensity. Regardless of the frequencies resonated, the harder the surface the more the

---

[13] The upper larynx, sinuses, trachea, and chest cavity are by some authorities considered effective resonators. Experimental research has neither established nor disproved their part in resonation.

sounds will reflect and the longer they will reverberate. The mega-
phone nature of the throat, mouth, and nose suggests that much of
our resonance is reflected. The hardness of the surface and the openness of the resonators, particularly the mouth, controls this reflected
resonance. Moreover, all three of the resonators are cavities, and
therefore act in accordance with the principle of sympathetic resonance, selecting sounds natural to themselves. It is highly questionable
how much forced resonance there is in the human vocal system. Experimental studies using microphones to pick up the forced resonance
of the body suggest that little or none of our resonance is of this kind.

Excessive resonance in one of the three chambers produces a voice
quality that is identified as throaty, oral, or nasal. These shall be discussed in the next chapter.

Articulation

The fourth and last step in the production of speech sound is
articulation, the formation and separation of speech sounds. Articulation takes place through the action of the tongue (the tip, the blade,
and the back), the lips, teeth, alveolar ridge (or upper gum ridge at
the front of the mouth), the palate, pharyngeal wall, and the velum
or palate. By various combinations of position and motion, these

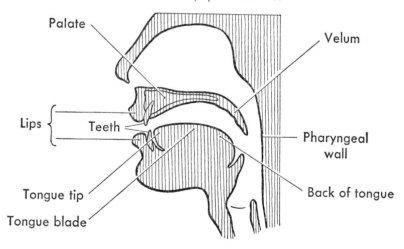

*The organs of the mouth and nose are impor-
tant in the creation of speech sounds.*

organs shape the mouth for both vowels and consonants. Good articulation means a flow of speech that is clear and understandable.

Unintelligible Articulation. When we can hear speech sound but cannot make it out, the articulators are not producing sounds distinctly enough, and we say that the articulation is poor or slovenly. The physical causes are four in number. The articulators may not be brought to bear upon the stream of sound with sufficient effort. For instance, the *d* sound is accurately formed by placing the tip of the tongue on the alveolar ridge, closing the nasal port by lifting the velum against the pharyngeal wall, and building up phonated air pressure in the mouth which is exploded through the mouth when the contact of the tongue and the gum ridge is broken by lowering the tip of the tongue. The force and clarity of the sound depends upon how well the nasal port is closed and how explosively the tongue is pulled down. Weak action causes the sound to be mistaken for an *n*.

Second, unintelligible sounds may be produced by the inaccurate placement and action of the articulators. An *s* is formed by closing off the air escape at the sides of the mouth and removing the tip of the tongue from the alveolar ridge just the right distance for producing the fricative, or hissing, quality we identify as a proper *s*. Lifting the blade a bit too high and/or improper side closure between the tongue and teeth causes variations more closely identified with the *sh* sound.

Third, faulty articulation may result from not opening the mouth wide enough and/or not shaping it accurately for the sound involved. The result is that sounds are muffled, much as if the hand were held over the mouth.

Fourth, and closely related, the speaker may talk out of one side of his mouth. The result is muffled speech.

There are a multiplicity of possible causes for these kinds of faulty articulation. Perhaps the chief causes are lack of effort, poor habits, regional or foreign dialect, rapid rate, poor hearing, nerve injury, defensiveness, and lack of self-respect. The assignments of Chapter 17 are designed to meet these problems.

Over-Precise Speech. While we may misunderstand speech that is not properly articulated, we do not listen to discrete syllables and words, but to ideas; and ideas come in phrases and sentences. Therefore a normal flow of words is necessary to intelligibility. When undue emphasis is placed upon producing every sound distinctly, the very preciseness gets in the way of ideas. Indeed, overdistinctness is just as much a fault in communication as unclear sound. Again the causes are many: undue regard for clarity of diction, a mind that gives exaggerated emphasis to isolated details, formal attitudes, imitation, habit.

THE SOUNDS OF ENGLISH

In civilized man, most speech is produced during the expiration phase of breathing. Only the smacking of the lips, clicks, and swillings such as the sucked-in *st* or *sh* remind us of a day when speech was a taking-in process and a hypnotic reaction to the world outside.[14] As man changed from the slave of an awe-inspiring universe to a creature that rose to conquer his environment, he began to breathe out upon the world, and the sharpness with which he forms his sounds is an index of his determination to control. In the evolution of outgoing speech man developed two classes of sounds, vowels and consonants.

Vowels

The vowels are more primitive than the consonants and therefore reflect man's essential inner state. The quality of voice — our finest index to the speaker's attitudes, and shortly to be discussed — is mainly carried by the vowels.[15] By definition vowels are the relatively open, full and continuous sounds, produced by air set in vibration at the vocal folds and resonated in the chambers of the head. They are generally classified in terms of the tongue position, mouth opening, shape and protrusion of the lips. For instance, ē as in *feet,* ĭ as in *fit,* ā as in *fame,* ĕ as in *bet,* ă as in *fat,* and à as in *ask* [16] are produced by arching the tongue in the front part of the mouth. As you move down through the sounds (ē, ĭ, ā, ĕ, ă) you will also note that the mouth gradually opens more widely.[17] At the same time, the lips

[14] Leopold Stein, *The Infancy of Speech and the Speech of Infancy,* London, Methuen & Company, Ltd., 1949, Chapter III.

[15] Jack Bloom, "An Experiment to Determine the Presence of Acoustical Cues in the Vowels Which Identify Familar Speakers," M.S. Thesis, University of Michigan, 1951.

[16] As pronounced in some places along the Eastern seaboard of the United States.

[17] Diacritical markings used here are those of Webster's *New International Dictionary.*

change in shape. For ē the upper lip seems to pull back and curl at the sides a bit, giving a sort of rectanglar shape to the mouth. The lower jaw juts out. As you proceed down through the above vowels the tensions seem to decrease, the squareness lessens, and the jaw drops back as it lowers. These maneuvers cause a gradual lowering of the dominant overtones as you proceed from ē to ă and it is this change that the ears hear and causes you to say "that is an ē, this an ĭ, etc."

Of this group the ĭ (*pin*) is often misused for ĕ (*pen*) and vice versa. You may have heard someone speak of a *fountain pin* or a *safety pen*. The ā may pass for ĕ, as in *dadication* exercises. The ă is often heard as ĕ, is *thet* not so?

When the tongue is arched in the midregion of the mouth and unobstructed sounds are permitted to flow, we produce the vowels ŭ as in *cut*, and the neutral vowel or schwa (a sort of shortened ŭ) like the "a" in *alone* or the "e" in *system*.[18] The mouth is relatively open for these sounds, and the lips are relaxed. These sounds do not usually cause much confusion. With the mouth slightly more closed and the lips a bit more tense we produce the ûr sound, as in *bird*, a difficult sound for many children, and for some adults.

With the back of the tongue arched, we produce the vowels ä (*father*), ô (*raw*), ō (*note*), ŏŏ (*look*), ōō (*boot*). As you run through these sounds you will observe that the mouth opening goes from the most wide-open position for ä (the reason why the doctor asks you to say "ah" when he wants to inspect your tonsils) to a relatively closed position for ōō. The lips in this process proceed from a large round opening for ō to a small and progressively protruded one for ŏŏ and ōō.

Whereas in the frontal sounds the upper lip comes back as the jaw protrudes, both the upper lip and the jaw protrude in the back vowels. You will also note as you go from front to back sounds (ē, ĭ, ā, ĕ, ă, à, ä, ô, ō, ŏŏ, ōō) that they are differentiated to the ear by an increasingly low characteristic overtone.

There is frequent interchanging of ä and ô. Consider the variations you hear in the way people say *father*. Often we can tell only by context whether a person is speaking about *Don* or *dawn*.

---

[18] The representation of speech sounds in written symbols may be confusing to you, for spelling often carries little suggestion of the way we speak the sounds. The same letter may represent two or more sounds (fast, paste) and one sound may be represented by two or more letters (many, men).

Diphthongs

A diphthong is a glide from one vowel to another within the same syllable. The movement of the mouth is from a more open to a less open position. Some diphthongs are distinctive, that is, have semantic significance; others are simply the indistinct slur that results from the fact that speech is formed by a plastic and moving mechanism. The non-distinctive glides are most common in words ending in a vowel (*be, so, to,* or *say*), though they also show up elsewhere. The most common vowels involved are those in the four examples above.

There are four clearly distinguished diphthongs common in English. The ī as in *cry,* the ou as in *now,* the oi as in *boy,* and the ū as in *use.* The first, ī, is a glide from the vowel ä (*father*) to ĭ (*bit*). The second, ou (*cow*), glides from ä (*father*) to oͦo (*look*). The third, oi (*toy*), glides from ô (*box*) to ĭ (*bit*). The last, ū (*use*) moves from ĭ (*bit*) to oͦo (*boot*).[19] Both the beginning and the ending of diphthongs vary from person to person and from region to region. Indeed this is true of all speech sounds. Symbolization can only approximate the actual sounds that people make.

Not every characteristic of vowels can be suggested in a single diagram. But relationships among the sounds may be indicated, and fixed in mind, by the following:

Positions in the mouth where vowel sounds are formed.

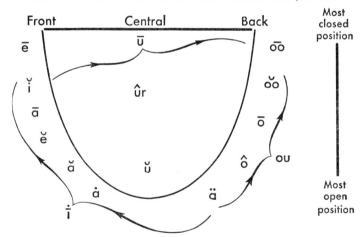

[19] Look in the mirror and watch the movement of your mouth as you glide from ä to ĭ, ä to oͦo, etc. If you reverse the glides, going from the less to the more

The structure of the diagram is indicated by the heavy lines. The horizontal line represents the position in the mouth in which each vowel is focused; ē (*feet*) is a front sound; o͞o (*boot*) a back sound; ă (*cat*) is half way between the frontal sound ē and the mid-mouth sounds ä and ŭ, etc. The heavy vertical line shows the relative mouth opening for each vowel. The ē and o͞o, for instance, are pronounced with the mouth relatively closed; the ä is formed with the mouth at its widest open position. Three of the diphthongs are suggested by brackets with arrows, showing the direction of the glide.

Perhaps all students, and surely those who have trouble with articulation, should study this chart, the diacritical markings, and the key words. Memorize the sounds and their key words from front to back, record your pronounciation of them, and listen to see whether you make the proper distinction in your speech and whether you hear them. Knowledge of all these sounds is basic to the use of a dictionary for the checking of pronounciation.

A study of any dictionary will soon indicate that the vowels noted above are not the only ones that may be identified. Only a minimum number has been mentioned, but these are sufficient for practice in improving articulation. The speech specialist, however, needs additional symbols for the finer discriminations in his work.

Consonants

Consonants are the attendants of vowels: "con" (with) + "sonare" (to sound). The vowel, being more sonorous, is the more dominant. We even have words that are isolated diphthongs such as "I" and "a." But the consonants are never spoken alone; they are always sounded with vowels. This is not to suggest that consonants are less important than vowels. If they are not clear, speech is not understood. But it does suggest the dependent marriage of consonants to vowels, and that actually the unit of speech is the syllable, made up of a vowel or a vowel and one or several consonants. As we said earlier, the first step in the development of outgoing human speech was the vowel. Primitive languages, even those that exist today, are heavily vocalic, and this is not strange, since the consonants require a good deal more muscular dexterity than the vowels. But as man's thinking

---

open mouth position, you produce either "y" or "w" as the initial sound. Moving from a relatively closed to a more open position, we identify the first part of the glide as a consonant.

became more precise, he needed a more extended code system than the vowels afforded, and hence the consonants gradually evolved.

Consonants are produced by a closure or a semi-closure at some point in the mouth. It is mainly because of this characteristic that consonants are distinguished from the more open sounds, the vowels. Thus the sound *b* is decidedly different in this regard from the sound ē. Yet because some consonants are only *relatively* closed they are hard to classify, and exist in a kind of twilight zone. This is particularly true of *r* and *l*.

The second distinction between vowels and consonants is also a relative matter. All vowels are phonated or voiced; that is, they originate with the action of the vocal folds. Some consonants are voiced too, for instance, *b, m, v, d, n, z, g*, etc. Others are surd, or voiceless, originating in an explosion or a friction of the air through a small opening. The consonants, *p, f, t, s*, and *k* are of this kind.

These complete or partial stoppages of air take place at eight points in the vocal track: between the lips (*p, b, m, w*), between the upper teeth and the lower lip (*f, v*), between the tongue and the upper teeth (*th*), between the tongue and the gum ridge behind the upper teeth (*t, d, n, s, z*), between the tongue and the palate (*sh, zh, l*), between the back of the tongue and the velum (*k, g, ng, r*), and between the open and motionless vocal folds (*h*). Other consonantal units are produced by combinations of the sounds formed at one point, for instance, *nts* as in "cents," or by combinations of sounds made at two points, such as *tsh* (spelled *ch*) or *dzh* (spelled *j*). But the essential features in the analysis of consonants are that consonants are determined by (1) the place in the mouth where (2) voiced or unvoiced air is (3) exploded or continued. We have already identified the places of stoppage or semi-stoppage. The chart on the next page classifies the consonants as to items (2) and (3).

In all, we produce about sixty-five sounds in spoken English. When we stop to consider the fine shades of difference among them, and the need to blend them into continuous speech, it is a wonder that articulation is not a greater problem than it is. The production of intelligible speech is a truly magnificent accomplishment.

In this chapter we have discussed the physics of sound and the four steps — breathing, phonating, resonating, and articulating — in the production of speech sounds. It is necessary to have some understanding of these things in order to make use of the suggestions for voice improvement given in the two following chapters.

THE CONSONANTS

Plosive			Continuants	
Voiced	*Voiceless*		*Voiced*	*Voiceless*
b	p		v	t
d	t		z	th
g	k		zh	s
			j (dzh)	sh
			wh (hw)	ch (tsh)
			m	w
			n	h
			ng	
			l	
			r	

QUESTIONS FOR STUDY AND DISCUSSION

1. What are some of the things we tell about a person by listening to his voice?

2. Why is the voice so revealing?

3. What is a sound wave?

4. What do we mean by frequency, overtone, resonance, intensity?

5. What are the three kinds of resonance? Which two are significant in voice production?

6. What are the four steps in the production of voice?

7. Can you explain the essential facts about each step?

8. What are the differences between vowels and consonants?

9. Can you diagram the vowels and identify the sounds by diacritical markings?

10. Can you divide the consonants into plosives and continuants and these into voiced and voiceless?

SUGGESTIONS AND ASSIGNMENTS

1. Write a paper analyzing your own voice as to: (*a*) breathing, (*b*) phonating attack, (*c*) resonation, (*d*) articulation.

Describe every important observation you have made of yourself on these matters. If you do not know your voice, first record and listen to it for characteristics that come under the above headings.

2. Write a paper describing (as in question 1 above) the characteristics of another student in the class. Do you do a better job analyzing your own or another person's voice? How do you account for this?

Language most shows a man; speak that I may see thee. It springs out of the most retired and inmost parts of us, and is the image of the parent of it, the mind. No glass renders a man's form or likeness so true as his speech.

Ben Jonson

16

The Meaning of the Voice

SPEECH SOUND has four characteristics: pitch, force, time, and quality. Varying combinations among these produce all the intellectual and emotional nuances of delivery. The delicate shadings of our thought are expressed when we pay full attention to hitting the speech target. When we are sufficiently immersed in the purposes of communication, and free within ourselves to speak, we need not be told how to express our meanings. But faulty habits, failure to hear ourselves, and inhibitions stemming from our self and social attitudes cause many of us to speak poorly. Learning to control pitch, force, time, and quality helps to form good habits and sharpens one's ear to the sound of his own voice.

PITCH

As we said in discussing sound in Chapter 15, pitch is the subjective interpretation of frequency. It refers to the rising and falling of the voice on the musical scale. Pitch may change gradually in a *slide* (an inflection), or suddenly in a *step* (a shift). The pattern of slides and steps is often referred to as the melody of speech.

As a rule slides occur within words and phrases, and steps occur between phrases or sentences. It is possible, however, to have both within a single phrase-sentence. To illustrate: "This *is* important." Here we have a sudden shift of pitch between "this" and "is," because of the dramatic emphasis on "is." As indicated by the unbroken line, pitch variations slide throughout the remainder of the sentence. As is true in the above illustration, shifts are generally upward, and usually about one-third of an octave. Shifts are predominantly upward because we tense in preparation for attack. The beginning of a phrase or sentence is a moment of anticipation and perhaps of anxiety. Most of the pitch variety in speech, however, is inflectional, the average being one-third of an octave. And most inflections are downward. Shifts and inflections, then, tend to complement each other. This seems to be borne out by a comparative regional study. The speech of the Eastern United States is characterized by more downward inflections than is that of other parts of the country.[1] Eastern speech also has a larger ratio of upward to downward shifts — that is, compared to the rest of the country Eastern speech uses more than the usual number of downward inflections and therefore compensates with a more than usual number of upward shifts.

Variety in Pitch

In American English, the characteristic melody follows a sort of roller-coaster pattern. We roll up or down from syllable to syllable and from word to word, the accented words and syllables usually receiving the rising inflections. The melody in the following words, for instance, is "constitution" and "Kalamazoo." In like manner we emphasize the important words of a sentence. Inflections within the word are relatively fixed by usage. We have considerably more freedom within the phrase or sentence. The guiding force *among* words is the particular meaning that has "a grip" on us. Thus we may say, "*This* is important," or "This *is* important," or "This is *important*," depending on the meaning we wish to stress.

One study revealed that on the average, the emphasized words were almost one semi-tone above the pitch level of the sentence as a whole. Approximately 40 per cent of the stressed words were above the sentence average in pitch and 20 per cent were below it.[2] Eighty-four per cent of the stressed words showed a greater magnitude of inflection than did unstressed words, 75 per cent reached a higher pitch, and 71 per cent descended to lower pitch. Although in English the higher pitches and wider range in slides more often characterize emphasized words, when we are dramatic we often use the lower

---

[1] T. D. Hanley, "An Analysis of Vocal Frequency and Duration Characteristics of Selected Samples of Speech from Three American Dialect Regions," *Speech Monographs*, March, 1951, pp. 78–93.

[2] Joseph Tiffin and Max Steer, "An Experimental Analysis of Emphasis," *Speech Monographs*, Vol. IV, No. 1, Dec. 1937, pp. 69–74.

pitches. This obvious variation from the general speech pattern gives the stressed words special emphasis by contrast.

Though variety in pitch is unquestionably an important means of emphasis, there is no one "right" pattern. The study cited above found all sorts of effective patterns, and in over 30 per cent of the stressed words no single pattern was used exclusively.

Good speakers use a pitch range of at least one octave and often as much as ten full tones (one and one-third octaves). Franklin

Roosevelt used about an octave and a half. We are seldom aware of the wide range of pitch we use in speech because we do not sustain a given pitch as we do in singing. Yet 5 per cent of our speech is pitched below what we can sustain in song.[3]

Intellectual and Emotional Meaning

Pitch, then, is a major tool of emphasis. Because changes in pitch help to lift out ideas and to show relationships, they are important in conveying intellectual meaning. This function of pitch was clearly illustrated by a study of the techniques of two famous Shakespearian actors. John Barrymore's interpretations have been thought intellectual as contrasted with those of Maurice Evans.[4] A study of their presentations of the same material, diagrammed by photo-electronic equipment, reveals that Barrymore's delivery was slow, relatively constant in rate, uniform in volume, and extensive in inflection. Obviously, the active agent in his speech was variation in pitch. The analysis of Evans' voice showed variety of rate, a play on the rhythm of the lines, and a wide variety of voice quality, but relatively constant pitch. It appears that it was the greater variation in pitch which reflected the intellectual quality in Barrymore's delivery.

[3] John C. Snidecor, "The Pitch and Duration Characteristics of Superior Female Speakers During Oral Reading," *Journal of Speech and Hearing Disorders,* March, 1951, pp. 44–51.

[4] Willard C. Booth, "An Analysis and Comparison of Vocal Techniques of the Delivery of Hamlet's Soliloquy (Act II, Scene I) as Recorded by John Barrymore and Maurice Evans," M.A. Thesis, University of Michigan, 1951.

Similarly, pitch is a powerful conveyor of emotion. Common experience indicates that intense emotions such as joy or extreme pain produce high pitch, while sadness and boredom, for instance, produce low pitch. One study of the relation of pitch and emotion, using the same verbal material for the expression of contempt, anger, fear, grief, and indifference, showed that the emotions were identifiable by the graph of pitch patterns.[5] There was more than an octave difference in the average pitch of the most and the least intense emotions. We have all had the experience of being controlled by an emotion we did not want to reveal and having our inflections leveled out or enlivened despite our efforts to deny or conceal the emotion.

Pitch and Personality

A low voice suggests intimacy, security, and confidence, a vocal characteristic cultivated by the physician. A high-pitched voice suggests distance, and is a characteristic attributed by stereotype to the military officer. The habitually tense person generally has a high-pitched voice, but without the intensity of the army officer's voice. Unresponsive people have little range in pitch, whereas excessively responsive people show abrupt and sweeping inflection. The speaker with a predominant falling inflection is usually assured and often dogmatic, whereas the timid soul will usually have an unusual number of rising inflections. A series of rising inflections in a sing-song pattern is associated with the gushing society woman. An overuse of subtle combinations of circumflex (a rising or falling inflection quickly followed by the opposite) and rising inflections on the part of a man suggests femininity.[6]

A humped inflectional pattern for a phrase or sentence suggests assurance and freedom from inhibitions: "You ⌒ shouldn't do ⌍ that.[7] Inhibited speech shows the reverse form: "You ⌍ shouldn't do ⌒ that." It is not unusual for tension to show itself at the beginning of speech, following a breath. As we noted before, this accounts for the preponderance of upward shifts over downward

[5] Grant Fairbanks and Wilbert Pronovost, "An Experimental Study of Pitch Characteristics of the Voice During the Expression of Emotion," *Speech Monographs*, Vol. 6, No. 1, Dec., 1939, pp. 87–104.

[6] Elise Hahn, *et al.*, *Basic Voice Training for Speech*, New York, McGraw-Hill Book Company, Inc., 1952, p. 84.

[7] Dwight Bolinger, "Inhibited and Uninhibited Stress," *Quarterly Journal of Speech*, April, 1945, pp. 202–207.

ones. But excessive inhibition is earmarked by the fact that both the beginning and the end of the sentence shows restraint. Conversely, the person who habitually begins and ends statements at a low pitch reveals assurance, both in anticipation and in conclusion.

Pitch and Sex

The most obvious difference between the voices of men and women is the difference in pitch level. As the previous discussion has suggested, there is a difference in the inflectional patterns of men and women. Women use more rising inflections than men and more circumflex or double inflections. But the inflections of men are more variable; that is, they use a wider range, they have more changes of direction, and they change more rapidly.[8] Women seem to use a much wider range of inflection, because the tendency to prolong their rising inflections inaccurately suggests a wider range.

Optimum Pitch

While variety of pitch is necessary for good speech, it should center on an average or mode. At one time speech educators would have said that the mode should be low. We recognize now, however, that individual differences should be taken into account. The important thing is to find a range that fits you. The prevailing notion now is that we all have an optimum pitch, an efficient pitch, at which we produce speech of good quality and maximum intensity with the least expense in energy. To discover your optimum or efficient pitch, sing "do" up and down the scale several times, going as low each time as you can and still produce a fully resonated tone. Then sing up the scale four or five full tones. In this area is your optimum pitch. If your voice is either too high or too low, you tend to court monopitch, for variety is then constrained by the limited distance you can go in one of the two directions. For men the optimum pitch, as may be seen in the graph on page 271, is about C below middle C. For women it is A below middle C.

While the concept of optimum pitch seems reasonable it should be pointed out that recent study indicates that competent judges cannot tell reliably when a voice is pitched at the optimum. This sug-

[8] John C. Snidecor, "The Pitch and Duration Characteristics of Superior Female Speakers During Oral Reading," *Journal of Speech and Hearing Disorders,* March, 1951, pp. 44–51.

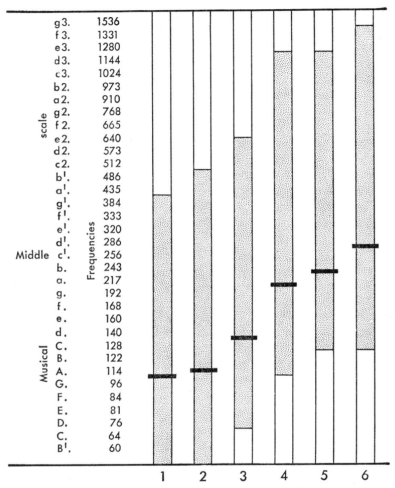

The ranges of the human voice, after Nadoleczny.
1. Bass. 2. Baritone. 3. Tenor. 4. Contralto. 5.
Mezzo-soprano. 6. Soprano. The horizontal lines
indicate the average pitch for each type. (Adaptation of chart by Robert Curry, *The Mechanism of the Human Voice*, New York, Longmans, Green and Company, Inc., 1940, p. 52)

gests the conclusion that there is no normal pitch, or that abnormality
of pitch is identifiable only when the pitch does not fit the force, quality, and time factors of the voice.[9] Pending further research, it would
seem wise to accept the latter conclusion. In fact, it is not clear that
the inability of judges to pick out voices abnormally pitched disproves
the concept of optimum pitch.

INTENSITY

Intensity refers to the energy or carrying-power of sound. The ear
interprets intensity as loud or soft. It scarcely needs to be said that
adequate intensity is indispensable to communication, for if speech is
not heard meanings cannot be conveyed. Yet one of the most common criticisms of beginning speakers and actors is that they cannot
be heard. In one study of a group of students, one-third were judged
to be deficient in loudness.[10] Indeed, intensity of voice is so important
to gaining and holding attention that a great many actors and speakers
talk much louder than they need to. The result may not be art, but
the fact still remains that it commands attention.

Determinants of Intensity

Intensity increases with an increase in the expenditure of air, the
tension of the vocal folds, the amplitude or distance through which
the vocal folds act, and the openness of the mouth.[11] According to
Grant Fairbanks, the last-named item is the most important.[12]

The power of sound fluctuates according to the formula: intensity
equals amplitude squared times frequency squared. Perhaps the formula can be clarified by an illustration. If a guitar string is plucked
so that it vibrates an eighth of an inch, a given volume will result.
If the string is plucked so that it vibrates one-fourth of an inch, the
volume becomes four times as great. If it vibrates three-eighths of an
inch, the volume becomes nine times as great. Accordingly, if the frequency of a speech sound remains constant and the amplitude of the

[9] John Dreher and Vernon C. Bragg, "Evaluation of Voice Normality,"
Speech Monographs, March, 1953, pp. 74–78.
[10] Jacqueline B. Benkley, "A Quantitative Measure of Vocal Loudness," M.A.
Thesis, Ohio State University, 1949.
[11] William W. Fletcher, "Vocal Fold Activity and Sub-Glottic Air Pressure in
Relation to Vocal Intensity: A Brief Historical Review," *Speech Monographs*,
Vol. XXI, March, 1954, pp. 73–78.
[12] Grant Fairbanks, "A Physiological Correlative of Vocal Intensity," *Speech
Monographs*, November, 1950, pp. 390–395.

vibration of the vocal folds increases, the volume increases with the square of the amplitude. Theoretically this is so, but there are important qualifications. In order to increase the vibration distance of the vocal folds, greater air pressure is necessary. The tension thus required usually increases the tension of the vocal folds, and this in turn raises the pitch. If we go back to the formula, then, we see that volume also fluctuates with the square of the frequency. Hence an increase in speech volume is usually produced by greater air pressure *and* higher pitch. The tension that produces air pressure tends to produce higher pitch, and both raise the volume.

The human ear is more sensitive to the higher frequencies of the voice than to the lower ones. The threshold for 400 cycles is 50 decibels; [13] that for 5000 cycles is 37 decibels, when the human voice is the sound instrument. [14] The intensity of consonants, which range in frequency from 400 cycles per second for 1 to 8000 for s, is lower than that of vowels, which range in frequency from 400 for o͞o to 3200 for ē. [15] Nevertheless, the increased sensitivity of the ear to higher frequencies blends consonants and vowels into intelligible sound groupings.

A third factor in intensity is resonance. In the human voice the higher pitches are often not so fully resonated as the lower ones. The total effect of these interacting factors is that consonants of the higher frequency level are often inadequately transmitted. This offsets the sensitivity of the ear to higher frequencies. It should be clear that we need to pay careful attention to intensity, particularly of consonants, if we wish to be heard.

Intensity and Emphasis

While it is necessary first to be heard, it is also necessary to vary our intensity in order to bring out the emphases intended. Superior speakers use a range of 20 decibels. [16] We can get some idea of the

---

[13] The decibel is the unit for measuring loudness. Sound power (intensity) increase is greater than the response of the ear. The decibel is a measure of hearing.

[14] James M. O'Neill, *et al.*, *Foundations of Speech*, New York, Prentice Hall, Inc., 1942, Chapter 8.

[15] Webster symbols. These frequencies are the *relative* principal frequencies of these sounds. No speech sound has a single or a fixed frequency. We speak or sing any sound at any point within the range of our voice.

[16] Joseph Tiffin and Max Steer, "An Experimental Analysis of Emphasis," *Speech Monographs*, Vol. IV, No. 1, Dec. 1937, pp. 69–74.

variation this range affords if we know that "very loud" speech is 20 decibels louder than "normal" speech, and normal speech is 20 decibels louder than "weak" speech.[17] In general, the stressed words of our speech are 9.3 decibels louder than the average of the sentence. The intensity range of good speakers can be diagrammed. Over 71 per cent of stressed words are louder than the average. This means that

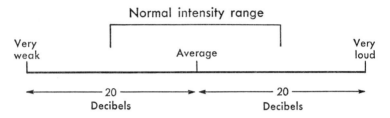

sometimes stress is gained without increased intensity, perhaps by variation in pitch, prolongation of sound, or pause. It also suggests that some ideas are better emphasized by decreased intensity. John W. Black found that the soft voice tends to accompany the more difficult idea.[18] Low intensity, then, is *at times* a more powerful agent than high intensity.

Adverbs tend to get the greatest intensity. Then come adjectives and nouns, followed by verbs and pronouns, and finally prepositions, conjunctions, and articles.[19] This analysis suggests that the qualifying words in our speech are the energy carriers. We can see how this works as we add adjectives and adverbs to an unembellished sentence.[20]

"A girl moved next door." (Yeh?)
"An *eighteen year old* girl moved next door." (Oh?)
"A *beautiful* eighteen year old girl moved next door." (Oh, boy!)
"A *very* beautiful eighteen year old girl moved next door." (Wow!)

[17] Giles W. Gray and Claude M. Wise, *The Bases of Speech*, New York, Harper & Brothers, 1946, pp. 121–122.
[18] John W. Black, "Relation of Message-Type, Vocal Rate and Intensity," *Speech Monographs*, September 1949, pp. 217–220.
[19] Max Steer and Joseph Tiffin, "A Photographic Study of the Use of Intensity by Superior Speakers," *Speech Monographs*, Vol. 1, No. 1, September 1934, pp. 72–78.
[20] In written style today excessive use of adjectives and adverbs is considered weak. This does not mean that written modifers necessarily lack energy; it means that we value a style in which nouns and verbs carry most meaning; long descriptive passages are felt to be "slow," and hence modifiers are used sparingly.

Intensity and Emotional Emphasis

Adjectives and adverbs (and descriptive nouns) with their varying shades of vividness are essentially tools of emotion. They are likely to express opinions, values, and judgments more than facts. Hence the intensity which stresses such words has a decided emotional coloration. This fact is borne out by the observation, made above, that low intensity accompanies the difficult task. When we are taking care to do a job deliberately, that is intellectually, we inhibit our energy.

Intensity and Pitch

The relationships between intensity and pitch are complex but well established. We have noted that intellectual distinctions are usually accompanied by high pitch but low intensity. Conversely, when emphasis is accompanied by lower than average pitch the effect is dramatic or emotional. Thus we can chart the following relationships:

Intellectual emphasis	*Emotional emphasis*
Low intensity	High intensity
High pitch	Low pitch

Other mixtures of emotional, intellectual, and physical state give different relationships between these two elements of speech sound. Thus:

Hysteria	*Exhaustion*
High intensity	Low intensity
High pitch	Low pitch

Intensity and Open Aggression

Since intensity suggests power, it might be expected to reflect the speaker's need for power. As we shall see later when we discuss fear and aggression, the person who feels a great need for power tends characteristically to speak in a loud voice. Conversely, the person who is afraid to exercise power over others will characteristically speak in a soft voice. These relationships were interestingly brought out in a study which reported that girls who came to a clinic attended by their parents spoke with less intensity than girls who came with other children.[21]

[21] Regina Tolshinsky, "An Analysis of Relative Intensity Characteristics Pertaining to Age and Sex of Elementary School Children," M.A. Thesis, Purdue University, 1951.

TIME

The factors of time usually identified are rate, quantity (length of sounds), pause, and rhythm. While variation in pitch is predominantly a medium of intellectual communication, and intensity is essentially emotional, factors of timing seem to convey both intellectual and emotional meanings.

Rate

Rate refers to the speed of speech flow. The determinants of rate are the difficulty of the task, energy, thoughtfulness, emotional tone, and the condition of the speaker's nervous system. Rate tends to increase if the speaking task is difficult. The amount of energy available also steps up speed, while thoughtfulness slows us down. The emotional tone, or mood, of the communication has a marked effect on rate. The more animated our feelings, the more rapid our speech; the more somber the mood, the slower. Since people differ from each other physiologically, each student should adjust to a change of rate that suits his own reaction time.

We often admire the speaking style of a friend, a teacher, a personality of radio, stage, or screen, whose total organization is different from our own. But it is dangerous to imitate, for we may unhappily come to feel that we are not "so skilled" as our model, whereas the truth is more likely that we are simply different. Because exhibitionists in the entertainment world often speak rapidly, many students identify rapid speech with success and excellence. The stereotype exists even though it is obvious that not all successful people are rapid speakers. The fact is that all of us have an optimum rate which suits our nervous system, and this rate is totally unrelated to success. There is a rate for each of us beyond which the necessary precision cannot be attained. To try to exceed this rate is to stumble. Tongue twisters dramatically illustrate the differences of rate among us. Pencil tapping tests do the same. Even the speed with which we walk, dress, read, and think suggests the natural tempo of the nervous system. As we noted in Chapter 14, there is generally a marked difference in the speed of movement between large people and small ones. There is a similar difference in their rate of speaking. Normal rate runs anywhere from 125 to 185 words per minute. Men and women speak at about the same rate. Most people feel that speech as slow as 80 words per minute is boring.

The Meaning of the Voice

277

When one considers rate in the light of communication values, it is difficult to see why the urge to rapid speech is so strong. Speed and glibness occur together so often that one may question the one as well as the other. Snidecor discovered that good speakers read more slowly than the average, a fact not surprising when we consider that thought is opposed to impulsiveness.[22] The right rate is that which fits the speaker's total personality, his physical make-up, and the immediate purposes and feelings of the communication.

While rate is often discussed in evaluating speech, it is very often inaccurately analyzed as a single element, rapidity.[23] Recent study indicates that rapidity is a combination of quantity and pause. The shorter the duration of sounds and the shorter the pause between words, the more sounds and words per minute. Obviously, the alteration of either quantity or pause affects the rapidity of speech.

Quantity

Quantity refers to the mass or amount of sound, and as suggested above, is a factor of rate. The determinates are the physical character of sound, the idea symbolized, and the emotions stirred. Vowels, continuants such as *m, n, r, l, th*, and sibilants such as *z, s*, and *sh* require more time for their production than do plosives such as *t, d, p, k*. But the major vehicle of duration is the vowel. Further, the sound that lends itself to holding lends itself to degrees of holding. The length of time a sound should be held depends on its contribution to the idea being symbolized. If the idea is important to the context, either holding the sound inordinately long or clipping it gives emphasis. The average length of syllables in normal American speech is .22 of a second.[24] If holding the sound suggests the idea, as in *flow* or *swing*, or if clipping the sound suggests the action described, as in *clip* or *strike*, the inherent meaning helps to determine the right quantity. Where the meaning has no quantitative suggestion, the variety of quantity itself aids both in lifting out the idea and in maintaining attention.

[22] John C. Snidecor, "Experimental Studies of the Pitch and Duration Characteristics of Superior Speech," Ph.D. Thesis, State University of Iowa, 1940.
[23] J. C. Kelly and Max Steer, "Revised Concept of Rate," *Journal of Speech and Hearing Disorder*, Vol. 14, September, 1949, pp. 222–226; Frederic W. Orr, *Voice for Speech*, New York, McGraw-Hill Book Company, 1938, Chapter VII.
[24] John W. Black, "The Effect of Delayed Side-Tone Upon Rate and Intensity," *Journal of Speech and Hearing Disorders*, March, 1951, pp. 56–60.

About 75 per cent of our total speaking time is spent in the phonation of sound, slightly more for men than for women.[25] For both
sexes, 98 per cent of the stressed words have longer duration than the
unstressed ones. This fact suggests that prolongation is a tool of
emphasis. In the South, stressed words are longer than in other regions
of the country. Unstressed words are longer in the East. These facts
suggest that the so-called Southern drawl prolongs stressed words but
not all words.[26]

Pause

Of the silent time in continuous speech, 80 per cent occurs between
phrases and sentences. The other 20 per cent takes place within
phrases, most of it in the formation of voiceless consonants such as
t, k, p. Only a small part of the silence within the phrase is directed
to emphasis. When used it either precedes or follows the emphasized
word.[27]

If the pause in speech is at a point where either or both speaker
and listener are puzzling over the thought, silence is essentially an
intellectual tool in communication. We are here referring to that 80
per cent that takes place between phrases. The good conversationalist,
story teller, teacher, or public speaker knows the value of a pause so
used. In addition, at points in lectures, interviews, and conferences
where the speaker thinks the listener will gain more meaning by completing the idea himself, the sensitive speaker purposely pauses and
searches for words. The listener then comes to the speaker's aid, and
in so doing makes his own creative associations.

If the pause occurs at a tense moment in speech, especially when
the tension is too great for controlled speech, the impact is dramatic
and emotional. The story is told of a teacher who at the climax of a
gripping story had the misfortune of arousing an impulsive giggle in
one corner of the room. The class broke into hilarious laughter. The
professor neither moved nor changed expression. There was a long
silence. When the pause became deafening he said quietly, "We
often laugh when we are afraid we may cry."

[25] J. C. Snidecor, "Experimental Studies of the Pitch and Duration Characteristics of Superior Speech," Ph.D. Dissertation, State University of Iowa, 1940.
[26] T. D. Hanley, "An Analysis of Vocal Frequency and Duration Characteristics of Selected Samples of Speech from Three American Dialect Regions,"
Speech Monographs, Vol. XVIII, March, 1951, pp. 78–93.
[27] Joseph Tiffin and Max Steer, "An Experimental Analysis of Emphasis,"
Speech Monographs, Vol. IV, No. 1, December, 1937, pp. 69–74.

Rhythm

Rhythm is the over-all pattern resulting from the peculiar combination of quantity and pause. The beat of primitive feet, the clapping of hands, childish jumping with joy, dancing, marching, the beat of the heart, the rocking of the baby, all suggest that rhythm pervades life. The beat of rhyme and alliteration ("Tippecanoe and Tyler too," "Better Buy Buick") indicate the way rhythm dominates our thinking and our language. The voice that flows like a river has a touch of magic in it.

The determinant of rhythm is the coordination of the perceptive and associative functions of the nervous system. Sometimes we do not clearly see the details of the mental picture we are trying to convey. This is a perceptive weakness. Sometimes we see many details clearly and distinctly, and as we speak of one the others stay faithfully in memory and in their proper relations. At such times, we may say that we "feel sharp." This is perceptive efficiency. On the other hand, we sometimes see clearly but cannot find the words, or they are irritatingly "just on the tip of the tongue." This is an associative problem. The neural connections of hearing and memory, and the motor aspects of speech, are not well synchronized. At other times words, and the right ones, come tumbling out almost without bidding. This is associative efficiency. We may have perceptual and associative difficulty at the same time. Either or both failures break the rhythm and flow of our speech. An echo delayed as little as .06 of a second on a single sound breaks the fluency of speech.[28] Normal rapid speech gets from twelve to fourteen impulse-feedback cycles per second.[29] So it is that the rhythm of the nervous system is closely related to efficiency and fluency. When the system is badly synchronized, speech "stutters." When the machine is in good order, speech is rhythmic and adjustable to the needs of the situation.

Normal Arhythmical Speech. There are two forms of arhythmical speech, hypertense and hypotense. Hypertense speech is excessively strained, rigid, inflexible. Hypotense speech is the opposite — sluggish.

Hypertension brings about blocks in the perceptive or the associative speech circuit, or in both. The behavior of the tense person is rather impulsive. Tension demands and insures action, but in its

[28] John W. Black, "The Effect of Delayed Side-Tone Upon Rate and Intensity," *Journal of Speech and Hearing Disorders*, March, 1951, pp. 56–60.
[29] Bernard S. Lee, "Artificial Stutter," *Journal of Speech and Hearing Disorders*, March, 1951, pp. 53–55.

drive for release it blocks off the deliberate exploration of all possible forms of action. Judgment is then not possible; therefore both the ideas and the language of tension are relatively impoverished. The speaker struggles with his idea because he knows there is more to say than is coming out. But try as he will, he fumbles, and the harder he tries the more involved he becomes.

In hypotense adjustment, the defense against tension drives the person to inhibit his inhibition, because he fears the conditions of fear. When students adjust this way, their rhythm is punctuated by long pauses and a general lack of responsiveness.[30]

The Standard of Fluency. The above discussion may suggest too much concern for fluency. Such over-concern would defeat our purpose, for while correction needs to be made for nonfluency which gets in the way of communication, a high regard for "smooth talk" may have two bad effects. First, as listeners, that standard may cause us to be unduly suggestible. Too much faith in fluency causes us to accept an easy speaker so readily that his ideas come along scot-free. The story is told of the man who returned from a political rally highly impressed by a fluent candidate:

"Well, what did he say?" asked a friend.
"Wonderful speech!"
"What did he say?"
"Well, he — gad! That man said plenty."
"What did he say?"
After several tries the questioner said, "I don't know, but it doesn't seem to me the Senator said much of anything."
To which the other responded classically, "Hang it all, a man that talks like he did, doesn't need to say anything."

Second, too much fluency does harm not only to critical listening but also to our thinking when we speak. The striving for fluency turns the search for words into a punishment when we cannot meet our standard. It causes us to resort to ambiguous language to escape the penalty of the search. It causes some of us to constrain our speech rather than face the hazard of a humiliating block. And finally, it causes a great deal of random activity in an effort to shake off the pervasive fear of those humiliating moments of blocking.

[30] See Chapter 19, pages 393–394.

A young man in a discussion class who showed these symptoms came gradually to understand that he was laboring under a false standard, and almost miraculously became acceptably fluent. Probably a third of our college students are in varying degrees caught in the struggle for fluency beyond any reasonable need.

QUALITY

Every voice can be placed somewhere along a continuum between pleasant and unpleasant. In such judgments we are considering the aspect of vocal sound called *quality*. In one study a group of business executives indicated that they considered "pleasant speech" fourth among the twelve most important characteristics of the desirable employee. By pleasant speech they meant good quality and articulation. They ranked only mental alertness, logical thinking, and ability to follow directions as more important.[31]

Two of your friends are talking in the hall; you cannot see them, but you identify them by quality of voice. This is a difficult thing to define, for though we have terms such as nasal, throaty, brilliant, thin, etc., to describe quality, the fact is that both your friends in the hall may have nasal voices, and yet you distinguish them. As Ortmann points out, quality is not an independent element.[32] Rather, it is a secondary attribute, an effect of the relationships of pitch, intensity, and duration.[33]

Four factors together produce vocal quality. First is the structure of the vocal mechanism. The shape and size of the larynx, throat, mouth, and nose is different in every individual. The second factor is the condition of the muscles, cartilages, and membranes of these parts. Varying degrees of mucus, inflammation, dryness, tension, and fatigue have their effect. Third, emotions affect the functioning of the speech organs. Finally, we are all creatures of habit, and our individual style in the use of the mechanism gives a distinctive, good or bad quality to the voice.

Though emotion is but one of the four determinants of quality,

[31] Ernest C. Fossum, "Speech and Occupational Needs," *Quarterly Journal of Speech*, December, 1943, pp. 491–498.

[32] O. Ortmann, "A Theory of Tone Quality," *Psychological Abstracts*, 1937, VII, p. 532.

[33] Quality is often restricted to timbre: the blend of frequencies that composes a sound. Both timbre and quality concern the pleasantness of sound, but quality when separated from timbre takes in more factors.

quality reveals our emotions more than does pitch, intensity, or timing. Your dog probably does not understand English, but he knows well your varying feelings. In like fashion the child understands the vocal quality of his mother's moods long before he can understand the meaning of the words she uses. From childhood on, voice quality is a vital force in our relations with others.

Brilliant quality is the mark of the healthy, energetic person. Harsh, irritating, strident, pompous, calculating qualities belong to people who are essentially aggressive. The ingratiating and satirical voices belong to the compulsive submissives who would influence by flattery or humor. Gentle voice belongs to the genuinely compliant. The cool and indifferent quality is a symptom of detachment.

Though all of us sound different, there are several classifications into which voice qualities tend to fall: the normal, oral, aspirate, throaty, and nasal.

Normal

By normal is meant that quality which has no deviant character, in which all factors blend. Attention goes to what is being said. The mechanics of such a voice are lost in the communication.

1. Ask the class after your next speech whether your quality is natural and normal. The key to analysis is whether you maintain the social position that the content of your speech calls for. If you are informative, normal quality is somewhat authoritative, assured, and final. If you are pleading, normal is somewhat indefinite and asking. If you are simply sharing experiences, normal is a neutral quality that suggests the same social position for yourself and the listener.
2. Record a speech and listen to it for emotional orientation. Try to detach yourself from the speech. What does quality say about the relation of the speaker to himself and his listener? Does it fit the role called for by the content?
3. If the quality is not what you want, discuss what it is and what you wanted. Record the speech again, consciously searching for the emotion you want to communicate. Listen to the recording. When you get the effect you want, listen to it a number of times. Try duplicating it.

Since quality is the result of so many features of voice, to be able to manipulate it effectively is to have mastery of the voice.

Other characteristics of voice, subnormal in one way or another, will be discussed with assignments in the following chapter.

HINTS ON ORAL READING

When exploring and improving our vocal skills, we can generally best concentrate on voice if we use the writing of others for content. Therefore, at the end of this chapter you will find a number of short selections which you may practice and read in class. Such practice lets you direct your energy to vocal improvement, but it also has at least two other purposes. Reading aloud well gives your esthetic urges another outlet. Human beings are restless creatures, with a strong demand for creative achievement. Man finds great satisfaction in using his voice as a medium of expression. Even though professional entertainers are accessible at the turn of a knob, we need active participation in imaginative expression. Oral reading can be a highly satisfying outlet.

Second, oral reading skill has practical applications. Public speakers often find it helpful to read a quotation or a few lines of poetry. Businessmen need to read reports with clarity, assurance, and good contact with their listeners. To learn the elementary skill of lifting ideas from the printed page while remaining in contact with the audience is of the highest value.

A few simple rules may help to direct your practice.

1. Get your materials into a form that you can handle with ease. If you are going to read a quotation from a magazine or a book, mark the places. A strip of paper inserted at the proper page will do. Place easily seen brackets around the material you are to read. Arrange your books and magazines on a stand in proper order. Skill in handling the printed page is important to continuity of thought. Practice handling your materials in the way you will use them in the speech situation. If you want to capitalize on the authoritative suggestion, it is always well to have the book or magazine on hand.

2. If recopying is necessary, type your material double spaced, particularly if you have difficulty in reading. If you have an outline for your speech in addition to the material you want to read, any one of three methods will be helpful. You may have all the material on cards, with quotations inserted at the appropriate places. If the quotations are long, make your notes on cards and type the quotations on $8\frac{1}{2} \times 11$ inch sheets. If you have several long excerpts to read, it is best to have all your material on sheets with the quotations inserted where needed in the outline.

3. The basic problem in reading aloud is to maintain contact with your audience. You need to become familiar enough with the language to "sweep up" a phrase or more and look at your audience as you say it. Otherwise you drift out of the target-set and read to your book. Only a part of the intended communication spills over the page, broadcast to a poorly visualized listener.

The skill of "lifting" phrases and saying them meaningfully may be increased if, in your practice, you do not insist upon reading accurately word for word. "Lift" an idea; if you alter the wording slightly, you will gradually learn to be more accurate. As in learning other skills, a free, uninhibited search for the goal is important, particularly at first. The poorest oral readers quake in the shadow of the author. If other students are looking at the same passage in their books, the commands of the language on the page grow even heavier. Remember, if you cannot give yourself the right to make a mistake, you have no opportunity to learn.

When you do not have time to learn the ideas well enough to raise your eyes from the page, you may compensate with exaggerated attention to vocal variety. Stepped-up vocal emphasis — greater care to intensity, pitch, duration, pause, and quality — will go a long way in commanding attention when the eyes are glued to the page.

4. Study long passages with two questions in mind. (1) What is the central idea? When you wander aimlessly in your reading, it is because you do not adequately sense your goal. (2) What is the dominant mood, emotion, or attitude? If you do not know the spirit of your material, you communicate no feeling or the wrong feelings. Write the central idea and the dominant mood in two separate sentences. This will help you clarify the purpose of your reading and fix it in your mind. For example, write out the idea and mood of the following:

> There is a pleasure in the pathless woods,
> There is a rapture on the lonely shore,
> There is society, where none intrudes,
> By the deep Sea, and the music in its roar:
> I love not Man the less, but Nature more
> From these our interviews, in which I steal
> From all I may be, or have been before,
> To mingle with the Universe, and feel
> What I can ne'er express, yet cannot all conceal.
> Lord Byron

Now compare your statements with the following:

> Central idea: I want to express the pleasure of intimate communication with nature.
> Dominant mood: I want to express stimulating thoughtfulness.

5. With these two purposes in mind, you are ready to relate your voice to the material. What can you do with your voice to communicate the pictures in the poem? Consider the words which naturally get emphasis: "There is a *pleasure* in the *pathless woods*" (see page 274). Experiment with the key words. How can you say "pleasure" with pleasure? How can you make the invitation of the "pathless woods"? Work out the mechanics of your interpretation and record the effect. Listen to it. Do you make the idea clear? Do you capture the emotion? Does your voice reveal it? Do your vocal mechanics lift out the pictures, yet blend them all into a unified flow of thoughtful expression? Or do you sing it? If so, is it because you express finality rather than continued rhythm at the ends of the lines? Write out the poem in regular prose form if you sing-song your lines.

6. Recorded music is an excellent aid in learning to read with feeling. Properly chosen music helps intensify the feeling we want to convey, and its rhythm coordinates the nervous system. Choose instrumental music in harmony with the emotions of a piece of poetry. After listening to it a bit, turn it low and begin to read. You will be amazed how much more responsive your voice becomes. This support should be used until it has released your expressive skills. Two or three rehearsals should be adequate. Then try reading a few lines with music, then fade it out and continue reading as expressively as possible. When you feel you are "dying emotionally," bring the music back in. In the end, it is sensing the muscular set of emotional expression that frees you from the need of the musical support.

Record this practice for later evaluation and objective ear training.

ORAL READINGS

Following are a number of selections in verse and prose, classified as submissive, aggressive, or withdrawing in their orientation. If you adjust more comfortably by "joining up," you will demonstrate more skill in reading the submissive selections. If you maintain more poise when you are making a vigorous attack, you will be more flexible and communicative in the aggressive passages. This does not mean you attack the audience. Aggressive rhetoric is usually directed against a third party, a foe common to both speaker and listener. If you find it difficult to reveal your emotions you will show more freedom in the withdrawing selections. The passages vary in the degree to which they express one of the three orientations. Some selections shift, or at least combine attitudes. This is to be expected, for human attitudes are highly complex. But any expression tends to be expansive and enthusiastic, aggressive and demanding, or self-searching and detached — just as each of us tends to orient to our world in one of these three ways.

Unless a voice is physically defective a poor voice is a non-responsive one. It follows (if the reader knows the meaning of what he reads) that voice is a reflection of the feelings he accepts in himself and therefore is willing to express freely. After you have developed reading skills within your orientation, try selections with attitudes more difficult to express. This is the road to flexibility in both voice and personality.

Submission

THE BUILDING OF THE SHIP

Thou, too, sail on, O Ship of State! Sail on, O Union, strong and great! Humanity, with all its fears, with all the hopes of future years, is hanging breathless on thy fate! We know what Master laid thy keel, what Workmen wrought thy ribs of steel, who made each mast and sail and rope, what anvils rang, what hammers beat, in what a forge, and what a heat, were shaped the anchors of thy hope! Fear not each sudden sound and shock; 'tis of the wave, and not the rock; 'tis but the flapping of the sail, and not a rent made by the gale! In spite of rock and tempest's roar, in spite of false lights on the shore, sail on, nor fear to breast the sea! our hearts, our hopes, are all with thee; our hearts, our hopes, our prayers, our tears, our faith triumphant o'er our fears, are all with thee, — are all with thee!

— Henry Wadsworth Longfellow

DOVER BEACH

The sea is calm tonight.
The tide is full, the moon lies fair
Upon the straits: on the French coast the light
Gleams and is gone; the cliffs of England stand,
Glimmering and vast, out in the tranquil bay.
Come to the window, sweet is the night air!

Only, from the long line of spray
Where the sea meets the moon-blanch'd land,
Listen! you hear the grating roar
Of pebbles which the waves draw back, and fling
At their return, up the high strand,
Begin, and cease, and then again begin,
With tremulous cadence slow, and bring
The eternal note of sadness in.

Sophocles long ago
Heard it on the Aegaean, and it brought
Into his mind the turbid ebb and flow
Of human misery; we
Find also in the sound a thought
Hearing it by this distant northern sea.

The Sea of Faith
Was once, too, at the full, and round earth's shore
Lay like the folds of a bright girdle furl'd.
But now I only hear
Its melancholy, long, withdrawing roar,
Retreating to the breath
Of the night-wind down the vast edges drear
And naked shingles of the world.

Ah, love, let us be true
To one another! for the world, which seems
To lie before us like a land of dreams,
So various, so beautiful, so new,
Hath really neither joy, nor love, nor light,
Nor certitude, nor peace, nor help for pain;
And we are here as on a darkling plain
Swept with confused alarms of struggle and flight,
Where ignorant armies clash by night.
                              — Matthew Arnold

The day is cold and dark and dreary;
It rains, and the wind is never weary;
The vine still clings to the mouldering wall,
But at every gust the dead leaves fall,
And the day is dark and dreary.
— Henry Wadsworth Longfellow, from "The Rainy Day"

At His Brother's Grave

My Friends: I am going to do that which the dead oft promised he would do for me.

The loved and loving brother, husband, father, friend, died where manhood's morning almost touches noon and while the shadows still were falling toward the west.

He had not passed on life's highway the stone that marks the highest point, but, being weary for a moment, lay down by the wayside, and using his burden for a pillow, fell into that dreamless sleep that kisses down his eyelids still. While yet in love with life and raptured with the world, he passed to silence and pathetic dust.

Yet, after all, it may be best, just in the happiest, sunniest hour of all the voyage, while eager winds are kissing every sail, to dash against the unseen rocks, and in an instant hear the billows roar above a sunken ship. For, whether in midsea or 'mong the breakers of the farther shore, a wreck at last must mark the end of each and all. And every life, no matter if its every hour is rich with love and every moment jewelled with a joy, will at its close become a tragedy as sad and deep and dark as can be woven of the warp and woof of mystery and death.

This brave and tender man in every storm of life was oak and rock, but in the sunshine he was vine and flower. He was the friend of all heroic souls. He climbed the heights and left all superstitions far below, while on his forehead fell the golden dawning of the grander day.

He loved the beautiful, and was with color, form, and music touched to tears. He sided with the weak, and with a willing hand gave alms; with loyal heart and with purest hands he faithfully discharged all public trusts.

He was a worshipper of liberty, a friend of the oppressed. A thousand times I have heard him quote these words: "For justice all place a temple, and all seasons summer." He believed that happiness was the only good, reason the only torch, justice the only worship, humanity the only religion, and love the only priest. He added to the sum of human joy; and were every one to whom he did some loving service to bring a blossom to his grave, he would sleep tonight beneath a wilderness of flowers.

Life is a narrow vale between the cold and barren peaks of two eternities. We strive in vain to look beyond the heights. We cry aloud, and the only answer is the echo of our wailing cry. From the voiceless lips of the unreplying dead there comes no word; but in the night of death hope sees a star, and listening love can hear the rustle of a wing.

He who sleeps here, when dying, mistaking the approach of death for the return of health, whispered with his latest breath, "I am better now." Let us believe, in spite of doubts and dogmas, and tears and fears, that these dear words are true of all the countless dead.

And now to you who have been chosen, from among the many men he loved, to do the last sad office for the dead, we give his sacred dust. Speech cannot contain our love. There was, there is, no greater, stronger, manlier man.

— Robert G. Ingersoll

Teach me half the gladness
  That thy brain must know,
Such harmonious madness
  From my lips would flow,
The world should listen then, as I am listening now.

— Percy Bysshe Shelley, from "To a Skylark"

It was many and many a year ago,
In a kingdom by the sea,
That a maiden lived, whom you may know
By the name of Annabel Lee;
And this maiden she lived with no other thought
Than to love, and be loved by me.

— Edgar Allan Poe, from "Annabel Lee"

And the night shall be filled with music,
  And the cares, that infest the day,
Shall fold their tents, like the Arabs,
  And as silently steal away.

Henry Wadsworth Longfellow, from "The Day Is Done"

Teach me to feel another's woe,
  To hide the fault I see;
That mercy I to others show
  That mercy show to me.

— Alexander Pope, from "Universal Prayer"

To Milton

Milton! thou shouldst be living at this hour:
England hath need of thee: she is a fen
Of stagnant waters: altar, sword, and pen,
Fireside, the heroic wealth of hall and bower,
Have forfeited their ancient English dower
Of inward happiness. We are selfish men:
Oh! raise us up, return to us again;
And give us manners, virtue, freedom, power.
Thy soul was like a Star, and dwelt apart:
Thou hadst a voice whose sound was like the sea,
Pure as the naked heavens, majestic, free;

So didst thou travel on life's common way
In cheerful godliness; and yet thy heart
The lowliest duties on herself did lay.
— William Wordsworth

The Chambered Nautilus

This is the ship of pearl, which, poets feign,
Sails the unshadowed main, —
The venturous bark that flings
On the sweet summer wind its purpled wings
In gulfs enchanted, where the Siren sings,
And coral reefs lie bare,
Where the cold sea-maids rise to sun their streaming hair.

Its webs of living gauze no more unfurl;
Wrecked is the ship of pearl!
And every chambered cell,
Where its dim dreaming life was wont to dwell,
As the frail tenant shaped his growing shell,
Before thee lies revealed, —
Its irised ceiling rent, its sunless crypt unsealed!

Year after year beheld the silent toil
That spread his lustrous coil;
Still, as the spiral grew,
He left the past year's dwelling for the new,
Stole with soft step its shining archway through,
Built up its idle door,
Stretched in his last-found home, and knew the old no more.

Thanks for the heavenly message brought by thee,
Child of the wandering sea,
Cast from her lap, forlorn!
From thy dead lips a clearer note is born
Than ever Triton blew from wreathèd horn!
While on mine ear it rings,
Through the deep caves of thought I hear a voice that sings:

Build thee more stately mansions, O my soul,
As the swift seasons roll!
Leave thy low-vaulted past!
Let each new temple, nobler than the last,
Shut thee from heaven with a dome more vast,
Till thou at length art free,
Leaving thine outgrown shell by life's unresting sea!
— Oliver Wendell Holmes

Break, Break, Break

Break, break, break,
On thy cold gray stones, O Sea!
And I would that my tongue could utter
The thoughts that arise in me.

O well for the fisherman's boy,
That he shouts with his sister at play!
O well for the sailor lad,
That he sings in his boat on the bay!

And the stately ships go on
To their haven under the hill;
But O for the touch of a vanished hand,
And the sound of a voice that is still!

Break, break, break,
At the foot of thy crags, O Sea!
But the tender grace of a day that is dead
Will never come back to me.

— Alfred Lord Tennyson

Sonnet XXIX

When in disgrace with fortune and men's eyes
I all alone beweep my outcast state,
And trouble deaf Heaven with my bootless cries,
And look upon myself, and curse my fate,
Wishing me like to one more rich in hope,
Featur'd like him, like him with friends possess'd,
Desiring this man's art, and that man's scope,
With what I most enjoy contented least;
Yet in these thoughts myself almost despising,
Haply I think on thee — and then my state,
Like to the lark at break of day arising
From sullen earth sings hymns at heaven's gate;
For thy sweet love remember'd such wealth brings,
That then I scorn to change my state with kings.

— William Shakespeare

They never fail who die in a great cause; the block may soak their gore;
Their heads may sodden in the sun; their limbs
Be strung to city-gates and castle walls;
But still their spirit walks abroad. Though years

Elapse, and others share as dark a gloom,
They but augment the deep and sweeping thoughts
Which overpower all others, and conduct
The world at last to freedom.

— George Gordon Lord Byron

Portia: The quality of mercy is not strain'd;
It droppeth as the gentle rain from heaven
Upon the place beneath: It is twice bless'd;
It blesseth him that gives, and him that takes:
'Tis mightiest in the mightiest: it becomes
The thronèd monarch better than his crown;
His scepter shows the force of temporal power,
The attribute to awe and majesty,
Wherein doth sit the dread and fear of kings;
But mercy is above this sceptered sway;
It is enthronèd in the hearts of kings,
It is an attribute to God Himself;
And earthly power doth then show likest God's
Though justice be thy plea, consider this, —
When mercy seasons justice. Therefore, Jew,
That in the course of justice, none of us
Should see salvation: we do pray for mercy;
And that same prayer doth teach us all to render
The deeds of mercy.

— William Shakespeare, from *The Merchant of Venice*

AT THE MID HOUR OF NIGHT

At the mid hour of night when stars are weeping, I fly
To the lone vale we loved, when life shone warm in thine eye;
And I think oft, if spirits can steal from the regions of air
To revisit past scenes of delight, thou wilt come to me there
And tell me our love is remember'd, even in the sky!

Then I sing the wild song it once was rapture to hear
When our voices, commingling, breathed like one on the ear;
And as Echo far off through the vale my sad orison rolls,
I think, O my Love! 'tis thy voice, from the Kingdom of Souls
Faintly answering still the notes that once were so dear.

— Thomas Moore

THE DAFFODILS

I wandered lonely as a cloud
That floats on high o'er vales and hills,
When all at once I saw a crowd,
A host, of golden daffodils;
Beside the lake, beneath the trees,
Fluttering and dancing in the breeze.

Continuous as the stars that shine
And twinkle on the milky way,
They stretch'd in never ending line
Along the margin of the bay;
Ten thousand saw I at a glance,
Tossing their heads in sprightly dance.

The waves beside them danced; but they
Out-did the sparkling waves in glee;
A poet could not but be gay,
In such a jocund company;
I gazed — and gazed — but little thought
What wealth the show to me had brought.

For oft, when on my couch I lie
In vacant or in pensive mood,
They flash upon that inward eye
Which is the bliss of solitude;
And then my heart with pleasure fills,
And dances with the daffodils.

— William Wordsworth

The leading distinction between dog and man, after and perhaps before the different duration of their lives, is that one can speak and that the other cannot. The absence of the power of speech confines the dog in the development of his intellect. It hinders him from many speculations, for words are the beginning of metaphysic. At the same blow it saves him from many superstitions and his silence has won for him a higher name for virtue than his conduct justifies. The faults of the dog are many. He is vainer than man, singularly greedy of notice, singularly intolerant of ridicule, suspicious like the deaf, jealous to the degree of frenzy, and radically devoid of truth. The day of the intelligent small dog is passed in the manufacture and the laborious communication of falsehood; he lies with his tail, he lies with his eye, he lies with his protesting paw; and when he rattles his dish or scratches at the door, his purpose is other than appears. But he has some apology to offer for the vice. Many of the signs which form his dialect have come to bear an arbitrary meaning, clearly understood by both his master and himself; yet when a new want arises he must either invent a new vehicle of meaning or wrest an old one to a different purpose; and this necessity frequently recurring must tend to lessen his idea of the sanctity of symbols. Meanwhile the dog is clear in his own conscience, and draws, with a human nicety, the distinction between formal and essential truth. Of his punning perversions, his legitimate dexterity with symbols he is even vain; but when he has told and been detected in a lie, there is not a hair upon his body but confesses guilt. To a dog of gentlemanly feeling, theft and falsehood are disgraceful vices. . . . He is never more than half ashamed of having barked or bitten; and for those faults into which he has been led by the desire to shine before a lady of his race, he retains, even under physical correction, a share of pride. But to be caught lying, if he understands it, instantly uncurls his fleece.

— Robert Louis Stevenson, from "The Character of Dogs"

Aggression

Villains! you did not threat, when your vile daggers
Hacked one another in the sides of Caesar!
You showed your teeth like apes, and fawned like hounds,
And bowed like bondmen, kissing Caesar's feet;
Whilst damned Casca, like a cur, behind,
Struck Caesar on the neck. — Oh flatterers!

— William Shakespeare, from *Julius Caesar*

Half choked with rage, King Robert fiercely said,
'Open: 'tis I, the King! Art thou afraid?'
The frightened sexton, muttering, with a curse,
'This is some drunken vagabond or worse!'
Turned the great key and flung the portal wide.

— Henry Wadsworth Longfellow, from "Robert of Sicily"

Shylock: How like a fawning publican he looks!
            I hate him for he is a Christian;
            But more, for that in low simplicity
            He lends out money gratis, and brings down
            The rate of usance here with us in Venice.
            If I can catch him once upon the hip,
            I will feed fat the ancient grudge I bear him.
            He hates our sacred nation, and he rails,
            Even there where merchants most do congregate,

On me, my bargains, and my well-won thrift,
Which he calls interest. Cursed be my tribe,
If I forgive him!
> — Shakespeare, from *The Merchant of Venice*

The World Is Too Much With Us

The World is too much with us; late and soon,
Getting and spending, we lay waste our powers;
Little we see in Nature that is ours;
We have given our hearts away, a sordid boon!
This Sea that bares her bosom to the moon,
The winds that will be howling at all hours
And are up-gather'd now like sleeping flowers,
For this, for everything, we are out of tune;
It moves us not.— Great God! I'd rather be
A Pagan suckled in a creed outworn, —
So might I, standing on this pleasant lea,
Have glimpses that would make me less forlorn;
Have sight of Proteus rising from the sea;
Or hear old Triton blow his wreathèd horn.
> — William Wordsworth

The advocates of Charles, like the advocates of other malefactors against whom overwhelming evidence is produced, generally decline all controversy about the facts, and content themselves with calling testimony to character. He had so many private virtues! And had James the Second no private virtues? Was Oliver Cromwell, his bitterest enemies themselves being judges, destitute of private virtues? And what, after all, are the virtues ascribed to Charles? A religious zeal, not more sincere than that of his son, and fully as weak and narrow-minded, and a few of the ordinary household decencies which half the tombstones in England claim for those who lie beneath them. A good father! A good husband! Ample apologies indeed for fifteen years of persecution, tyranny, and falsehood!

We charge him with having broken his coronation oath; and we are told that he kept his marriage vow! We accuse him of having given up his people to the merciless inflictions of the most hot-headed and hard-hearted of prelates; and the defense is, that he took his little son on his knee and kissed him! We censure him for having violated the articles of the Petition of Right, after having, for good and valuable consideration, promised to observe them; and we are informed that he was accustomed to hear prayers at six o'clock in the morning! It is to such considerations as these, together with his Vandyke dress, his handsome face, and his

peaked beard, that he owes, we verily believe, most of his popularity with
the present generation.

For ourselves, we own that we do not understand the common phrase,
a good man, but a bad king. We can as easily conceive a good man and
an unnatural father, or a good man and a treacherous friend. We cannot,
in estimating the character of an individual, leave out of our consideration
his conduct in the most important of all human relations; and if in that
relation we find him to have been selfish, cruel, and deceitful, we shall
take the liberty to call him a bad man, in spite of all his temperance at
table, and all his regularity at chapel.

— Thomas Babington Macaulay, from the "Essay on Milton"

O, ye that love mankind! Ye that dare oppose not only the tyranny,
but the tyrant, stand forth! Every spot of the old world is overrun with
oppression. Freedom hath been hunted round the globe. Asia and Africa
hath long expelled her. Europe regards her like a stranger, and England
hath given her warning to depart. O, receive the fugitive, and prepare in
time an asylum for mankind!

— Thomas Paine, from *Common Sense*

Writing is not literature unless it gives to the reader a pleasure which
arises not only from the things said, but from the way in which they are
said; and that pleasure is only given when the words are carefully or
curiously or beautifully put together into sentences.

— Stopford A. Brooke, from *Primer of English Literature*

THE GHOST TO HAMLET

Ghost: I am thy father's spirit,
        Doom'd for a certain term to walk the night,
        And for the day confined to fast in fires,
        Till the foul crimes done in my days of nature
        Are burnt and purged away. But that I am forbid
        To tell the secrets of my prison house,
        I could a tale unfold whose lightest word
        Would harrow up thy soul; freeze thy young blood;
        Make thy two eyes, like stars, start from their spheres;
        Thy knotted and combined locks to part,
        And each particular hair to stand on end,
        Like quills upon the fretful porpentine:
        But this eternal blazon must not be
        To ears of flesh and blood. List, list, O list!
        If thou didst ever thy dear father love —
        Revenge his foul and most unnatural murder.

              ·   ·   ·   ·   ·   ·   ·   ·   ·   ·   ·   ·

Fare thee well at once!
The glow-worm shows the matin to be near,
And 'gins to pale his uneffectual fire;
Adieu, adieu! Hamlet, remember me.
— Shakespeare, from *Hamlet*

SHYLOCK'S REPLY TO SALARINO

If it will feed nothing else it will feed my revenge. He hath disgraced me, and hindered me half a million; laugh'd at my losses, mock'd at my gains, scorned my nation, thwarted my bargains, cooled my friends, heated mine enemies; and what's his reason? I am a Jew. Hath not a Jew eyes? Hath not a Jew hands, organs, dimensions, senses, affections, passions; fed with the same food, hurt with the same weapons, subject to the same diseases, healed by the same means, warmed and cooled by the same winter and summer, as a Christian is? If you prick us, do we not bleed? If you tickle us, do we not laugh? If you poison us, do we not die? And if you wrong us, shall we not revenge? If we are like you in the rest, we will resemble you in that. If a Jew wrong a Christian, what is his humility? Revenge. If a Christian wrong a Jew, what should his sufferance be by Christian example? Why, revenge. The villainy you teach me, I will execute; and it shall go hard, but I will better the instruction.
— William Shakespeare, from *The Merchant of Venice*

WARREN'S ADDRESS

Stand! the ground's your own, my braves!
Will ye give it up to slaves?
Will ye look for greener graves?
    Hope ye mercy still?
What's the mercy despots feel?
Hear it in that battle peal!
Read it on yon bristling steel!
    Ask it — ye who will.

Fear ye foes who kill for hire?
Will ye to your *homes* retire?
Look behind you! — they're afire!
    And, before you, see
Who have done it! From the vale
On they come! — and will ye quail?
Leaden rain and iron hail
    Let their welcome be!

In the God of battles trust!
Die we may — and die we must:
But, O, where can dust to dust
   Be consigned so well,
As where heaven its dew shall shed
On the martyred patriot's bed,
And the rocks shall raise their head,
   Of his deeds to tell.

                                        — John Pierpont

      So live, that when thy summons comes to join
The innumerable caravan, which moves
To that mysterious realm, where each shall take
His chamber in the silent halls of death,
Thou go not, like the quarry-slave at night,
Scourged to his dungeon, but, sustained and soothed
By an unfaltering trust, approach thy grave,
Like one who wraps the drapery of his couch
About him, and lies down to pleasant dreams.
            — William Cullen Bryant, from "Thanatopsis"

      Strike — till the last armed foe expires;
      Strike for your altars and your fires;
      Strike for the green graves of your sires;
            God — and your native land!
            — Fitz-Greene Halleck, from "Marco Bozzaris"

Beat! Beat! Drums!

Beat! beat! drums! — blow! bugles! blow!
Through the windows — through the doors — burst like a ruthless force,
Into the solemn church, and scatter the congregation,
Into the school where the scholar is studying;
Leave not the bridegroom quiet — no happiness must he have with his
      bride,
Nor the peaceful farmer any peace, ploughing his field or gathering his
      grain,
So fierce you whirr and pound you drums — so shrill you bugles blow.

Beat! beat! drums! blow! bugles! blow!
Over the traffic of cities — over the rumble of wheels in the streets;
Are beds prepared for sleepers at night in the houses? No sleepers must
      sleep in those beds,

No bargainers bargain by day — no brokers or speculators — would they
      continue?
Would the talkers be talking? Would the singer attempt to sing?
Would the lawyer rise in court to state his case before the judge.
Then rattle quicker, heavier drums — you bugles, wilder blow!

Beat! beat! drums! blow! bugles! blow!
Make no parley — stop for no expostulation,
Mind not the timid, mind not the weeper or prayer,
Mind not the old man beseeching the young man,
Let not the child's voice be heard, nor the mother's entreaties,
Make even the trestles to shake the dead where they lie awaiting the
      hearses,
So strong you thump, O terrible drums — so loud you bugles blow.
                     — Walt Whitman

Deep personal emotion can make men eloquent who are not noted for
their eloquence. It did this to Calvin Coolidge when, crushed by the death
of his son Calvin, he inscribed a friend's book with these words, "To my
friend, in recollection of his son and my son, who, by the grace of God,
have the privilege of being boys throughout Eternity."

Moral passion even more than sorrow can fuel the minds and spirits,
and hence the language, of those fired by it. It is moral passion of the
finest sort which has directed the considerations and ignited the prose of
the great judges, including those I have named. Light and heat, Shaw
insisted, are the two vital qualities demanded of literature, adding that he
who has nothing to assert has no style, and can have none. The great
judges have never lacked something to say and, at their best, have said it
with light and heat.

They have loved words. They have realized the adventure which the
quest for the right one represents. They have known that there are no
such things as wilted words; there are only wilted people who use them.
They have hated verbosity and taken pains, when expressing themselves,
to clear away the thick underbrush and ugly weeds which obstruct most
legal language. . . . They have had Churchill's veneration for the structure
of a sentence. They have known better than to believe, as someone tried
to prove a few years ago, that the ideal sentence is seventeen words long.
Part of their wisdom is that they have recognized that a good sentence is
as long as it needs to be and no longer, and that a long sentence is more
than acceptable if only it seems short.

The beauties of the law are not the only ones the great judges have
opened up to us. They, like their blood-relations the great word-men in
literature, have lighted up the world for us by using language as a beacon.

The shadows will always be with us. They are a part of the health of our thinking. They mean that we recognize gradations, that we keep even our certainties open to question, and do not sink into the dangerous over-simplification of believing everything is either black or white. Shadows and darkness, however, are not the same thing. Illumination, the kind of illumination which banishes darkness though it leaves shadows, is among the paramount obligations of literary no less than legal writing. It has never been more needed than now when so many are tempted to lose hope and to surrender to despair. . . .[34]

— John Mason Brown, from "Language, Legal and Literary"

SHYLOCK TO ANTONIO

Signior Antonio, many a time and oft
In the Rialto you have rated me
About my moneys and my usances
Still I have borne it with a patient shrug,
For suff'rance is the badge of all our tribe.
You call me misbeliever, cut-throat, dog,
And spit upon my Jewish gaberdine,
And all for use of that which is mine own.
Well then, it now appears, you need my help.
Go to then! You come to me, and you say,
"Shylock, we would have moneys;" you say so;
You, that did void your rheum upon my beard,
And foot me, as you spurn a stranger cur
Over your threshold; moneys is your suit.
What should I say to you? Should I not say,
"Hath a dog money? Is it possible
A cur can lend three thousand ducats?" Or
Shall I bend low, and in a bondman's key,
With bated breath and whispering humbleness,
Say this:
"Fair sir, you spat on me on Wednesday last;
You spurn'd me such a day; another time
You call'd me dog; and for these courtesies
I'll lend you thus much moneys?"

— William Shakespeare, from *The Merchant of Venice*

And let the sacred obligations which have developed on this generation, and on us, sink deep into our hearts. Those who established our liberty

[34] Reprinted by permission from *The Saturday Review*, June 28, 1952, pp. 25–26.

and our government are daily dropping from among us. The great trust now descends to new hands. Let us apply ourselves to that which is presented to us, as our appropriate object. We can win no laurels in a war for independence. Earlier and worthier hands have gathered them all. Nor are there places for us by the side of Solon, and Alfred, and other founders of states. Our fathers have filled them. But there remains to us a great duty of defence and preservation; and there is open to us also, a noble pursuit, to which the spirit of the times strongly invites us. Our proper business is improvement. Let our age be the age of improvement. In a day of peace, let us advance the arts of peace and the works of peace. Let us develop the resources of our land, call forth its powers, build up its institutions, promote all its great interests, and see whether we also, in our day and generation, may not perform something worthy to be remembered. Let us cultivate a true spirit of union and harmony. In pursuing the great objects which our condition points out to us, let us act under a settled conviction, and an habitual feeling, that these twenty-four States are one country. Let our conceptions be enlarged to the circle of our duties. Let us extend our ideas over the whole of the vast field in which we are called to act. Let our object be, OUR COUNTRY, OUR WHOLE COUNTRY, AND NOTHING BUT OUR COUNTRY. And, by the blessing of God, may that country itself become a vast and splendid monument, not of oppression and terror, but of Wisdom, of Peace, and of Liberty, upon which the world may gaze with admiration forever!

— Daniel Webster, from "First Bunker Hill Oration"

The Crime of *Et Cetera*

Miscellaneous and *et cetera* are chief causes of the decline and fall of the power of the mind. With many people, no matter where they went to school, the curriculum was mainly *et cetera*, in which they took their degree *magna cum miscellaneous*. When they tackle a job, their vision is so all-inclusive that they cannot focus the eye on a limited target. The night has a thousand eyes, and so have they, and they use them all simultaneously.

Too many speeches suffer from acute and chronic *et cetera*. The speaker, instead of returning from the hunt with a fox's tail, brings back a spray of huckleberries. Many speeches (and may we say under our breath, some sermons) follow the approved pattern of speech of Aunt Minnie, giving a blow by blow description of a half-hour trip on a boat. "It was a lovely trip; we met some folks from Iowa; Iowa is a lovely state, but it is cold in winter; still, I think the winters are getting warmer, don't you? These new thermostats are wonderful; I have a cousin in Maine and they keep it at

70 degrees all winter; except when they go to Florida; I wouldn't like
Florida, because I can't play croquet or shuffleboard" — *et cetera*.

If you have any doubts about this, listen carefully to the next five
speeches you are exposed to. Or, if you are tough and can take anything,
read the letters of [35]

Yours,

Simeon Stylites

Stanzas on Freedom

Men! whose boast it is that ye
Come of fathers brave and free,
If there breathes on earth a slave,
Are ye truly free and brave?
If ye do not feel the chain
When it works a brother's pain,
Are ye not base slaves indeed,
Slaves unworthy to be freed?

Women! who shall one day bear
Sons to breathe New England air,
If ye hear without a blush,
Deeds to make the roused blood rush
Like red lava through your veins
For your sisters now in chains, —
Answer! Are ye fit to be
Mothers of the brave and free?

Is true Freedom but to break
Fetters for our own dear sake,
And, with leathern hearts, forget
That we owe mankind a debt?
No! True freedom is to share
All the chains our brothers wear,
And with heart and hand to be
Earnest to make others free!

They are slaves who fear to speak
For the fallen and the weak;
They are slaves who will not choose
Hatred, scoffing, and abuse,

[35] Reprinted by permission of *The Christian Century* from the issue of August
8, 1951, p. 911.

Rather than in silence shrink
From the truth they needs must think;
They are slaves who dare not be
In the right with two or three.
— James Russell Lowell

Withdrawal

A Musical Instrument

What was he doing, the great god Pan,
Down in the reeds by the river?
Spreading ruin and scattering ban,
Splashing and paddling with hoofs of a goat,
And breaking the golden lilies afloat
With the dragon-fly on the river.

He tore out a reed, the great god Pan,
From the deep cool bed of the river:
The limpid water turbidly ran,
And the broken lilies a-dying lay,
And the dragon-fly had fled away,
Ere he brought it out of the river.

High on the shore sat the great god Pan,
While turbidly flowed the river;
And hacked and hewed as a great god can,
With his hard bleak steel at the patient reed,
Till there was not a sign of the leaf indeed
To prove it fresh from the river.

He cut it short, did the great god Pan
(How tall it stood in the river!),
Then drew the pith, like the heart of a man,
Steadily from the outside ring,
And notched the poor dry empty thing
In holes, as he sat by the river.

"This is the way," laughed the great god Pan
(Laughed while he sat by the river),
"The only way, since the gods began
To make sweet music, they could succeed."
Then, dropping his mouth to a hole in the reed,
He blew in power by the river.

Sweet, sweet, sweet, O Pan!
Piercing sweet by the river!
Blinding sweet, O great god Pan!
The sun on the hill forgot to die,
And the lilies revived, and the dragon-fly
Came back to dream on the river.

Yet half a beast is the great god Pan,
To laugh as he sits by the river,
Making a poet out of a man:
The true gods sigh for the cost and pain, —
For the reed which grows nevermore again
As a reed with the reeds in the river.
                                   — Elizabeth Barrett Browning

All heaven and earth are still, — though not in sleep,
But breathless, as we grow when feeling most;
And silent, as we stand in thoughts too deep: —
All heaven and earth are still: From the high host
Of stars to the lulled lake, and mountain coast,
All is concenter'd in the life intense.
          — George Gordon Lord Byron, from "Stillness of Night"

Away, away, from men and towns,
To the wild wood and the downs —
To the silent wilderness
Where the soul need not repress
Its music lest it should not find
An echo in another's mind,
While the touch of Nature's art
Harmonizes heart to heart.
          — Percy Bysshe Shelley, from "The Invitation"

The curfew tolls the knell of parting day,
The lowing herd winds slowly o'er the lea,
The plowman homeward plods his weary way,
And leaves the world to darkness and to me.

Now fades the glimmering landscape on the sight,
And all the air a solemn stillness holds,
Save where the beetle wheels his droning flight,
And drowsy tinklings lull the distant folds.
— Thomas Gray, from "Elegy Written in a Country Church Yard"

Out of the night that covers me,
    Black as the pit from pole to pole,
I thank whatever gods may be
    For my unconquerable soul.

In the fell clutch of circumstance
    I have not winced or cried aloud;
Beneath the bludgeonings of fate
    My head is bloody but unbowed.

It matters not how strait the gate,
    How charged with punishment the scroll;
I am the master of my fate,
    I am the captain of my soul.
                    — William Ernest Henley, from "Invictus"

THRENOS

O World! O Life! O Time!
On whose last steps I climb,
    Trembling at that where I had stood before;
When will return the glory of your prime?
    No more — Oh, never more!

Out of the day and night
A joy has taken flight:
    Fresh spring, and summer, and winter hoar
Move my faint heart with grief, but with delight
    No more — Oh, never more!
                    — Percy Bysshe Shelley

SHE WALKS IN BEAUTY

She walks in beauty, like the night
Of cloudless climes and starry skies;
And all that's best of dark and bright
Meet in her aspect and her eyes:
Thus mellow'd to that tender light
Which heaven to gaudy day denies.
One shade the more, one ray the less,
Had half impaired the nameless grace
Which waves in every raven tress,
Or softly lightens o'er her face;

Where thoughts serenely sweet express
How pure, how dear their dwelling-place.
And on that cheek, and o'er that brow,
So soft, so calm, yet eloquent,
The smiles that win, the tints that glow,
But tell of days in goodness spent,
A mind at peace with all below,
A heart whose love is innocent!

— George Gordon Lord Byron

To the Moon

Art thou pale for weariness
Of climbing heaven, and gazing on earth,
Wandering companionless
Among the stars that have a different birth,
And everchanging, like the joyless eye
That finds no object worth its constancy?

— Percy Bysshe Shelley

Crossing the Bar

Sunset and evening star,
And one clear call for me!
And may there be no moaning of the bar,
When I put out to sea,

But such a tide as moving seems asleep,
Too full for sound and foam,
When that which drew from out the boundless deep
Turns again home.

Twilight and evening bell,
And after that the dark!
And may there be no sadness of farewell,
When I embark:

For though from out our bourne of Time and Place
The flood may bear me far,
I hope to see my Pilot face to face
When I have crossed the bar.

— Alfred Lord Tennyson

To Sleep

A flock of sheep that leisurely pass by
One after one; the sound of rain, and bees
Murmuring; the fall of rivers, winds, and seas,
Smooth fields, white sheets of water, and pure sky;
I've thought of all by turns, and yet do lie
Sleepless; and soon the small bird's melodies
Must hear, first utter'd from my orchard trees,
And the first cuckoo's melancholy cry.
Even thus last night, and two nights more I lay,
And could not win thee, Sleep! by any stealth:
So do not let me wear tonight away:
Without Thee what is all the morning's wealth?
Come, blessed barrier between day and day,
Dear mother of fresh thoughts and joyous health!

— William Wordsworth

The Lord is my shepherd; I shall not want.
He maketh me to lie down in green pastures: he leadeth me beside the
    still waters.
He restoreth my soul: he leadeth me in the paths of righteousness for
    his name's sake.
Yea, though I walk through the valley of the shadow of death, I will fear
    no evil: for thou art with me; thy rod and thy staff they comfort me.
Thou preparest a table before me in the presence of mine enemies; thou
    anointest my head with oil; my cup runneth over.
Surely goodness and mercy shall follow me all the days of my life and I
    will dwell in the house of the Lord for ever.

— Psalm 23

Bound on the Wild Horse

Away! — away! — and on we dash!
Torrents less rapid and less rash.
Away, away, my steed and I,
Upon the pinions of the wind,
All human dwellings left behind:
We speed like meteors through the sky,
When with its crackling sound the night
Is checkered with the northern light: —
From out the forest prance
A trampling troop, — I see them come!
A thousand horses — and none to ride! —
With flowing tail, and flying mane,

Wide nostrils, never stretched by pain,
Mouths bloodless to the bit or rein,
And feet that iron never shod,
And flanks unscarred by spur or rod, —
A thousand horses — and none to ride! —
Like waves that follow o'er the sea,
Come thickly thundering on: —
They stop, — they start — they snuff the air,
Gallop a moment here and there,
Approach, retire, wheel round and round,
Then plunging back with sudden bound, —
They snort, — they foam — neigh — swerve aside,
And backward to the forest fly,
By instinct, from a human eye.

— Byron, from "Mazeppa"

To A Waterfowl

Whither, midst falling dew,
While glow the heavens with the last steps of day,
Far, through their rosy depths, dost thou pursue
    Thy solitary way?

Vainly the fowler's eye
Might mark thy distant flight to do thee wrong,
As, darkly seen against the crimson sky,
    Thy figure floats along.

Seek'st thou the plashy brink
Of weedy lake, or marge of river wide,
Or where the rocking billows rise and sink
    On the chafed ocean-side?

There is a Power whose care
Teaches thy way along that pathless coast —
The desert and illimitable air —
    Lone wandering, but not lost.

All day thy wings have fanned,
At that far height, the cold, thin atmosphere,
Yet stoop not, weary, to the welcome land,
    Though the dark night is near.

And soon that toil shall end;
Soon shalt thou find a summer home, and rest,
And scream among thy fellows; reeds shall bend,
    Soon, o'er thy sheltered nest.

Thou'rt gone, the abyss of heaven
Hath swallowed up thy form; yet, on my heart
Deeply has sunk the lesson thou has given,
    And shall not soon depart.

He who, from zone to zone,
Guides through the boundless sky thy certain flight,
In the long way that I must tread alone,
    Will lead my steps aright.
               — William Cullen Bryant

Concord Hymn

By the rude bridge that arched the flood,
    Their flag to April's breeze unfurled,
Here once the embattled farmers stood
    And fired the shot heard round the world.

The foe long since in silence slept;
    Alike the conqueror silent sleeps;
And Time the ruined bridge has swept
    Down the dark stream which seaward creeps.

On this green bank, by this soft stream,
    We set today a votive stone:
That memory may their deed redeem,
    When like our sires, our sons are gone.

Spirit that made those heroes dare
    To die, and leave their children free,
Bid Time and Nature gently spare
    The shaft we raise to them and thee.
               — Ralph Waldo Emerson

Jaques' Seven Ages of Man

               All the world's a stage,
And all the men and women merely players:
They have their exits, and their entrances;
And one man in his time plays many parts,
His acts being seven ages. At first, the infant,
Mewling and puking in the nurse's arms.
And then, the whining school-boy, with his satchel,
And shining morning face, creeping, like snail,
Unwillingly to school. And then the lover,
Sighing like furnace, with a woeful ballad
Made to his mistress' eyebrow. Then the soldier,

Full of strange oaths, and bearded like a pard,
Jealous in honor, sudden and quick in quarrel,
Seeking the bubble reputation
Even in the cannon's mouth. And then, the justice,
In fair round belly, with good capon lin'd,
With eyes severe, and beard of formal cut,
Full of wise saws and modern instances,
And so he plays his part. The sixth age shifts
Into the lean and slipper'd pantaloon,
With spectacles on nose, and pouch on side;
His youthful hose well sav'd, a world too wide
For his shrunk shank; and his big manly voice,
Turning again toward childish treble, pipes
And whistles in his sound. Last scene of all,
That ends this strange, eventful history,
Is second childishness, and mere oblivion;
Sans teeth, sans eyes, sans taste, sans everything.
— William Shakespeare, from *As You Like It*

QUESTIONS FOR STUDY AND DISCUSSION

1. What is meant by pitch? By variety of pitch? What relation has pitch to intellectual and emotional emphases? What about personality is shown by pitch patterns? What is optimum pitch? How do you determine it? What is yours? What is the difference between the melody of speech and song?

2. What do we mean by intensity? What is the relation between intensity and intellectual emphasis? Between intensity and emotional emphasis?

3. What emotional and intellectual communications are produced by the relationships between pitch and intensity?

4. What do the timing elements convey? What is meant by "a good rate?" What does quantity contribute to communication? What does pause contribute? Rhythm?

5. What are the values of fluency and the dangers of over-emphasizing it?

6. What is the role of vocal quality in communication?

7. Can you state the techniques for improving reading ability? Why do we discuss reading in connection with vocal improvement?

Mend your speech a little,
Lest you may mar your fortunes.

Shakespeare, from *King Lear*

17

The Faults of Voice
and Their Correction

THE TWO PRECEDING chapters discussed the principles of sound, voice production, and the tone code — the meanings and personality traits implied and expressed by voice. Against this background, we come now to a series of suggestions for the correction of particular faults in the use of voice. Voice is a product of many factors operating at once, and its faults are seldom to be found in a single cause. For instance, if a person lets out most of a breath before he speaks, his fault is not merely one of phonation or of breathing, but of both. If one has excessive nasality, his problem may be one of tension, breathing, articulation, and still other causes. We are concerned now with seeing how we may improve the voice.

How to Use This Chapter

This chapter is intended not for complete reading but for selective study and practice, and the assignments are designed on the following principles.

1. By yourself, or with the help of your instructor, find those problems on which you need particular work. Study and work with them in the order of importance.

2. Daily practice is necessary. Spasmodic attention to a speech problem is wasted. Daily practice for half an hour will produce results.

3. You should keep a written record of your daily practice. This will help you see what you are concentrating on, and will organize your effort. This record may be checked by your instructor periodically to see if you are emphasizing the right details at the right time. Progress determines what your point of concentration should be.

Projection is not good unless . . .

the elements of sound are a happy blend.

4. In the following assignments you will note considerable emphasis upon recording your voice. This should be frequent — daily if possible. To hear your voice as others do, completely removed from the act of speaking, is perhaps the best way to judge it objectively. Besides, any change is a deviation from habit, and you will tend to think the change much greater than it actually is. You need to keep recording your voice to see if you are changing as much as you think you are.

5. The assignments for each problem are organized to take care of the following:

   a. Relaxation of muscles at the beginning of each practice period.

   b. An understanding of the psychological aspects of the problem and related assignments.

c. Practice in hearing and in recognizing kinesthetic, that is, internal bodily sensations.

d. Location of the target. You need classmates and teacher to verify when you are "on the beam."

e. Repetition when on the target.

f. Practice in different situations to test your ability to hold the target in view. Sometimes the change in situation is only from syllables to words or from words to sentences. Sometimes it is from room to room, or from person to person.

One comment should be made about the transition from *d* to *e*. In your search for the execution of a quality, sound, inflection, attack, or whatever you are trying to achieve, you will narrow the range of error and then suddenly locate your target. This is a crucial moment. To respond with satisfaction or relief to your success is fatal, for you lose the set. Do not move a muscle, except those needed to take a breath, and not even that unless necessary. Hold your set and repeat over and over again. Then relax and repeat the performance. This care is basic to fixing on the target.

Projection

All voice correction is intended to improve projection. *Projection,* simply defined, means "putting it across," and is the aim of all speaking. It refers to the actual transmittal of the communication signals from the speaker's mind to the listener's. When, as a listener, you are unaware of pitch, intensity, time factors, variety, quality, and articulation because of the impact of the speaker's ideas, he has pro-

Bad projection

jected. Conversely, if you say, "I can't *listen* to him. I just hear the way he talks," his projection is faulty for at least two reasons.

First, poor projections may result from a lack of balance among the elements of voice production. Intensity may be too great or too varied for pitch and time. If so, instead of receiving the impact of the idea, the listener's attention is directed to intensity, which gets in the way of listening. Any of the other elements of speech may be out of balance — pitch may be too much or too little varied. Pauses may be too long or too short. Speech may be too rapid or too slow. And so on. But generally the failure to project because of a fault in speech production is associated with "unbalanced intensity," probably because the public speaker and the actor are often urged to speak louder. The speaker who simply speaks louder without adjusting volume to the other elements of speaking gives the effect of broadcasting to nobody.

A second reason for faulty projection, though involving the above elements, seems to be of psychological origin. It is failure in target set (Chapter 3). Some people talk to an audience as if one person were present. This is good for radio, but bad on the public platform. While we desire the conversational mode in all speech, the public speaker is nevertheless conversing with an audience. He seems smaller than his task if he does not seem to perceive the size of his audience. Some people seem to speak to a larger audience than the one present. Queen Victoria said of her prime minister that "Mr. Gladstone always addresses me as if I were a public gathering!" Perhaps the best answer to the problem of correct projection was given by the actress who, when asked how it was that she seemed to talk with each member of her audience, replied, "I intended that I should!"

All improvement of the speaking voice is in the interest of better projection, and hence of better communication.

PROBLEMS OF BREATHING AND PHONATION

In the discussion of breathing (pages 252–254), we noted that speech requires an adequate quantity of air and control in releasing it to fit the phrasing of ideas. The person who has insufficient air does not inhale deeply; he lifts his shoulders slightly and expands the upper chest. The lack of control may result from trying to hold in too much air during speech, or from letting out too much before the vocal folds are brought into position for phonation. These problems are alike in that they indicate improper use of breath. The machinery is out of time. The most common cause is fear.

When we are afraid we spend 2.65 times as long inhaling as exhaling.[1] In confident speaking we use from 6 to 16 times as much time exhaling as inhaling. No other emotion requires so much inhalation time, and therefore so upsets the breathing rhythm.[2] Excitement, and particularly fear, uses oxygen rapidly. The resulting carbon monoxide reacts upon the phrenic nerve which trips off the contraction of the diaphragm. Conscious control of normal speech is then impossible. These are the physiological relations of fear to breathing.

But there are important psychological factors. When we become apprehensive we take on a protective posture and the related mode of breathing. We are vulnerable when we are expelling air for two reasons. First, when exhaling we do not have the oxygen ready for maximum action. We are much in the same position as the boxer on his heels. Second, when we are exhaling the diaphragm and abdominal muscles are moving in, and are thus unprotected. Civilized speech is carried on in the exhaling phase of breathing, whereas during the primitive reflexes of the protective posture, we breathe in. Therefore when we are on guard we use our breath for speech in such a way as to be ready for attack. As mentioned before, this defensive kind of speech may enforce one of four forms of breathing.

Hypertense Adjustment

Talk at the Top of a Complete Inspiration. When the reaction is extremely high tension, the speaker takes a deep breath and speaks without using it. When he needs another breath, he quickly lets out the air (so as to be vulnerable for a minimum time) and takes another breath. The most obvious symptom of this kind of breathing is the sigh that comes at pauses in speech.

To speak this way requires great control over the relaxing tendencies of the muscles that increase the size of the rib cage, for tension must be maintained. Accordingly, the tension produces speech in the upper part of the potential range. The voice is harsh; that is, the higher overtones of the fundamental are dominant, giving the voice a metallic

[1] Lyman Judson and Andrew T. Weaver, *Voice Science*, New York, F. S. Crofts, 1942, p. 28, footnote 11.
[2] Only the emotion of *wonder* taxes the breathing rhythm for speech to a degree comparable to fear. Anger and pain require a little more time for inspiration than for expiration.

ring. The voice is loud and has little variation in force. The speaker
usually talks rapidly. He generally attacks words sharply, and his attack is harder at the beginning than at the end of phrases.

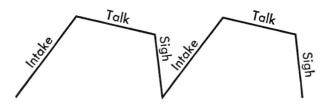

Such speakers are openly aggressive, holding the listener at a distance by force, harsh quality, high pitch, and the hard attack. Consider the voice stereotype of the army sergeant.

Talk Between Ascending Inspirations Followed by a Sigh. This
breathing adjustment, also hypertense, is an effort to escape the
normal intake-outgo cycle of breathing. Instead of stopping to release
the carbon monoxide, these speakers keep adding fresh air to the old
until the need for oxygen trips off the exhalation response. They then

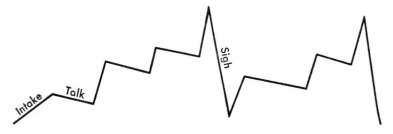

let out the air with a blast, gasp for part of a breath, and start talking
again. Both the breathing pattern and the attitudes suggest that the
speaker cannot reconcile himself to his biological needs. He is going
to talk and adjust his life to that all-embracing purpose. This speaker
is seldom a listener.

Such speakers are excitable. They speak at a high pitch level, with
a wide range of inflection and intensity, and at a rapid rate. They are
generally optimistic in their speech and show little distrust of the listener; otherwise they would not air their thought so profusely.

Of course, excessive speech has its motivation in fear. It indicates
a fear of self, an impulsive, disorganized effort to find equilibrium

through exhaustion. Such people have an abundance of "nervous" energy and are highly stimulated by other people. Their whole lives suggest energy without direction.

1. Speak before a lighted candle. Do you tend to blow out the flame at the ends of phrases and sentences?
2. If you do, practice trying to expel the air so that as you close a period of speech, you breathe in without first expelling pent up air.
3. Practice alternately expelling and not expelling air, after speech, before you take in breath.
4. If you have trouble doing this, read for a few minutes some pleasant and placid poetry before you try the above exercise again.

Hypotense Adjustment

Talk on Incomplete Inspiration. Some people do not breathe deeply enough to prolong sufficiently the exhaling period required for normal speech. There are several symptoms of this fault. Such

speakers usually lift the shoulders when taking in air, filling only the upper part of the rib cage. They tend to speak with a soft, weightless, and often breathy quality. And they usually show little emotion in voice, action, or facial expression.

This kind of shallow breathing is generally attended by attitudes of extreme submission or withdrawal. Unconsciously, the speaker keeps himself in readiness for a quick protective intake of air. So long as he is speaking, however, he guards against taking a deep breath and "throwing it away" in speech. Moreover, he is not strong enough in his interactions with others to throw himself with energy upon his listeners.

Talk at Bottom of Expiration Phase. Some speakers take a breath, perhaps a deep one, let it out, and then speak. They do not use the air pressure that is the natural result of relaxed muscles which during inhalation increased the size of the rib cage. Having dissipated this air, they speak on the residual, forced air. The pressure is low, and the vocal muscles of the larynx must be relaxed and toneless in order to vibrate at all. The result is a dissonant, gravelly sound in the

throat known as "glottal fry." Because of the lack of air pressure, the tone is resonated in the throat. The resulting speech is low in pitch, guttural, and usually weak in force. Often such speech causes a swelling of the throat, a distention of the arteries of the throat, muscular distention around the eyes, and a slightly flushed face.

Such speakers are defensively aggressive in their attitudes, and suggest by their "growl" that the listener hold his distance. They are always ready for the protection of a quick intake of air.

1. You may test to see whether you expend air before you speak by talking near a candle flame. A little practice will let you see whether you dissipate the breath and how to synchronize the actions of expelling it and phonating.
2. After you feel you have learned when you control the air and when you do not, speak before the candle with your eyes closed. Have your roommate check whether air escapes before you initiate sound.
3. Practice alternately "attacking the air with sound" and dissipating some of the air before you speak. In the end it is the kinesthetic feedback of the difference between the two habits that makes you aware when you are using the air at the moment you start releasing it.

The assignments above are mainly analytical. When breathing is out of phase with speech, in one of the four patterns mentioned, the following corrective suggestions should be helpful.

1. With the aid of your instructor and the class, determine whether your analysis is correct.
2. Study Chapter 19, "Fear and Confidence," particularly those sections that deal with the attitudes and assignments related to your breathing style.

3. Study the suggestions particularly under "What to Do About Physical Tension," pages 392–394, Chapter 19. This deals with hypo- and hypertensions.

4. Imitate the breathing of sleep.

5. Stand and place your hand on your abdomen. The more your hand moves as you breathe the greater the diaphragmatic action.

6. When you take a deep breath to trip off relaxation, remember to inhale again before speaking. A cycle and a half, two and a half, or three and a half is necessary. Otherwise you will begin speaking when you are out of breath, only to gasp and run into additional trouble. This inhalation-exhalation-inhalation sequence should be practiced in private until the pattern is set.

7. Practice reading or speaking in a loud but unstrained whisper. This demands a greater quantity of air than normal speech and adjusts the breathing muscles to more vigorous action.

8. Arrange some material which you care to read well into breath groupings, separating the groups by lines or dashes. Read the material, taking in breath at the marked points. These groupings should fit the meaning of the material. A little experiment will soon tell you where meaning permits pauses. Charles Van Riper has found that good breathing is automatically developed by eliminating the faulty habit. If you have trouble reading material broken into short groupings, you are trying to speak on the intake. Consistent practice at speaking on the expiration phase and breathing in "on the dashes" will at once eliminate the more common breathing error and establish an adequate pattern. *If you consistently run out of air when the material has been broken down into short groupings, the problem is probably one of phonation,* to be discussed next.

PROBLEMS OF MONOTONY

Some people speak too high or too low, too loud or too soft, or too high and loud, too low and soft, and so on. With these faults the problem is one of monotony. There are a number of reasons why it should be corrected and a number of ways of doing so.

Vocal Variety and Health

The vocal folds are many muscles made up of countless fibers. As with any muscle, stimulation of a fiber produces either no contraction or the maximum of which it is capable. Consequently the tension — the hardness and firmness of the muscle — depends upon the *number* of fibers that are activated. Since fibers must be exercised in order to maintain their capacity to respond, increasing the number of fibers in action is desirable. In addition, with a large number of fibers at one's disposal, there is opportunity to relieve some of them from time to time. Conversely, any muscle or set of muscles which is used to the same degree of tension employs practically the same set of fibers. Fixed tension for a prolonged period produces fatigue and eventually strain. Both non-use and over-use create unhealthy conditions, non-use causing atrophy (wasting away) and excessive use causing strain, soreness, and swelling.

These facts suggest the importance of good phonation. As one alters pitch or intensity, he increases or decreases the number of fibers in use. If a person speaks with monopitch, or monoforce, he overuses some fibers and underuses others. Consequently it is monotonous speech that produces fatigue. Strained, strident, harsh, and raspy voices result. One should, therefore, exercise a wide range of the elements in his speech in order to maintain healthy vocal folds. Moreover, one must live at a reasonable state of tension in order to be able to maintain the conditions for a flexible voice.

To relax vocal muscles means, first, relaxing the muscles of the body as a whole, then the smaller muscles more directly associated with speech.

1. Busy people often find it helpful, for a few minutes at midday, to lie flat on the back, arms and legs dangling, relaxing the whole body. Clothes should be loose and eyes closed. It helps to lift and let fall the arms and legs, one at a time, and to roll the head back and forth.

2. Sit up and roll your head back and forth, up and down, gently.

3. Yawn, waggle your jaw, and slowly stroke the sides of your throat. Repeat several times.

These exercises should be used when you are tense in order to improve your overall efficiency and enjoyment of life. They also have an effect on your voice, for they teach you the state of relaxation desired in the speech situation. But relaxation should not be enforced. The hypotense guard of the compulsively submissive or independent person produces monotony at a low pitch and low intensity. Monotony at any tension level entails a constant use of some muscle fibers and disuse of others.

Monopitch

When Pat speaks before the class, the major impression is that of a droning machine. The voice is pleasant, but it is dominated by the monotony of an unvaried low pitch. Mary's voice is monotonous, and more irritatingly so, for it is high-pitched. Gerald is tense and alert. He tends to cow you with verbal cross-fire. His pitch is monotonous too, but he commands better attention because his high pitch is coupled with a sharp attack upon words.

When a person is inclined to speak in a very limited range, we refer to the tendency as *monopitch*. A pitch range of one-third octave or less is interpreted as monotonous. We have explained the harmful fatiguing effect of monopitch upon the larynx. In addition, such a pitch pattern makes it difficult for the listener to get the meanings, reducing comprehension by some 10 per cent.

Monopitch takes two forms. The first may be high or low, but it is weak and may be accompanied by slovenly diction. Such speech is associated with compulsive submission or withdrawal, or with a habit that has persisted after security has been established. If physical tensions are not present, the faulty voice is due to habit. The second type of monopitch is coupled with a strong monoforce, which stems from aggressive attitudes.

Corrective assignments involve readjustment of attitudes, ear training, and motor control.

Assignments for All Forms of Monopitch.

1. If you are in doubt whether your speech is limited in pitch variety, have the instructor and class judge your next speech. Ask them to label the monotony as submissive, withdrawing, or aggressive. Examine your self and social attitudes. Read Chapters 18 through 21.

2. Record your voice, preferably along with that of at least one other student whose pitch patterns are different from yours. It is desirable to record both discussion and public speaking situations. Listen to the recordings a number of times, until your voice rings in your ears, until you understand your pattern.

3. After you get the pattern well in mind, listen to the recording of a speech that your instructor recommends for excellence of inflection. Study this until you sense the freedom and spontaneity of varied speech.

4. Prepare and record some remarks that experiment toward the accepted pattern. Study these by frequent replaying.

5. If you find it hard to change your pattern, use one of the self-hearing devices as you speak. Some tape-recorders operate as a recorder and a public address system simultaneously. Should you still have trouble, use ear phones instead of the speaker.

6. If a pitch meter or ossiloscope is available, practice your speeches with this equipment. A visual feedback of your pitches as you speak supplements your hearing and lets you see when you are speaking high or low, when you are flexible and when monotonous.

Assignments for Low Monopitch. Low monopitch is one of the easier faults to overcome and the correction of it is often instrumental in the elimination of other lesser faults of the voice.

1. You will tend to raise your voice and alter the inflection patterns if you talk on a subject that you consider difficult to make clear. Set yourself for the anticipated change by establishing the purpose and expectation of being understood. We use a wider range when we are trying to make ourselves clear.

2. Imagine you are speaking or reading to an audience of children, for we speak with greater inflection to children.

3. If possible speak to an actual audience of children.

4. Practice reading a dramatic story or poem. To express the action, your voice must rise and become flexible.

5. Develop a speech that tells of an exciting experience. Record it for study and additional change.

6. Practice a speech after it has been well developed, with the idea of raising your pitch level. Then practice the same speech with the purpose of varying your range more than usual. Either alteration will advantageously affect the other. Bringing both into focus doubly sensitizes your self-hearing.

7. Take part in conversations or interviews with a student whose voice is more flexible than yours, particularly if you admire his speech. In the interaction you may adopt a more flexible voice.

8. Play a dominant role such as the boss or a salesman opposite a student of more dominant speech, then opposite a student of less dominant speech. In which are you more flexible? How do you account for this?

9. Practice and deliver several short speeches to the accompaniment of a masking tone. The pitch of the tone is not important, but it must

be loud enough for you to "fight" it. The louder it is, the more you will raise your voice and make it flexible. Diminish and fade out the tone in accordance with your ability to maintain the desired speech on your own.

10. Read a poem or speech that has harsh, dynamic, or aggressive attitudes. To express such attitudes demands a hard attack. The vowel following hard attack rises. As your voice rises, it will become more flexible.

11. Practice a well prepared speech before the mirror. Watch your mouth and focus attention upon opening it wider than usual. Pitch rises as we open our mouths wider in the process of articulation. Record your voice in practice for a check on the effect.

Assignments for High Monopitch. The task of lowering pitch and increasing range is somewhat more difficult. We tend to work at cross-purposes, since lowering the voice accentuates monopitch. Pronovost suggests lowering the pitch level below that desired, then raising it to the right level, to increase flexibility.[3] The following assignments are designed to lower the voice:

1. Practice to acquire the glottal fry, a "dead groan." When you can produce this sound at will, practice ten minutes a day, speaking first vowels with the glottal fry, then syllables, words, and finally phrases and sentences. When glottal fry dominates the voice, the pitch level is excessively low.

2. Once you are able to speak whole sentences easily with the glottal emphasis, add more breath to the voice. This can be done by speaking in a slightly breathy voice. Aspirate attack, also, tends to lower the vowel that follows it. Alternately speak phrases with glottal fry and a breathy quality of the same pitch level. Gradually eliminate the "fry" as you are able to maintain the low pitch.

3. Once you speak at will in a low, breathy voice, alternate phrases breathily and in normal quality at the same pitch level. Gradually eliminate the breathy voice. Record often to check both pitch level and quality. You have now acquired a very low voice of normal quality.

4. As a challenge to the stability of your newly acquired speech, practice in conversation and interviews with students of varying pitch patterns and dominance levels. If you return to your "higher voice," go back to assignments 1, 2, and 3 to reestablish the technique.

[3] Wilbert Pronovost, "Research Contributions to Voice Improvement," *Journal of Speech and Hearing Disorders*, Vol. 7, 1942, pp. 313–318.

5. Read prose or poetry in which the emotions are gentle, subdued, and serene. To capture the mood in voice, you must use a soft attack. Vowels become lower after the soft attack. To help capture the technique, notice that such material calls for the prolongation of many sounds. Such material will give you confidence in your low voice, for it will not seem monotonous, since the meanings call for a low narrow range.

6. Practice speaking before a mirror, focusing attention upon opening the mouth no more than is necessary to articulate clearly. Low voice and small mouth-opening are compatible. The use of one tends to produce the other.

When your voice is stable and low, a condition which, as suggested, will require persistent daily practice with these assignments, turn to the assignments for raising the voice. Check with your instructor and use frequent recordings to locate and stabilize the desired pitch level and flexibility.

Monoforce

Where the problem of force seems essentially to be one of monotony and where, as is usual, the voice is also marked with mono-pitch, you should work with the assignments designed for that difficulty. To correct one aspect of an inadequate voice very often corrects the whole problem. The following analysis and assignments are a direct attack upon faults of intensity.

Low Intensity. Vera, in all speech situations, is scarcely audible. The central observation is that she does not talk loudly enough. Her breathing is usually very shallow, and when she does take a deep breath, she sighs before she speaks. Her face tells nothing. She seldom shows strong emotions, though she shows some inclination to oppose. Her voice is basically oral and weightless. Her rate is average and she prolongs all sounds about equally. She is bright and sensitive, but gives the impression of standing on the sidelines.

Obviously, not everyone who speaks with characteristically low intensity fits this description in detail, but this is the general picture. What can we recommend?

1. If you are usually low in energy, which of course may be a cause of low vocal intensity, you should see a doctor and have a physical check-up.

2. As indicated, attitudes also may be involved. If you cannot assert yourself even though you want to, the chapters and assignments on fear, personality, images, and interaction need to be examined carefully. Perhaps some counseling aid is in order.

The following assignments will help break the habit regardless of cause:

3. Take part in conversations and interviews with a person who characteristically or intentionally speaks (as you do) in an extremely low, almost inaudible voice. Most of us tend to interact with increased intensity to low intensity in others.[4]

4. If possible, practice your speeches in a large and preferably "dead" room, a room that does not resonate. Lock the door if you are afraid of being caught. Imagine your audience is sitting in the last row. It will help to record your voice, study it, and evaluate the increased intensity.

5. Again, the masking tone is of value. We tend to increase our intensity in direct proportion to the loudness of the interference. Practice and deliver speeches against the competition of the masking tone if your voice is low in pitch and in force. Do not use this assignment if your voice is high in pitch.

6. Prepare a speech of demonstration or one in which you will naturally exercise considerable action and gesturing. We tend to speak louder as we increase our body activity.[5]

7. Practice your speeches before a mirror, emphasizing an open mouth. Since the open mouth tends to raise the pitch, do *not* use this assignment if your voice is already too high.

8. Practice your speeches with cotton in your ears, to decrease your sidetone hearing. We usually compensate one-half as much in intensity as the amount of temporary loss in hearing.[6] As we have suggested for other external stimuli, after you have accustomed yourself to speaking with greater force, occasionally remove the cotton and speak, now guided by kinesthetic sensations.

---

[4] John W. Black, "A Compensating Effect in Vocal Responses to Stimuli of Low Intensity," *Journal of Experimental Psychology*, Vol. 40, No. 3, June, 1950, pp. 396–397.

[5] Alan Monroe, "The Effect of Bodily Action on Voice Intensity," *Journal of Applied Psychology*, Vol. 13, 1929, pp. 516–532.

[6] John W. Black, "The Effect of Noise Induced Temporary Deafness Upon Vocal Intensity," *Speech Monographs*, March, 1951, pp. 74–77.

9. Since a slight side-tone delay (up to .09 of a second) will excite effort to speak louder, it helps to practice speaking in a large echoing room or auditorium. A room fifty feet deep gives the maximum stimulation.

10. In all the foregoing assignments it is well to add the visual feedback of a gain or intensity meter. Some tape and disc recorders are equipped with a needle and dial that tell the range of normal intensity. Determine the power and distance from the microphone that is needed for a voice of average power. Set the volume control and let the meter serve as a simultaneous feedback while you speak.

11. Practice and deliver your speeches on a public address system. *If you like to hear your voice when it is loud,* you will tend to exercise additional energy as the instructor decreases the volume of the machine. If you dislike a loud voice or are afraid to exercise additional power, this technique is not effective. If you find yourself moving up to the microphone as the power is decreased, the technique is well designed for you.

12. The following assignment does not increase intensity but does help to compensate under conditions where you cannot add further power. Hold the sounds longer and you will be judged as having additional intensity. The prolongation of sounds gives the listener more assurance that he has heard correctly. He interprets this as an improvement in your intensity.

High Intensity. One of the marks of decided and open aggressiveness is the loud voice. What can you do if you evaluate your speech as too loud?

1. It is obvious that the first need is to reconsider your competitive attitudes. If, of your own volition, you decide you speak with too much energy, you probably have started already to renounce the values which make you do so. More reading in the area of human relations will help you clarify your new position and attitudes.

2. It is possible that you have a hearing loss which steps up your intensity. If there is any evidence of this, you should have a hearing examination, at the speech clinic if your college has one.

3. Practice your speeches in a small room. This will condition you to lowered intensity.

4. Practice before a mirror, opening your mouth less wide as you speak. Check with a recorder occasionally to see that the articulation, pitch, and flexibility of your voice are not suffering.

5. Take part in interviews and discussions in which you express tact, mediation, or good will.

PROBLEMS OF RATE

Extremely Rapid Rate. If you speak too rapidly, according to the judgment of your instructor and fellow students:

1. Record your voice and listen to it. Listen to the recording of another student, judged as average in rate. Compare the two. Is the difference in the prolongation of sounds, or the pause between words? Try to alter the factors involved. Record your efforts and listen to them.

2. Again, a masking noise is of aid, if you cannot wilfully slow your rate. A masking noise will slow you down.[7] As you slow down, fade out the noise in order to develop your power to control rate. Bring in the masking noise as you develop excessive speed. With daily practice you will gain the ability to hear, monitor, and control your rate.

3. Practice your speeches at an excessively slow rate to "face up" to your fear. Give a short speech or two in class at this extremely slow rate.

4. Practice your speeches in very large rooms. This will force you to speak more slowly.[8] One factor induced is the prolongation of sounds. The delay in the reflection of the sound from distant walls will increase the length of your pauses, also.

5. The effect of side-tone delay may be increased by the use of a public address system in which the speaker is placed some distance from you. Even a delay of .03 of a second will slow your speed. This can be achieved by placing the speaker at a distance of 33 feet. A delay of .18 of a second or a distance of 198 feet produces the maximum slowing down. It is not often possible to find so large a room, of course. If your speech department has a tape recorder with a time delay device on it, you may produce the effects of delayed feedback in a room of any size. Side-tone delay has a carry-over effect, slowing down speech for a period after normal conditions have been re-established.[9]

6. Read poetry or prose that is thoughtful or conveys emotions that slow the speech — longing, sadness, grief, weariness, awe. Capturing the mood helps to develop appropriate rate.

[7] T. D. Hanley and Max Steer, "Effect of the Level of Distortion Noise Upon Speaking Rate, Duration and Intensity," *Journal of Speech and Hearing Disorders,* Vol. XIV, December, 1949, pp. 363–368.

[8] John W. Black, "The Effect of Room Characteristics Upon Vocal Intensity and Rate," *The Journal of Acoustical Society of America,* Vol. 22, No. 2, 1950, pp. 174–176.

[9] John W. Black, "The Effect of Delayed Side-Tone Upon Vocal Rate and Intensity," *Journal of Speech and Hearing Disorders,* March, 1951, pp. 56–60.

Extremely Slow Rate. Should the appraisal of others indicate that you need to increase your rate, you may devote fifteen minutes to a half hour each day on the following exercises:

1. Rate of speech is related to physical activity. To speak with more energy and to incorporate gestures will accordingly cause you to step up your rate. Record your speech and study the rate, both with and without activity. This will give you an awareness of the degree of change and the desirability of the effect.

2. To practice your speeches in a very small room will tend to increase your rate.

3. Practice reading prose or poetry that is dynamic, that calls for action, tense emotions, and therefore more rapid rate.

PROBLEMS OF FLUENCY

Hypertense Nonfluency. If you tend to become over-tense in the speech situation, you are hypertense. Attending symptoms are shortness of breath, high pitch, harsh attack, excessive intensity, rapid rate, clipped speech, and very little pause. You may display several or all of these characteristics. The end effect is that words and ideas tend to "jam the circuit." You may try the following assignments:

1. Practice reading daily lyric poetry or prose that appeals to you. The rhythm of the material will help you establish nervous order.

2. Try reading poetry to low background music that seems to fit the mood. These assignments not only have a carrry-over effect but bring to your consciousness the kinesthetic sense of coordinated speech.

3. As you approach tense situations, utilize a soft attack on sounds. Not only does a soft answer turn away wrath, but it inhibits the building up of internal tensions that result in arhythmical speech. As you proceed with an "easy" approach to speech, a coordination of speech elements takes place. Practice your speeches with this soft attack in order to condition your nervous system to the way it feels. You cannot expect to learn the technique under pressure.

4. See the assignments for hypertension on pages 392–394.

Hypotense Nonfluency. The person who controls his fear responses by over-relaxing often dulls his processes to the point where he loses rhythm. The attending symptoms are low monopitch, low intensity, long pauses, aspirate and sometimes hoarse voice.

1. Practice your speeches daily with energy and hard attack.
2. Use the assignments designed for extremely slow rate, page 328.
3. Use the assignments designed for hypotension in Chapter 19, pages 393–394.

PROBLEMS OF QUALITY

Breathy or Aspirate Voice. If you waste air as you speak, giving the voice a breathy, whispery, or aspirate quality, the physical cause is improper closure of the vocal cords. Breathy quality, not always unpleasant to the ear, is produced either by permitting too much air to escape before phonation or by permitting an excessive amount of air to escape during phonation. A lag of more than one-hundredth of a second in the closing of the vocal folds will give a breathy effect.[10] Usually breathy speech has a glottal opening two and one-third times as wide, at the point of greatest opening, as normal speech.[11]

It is obvious that breathy voice involves the interaction of breathing and phonation. Since the attack of the vocal folds upon the air is soft, and since air pressure is partly wasted, the intensity of breathy speech is usually low. The reason for speaking this way is not always clear. Imitation, a confidential attitude, poor self-hearing, admiration of a soft voice, early criticism for speaking harshly, a "tip-toeing" personality,[12] and physical condition are among the possible explanations.

1. Try reading as long as you can before you run out of breath. Note that near the end of this span you produce more sound per unit of air than at the beginning. Indeed, you will reach a point where there is decided raspiness or glottal click in the sound.

2. As you become sensitive to the muscular set for the conservation of air try reading a sentence, (*a*) in a whisper, (*b*) as you normally do, (*c*) at a point where you get the maximum volume at the minimum expenditure of air. Record these efforts and listen to them. This will tell you whether you are approximating in the third effort the kind of phonation you want. It is important to recognize that you will not like the feel of it. Only by hearing can you determine the wisdom of the change. If you are in doubt, have your instructor listen with you

10 Robert Curry, *The Mechanism of the Human Voice*, New York, Longmans Green and Company, 1940, p. 64.

11 William W. Fletcher, "A High Speed Motion Picture Study of Vocal Fold Action in Certain Voice Qualities," M.A. Thesis, University of Washington, 1947.

12 Wilbur E. Moore, "Personality Traits and Voice Quality Deficiencies," *Journal of Speech and Hearing Disorders*, Vol. IV, 1939, pp. 33–36.

and help you in your judgments. Once you locate the proper vocal tension, you must practice a few minutes daily, alternating, from word to word, the old and new habits. As you learn to adjust accurately from word to word, try alternating from phrase to phrase, then from sentence to sentence.

3. When you locate the desired voice at will, practice reading with varied inflections and force in order to stabilize the habit in flexible speech.
4. Increased volume counteracts breathiness. Work with the exercises for increasing intensity, pages 324–326.
5. Besides carrying out these exercises, you need to examine your attitudes to see if you have an urge to speak in an aspirate fashion. If so, talk it out with yourself to see if the attitude is desirable. In the end, if the attitude persists there will be no change in the voice. Or if there is, it will be a "speechy" change.
6. If in your practice you find it impossible to become less breathy, you should consult your instructor on the advisability of a physical examination of the vocal cords.

Throaty Voice. As the word suggests, a throaty voice over-emphasizes throat resonance. It is attractive to the owner of the voice because throaty sounds, low in pitch, are usually pleasant in self-hearing. It is only by listening to a recording of his voice that the speaker understands the unpleasant effect on others. Throatiness is more common among men than women, for we tend to identify the deep voice with masculinity. During puberty the male voice often deepens dramatically, and if the boy associates this new quality with his introduction to manhood, the habit of throatiness is easily established. As might be suspected from the foregoing, throatiness is generally associated with dominance.[13] Sometimes, however, it is adopted by the person who feels the need for more dominance, a need to hold others at bay. In this case he generally shows a number of defensive and inhibiting mannerisms along with throatiness. The throaty speaker often has aggressive attitudes and values.

Throatiness takes four related forms, guttural, glottal, orotund, or metallic. The voice may be guttural, as in the movie stereotype of the "tough guy." The speaker usually does not breathe deeply. Though not particularly tense, he is on guard and ready for a quick breath for emergency action. Second, if he relaxes too much for the

[13] Wilbur E. Moore, "Personality Traits and Voice Quality Deficiencies," *Journal of Speech and Hearing Disorders*, Vol. IV, 1939, pp. 33–36.

air pressure, or talks on residual air, the distinguishing element of the quality shifts from a guttural to a gravelly sound. The edges of the vocal folds act to produce the glottal fry or glottal click. Third, if the speaker takes a deep breath and adjusts the muscles of the throat to get a big full-throated quality, the voice, called orotund, takes on the quality we think of as oratorical. There was a time when it was popular for radio announcers to cultivate this quality. Finally, when throaty resonance is accompanied by a great deal of muscular tension, the quality is identified as harsh, metallic, or strident.

The following exercises are useful for all types of throatiness:

1. At the beginning of each daily practice session, do the exercises for relaxing, page 320.
2. Vocalize a sigh several times at each daily practice session.
3. Chant a few vowels (ä, ä, ä; ă, ă, ă; ē, ē, ē; ōo) for several minutes. Fade back and forth between chanting and singing the vowels.
4. In daily practice sessions before the mirror, speak with attention to opening the mouth wider, both laterally and vertically.
5. Work on the exercises for raising pitch, pages 321–323.
6. Experiment with altering the muscle tension of the throat. This can be done by imitating the voice qualities of other people, particularly those whose speech is just the opposite of your own. A thin mouthy voice or a weak nasal voice enforces muscle tensions considerably different from throatiness. As you learn to imitate voice qualities, you achieve discrimination by ear and sensation as well as control of the muscles involved in the desired change. Record these imitations frequently to check your accuracy.
7. After you have learned to discriminate between vocal extremes, imitate what you think is a desired quality. Record it and compare it with your throaty voice. Read from phrase to phrase, changing from the throaty to the desired quality. Record and study.
8. Practice reading pleasant, outgoing, warm poetry and prose.
9. Give a speech in which your basic purpose is to gain good will. Choose a topic and point of view likely to clash with the audience attitudes. Instruct your audience to show disapproval at any moment you arouse negative attitudes. Then try earnestly to gain their approval. The direction of this self-adjustment is opposed to throatiness.
10. Play the role of trying to placate the anger of an irate superior or an indignant customer.

11. Lead a discussion on a controversial topic in which your purpose is to bring the group to a conclusion on a course of action that all will subscribe to. It may be well to record the discussion and listen to it for your successes and failures in the role. Analyze the voice qualities attending these successes and failures.

Guttural Voice. A throaty voice which may be described as guttural is often produced in part by depressing the chin against the throat. If your speech has this quality you should in addition to the assignments above:

1. Check your posture and stand erect in your daily practice sessions.
2. Watch the mirror and speak alternately with your head depressed and held up.
3. Practice consciously holding your chin down and back for a few minutes a day until the learned muscle tension gives you a cue when you are speaking gutturally.

Glottal Fry or Gravel Voice. The causes of glottal fry are many. Extreme weariness, ill health, hypotension, imitation, defensiveness, and desire for a low voice, are the most common causes. Probably the first three account for the occurrence of this type of voice among women, though any of these causes may explain the fault in men. It is true that women often strive for low voices. When they do, their purpose is a pleasant voice; most women, therefore, are sensitive to vocal fry and adjust to avoid it. But to men who want depth of voice, the roughness of glottal dissonance may seem to make for greater depth and "manliness." As with any behavior, the habit may persist after the cause is dead. You should practice daily the following exercises to eliminate glottal fry.

1. Read or speak for a ten-minute practice period more energetically than is your custom. This should reinforce the pitch-raising exercises and lift your pitch level three or four tones, thereby producing muscle tension in which the "fry" is impossible.
2. Practice reading a sentence, (*a*) in a whisper, (*b*) in a breathy vocalized tone, (*c*) in your usual manner. As suggested for the breathy person, record these three voices and analyze them. Experiment, record, and listen until you find that tension which produces the "right" sound. Practice alternating the tension until you can produce, at will, the vocal tension you want.

3. Practice reading and speaking with a variety of inflections and intensities to test your capacity to maintain the tension that eliminates the fault.

Orotund Voice. The orotund is the voice with its biggest, fullest, and richest resonance. Since it is bigger than the normal, it seems pompous to modern tastes. The orotund voice rightfully belongs to the hero in the battle of giants. Democratic concepts do not idealize leaders to such godlike proportions. The orotund orator therefore belongs to a past age, and those who adopt the style do not generally fare well today. The orotund speaker usually develops an attending grandiloquent vocabulary and sentence structure.

If evaluation suggests that you tend (perhaps by limitation) to be orotund in normal situations:

1. Prepare a speech in which your major purpose is to gain the good will of the audience. Choose a topic and point of view that you know is likely to clash with audience attitudes. Instruct your audience to show disapproval at any moment you arouse a negative attitude. Then try earnestly to gain their approval. The direction of this adjustment will alter your quality accordingly.

2. Lead a discussion on a controversial topic in which your purpose is to bring the group to a conclusion that all will agree to.

3. Act out the role of asking for a job.

4. Act the role of placating the anger of an irate superior or an indignant customer.

5. In public speech situations stand close to the audience.

Metallic or Harsh Voice. Van Dusen says that 27 per cent of voices are judged as metallic, cutting, piercing, harsh, strident.[14] In women this means a voice with few overtones. The male quality that is judged to be metallic shows a great deal of its energy in the high overtones. There appear to be two conditions that produce metallic voice. The larynx is usually raised up under the hyoid, a U-shaped bone directly above the larynx.[15] When this happens the false vocal folds are pressed down on the true folds. Only a small strip of the vocal fold is then free to vibrate, so that the deeper tones are not developed.

14 Clarence R. Van Dusen, "Laboratory Study of Metallic Voices," *Journal of Speech and Hearing Disorders*, December, 1941, pp. 137–140.

15 G. O. Russell, "Physiological Causes of Guttural and Piercing Deaf Voices," *Oralism and Auralism*, July, 1929.

If your voice is metallic in quality, in addition to the general assignments for throatiness:

1. Stand before the mirror and note the tendency to raise the larynx when you speak. Experiment with other voice qualities to find muscle action that does not raise the larynx. Record and listen daily. Practice the vocal qualities that alternately raise and lower the larynx until you can raise or lower it at will.

2. Harshness is generally associated with hard attack. Therefore practice and record its opposite, a whispery voice. When you can alternate easily between your normal voice and the whispery one, try "hitting" the normal quality between the two. Record your efforts, listen, and repeat until you can use all three voices at will. Try alternating among these first with sounds, then words, then phrases and sentences. When you know the muscle tension of the right voice, try it in a class speech. Test it under adverse conditions.

3. Harshness is often associated with rapid rate. Therefore practice the exercises for rapid speech, page 327, if this is your problem.

Hoarseness. The hoarse voice is usually a combination of the breathy and the harsh voice. It can be produced by the phonation of the false vocal folds. The quality is associated with muscular constriction at the root of the tongue, just above the larynx and the back pharyngeal wall. The pitch, unusually low, may be one cause of hoarseness, for low pitch requires greater intensity than normal speech which, in turn, causes greater tension and additional air. Laryngitis and continued irritations of the vocal folds may cause it. A check for physical causes should be made before it is treated as a functional disorder. As Van Riper points out, persistent strenuous exercise may cause hoarseness, for great muscular effort requires a rigid thorax.[16] This condition can be produced only by an excessively tight closure of the glottis. However, Williamson found that of seventy-two cases an extremely small percentage showed any physical causes.[17]

Often undue admiration of low voice and emotional adjustment are involved.[18] Shyness, self-consciousness, and feelings of inadequacy can

[16] Charles Van Riper, *Speech Correction, Principles and Methods,* Third Edition, New York, Prentice-Hall, Inc., 1954, pp. 321–323.

[17] Arleigh B. Williamson, "Diagnosis and Treatment of Seventy-two Cases of Hoarse Voice," *Quarterly Journal of Speech,* April, 1945, pp. 189–202.

[18] Melba Hurd Duncan, "Personality Adjustment Techniques in Voice Therapy," *Journal of Speech and Hearing Disorders,* Vol. 12, 1947, pp. 161–167.

also cause hoarseness. When physiological reasons are ruled out the following assignments may be used:

1. Study Chapter 19 for information and suggestions pertinent to your attitudes.
2. Work on the assignments for relaxing tension, page 320.
3. Work on the assignments for raising the voice, pages 321–323.
4. To locate the quality desired, place the tip of your tongue behind the lower front teeth and say, "ah." Since hoarseness involves constriction of the root of the tongue and the adjacent pharyngeal wall, this exercise, if you are relaxed, should start you in the right direction. Practice alternately with "ah" the other vowels in a chanting fashion.
5. Imitate other voice qualities to readjust the muscular tensions and to give you hearing and kinesthetic discriminations. Record and study the results. Then practice imitating the breathy and harsh voices. Record and study. Alternate practice between the two until you do either with assurance. Then repeat vowels aspirately, harshly, and half way between the two (see exercise 4 above). Record and study. When you locate normal quality, practice it alternately with the other two qualities until it is fixed, first with vowels, then syllables, words, and short sentences.
6. Read poetry or prose of outgoing, friendly, and generous tone.
7. Carry on a conversation with a classmate who speaks in a hoarse voice.
8. Take part in interviews. Try playing cooperative, submissive, and aggressive roles. Which is the easiest to play and maintain the desired voice? Repeat it. Try the more difficult roles as you progress.

Nasal Voice. The nasal voice may be characterized as "twangy." The quality is caused by adjusting the musculature of the resonators so that there is a larger opening between the velum and the nasal pharyngeal wall (8.8 mm) than between the velum and the tongue (3.1 mm). The opening to the nasal passages is almost three times as great as the opening to the mouth. In normal speech the opening to the nose is 1 millimeter while the mouth opening is 11.[19] This means nasal speech is produced in part by a muted throat opening to the mouth; that is, the tongue is pulled back and up. The correction for nasal speech, in part then, calls for a lowering of the tongue

[19] Arthur Kaltenborn, Jr., "An X-ray Study of the Velopharyngeal Closure in Nasal and Non-Nasal Speakers," M.A. Thesis, Northwestern University, 1948.

in the mouth. Along with this, the mouth needs to be opened more widely.[20] Nasal speech is spoken between nearly closed teeth, which at the open position are often only one-eighth of an inch apart. In normal speech the opening is twice this or about one-quarter of an inch. The guide to these muscular changes is listening, and devices for its improvement are proposed in the assignments.

The tensions that produce the resonator openings peculiar to nasality also affect the action of the vocal folds. The folds in hyper-nasalization are slower and more abrupt in opening, the glottis is slanted to one side, so that there is a difference in the width of the folds.[21] Williamson found that in almost all cases of nasal speech the breathing was shallow, compensated by resonator tensions to secure the needed intensity. This entire description indicates that the peculiar character of nasality is abnormal tension throughout the vocal musculature. Nasality is not basically a problem of eliminating or perhaps even reducing nasal resonance. It is essentially a case of eliminating constriction so as to produce pleasant nasal resonance.

In certain areas, particularly in the Midwest and New England, a certain amount of nasality is characteristic and therefore normal. It is different in the two regions, however. In the Midwest, nasalization is assimilative, that is, it takes place with vowels preceding and following *m*, *n*, and *ng*, sounds that are nasal by nature. The typical Midwesterner therefore nasalizes "my," but not "I" or "cry." But nasalization in New England is complete, giving a twanginess to all vowels. We are usually most comfortable if we speak like our neighbors, so that nasalization needs correction only in so far as we sound different from the people we talk with.

Aside from the environmental force that causes us to nasalize, emotional attitudes may accentuate the quality. Both primitive speech and the speech of childhood are characterized by nasality, so that "whiny" nasalization is often characteristic of a person under the urge to be more irresponsible and dependent. Here again the habit may long outlive the need.

The physics of nasality is a matter of overtones. The nasal sound spreads its energy over a wider span of frequencies than does the non-

[20] Aleigh B. Williamson, "Diagnosis and Treatment of Eighty-Four Cases of Nasality," *Quarterly Journal of Speech*, Vol. 30, 1944, pp. 471–479.

[21] William W. Fletcher, "A High Speed Motion Picture Study of Vocal Fold Action in Certain Voice Qualities," M.A. Thesis, University of Washington, 1947.

nazalized sound, and emphasizes especially those frequencies between 1000 and 2000 cycles.

Since nasality is the accentuation of overtones resonated in the nose, it is commonly believed that nasal quality and the nasal emission of air in speech are two symptoms of the same thing, though voice scientists have known for a long time that it is possible to have nasal speech without nasal emission. Recent study suggests that there is no relation between the two phenomena.[22] The cold mirror under the nose is therefore a questionable monitor of nasality. The following exercises may be recommended:

1. Since tensions attend nasality, you should practice relaxation, particularly using those exercises suggested on page 320.
2. Blowing up a balloon or playing a wind instrument tends to emphasize the muscular action that allows mouth opening to exceed nasal opening. These exercises also excite deeper breathing. In blowing a balloon, let the air escape (if you do not have a cold) back into the mouth and then dam the air by glottal and velar closure. This will sensitize you to the nature of velar closure. To practice a very hard explosion of the *k* sound produces a similar sensitivity.
3. In searching for the proper quality, select that vowel, with the help of your instructor, which in your speech is least stabilized, which you sometimes over-nasalize and sometimes do not. Place your tongue low in your mouth with the tip behind the lower front teeth. Open your mouth wide. Say the vowel for a prolonged period, adjusting the above positions only to the degree necessary for its production. Record and listen with a competent helper to determine whether the vowel has the desired quality.
4. Alternate saying nasalized and non-nasalized sounds until you sensitize yourself to the difference: *m, o, n, e, ng, i, m, b, n, d, ng, g.* This sense of difference is the key to making desired changes in oral and nasal resonance.
5. Imitate throaty and "mouthy" speech in order to produce both hearing and kinesthetic discrimination. Record these samples and study them.
6. Have your roommate or a classmate produce various vocal qualities for a given phrase. Then imitate him. Have him help you decide your successes and failures in imitation.

[22] Jack Bensen, "An Experimental Study of Relationships Between Amount of Nasal Emission of Air and Judged Nasality," M.A. Thesis, West Virginia University, 1951.

7. Record, trying alternately to nasalize and de-nasalize, first a single vowel, then a vowel with a consonant, then words without nasals (*m, n,* and *ng*), then words with nasals in them, then short sentences without nasals, such as "This is good," then sentences with nasals, such as "Time is fleeting." Words with nasals, of course, must be nasalized. The problem is not to eliminate nasalization, but to use it pleasantly and to the degree acceptable in your environment. Study your recordings. Repeat daily the successful efforts in order to establish habits. Repeat, with the effort to change unsuccessful combinations.
8. Bullen believes that emphasis should be placed upon the sharpening of the plosives (*p, b, t, d, k, g, ch,* etc.).[23] Work on the exercises for articulation, pages 339–342.
9. After you have learned how to discriminate and manipulate the quality in isolated sounds and words, practice interviews and conversations with a person who speaks nasally. Usually the mirror of your fault helps to reinforce the quality you are trying to develop.

Denasal Voice. Voice without adequate nasal resonance is that which we stereotype as the voice of a person with a head cold. It may be caused by an obstruction in the nasal passages, in which case the problem is one for the physician or surgeon, though often such speech persists after a physical correction has been made. For correction Van Riper recommends:[24]

1. The snorting of vowels and the nasalization of all speech in order to direct the musculature to include nasal resonance.
2. Humming with and without closing the nose with the thumb and forefinger.
3. With the opposite objective in view, practice daily exercise 5 under nasalization.
4. Work on the articulation assignments, pages 339–342.
5. Practice conversations and interviews with a person who speaks without adequate nasalization. This mirror of your error will steer you.

Oral Voice. An oral or "mouthy" voice is one that over-emphasizes the mouth resonance. As Weaver points out, this kind of speech is

weak and ineffective. Usually it indicates a lack of emotion. It is practically impossible for anyone to feel deeply and at the same time speak

[23] Adaline Bullen, "Nasality: Cause and Remedy of Our American Blight," *Quarterly Journal of Speech,* February, 1942, Vol. 28, pp. 83–84.
[24] Charles Van Riper, *Speech Correction, Principles and Methods,* Third Edition, New York, Prentice-Hall, Inc., 1954, p. 318.

in his oral quality, which suggests affectation, boredom, and ennui. . . .
It has one virtue only; it is likely to be clear and coupled with good
articulation. It always lacks volume and power.[25]

As suggested by the above description the oral quality is a mark of
self-concern and withdrawal.

This may all sound paradoxical. We advocate good articulation
and correction of throatiness and nasality; yet we deplore this highly
corrected speech. The point is that mouthy speech is proper, formal,
and weightless. This over-emphasis on propriety indicates that virile
energy in communication has been supplemented by correct form —
which, in the end, is all wrong.

For those who have this self-conscious withdrawing way of speaking,
we recommend the following:

1. Give careful attention to Chapters 18 through 21.
2. Take part in a discussion with one of two purposes. Try to further a
   point of view that seems highly important to you. This aggressive position is opposed to the oral quality. Or, try to establish a group spirit
   among the discussants, to work for common agreement. This attitude
   also is opposed to oral quality.
3. In interviews you may play comparable roles — say, a superior giving
   orders or a social worker investigating a hardship case.
4. Prepare a speech, pleading a cause or denouncing a social ill.
5. Imitate nasal and throaty speech, as well as your oral quality, in order
   to get the feel of the muscle-set you are trying to eliminate. Imitate
   the postures of these kinds of speech. This will help fix your quality
   in mind. Record these efforts and listen carefully. When you feel you
   sense the character of these distinctive types, prepare a few comments
   on a topic that you would like others to appreciate. Record them. Are
   you able to hear the desire to be understood, or do you still hear that
   formal correct diction? In your practice, try speaking on a public address system. If you search for change, guided by the desire to communicate with others, the oral quality will give way to vigorous speech.

PROBLEMS OF ARTICULATION

In the discussion of articulation (pages 258–265) we pointed out
that inaccurate use of the articulators or over-precise usage was faulty.
We offer the following assignments under separate headings:

[25] Andrew T. Weaver, *Speech Forms and Principles*, First Edition, New York,
Longmans, Green and Company, 1942, p 206.

Inaccurate Articulation

1. If you are criticized for unclear speech, you should ask for an appointment with your instructor to determine whether your speech is generally mushy, or faulty on particular sounds.

2. Probably your greatest need is ear training. Record your voice in as nearly normal a speech situation as possible and study it. With the aid of your instructor determine whether you can identify the faulty sounds.

If you have trouble with only one or a few sounds, concentrate on one sound at a time, preferably starting with the one on which you are least stable. This very instability means that it is amenable to change. When you have gone through the following procedure and reached the point where you can at will pronounce the sound by itself, at the beginning, middle, and end of words, and in continuous speech, move on to the next sound.

1. Have the instructor explain how the sound is formed by most people. Study a diagram of the articulators in the set which produces the sound. Write a paper explaining how the sound is produced. Have the instructor check the paper for accuracy.

2. Practice the faulty sounds in isolation, in words, in phrases, and in sentences. Record the efforts and compare them. Have a competent person listen with you to see if your corrections are accurate or are moving in the right direction. In this study determine at what level you should first concentrate. It is, of course, easier to correct the sound in isolation. If you cannot produce it correctly, then this is the place to start. If you can say the sound accurately in isolation, move on to individual words.

3. At whatever level you have difficulty with the sound, say it as accurately as you can. Have your helper say it accurately right after you. Record a series of these repetitions. Listen and compare them.

4. If you still cannot hear the difference, try saying the troublesome sound three different ways. Record and listen for the difference. With the aid of another person try to determine which of the three efforts is more accurate. If you have trouble changing, try some babbling for a few minutes. See how many sounds and combinations of sounds you can make that have no meaning to you. Simply waggle your tongue around in your mouth and change the shape and size of mouth and lips. For the utmost freedom, do this by yourself and where no one can hear you. Now try saying your faulty sound in three different ways as above suggested.

5. When you hit the target and say the sound correctly, or nearly so, in these practice sessions have your helper give you a signal. At this signal freeze and repeat the sound over and over.

6. At whatever level you are working now, say the sound alternately as it should be and as you have been saying it. Record these efforts and study them.

If your speech is not particularly inaccurate on particular sounds but is generally unprecise by usual standards, you may work on the following. Those who have had difficulty with individual sounds may also practice the following after mastering the above drills.

1. Under-emphasized speech tends to be less intelligible than stressed speech.[26] Give a speech in which you have a reason for getting your point across. Choose the subject because it concerns an important conviction or because you know that the idea is difficult to communicate. Prepare it carefully from the standpoint of arrangement and evidence. Practice the delivery with particular attention to proper emphases. You will find an energetic effort will sharpen your diction. The increasing of sound duration and intensity, motivated by the assignment, will add to your intelligibility.[27]

2. In the preparation and delivery of a speech, pay particular attention to slowing your rate. Improved articulation attends the slower rate.[28]

3. Use a masking noise in practice sessions and occasionally in the speech situation. This demands more energetic action of all the vocal muscles, prolongs your sounds, and increases your intensity, all of which improve intelligibility.[29] A word of caution is probably in order. Quite often the person with poor diction has the attitude that he cannot interest his audience. This feeling, that his communication does not get a response, is a restraint that helps produce poor articulation. If the masking sound in the classroom situation makes you feel that you are less able to make your impact on the audience, you should use the technique in practice only.

[26] L. Baker and J. S. Harris, "The Validation of Rorschach Test Results Against Laboratory Behavior," *Journal of Clinical Psychology*, 1949, Vol. 5, pp. 161–164.

[27] Gayland L. Draegert, "Relationships Between Voice Variables and Speech Intelligibility in High Level Noise," *Speech Monographs*, November, 1951, pp. 272–278.

[28] John W. Black, "Precision of Articulation in Repeated Phrases," *The Central States Speech Journal*, Vol. 1, November, 1949, pp. 8–11.

[29] James C. Kelly, "Effect of Training in Voice Communication Through Synthetic Noise Barriers," Ph.D. Thesis, Purdue University, 1948; Gayland L. Draegert, "Intelligibility Related to Articulation," *Speech Monographs*, Vol. XIII, No. 2, 1946, pp. 50–54.

4. Practice talking with cotton in the ears or a finger closing each ear. This decreasing of the side-tone not only alters self-hearing but increases kinesthetic sensitivity. Record your speech under these circumstances. Some students become more precise, others less, depending upon whether they respond to or try to lessen the sensation of feeling the formation of sounds.

5. Practice speaking in a whisper. This stimulates more active use of all the speech mechanism, and is particularly effective in improving the stop consonants *p, b, t, d, k, g, j,* and *ch.* (This device may be used with closed ears.) After you have begun to respond more energetically, speak alternate sentences with the device. Record and study, to determine whether you are sharpening your diction. It is highly important to learn by kinesthetic sensation and by hearing when you are speaking precisely enough.

6. Speak before a mirror. Those who articulate poorly often do not open the mouth wide enough. Your teeth ought to part at least a quarter of an inch in the open position. The muscles about the mouth should be relaxed and flexible. If they are not, practice tongue and lip exercises as well as babbling. See exercise 4, page 340. Try normal speech again and study your face in the mirror.

7. If in the mirror you notice that you talk out of one side of your mouth, place a pencil or pipe in the side you speak out of, and practice talking. This will enforce the action of the unused side.

8. When the present cause of poor articulation is habit, the foregoing exercises produce favorable and lasting results in a semester of daily practice. If you are driven to speak inaccurately by tensions and attitudes, you should in addition to the above work go to Chapter 19.

Part Five

Speech and Personality

———

The crux of mental health rests upon one's beliefs, and the ability to integrate his conflicts around a master sentiment that points beyond immediate and self-centered gratification to larger relationships, more decisive action and deeper assurance in the realization of permanent values.

Gordon W. Allport

18

Speech and the Self

IN CHAPTER 2 we pointed out that the first step in scanning is to get the feeling of the machine with which you work. The beginning golfer has little notion what he is in for until he takes up a club, gets the feel of its weight, balance, and of the way it affects him as he begins swinging. But he then almost unconsciously gets some idea of how to go about hitting the ball. We need to get this "feel of the machine" in speech also, and because we are dealing with something less tangible than a golf club, the task is the more difficult.

Speech and the Whole Person

The difficulty comes into sharp relief when beginning students are asked what speech is. Usually they conceive of it as spoken words plus gestures, with the emphasis on words. They generally find it hard to think of talk as all the meaning produced by the body. Yet we refer to deaf and dumb "speech." We all recognize that we receive important messages by a lift of the eybrows, a hesitation, a turn of the head, a "blank stare," a set of the facial muscles that preludes screaming, weeping, or cursing, a random searching movement of the hands, a listless, bowed, or energetic walk, a sigh, or a tremulous, booming, or rasping voice. These and a host of other signals sent by the body — all directed by "thinking" — are a part of speech. Speech is all "language which man produces *without resorting to agencies outside of his own organism.*" [1]

If such is the scope of speech, it follows that the study of speech

[1] Jon Eisenson, *The Psychology of Speech*, F. S. Crofts and Company, New York, 1947, p. 5.

is the study of man. Yet even with the recognition that speech involves the whole person, we may have but a vague idea of the speech
machinery. Until we gain a picture of ourselves which takes in everything that affects the listener, we are merely lucky if we handle ourselves well.

The purpose of this chapter, and the ones that follow, is to describe
the self, the person. The result will be that as you gain a more definite
picture of what you, the speaker, are, you will *hear* the *difference*
between your present speech and the speech you are trying to attain.

Uncertainty about this difference is indicated by such questions as,
"What will they think of me if I talk about myself?" "Am I talking
to myself or are they interested?" "Am I too dogmatic?" "Do other
people think so?" You will develop good speech about as fast as you
attain a stable and acceptable picture of a proper self.

What Is the Self?

A proper picture of the self comes into focus if we keep in mind
the following point of view. A person is motivated healthfully only
as a part of society. Yet he is a *self-centered creature in that social
whole.* There is nothing cynical about this observation. The blending
of self and society into one whole is a natural process. The ears hear
both self and others from almost the beginning.

It is of the first importance to keep in mind that if one is going
to express words and actions, perforce he is going to express himself.[2]
Consequently it follows that all of one's behavior is motivated by
the need for self-approval. Because of the tendency to overlook these
plain facts, the words "selfish" and "selfless" are unfortunate. This is
not to deny the existence of selfish behavior; it is all too apparent,
even in those who deplore it. By selfishness, we here mean self-
expression that restrains another's self-expression. But selflessness is
the really disturbing concept. Selfless action simply does not exist,
except in slaves.

Part of our trouble with these words is a matter of language. Most
of what we in Western culture identify as "other," the Wintu Indian
identifies as a part of the self.[3] This is a remarkable notion to us.

---

[2] G. Adler, "Notes Regarding the Dynamics of the Self," *British Journal of
Medical Psychology*, 1951, Vol. 24, pp. 97–106; Bonaro W. Overstreet, *Under-
standing Fear in Ourselves and Others*, New York, Harper and Brothers, 1951,
Chapter 3.

[3] Dorothy Lee, "Notes on the Conception of the Self Among Wintu Indians,"
Journal of Abnormal Social Psychology, 1950, Vol. 45, pp. 538–543.

To the Wintu, "self" is his physical being, but it is also much more. It is all that he has come in contact with. He quite naturally sees that

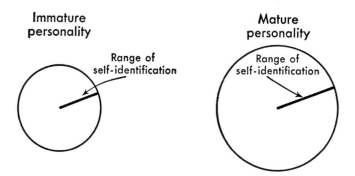

poise, self-confidence, and self-satisfaction rest in ever expanding identifications of the "self" with the people he talks to. While this is basic in our behavior too, our language, with its "self" and "other," masks the essential unity of the two. Since the Wintu does not sense this difference, he obviously has less trouble getting himself into harmony with his society.

Ways of Looking at the Self

The self may be defined in three ways, which show how impossible it is even in definition to separate a person from other persons.

1. Personality is a person's total reactive capacity, the ways he responds to others and to the situations he meets. From this point of view the person is everything he says and does.

2. Personality is the meaning others gain from a person's speech. From this point of view the emphasis is not so much upon what the behavior is, as upon what other people say it is. The writer recalls hearing a girl seriously criticized by a speech instructor for not thinking in a speech. "You were just saying words. You were not thinking at all," said the instructor.

"But that couldn't be," replied the student. "I had never given that speech before; I had to be thinking."

After some discussion of the point, the teacher spoke with finality, "But I didn't know you were thinking. It therefore did not stir me to think with you. I don't care what you were doing that I didn't know about. If you didn't reveal you were thinking, so far as I am concerned you were not thinking."

Here personality was interpreted in terms of what was communicated.

3. Neither of the foregoing definitions is analytical. Allport explains that personality is "The dynamic organization within the individual of those psychological systems that determine his unique adjustments to his environment." [4] Such a point of view sees a person as a "solid organization" of traits. The peculiar combination of these give a person his individuality, his style, his "personal idiom."

Some of the personality traits implied in the above definition are: ascendance or dominance, emotional breadth, emotional strength, emotional stability, esthetic appreciation, talkativeness, humor, gregariousness, insight, intelligence, introversion, extroversion, radicalism, social adaptability, conceit, suggestibility, masculinity, femininity, religious interest, economic interest, theoretical interest, will to power, vitality, persistence, tact, curiosity, impulsiveness, and reliability. One could list many more.

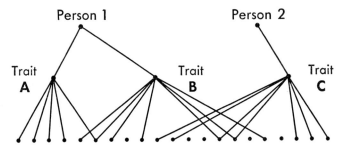

Each of these is itself a complex, so that a trait analysis does not communicate the precise behavior of a man. Perhaps the diagram explains the idea. The dots represent the speech or other specific acts of a person. To tell accurately what a person is, is to tell what he does, to present a complete movie of his life. But total description is not understanding. The opposite extreme is to say, "Joe's a good Joe," or "I don't like him." This is too crude, for it divides people into just two classes. Between these extremes is the trait approach to analysis.

[4] *Personality, a Psychological Interpretation*, New York, Henry Holt and Company, Inc., 1949, pp. 47–48.

We use this method in our daily affairs. "I don't know. I can't quite figure him out. He's pretty smart, but he doesn't stick to anything. Boy! Does he have a temper! Most of the time he has a good sense of humor, though he doesn't talk very much. Sure is good-hearted. . . ." The wisdom of the workable becomes the basis of our analysis. If you keep an open mind and carefully appraise any personality inventories, student ratings, self ratings, and instructor ratings that may be incorporated into your course, you may "hear" yourself better.

WHAT WE ARE JUDGED BY

People judge us by our appearance, actions, voice, intelligence, temperament, beliefs, and attitudes. These are the aspects of our personalities we want first to become acquainted with.

Appearance

It is obvious that appearance is of prime importance in first impressions. We tend to ascribe to large people more prestige, authority, and leadership than we do to small ones. We classify people as intelligent or dull, good-natured or irritable by what we see. It is of the first importance to remember that because we tend to type people, each of us learns unconsciously to respond in harmony with the type into which he is cast. You can tell how you have been typed by the roles people ask you to play. Are you looked upon as easy-going, hard to approach, energetic, languid, strong, weak, intelligent, sociable? How much of this appraisal is the result of your appearance?

Since "looks" come without effort, the person who is handsomely endowed is likely to coast on his good looks. As a result it is not uncommon for the more animated to be less blessed by nature. And appearance is often a matter of grooming and dress as much as it is of native endowment. Good taste in clothes and proper grooming are most important.

What response do you have to your grooming before you meet the speech situation? Does your dress aid or disturb you?

Action

Closely allied to appearance is action. Indeed, action is living, moving appearance. If you will for the moment let your mind drift to a picture of the first well-known person that appears upon your "memory screen," you will sense that his individuality and your attitude toward him cannot be separated from his movement. By movement we mean the total symphony of action, the way the whole body organizes itself about a bit of purposeful motion. Walking is just placing one foot ahead of the other, yet the variation in timing and the coordination of all the muscular movements involved in a single step give each man his personal idiom. A man pours himself into his walk, as indeed into all his actions. The way we balance our weight as we stand, take hold of a pencil, or purse our lips in thought gives each of us distinction. Our action is important, not only to the listener, but also to ourselves.

What feedback do you have to your actions? What do others say?

Voice

Your voice also is the shape of your personality. Your body takes the set of your internal world, and your voice, which is part of your body, takes the set of your body. If a truck bears down on you, your body becomes like one tense muscle — and you scream, not yawn. Likewise, when you know and believe what you are saying, your body and voice suggest a major key. If you doubt what you are saying, your body and voice reflect indefiniteness. As you move from sadness to joy, from joy to meditation, from meditation to decision, your voice moves with you.

How do you hear yourself? What do others say they learn from your voice? The recording machine is the mirror of the voice. The student of speech should use it frequently.

Intelligence

Much of what a person is, and, of course, much of what he means to others, is determined by his intelligence. Intelligence involves sensitivity, alertness to and interpretation of the world around one. Sensitivity has both breadth and depth, and varies from person to person, from hour to hour, and from activity to activity within the same person.

Two kinds of intelligence are especially related to speech growth — verbal and social. The former, the capacity to use symbols, to arrange them in striking, meaningful, and creative forms, is quite obviously important to speech development. Social intelligence is the other side of self-sensitivity or insight. Insight is a problem to college students. While they are generally considered by psychologists to be relatively poor self-analysts, in one study 96 per cent said they felt they had better than average insight. The fact is, of course, that all of us are in varying degrees blind to our own limitations and even to our finest abilities. Familiarity is not an aid to observation. The test of insight is the correlation between what you think you are and what others think you are. The nearer the two ratings coincide the more insight may be ascribed to you.

Generally accompanying insight is a sense of humor. (In one study the correlation was .88, which is very high.) Humor, says the novelist George Meredith, is the ability to laugh at the things you love most. Allport says it is that emotion which arises when you compare your pretenses with your performance. Humor is, therefore, a matter of seeing yourself as others see you. It should be clear that the quality discussed here is not the sense of the comic, so often built upon the degradation of another. Humor, insight, and language skill are the aspects of intelligence most significant to speech development.

What echo do you have of your intelligence? Can you accept it? What do others think?

Temperament

Of temperament, Allport offers the following definition:

> Temperament refers to the characteristic phenomena of an individual's emotional nature, including his susceptibility to emotional stimulation, his customary strength and speed of response, the quality of his prevailing mood, and all peculiarities of fluctuation and intensity in mood; these phenomena being regarded as dependent upon constitutional make-up and therefore largely hereditary in origin.[5]

The phenomena of temperament have fascinated men since early times. The Greeks divided temperament into four classes: The person of many and intense emotions was labeled *choleric*. The person with a variety of emotions of moderate strength was known as *sanguine*. The person of narrow emotional range but great intensity was called *melancholic*. And the person of few and weak emotions was said to be *phlegmatic*. Temperament refers to characteristic emotional state, and as applied to speech, means especially the degree and range of calmness or irritability expressed.

[5] *Personality, a Psychological Interpretation.* New York, Henry Holt and Company, 1949, p. 54. By permission of the publishers.

Temperament finds its roots in the nervous structure. But it is subject to control in a way appearance and intelligence are not. Hence temperament· is one of the areas in which we find personality virtues

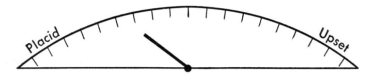

that are isolated and universally admired — particularly such qualities as self-control, patience, and good nature. Note the qualities most commonly cited in speeches in which students talk about people they admire.

Beliefs

Another part of you which powerfully shapes and directs your speech is your beliefs. Belief is the credence, assurance, confidence, or faith shown in an idea. Beliefs rise out of perhaps the most intellectual aspect of thinking, and direct the conscious content of speech.

The cluster of your beliefs determines whether you may be classified as a *radical*, a *conservative*, or a *reactionary*. The radical is one who sees great need of social change; the conservative sees virtue in keeping things as they are; the reactionary would go back to yesterday. Your position between the extremes probably depends upon that point at which you feel most secure. This urge is particularly clear in the radical, the person who calls for change. Security is no less a motive with those who fear change.

We are likely to associate radicalism with instability, but a recent study indicates that it is probably wrong to do so.[6] What is perhaps more important, radicals and reactionaries have more insight into current social problems than do "middle of the roaders" — and no man clearly sees the weakness in his own beliefs.

This is a world of events; all is in motion. Who then is right? He who would stop change defies the order of things, and he who would race events fails to understand the tempo of society. The speaker whose beliefs are adjusted to reality keeps them close to his culture, yet different enough to offer leadership. Even the giants of history have been the instruments of total cultural movements.

[6] H. H. Eysenck, "Primary Social Attitudes and the 'Social Insight' Tests," *British Journal of Psychology*, Vol. 42, 1951, pp. 114–122.

As we have seen, beliefs tend to cluster in such a fashion that we may type people. Spranger divided all men into six classes.[7] (1) The *theoretical*, or thinking person, finds his greatest satisfaction in discovering an idea. (2) The *economic* man stresses material things and therefore directs much of his energy to their acquisition. (3) The *esthetic* channels his energy into artistic creation and appreciation. (4) The *social* lives for contact with other people. (5) The *political* man wants power and thinks of it as the major instrument for solving problems. (6) The *religious* person looks upon all experience in terms of universal purpose. Most of us are complex enough so that several or all of these types are intermixed in us. With Spranger's types as a springboard, we may look into the dominant motives behind the beliefs that shape the speech of most college students.

Possessions. When a student's speech centers on the joy of a vacation in Florida, the luxury of the Waldorf-Astoria, the magnitude of the Lever Brothers Corporation, or the smooth power of a Cadillac, his speech is obviously shaped by the value he attaches to material things. In essence, the attraction to things is the urge for comfort.

America is the industrial nation of the world, a fact which means that our fathers had a strong urge for things. Today the child learns to build his play world around a multitude of toys, and our adult world could not exist without a profusion of gadgets. Through newspapers, magazines, radio, television, and store windows, we are constantly bombarded by stimuli that excite the desire for more. Indeed, it is not the possession of goods that makes peoples materially minded; rather, it is the belief that the absence of things means shame or inadequacy. As individuals we vary considerably in the degree to which worldly goods color our thinking and our speech. That our forefathers, at the price of terrible hardship and a heavy toll of life, swept over and laid possession to a continent in the course of a century, suggests the importance of material wealth to America.

How much does your speech echo the desire for things? What does your listener feed back to you about your urge for things?

Power. Directly related to the value placed on things is the love of power. When men accumulate more than they can use, their pur-

---

[7] Elaard Spranger, *Types of Men.* Description here taken from G. W. Allport, *Personality, a Psychological Interpretation*, New York, Henry Holt and Company, Inc., 1949, pp. 228–230.

pose is to turn these goods into an instrument of power over others.
Yet it is possible to want power through other means than the force
of material wealth. Some men choose politics, shaping and executing
the law that directs the lives of millions. Others strive for intellectual
leadership, and so write books, lecture, analyze the news, predict the
future. Still others turn to society, where smart clothes and proper
language, and being seen with the right people at the right places,
are tools of power.

John's speech is essentially determined by his belief in power. He
lost in a state oratorical contest, receiving the disturbing criticism that
he "slugged his audience." This he could not understand, because he
had just conducted a group of political lieutenants in his community
with considerable success. He said, "I bombarded my workers with
the political information that was given me and they liked it. Now I
find people rebelling against my style." John believes in power just
a bit too much to suit the average American audience.

Does your speech echo the love of power? How does your audience
react to your efforts to influence it?

Prestige. Prestige is power derived from the attention or esteem of
others. Psychologically it reflects the pleasure of viewing oneself in
the mirror of other people. It may be felt on seeing one's name in
the paper, being called upon to speak, having a building or a foundation named for one, being "boss," driving a big car, living in a fine
house, knowing the "right" people. The tools of power and of prestige
overlap, just as do those of power and wealth, or of wealth and prestige.
But there are important differences. Mark Hanna, the dominant
political power of President McKinley's time, was apparently more
concerned with controlling people than with being noticed. A movie
actor may give away the controlling interest in a corporation, losing
both power and wealth, but be anguished when the public ceases
crowding the theatres where his name flashes on the marquee. Often
a business quarrel is solved by creating a new title — supervisor, director, or associate manager — while power and income remain as before.

How much does your speech echo the search for position? What do
your listeners think about your interest in prestige? How do you know
what your listeners think?

The Welfare of Others. Earl brought considerable criticism upon
himself by displaying in speeches general indifference to the experi-

ences most students value. He committed the cardinal sin the day
he admitted that sports bored him, particularly baseball. The audience maintained a negative set toward him until a later impromptu
speech, in which he told of returning to his room one day to find
his roommate sprawled upon the bed, crying. His mother had just died.
In an unadorned description of an impressive moment, Earl explained
how he took over and helped his friend arrange his affairs. The audience responded with genuine warmth, because they valued identifica-
tion with the other fellow.

How much does your speech echo an interest in others? What do
others think of your social concern?

The Value in Belonging. While the American talks a great deal
about his love of independence, what he means is a group independence, and this is what he fought for in 1776. In fact, the American
often hates and fears individual independence, a state of mind which
reflects a dislike of one of the prime conditions of frontier life. In
pioneer days, he had all the physical conditions for the hermit's life —
he had individual independence, and the whole West was open to
him. Yet the more important value was to have others close by for
both companionship and safety. This is reflected in the way, with land
as free as air, he built his home close to his neighbor's. Energies were
concentrated on the building of canals, steamboats, the pony express,
railroads, telegraph lines. The great belief in America has not been
in individual independence but in a community (rich in opportunity)
to which we might belong. We are an affectionate people, a nation
of joiners, a people who fear to be different from our neighbors.

This being our value, American speech is driven to gain a favorable
response from the audience. It is not strange that as American speech
education developed, it built its concepts of persuasion around audience analysis. We need not overlook the fact that part of the energy
used to understand the audience is spent because of desire to control.
Yet if speaker and listener interests are at variance, the average American will compromise his own purposes in preference to maintaining
a course that encourages boos. Indeed, rejection is considered such a
serious penalty that the American audience is slow to show discourtesy
to the speaker. If a speaker (due to ignorance) sponsors an idea opposed by his listeners, or is downright boring, the worst he generally
receives is silence and a lack of response. In a beginning speech class

it is hard, at first, to get the audience to feed back disapproval to the speaker. Only when the speaker is aggressive will he elicit open rejection. The sensitivity of American audiences is also indicated by the fact that the college student generally demonstrates no disapproval of the professors' beliefs, whereas in some European universities it is accepted practice for a student to shuffle his feet when the professor expresses a conviction the student doubts or cannot accept. Though audience courtesy encourages poor speech, the strong desire to belong motivates American speakers to do a job that will receive approval.

How much does your speech echo the need to belong? How much of this need do your listeners think you show?

Artistic Language. Earlier we mentioned the man who defended a speaker who had said very little but said it in fine style: "A man who can talk that well doesn't need to say anything." This respect for language is expressed every day in speech classes. The student who talks glibly is often too well satisfied with himself to learn the hard lessons of thought, and he will be encouraged to maintain his faith by the large number of students who drop their mouths in open approval. This is not strange, of course, for man has always been carried away by the music of his speech. Critical appraisal is a mark of sophistication.

How much does your speech feed back the love of language? What does the listener reveal to you about your language?

Ethical Principles. Belief in the rules of society is common to all men. Without it there could be no social order and no standard against which to compare one's speech. But this is not to say that all people believe in the same rules, even in the same society. All we have been saying about beliefs and their relation to speech is designed to show that we each speak in accordance with that part of the body of social rules which most impresses us.

The wise, or at least the democratic, speaker is the one who understands the beliefs current in his environment, who can sense their intensity, worth, conflicts, and dangers, who says what he himself can accept and who influences others without dominating them.

Attitudes

As we have said, the conscious director of your speech is the constellation of your beliefs. Your beliefs are related to your attitudes, and to those we now turn our attention. Beliefs take shape out of what you know or think you know, and the relationships you see among these things. Attitudes are responsible for the specific ways you act in particular situations. We might say that your attitudes are ways you are inclined to act when you are thrown into a situation. You may act on the beliefs expressed in your talk — or you may not.

Attitudes are thus akin to habits, differing in that they are not so fixed. That is, your "sets" to words such as mother, communism, history, dates, education, religion, professors, etc., tend to change with your experiences. Since experience is always in progress, attitudes are plastic. But when a reaction has become automatic, we say the attitude has become a habit. The following attitudes are the ones most observable in human speech. It will be noted that they are explained in terms of a continuum between two extremes.

Positiveness-Negativeness. A person's speech varies in the degree of positiveness or negativeness it communicates. At the extreme are some persons who are always for something and others who are always against something. We tend to be attracted to persons of the former kind. When students are asked to describe the personality they most admire and to name the admired characteristics, those most often cited are generosity, diligence, tolerance, the ability "to take it," and "a good sense of humor."

Following is an excerpt from a freshman speech that suggests the positive tone of the attractive personality:

> Somewhere in one or another of your English classes you have probably heard of Louis Adamic, who wrote about families from Europe who came here to make good. In his book *From Many Lands* he wrote about Frank and Helen Karas from Czechoslovakia. I had the privilege of knowing this family and would like to tell you about them.
>
> Before his death several years ago "Pa" Karas was the instrumental music teacher in the grades and junior high. "Pa" was a very understanding and patient teacher. When we had too much school work to do and didn't get around to practicing very much, "Pa" wasn't mad; instead, he'd encourage us to do better next week. To develop a love for good music in his students "Pa" used to have us over to his house on Sunday evening to play Haydn quartets and other good chamber music. Of course there was also an element of bribery present. If we played well, "Ma" would treat us to a great big double-dip ice cream cone.

Just as we were beginning to understand our instruments better, "Pa" became very ill. Soon it was evident that both his legs must be amputated above the knee to prevent the spread of cancer. We were all terribly shocked and unhappy, but when we saw "Pa" out in his garden, tending the flowers, pulling himself along on his hands, we realized that he had more spunk and courage than we did. His special students were allowed to see him that winter, and we were always encouraged to keep on practicing and trying to make it easier for the new teacher.

Our whole town mourned the passing of our teacher and friend last July, but his spirit lives on in his daughter Clara who is teaching in his place, a living memorial to this man who taught so many people to love music. Her interpretation and directing are just the same as his, and once in a while we forget it's Clara directing and think of our beginning days with "Pa."

This student's worship of her old teacher reflects the universal response to the affirmative and the secure personality.

What does your self-hearing tell you? Do your listeners interpret you as positive or negative?

Introversion-Extroversion. The original description by the psychologist Jung held that the introvert takes a subjective view of things and is governed by the relationships of things to self, whereas the extrovert is dominated by external social values. These terms have been so widely and loosely used in recent years that they have come to carry a variety of meanings. Gradually the notion has developed that the introvert tends to be a sedentary, thoughtful, introspective, self-conscious, artistic, and sensitive person, and that the extrovert is active, boisterous, well-met, and at his worst, ruthless and crude. We shall use the terms in the latter sense.

The speech of the extrovert is abundant and revealing.[8] Since he is a person whose life is inseparable from his external environment, his speech becomes the "nerve" connecting his physical and his environmental selves. The extrovert easily strikes up a conversation with whomever he is with. At the extreme, he cannot keep a secret, and he wears his emotions on his sleeve. When the speech of the extrovert is unresponsive, it is so because he has no interest in the topic and speaks

[8] S. G. Estes, *The Judgment of Personality on the Basis of Brief Records of Behavior,* Cambridge, Harvard University Library, 1937.

only because the occasion calls for it. Generally he enjoys all aspects of speech, for speech is an essential part of his existence.

The introvert is reticent. Speech to him is a tool to be exercised in establishing the necessary contacts with others. Seldom, even with

The introvert and the extrovert. Where <u>do</u> the most interesting messages come from?

his closest friends, does he pour out all his reactions. His speech is accordingly not so vivacious and emotionally alive as is the extrovert's. Both the actions and the voice of the introvert tend to be impenetrable. Even in great joy or sorrow, the extreme introvert will tend more than the extrovert to present to the world a calm and unmoved spirit. Obviously, on first contact he is much more difficult to judge.

What does your self-hearing tell you about yourself in regard to introversion and extroversion? What do your eyes tell about the interpretation of you made by your listeners?

Emotional-Factual Attitude. Two students give speeches about a frightening experience. One emphasizes the way he felt about it, what the encounter did to his reactions. The other describes events, and becomes a reporter of observed facts. A person who is predominantly emotional in his thinking is motivated to act in accordance with his feelings rather than external circumstance. A person who tends to focus on facts will tend to act only after a proper study of them. Both kinds of orientation may bring satisfactory action; both may fail. The result depends on the purpose involved. A scientific search demands a factual approach, but the artist is poor indeed who has no internal response. It goes almost without saying, however, that we make fewer unhappy judgments when we try to go by the facts.

How factually oriented is your everyday speech? Do your listeners trust the observations you report?

Gregariousness — Solitude. All other things being equal, the less you like to be with people the less speech skill you will have. As in games, the skills of speech come with practice. You can evaluate your own gregariousness in several ways. First, in reviewing your time budget, how much of your free time is spent with people? How many clubs do you belong to? The size of your correspondence is also an index. Finally, the range of your general information and gossip suggests how gregarious you are.

It should be noted that the degree of gregariousness or solitude is not an index of cooperativeness or love of people. Some very belligerent people like to be with others; in fact, you cannot well be aggressive if you have no one to control. Still others like to be with people because the dominant self-feedback, when they are alone, is not pleasant to them.

How gregarious are you? How gregarious do others think you are?

Expansiveness — Reclusiveness. Closely allied to gregariousness is the desire to talk. Obviously, how much you talk of your own accord is an important speech attitude. This may be tested by observing how much of the time you monopolize a speech situation.

Persistence — Vacillation. Speech is affected by the degree of persistence you have. The best speech adjustment is the one that leans to neither extreme. The over-persistent person cannot adjust readily enough to group fluctuations. He is inclined to talk on a point after others have lost interest. His internal echoes are too great, decreasing his alertness to others and to the environment. He will reveal a peculiar kind of disorganization which results from his tendency to say something, then feed in a number of self-echoes to what he has just said. For instance: "First I got a job in a steel mill. *Boy! What a job! You can have the steel industry.* Well anyhow I got the job on May 15. *That's the day before my birthday.*" Or if he sticks to the point, he wears the listener out. He may go over and over a point, with or without new evidence. The average radio or television commercial shows what can happen.

The opposite extreme is quite as troublesome. Vacillating speech lacks constancy of purpose; under the pressure of people and events, the vacillating mind skips so much from one thing to another as to become incoherent and superficial. The feedback from others and from the environment causes the immediate stimulus to be too impelling. We say of such a person that "he never follows through," or that he is weak.

How persistent are you? How do others evaluate you in this regard?

Independence — Dependence. Independence is indispensable to the lonely pioneer. But the frontier is gone, except in creative thought and work, and even in the realm of ideas and research we all must borrow more heavily than the individual may find it comfortable to admit. Everything we know, as suggested by our manners, speech, dress, patterns of thinking, values, and knowledge, is taught us. We are even more dependent in the physical conditions of our lives. Who builds his own house, makes his own car, refrigerator, radio, television set, table, chairs, and clothes, and grows his own food?

A person is essentially, as we have said elsewhere, a set of interpersonal relationships. The creative force in personality, then, is dependency. We are not talking here about childish dependence, reliance upon others for assistance. As we mature, this kind of dependence develops into communication and cooperation with contemporaries.[9] This mature dependence — or interdependence — is in essence the development of the capacity to love. As Ashley Montagu points out, "We love only those things upon which we are dependent — not, however, all things upon which we are dependent: those which are associated with frustration we hate, but those that are associated with pleasure, either present, recollected, or anticipated, we love." [10]

Another evidence that we are dependent by nature is that we all have needs. It follows that our frustrations and conflicts arise from our failure to accept the satisfactions of dependence. Men "want to feel dependent, either upon some mother-ideal, deity, or other persons, or pathologically, narcistically upon themselves, but dependent

[9] J. Ruesch and G. Bateson, *Communication: The Social Matrix of Psychiatry,* New York, W. W. Norton and Company, 1951, p. 35.
[10] *On Being Human,* New York, Henry Schumann, 1950, p. 82.

they must feel." [11] Self-dependence is the disease of society. At best the ideal of complete independence is a false image when men live in close touch. The only possible freedom in our society lies within the structure of dependency. It is only as we learn to appreciate this that we can hope to build a speech personality commensurate with the needs of our day.

The speech of the highly independent is cold, diffident, and distant. The speech of the healthily dependent is warm, sensitive to the listener, and outgoing. The dependent speaker has a high degree of audience feedback to which he adjusts very readily. In other words, he identifies himself with the interest of the listener and organizes his thoughts around the needs and desires of the listener, often quite unconsciously.

As you listen to yourself, do you sound independent or normally dependent? What do others think?

Dominance — Nondominance. One of the more obvious features of a person's speech is its dominance level. By dominance we mean the ability to maintain purpose in face-to-face situations. This should not be confused with the control of others. Rather, it refers to the capacity to keep from being controlled. There are probably a number of factors that shape this trait. Self-assurance, knowledge of "where you are going," energy, suggestibility, faith in others are some of the variables that determine dominance. Thus your dominance level changes with the situation and with the people around you. Yet the range for each of us hovers around an average, so that we may say that any person's speech is relatively dominant or non-dominant.

The more noticeable features of the dominant person are the decisiveness of his actions and the poise of his behavior. His "easy does it" style is the key to our judgment.

How much dominance do you hear in yourself? How do others evaluate you?

Aggressiveness — Submissiveness. We all range somewhere between a superior and an inferior attitude toward the person with whom we are in communication. There is no right or wrong relationship so far as successful communication is concerned; it all depends upon the related role the listener wants to play. The boss is usually quite willing to listen to an employee who plays a role inferior to him. Conversely,

---

[11] *Ibid.*, p. 80.

the sick man may be happy to be given orders by his doctor; in fact, the doctor who does not learn this fact is likely to be unsuccessful. In between are all the relationships where people communicate on an equal basis — pals, friends, sometimes even husbands and wives.

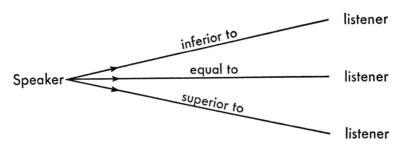

The continuum stretching between aggressiveness and submissiveness has a· clear relation with those of dominance-nondominance and independence-dependence. But these inter-relationships are too complex to take up here and will receive treatment in later chapters.

Interest — Lack of Interest in a Topic. Because of his peculiar combination of the preceding attitudes, a speaker reveals varying degrees of interest in what he is talking about. Of course, a student can choose a topic in which he is not interested. But it is usually safe to assume that he selects topics as vital to himself as he can. The fact that a subject echoes in his mind and is developed indicates that it has stirred a certain energy. The more independent person has little need of sharing even his most important reactions. The aggressive, submissive, or dependent person must have communication to satisfy his needs. Whatever the cause may be, it is quite apparent that the student who has enthusiasm for "getting an idea across" has a set extremely advantageous to the speech purpose, for enthusiasm is contagious.

How much enthusiasm do you hear in your own speech? How much do others hear?

One's appearance and temperament start him in the direction he takes in life. Interacting with his environment, he becomes sensitive to certain "facts." Whatever facts his intelligence sees build the structure of his beliefs. These things produce attitudes, tendencies to express himself in a given manner in a given situation. All this, the total personality, is communicated and interpreted through action and voice — which are not separate forces, but interacting parts of a single thing, the person.

How much feedback have you of the way your speech operates?

QUESTIONS FOR STUDY AND DISCUSSION

1. What are the differences between self-expression, selfishness, and self-lessness?

2. Explain the Wintu Indian concept of self.

3. Give three definitions of personality.

4. Discuss these seven aspects of personality: appearance, intelligence, action, voice, temperament, belief, and attitudes.

5. Discuss the relation of humor to intelligence.

6. What is meant by choleric, sanguine, melancholic, and phlegmatic?

7. Discuss belief from the standpoint of (a) radical-reactionary, (b) Spranger's types of men.

8. Explain each of the expressive attitudes.

9. Can you defend the following statement: All we know about a person we learn from his actions and voice?

DISCUSSION TOPICS FOR PANELS, SYMPOSIUMS, AND FORUMS

1. List in parallel columns the desirable and undesirable attitudes expressed by college students. Discuss with a group of four or five, before the class, the attitudes that each of you have assembled. From this discussion you may recognize the attitudes you need to capitalize upon and those you need to restrain in the interest of being accepted.

2. Discuss the fundamental beliefs and attitudes of Americans, Germans, Russians, Englishmen, Chinese, etc. Which of these nations is the easier for the group to understand? Why?

SUGGESTIONS AND ASSIGNMENTS

1. Give a five minute speech describing the best speaking personality you know. What are the person's outstanding characteristics?

2. Write a description of your own personality, using the analysis of this chapter. Pay attention to your beliefs about worth-while things in life and your appraisal of other people. Be as honest as you can. Have a friend evaluate it for objectivity before you hand it in.

3. Prepare a five minute speech from this material. In this speech see if you can talk about "I" without boasting, defending, or apologizing for him.

4. Give a five minute speech about your father's (or mother's) beliefs. Make a list of dominant ones. Tell how he or she is integrated around these beliefs, how his or her life is propelled by them. Give examples of the way you predict his behavior by your knowledge of his beliefs.

5. Construct a speech describing an interesting personality that you know very well. Apply the analysis of the chapter. Use vivid language and specific examples so that we may come to know this person.

6. Develop a five minute talk about the expressive attitudes of a person well known to the class: a well-known senator, foreign diplomat, the President, a well-known campus personage.

7. Prepare a five minute speech about an unpredictable person you know. Use clear-cut examples. List the beliefs that he reveals in his behavior, pointing out the conflicting beliefs that result in one kind of behavior in one instance and its opposite in the next.

8. Describe a well-known personality from history, but do not tell who he is or what he did, but rather what he *is*, using the analysis of the chapter. See if the class can identify him after you have finished.

9. Since belief is so central in speech, prepare a five minute talk about a belief that is the core of your own life. The following subjects are suggestive:

1. Prejudice and Tolerance
2. Unethical Speech
3. Sincerity and Friendship
4. Twisted Thinking
5. Ethical Salesmanship
6. Emotional Speech
7. The Mark of Character
8. How to Deal with the Enemy
9. Christian Ethics
10. You've Got to Take Care of Yourself
11. Survival of the Fittest
12. The Nature of Man
13. The Hopes of the Future
14. Why I Go to College
15. What a Religion Is For

As a reaction to these speeches list the beliefs that each speaker identifies himself with in addition to the one implicit in his subject. Evaluate how consistent his beliefs are. Tell the speaker how convinced you are that he lives the beliefs he states.

10. Give a five to ten minute talk analyzing yourself as to the expressive attitudes. Before you begin have the students evaluate you on the following scales:

Positiveness									Negativeness
1	2	3	4	5	6	7	8	9	10

Introversion									Extroversion
1	2	3	4	5	6	7	8	9	10

Factual									Emotional
1	2	3	4	5	6	7	8	9	10

Gregariousness									Solitude
1	2	3	4	5	6	7	8	9	10

Expansiveness									Reclusiveness
1	2	3	4	5	6	7	8	9	10

Persistence									Vacillation
1	2	3	4	5	6	7	8	9	10

Independence									Dependence
1	2	3	4	5	6	7	8	9	10

Dominance									Non-Dominance
1	2	3	4	5	6	7	8	9	10

Aggressiveness									Submissiveness
1	2	3	4	5	6	7	8	9	10

Interest in Topic									Lack of Interest
1	2	3	4	5	6	7	8	9	10

Answer any questions after your talk that may arise as to your self-evaluation. Check the student evaluations after class to see how closely they approximate your own. If they are not close or if the evaluations disturb you, see your instructor. Obviously the more your evaluation and that of the class coincide, the better. Agreement indicates that you communicate as you think you do. It means you will get the interpersonal feed-back you expect.

11. Attend the next lecture by a famous person who visits the campus. Analyze his personality and prepare a speech describing his speech behavior and the conclusions you have drawn about him. This is a particularly valuable assignment if the entire class has attended the lecture.

12. Prepare a ten minute speech demonstrating the power of visual aids in producing belief. This may be achieved by trying to convince your audience of two ideas, one for which you use the visual aids. What does this tell you about the power of what the listener sees?

13. Give a five minute talk on two conflicting beliefs in American life. Following are some suggestions:

1. Take Care of Number One First *vs* Love Thy Neighbor
2. Tell the Truth *vs* Be Diplomatic
3. Be Aggressive *vs* Be Kindly
4. Be Intelligent *vs* Don't Be an Egg Head
5. Work Hard *vs* Don't Be an Eager Beaver
6. Get Ahead *vs* Don't Be Pushy
7. Be Honest *vs* Don't Be Naïve
8. Discipline the Child *vs* Give the Child Freedom
9. Isolation *vs* Intervention
10. Intervention *vs* Freedom
11. Freedom *vs* Peace
12. Human Nature Is Good *vs* People Have to Struggle Against Their Baser Nature

14. Work out a skit with several classmates in which you demonstrate speech attitudes which are particularly objectionable. Be faithful to the attitude that you want to demonstrate. Do not exaggerate. Make your selection from the common complaints made by students about people that irritate them.

15. Observe the attitudes revealed in the way students walk to and from the platform. Prepare a three to five minute talk demonstrating the good and bad attitudes revealed.

16. At the student union or the next social affair observe the attitudes of the students who, in your judgment, command the most favorable attention. What are these attitudes? What attitudes are expressed by those less popular? Draw up a five minute speech from your observations.

17. Study the walk of another person carefully. Walk like that person. What feedback do you get? What can you say about the person? By sensing the difference from your usual walk, what have you learned about yourself?

18. Evaluate your echoes to your appearance and dress. Do you get too much feedback, or just enough to keep yourself socially acceptable, or too little? What reactions have you received from your friends?

19. Read three popular magazine stories. Select the values extolled by the "good" and "bad" people. Prepare a five minute speech explaining the American sense of values as evidenced by these stories.

20. Go to three popular movies and prepare a speech from the values set forth. The same thing can be done by analyzing several television or radio plays. What of the American comic strip?

*Of all the emotional forces that pattern our indi-
vidual and interpersonal behavior, fear has the
most insidious power to make us do what we
ought not to do and leave undone what we ought
to do. . . . No other emotion wears so many
disguises — convincing disguises that make us,
time and again, treat it as something other than
itself.*[1]

Bonaro W. Overstreet

19

Fear and Confidence

HUMAN PERSONALITY is magnificent in complexity, as suggested by
the previous chapter; and fear, to which we now turn our attention,
adds confusion to the complexity.

What Is Fear?

Fear is an emotion — the dread of harm, the desire to escape from
something conceived as injurious. Fear is a spring of action, directed
to the avoidance of pain. In animals, it is a simple and direct mechanism for self-preservation. In human beings, it is this but it is more.
At its worst it builds a defensive wall around the self which warps our
view of the world and cuts us off from effective contact with our fellows. Because it is dead set against expressiveness, it should be of
interest to all students of speech.

Here is a vivid picture of fright in action.

> One morning last summer I saw a deer grazing at the edge of our
> hayfield. At intervals, it raised its head, listened in one direction and
> another, sniffed . . . and went on grazing. Then its delicate senses
> recorded some threat; and it bounded off across the field, over the
> stone wall, and into the woods.
>
> From the direction it took, I could guess where it went: to a spot
> among the tamaracks, down by the spring, where ferns have been
> leveled by deer that have lain there. But with even more certainty I

---

[1] *Understanding Fear in Ourselves and Others*, New York, Harper and Brothers,
1951, pp. 3–4.

369

could guess something else about that deer: that in its ferny thicket it
did not reproach itself for having run away. It did not call itself a
timid fool, nor think up belatedly some more dramatic role it might
have played. It did not take out its self-contempt upon some smaller
deer, nor dance up and down in hoofed rage upon the unoffending
ferns — these symbolically cast as the enemy it would like to trample.
It did not convert into bodily illness a brooding sense of having been
humiliated. With danger temporarily past — but with alertness unim-
paired and ready on demand — it lent itself to the positive business of
staying alive: to rest and nourishment. In short, it remained a deer.[2]

To understand the difference between the simple reaction of the
deer and the tortured complexity of many human beings under similar circumstances is to understand the way fear shapes human life
as it does no other animal's. Fear is a healthy protective power in the
deer. He does not praise, denounce, or in any way put value on it.
In fact, he does not put value on anything. He simply does what nature impels him to. That is because he does not talk. But man speaks
and passes judgment. The power to create words and build a life out
of them is the thing that makes him human and gives him unique
command over his actions. Unfortunately, this same power permits
him to say some things about his behavior that are not so. As Mrs.
Overstreet suggests, if the deer were human he might hate his fear
and therefore despise himself. Or he might believe that being tough
proves he is not afraid, not knowing that toughness is the very proof
of fear.

Extent and Kinds of Fear

In our society most of us suppress our fears because we do not want
to be labeled with the penalty word "coward." As a result, the college student is often amazed to find that he is not alone with his
anxieties, but that the majority of his fellows have very similar feelings. One study, of 175 college men and 100 college women, indicates
that about half of the men feel inferior, physically, socially, and intellectually; 17 per cent said they felt morally inferior, and 37 per cent
said they had felt so at one time or another. Over half the women
said they felt inferior physically, socially, and intellectually; 18 per
cent felt morally inadequate; 25 per cent had at one time. Only 10

2 *Ibid.*, p. 17.

per cent of both the men and women reported that they did not feel inferior.[3] Karl Menninger reports substantially the same conclusion — that 90 per cent of the college population has feelings of inadequacy.

Status Anxiety. Most persons in our culture are alert to social pressure, and the college student particularly. Belonging to those of his own age (institutionalized in the fraternity and sorority) is a maturing step from the home world to adult social life. In this new world the student must be able to attract people of no kinship. "Popularity" becomes a high goal. He must learn to say the right things at the right time in the right language and with the right manner. But there is a great danger in learning these skills — the danger of being laughed at.

The college student is learning to play new roles in life; in a sense he is pretending to be more than he is. The new role, because of its very *newness,* is not yet familiar, and his self-consciousness about it tends to keep the role separate from his more accustomed self. There are so many firsts: the first day in college, the first speech, the first dance, the first trip to a large city, the first stay at a hotel, the first time to be called "Mister," that much of him does not really seem genuine. He so often feels like a "bluff" that he is afraid to talk freely with others lest they see him for what he fears he is.

The Anxiety of Conflicting Values. The college student's value system is a mixture of those both younger and older, and is therefore the more confusing. He wants to feel that he can handle his own affairs, but he wants to run home to parents who will shoulder his responsibilities when "the going gets rough." He still wants to play, but he needs a sense of achievement. Consequently he cannot decide how much to work and how much to play. He wants to make independent financial decisions but he has to ask his father for money. He wants to feel adult but he wants others to plan his assignments day by day.

Little difficulty arises from the fact that he cannot entirely retain the values of childhood, but much comes from his inability to become fully adult all at once. Because he is physically mature, older people

[3] Gordon W. Allport, *Personality, a Psychological Interpretation,* New York, Henry Holt and Company, 1949, p. 174. Reprinted by permission of the publisher.

all too often expect him to see things as they do, having forgotten much of their own youth.

Further, the college student is the unconscious victim of a value system which holds that some people are worth more than others. He must therefore try to demonstrate that his speech is better than his neighbor's, and fearing that it is not, he must curry the favor of the instructor who holds the reins of power. In addition, he must compete for friends, compete for social position, compete for a friend of the opposite sex.

All this is extremely important to his speech development. Honest speech comes of the energy to share one's life with others as well as to reach out and accept the internal worlds of others. We cannot at the same time share and compete with others without bringing into the act varying combinations of love and hate. As long as this conflict exists, fear persists. That is why much of youth's social fear arises from this conflict of opposing values that ricochet about within him.

Anxiety Over Strained Relations With Parents. Parents are accustomed to having their children look upon them as the source of all power, resources, and knowledge. But due to the growth patterns in our culture, as early as the age of two a child begins to develop self-identification and a sense of separateness from all other selves. The cleavage is first marked by the negative stage, an effort to stop all those huge and powerful adults from sculpturing his personality as if it were clay. Professor Andrew Weaver tells the story of a little boy wandering across the street to his grandmother's house after breakfast, entering the kitchen and announcing without any immediate provocation, "Grandma, no!" Whatever the forces of separation may be, by the time a person reaches his teens he generally considers his total environment a rather harsh force to bend and shape to his own purposes. So it is that parents who were once gods are now viewed with a critical eye, and appraised as assets or liabilities. Relations already strained are often further impaired by the resulting defensiveness of parents; it is never easy to take on the role of a "has been."

Anxiety About the Future. The college student, with energy to burn, has not yet fully learned how to use it. Quite understandably, he does not know what occupation to choose, what beliefs and causes to stand for. He is doubly distressed at these uncertainties because it is urgent with him to "go places," and it is disturbing when he does not know where. Norman Cousins has said, "where man can find no answer, he will find fear." [4]

The physical and social pressures of our civilization, and indefinite purpose, cause extreme sensitivity during youth. Generally full adulthood brings an intricate balance between caring and not caring, as well as clarity of purpose. However, A. A. Roback says that as many as one-third of our adults are hampered in all they do by a chronic sense of self-consciousness which is their chief source of worry.[5]

Speech Fear

Fear can warp and color every aspect of our behavior, and speech is no exception. A study of 420 college students enrolled in a beginning speech course reveals the prevalence of fear specifically associated with the public speaking situation.[6] Here are some of the ways in which students described their states of unease:

I am in a state of nervous tension before getting up to speak. (70 per cent)

It is difficult for me to search my mind calmly for the right word to express my thoughts. (57 per cent)

I feel more comfortable if I can put my hands behind my back or in my pockets. (45 per cent)

I feel awkward. (46 per cent)

Fear of forgetting causes me to jumble my speech at times. (40 per cent)

My voice sounds strange to me when I address a group. (37 per cent)

My legs are wobbly. (26 per cent)

I gasp for breath as I begin to speak. (11 per cent)

I am so frightened I scarcely know what I am saying. (9 per cent)

Speech fear is self-consciousness, a feeling of tension about social relations that causes a person to isolate himself from the activity at hand and turn the spotlight of his attention upon himself. It is most acute when we are "on stage," but it exists in varying degrees whenever we feel doubts, irritations, or frustrations about speaking. It comes into being when the response of self and audience is not predictable: when we speak on the radio, pass the time of day with a

[4] *Modern Man Is Obsolete*, New York, The Viking Press, 1945, p. 7.

[5] *Self-Consciousness, Self-Treated*, Cambridge, Science-Art Publishers, 1936, p. 41.

[6] Lester Thonssen and Howard Gilkinson, *Basic Training in Speech*, Boston, D. C. Heath and Company, 1947, p. 34.

stranger, ask for a raise, argue with the teacher, or propose to that dream girl.

CAUSES AND FORMS OF SPEECH FEAR

Punishment

We get our first insight into the workings of speech fear when we recognize that it stems from the memory of punishment in a speech situation, and punishment can be anything from a harsh word or a de- risive laugh to a facial expression we cannot understand. This memory arouses fear when we speak in a new situation. Each time the "evil" memory is aroused, it adds one more incident to the hidden store. The recollected experiences are seldom complete and vivid pictures, but are more likely to be body sets and posturings. The unconscious- ness of the process, however, does not lessen its effect, but tends to make correction the more difficult. We are generally awkward in hand- ling what we do not understand.

Conflict

The memory of punishment produces conflict, between the desire to talk and the desire not to talk. By nature human beings derive sat- isfaction from talking with one another. But if they have received punishment in the process, they are conditioned in one of three ways: to avoid talking, to search for approval, or to struggle for domination.

Speech conflicts are often most intense in the student who cannot release tension, as most speakers do, near the beginning of a speech. Such speakers report that they feel more emotion when they have finished than at an earlier time. Strangely, these speakers generally appear to be completely at ease, for they adopt a flaccid and indifferent posture. It is after they return to their seats that they grow jittery and shake. They quake because they are relaxing from an enforced relaxation. Their trouble is that proceeding to speak does not end the feeling of danger. Their conflict remains deadlocked.

Or consider Neal, who strives to dominate by his speech. Neal paces, and speaks loudly and emphatically. He is not arrogant or belligerent, but is somewhat oppressive and overpowering. He says he feels surest when he walks right up to the audience, but in general he is not satis- fied with his speech. "I walk around too much. I don't seem able to talk calmly." After a speech on — ironically enough — the cementing power of cooperation in society, he evaluated his performance calmly and communicatively. And the gist of his appraisal was, "I don't seem able to get my points across." The class was amazed, for they could phrase his points clearly and felt that he had organized his ideas well.

One can but dimly understand this boy's dissatisfaction with himself without knowing his background. Neal grew up in a family of dynamic speakers. Several of his brothers are successful lawyers. At seventeen he felt insecure and "fired up" because they could always talk him down.[7] He therefore had to "talk down" the class. But the students, while they listened well and with a certain admiration, maintained their independence by keeping their feelings well concealed. So the harder Neal worked to get a much needed response, the less reaction he got. His speech conflict, then, was between the need to speak well, which for him meant complete mastery, and his feeling of failure, that the audience did not submit but evaded him, as indeed it did.

Standards

Conflict always takes shape around our values and standards. While our standards often reflect the best that is in us, when they are impossibly high they produce fear and tension, and defeat both themselves and us. From a life-long barrage of preaching and teaching, young people develop two convictions: first, that growth comes from lashing themselves; and second, that they must lash themselves with those standards that have been impressed upon them.[8]

Thus the student exhorts himself not to stumble, to pronounce words correctly, to articulate well, to get the right inflection, the right rate, to be forceful and effective, to stand erect, to "push the words out from the belt," to finish in five minutes, and to strive for freedom. He finds it easy to believe that the more numerous the rules and the higher his standards, the more likely he is to achieve good speech.

Failure and Shame. Some students can live up to all these standards without tension, but the vast majority, in the great effort to stretch their powers, tighten up. To tighten up is to make some kind of error. Obviously to stumble, forget, and ramble is undesirable, and so

---

[7] One investigation indicated that students from large families show more "nervousness" in the public speaking situation, perhaps from the fear of losing attention at home. Stanley Ainsworth, "A Study of Fear, Nervousness, and Anxiety in the Public Speaking Situation," Ph.D. Dissertation, Northwestern University, 1949.

[8] Floyd Greenleaf, "An Exploratory Study of Speech Fright," *Quarterly Journal of Speech*, October, 1952, p. 328.

the speaker feels ashamed. His shame has nothing to do with what he has to say, but his attention is now focused on his shame instead of his speech. If he does not give up his unrealistic standards, he inevitably builds one of three defenses to keep his feelings of unworthiness to himself: (1) a masterful over-easy control, (2) a tense over-control, or (3) an impenetrable mask. There are subtle combinations of two or all three of these reactions. Half hidden in the defense is the awareness of bluff, and of this too he is ashamed.

The shame we reveal in speech is not due only to failure to meet speech standards. Other standards may be involved. A student may feel ashamed to speak because he is five-feet four instead of five-ten, or six-feet six instead of five-ten. The girl who is twenty pounds overweight hangs her head, and the stately Amazon weeps in misery. In like fashion a student may reflect shame in his speech because his intellectual, social, or moral behavior does not match his standards.

Failure and Inferiority. Under this stress we do not feel equal to the speech situation; we feel inferior, insecure, inadequate. The end result is that we attach too much importance to other people in the situation, or at least we question what they think of us. Seeing ourselves near the bottom of this ever-present social ladder, the lower rungs of which are "bad," can create severe stress. No man, however humble his speech, suffers feelings of inadequacy when talking to his dog — or to a baby, unless another older person is present. It is only when we are speaking with or in the presence of persons whom we regard as a challenge to our own significance that we suffer the need to attain standards beyond our performance level.

Standards and Ambition. The peculiar structure of most of our standards assigns worth in accordance with the ability to excel. The resulting stress shapes speech, most apparently in two ways. The extremely aggressive speaker is obviously driven by his need to dominate the listener and to excel others who are competing for an A. At the other extreme, the person who is convinced that he cannot compete successfully either withdraws and becomes indifferent to the task of learning to express himself better, or succumbs to the "shame" of not being able to do the job.

Day by day, month by month, the evidence accumulates: modern man is afraid and is guilty and hostile in his fears, because the standards by which he is asked to prove his worth are standards that convert all other men, and all groups of men other than his own, into actual or potential enemies.[9]

To be ambitious is to be fearful.

Forms of Conflict

Avoidance. The conflict so often generated by unrealistically high standards may take many forms. Perhaps the most extreme is complete avoidance, but we seldom see this in the classroom, for generally those who take speech have decided to face the problem and try to correct it. But even in the speech course an occasional student will flee from the room in the middle of a speech, or stop in tears, or drop the course after several efforts. More frequently, fearful students speak as little as possible, or complain that certain members of the class are too critical.

Approach-Avoidance Conflict. When the student speaks but fears the responses of the audience he has what is known as internalized fear. Then, no matter what action is decided upon, there is a certain amount of avoidance of that action. When the student wants to speak but *knows* he will be punished for it, his stage fright is of this form. To speak is to meet the punishment of the external force and to avoid the pain of not talking. Not to speak is to meet the pain of self-suppression and to avoid the external punishment. Either decision is, in part, directed by fear, for the conflicting force is not eliminated.

While many external sources of pain may be internalized, it is important for our understanding of communication to recognize that the conflicts which involve other people cause us our greatest speech concern. Psychologists are pretty much in agreement

> that disruptive emotional problems always have their root in interpersonal relations. The human being experiences fear when his car skids on an icy highway but such fear does not distort his personality. . . . The one loss he cannot tolerate and remain in emotional health is the loss of goodwill between himself and his fellow humans. The fear and pain that distort his personality are those that come from actual or anticipated rejection.[10]

[9] Bonaro W. Overstreet, *Understanding Fear in Ourselves and Others,* New York, Harper and Brothers, Inc., 1951, p. 121.
[10] *Ibid.,* p. 137.

Avoidance — Avoidance Conflict. Conflict does not have to be between self and an external force or person. It may be between antagonistic motives within the self. Of course, internal conflict is not divorced from the social world, for we learn our beliefs from other people. We learn rules of conduct which do not conform to the sex drive. We learn to be both generous and selfish, to love and to hate, to value both saving and spending. We learn to respect both material and spiritual values, to value both aggression and submission, to value experimentation and to avoid failure. Every time we speak, then, when we do not know what standards or values to stand for, we are afraid of ourselves.

Unless one is sure that his speech in a given situation is going to bring rejection, which is not usually the case, stage-fright is of this form. The fact is that most audiences "pull" for the speaker who is caught in fear, and students learn this long before their fear goes.

Compulsiveness

Regardless of the nature of our conflict, when we speak in such a state, one of these drives opposes the other. The resulting behavior is compulsive. By this we mean that action is the composite result of

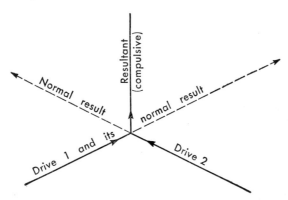

two or more opposing forces and is different from the expression of any one of them acting alone.

An illustration will clarify. Jerry grew up without an adequate regard for grammar, and at times produced some original, if not polished, speech. One morning during his freshman year at college he was asked to make an announcement to the assembly. Directly afterwards an English professor stopped him in the hall and said, "Son, I counted twenty grammatical errors in the first two minutes of your announcement and then gave up in despair!" Jerry, never before fully aware of his deficiency, was shocked into a paroxysm of hate and self-contempt. It required his greatest command to face the rest of his classes that day. Thereafter in public speech or in any situation where there were a number of listeners, fear swept over him and he was incapable of constructing a sentence rationally. The harder he tried the more compulsively he was driven to frame awkward sentences.

Fear Reward

Among the causes of fear are the rewards that it provides. To understand how fears keep themselves alive we need a knowledge of the structure of a motive. Motives, or drives, the things that "make us tick," are not isolated engines. They are cycles of action. Thus in hunger, the craving for food (stage one) leads to eating (stage two) which leads to the satisfaction of not being hungry (stage three) which leads again to hunger (stage one). The action of the drive temporarily destroys the motive, but in the long run restores it to full strength and may even cause it to grow.

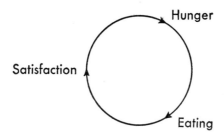

Similarly, fear is a craving to avoid pain, which leads to the avoidance, which leads to the satisfaction or reward of relief from the pain, which leads to the craving to avoid the pain. The last stage may at first sound illogical, but only because we fail to take into account that the stage before, the satisfaction of having escaped fear, is a reward — a lowering of tension and a pleasure. While most of us generally find other forms of reward more satisfying, we all do precisely this sort of thing when we follow the dictates of fear. The person who most fears speech is the one who will not meet the fear of speaking. If not-speaking did not produce a pleasurable lowering of tension, the action-of-not-speaking would lessen fear of speaking. But just the opposite is true: escaping the fear of speaking produces temporarily a comfort that in turn makes it desirable to fear. This may

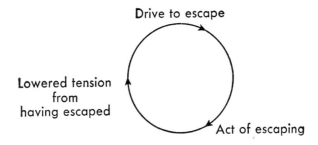

be hard to see, but a similar response prevails in many problems in life. Consider the unhappy lot of the drug addict or the alcoholic. Neither places value on his affliction — but its rewards he cannot deny.

The Nervous and Endocrine Systems

The recognition of any danger, social or physical, external or internal, alerts the nervous system for emergency action. Certain glands, known as the endocrines, can produce instantaneous charges of immense energy through the release of hormones into the blood stream. The effect is comparable to what happens in an automobile equipped with overdrive when the accelerator is suddenly pushed to the floor. In a car this is fine, and in primitive man it is efficient, for he is essentially an animal of gross action; nature protects him by providing "violent" energy for crucial moments.

The same mechanism goes into action when we meet the crucial moments in speech. Breathing speeds up. The heart accelerates. Students complain, "I thought my heart would burst. It pounded through my whole body." One speaker's pulse leaped from 72 to 105 when he was called on for an impromptu talk. He was geared for gross action. But speech in our highly discriminating society calls for precise and refined muscular movements. It calls for very careful combinations of memory patterns; it places a premium on control. The emergency mechanism of the nervous system is therefore set against the need.

Such are the causes of our speech fears.

ESCAPE FROM CURE

Since fear commands us to escape, it is little wonder we develop subtle mechanisms that permit us to feel we have solved the problem without facing it.

Over-Compensation

Jack runs away with a discussion, talking loudest and longest in any group. Ethel is a bubbling conversationalist. She hangs on every word you say, and by her responses builds up your sense of importance. Dick is clever, sweeping away all honest emotions with a wisecrack. Joe laughs too loudly. These are common examples of over-compensation.

Because the blind victory is better than none, many develop the quality of exhibitionism. It is said that we talk to show off. More accurately, we talk because we are afraid not to talk. We over-react in order to quiet the voice that says, "Don't talk."

Defense

Or we may meet the feared situation, like a knight of old, well protected with armor. Defense is similar to over-compensation, the difference being that the defensive person does not seem to enjoy himself so thoroughly. He may be rough, belligerent, foolishly courageous, contemptuous of social popularity, snobbish, prejudiced, critical, superior, evasive, flippant, quiet, timid, unduly humble, over-loyal, excessively generous, self-sacrificing, all too smiling, or just plain unresponsive. These are defenses, forms of camouflage or "protective coloration," raised by fear. They often deceive others, and more often ourselves. This is not surprising, for fear is not an isolated force in personality but is intermingled with all our other emotions.

In addition, defenses create tremendous hurdles for "honest" communication, a condition that sets up the need for further defenses. People react to what they see and hear. If our real motives are not apparent to others, we in turn receive a reaction not expected. Thus people learn to mistrust each other. And since we do not usually recognize our own defensive expression, we are forced to live in deception about both ourselves and others.

Substitution. Defenses take many forms, of which a common one is substitution. A boy who is too small to be a football player may strive to become an outstanding speaker. While this goal is healthy if kept in bounds, our lad may become troublesome to himself and others if he is ready to give a speech "at the drop of a hat." Substituting speech for a well-rounded life, he limits his fullest development. Thus limited in experience, his speech becomes relatively worthless. Or he may, as a substitute for action, develop just one kind of speech in which he is most effective. He may become a great story teller, a good arguer, a good order-giver. He may even go a step further, substituting words that give him an emotional release for the objective facts those words stand for. This is dangerous, for daydreams work out so perfectly that we come to put faith in a self which does not exist. To save ourselves from the painful truth we are then driven to create still more dreams, and to suffer still more disillusionment. Fantasy is quicksand.

Other substitutions are revealed in the classroom every day. Slumping, trembling, nervously rolling a pencil between the hands, not moving, moving nervously all the time, looking out the window, looking at the audience but not seeing it, stumbling, blocking, monopitch, monoforce, inaudible volume, hurried rate, forgetting, rambling, awkward sentences — all these are symptoms of a conflict which has not been met and solved.

Instead of solving the conflict, one frequent pattern is to seek cleverness. One may, eventually, become "a polished speaker," but his speech, with its subtle substitutions, becomes more and more divorced from the inner person. In truth, it is not then the speech that is polished; rather, fear takes on such a high gloss that to both himself and the untrained observer the speaker seems improved. The sophisticated behavior that causes people to ask "what kind of person lives behind this front" comes of substituting standardized but tense speech patterns for an earlier unvarnished display of fear.

Rationalization. Since we tend not to recognize our defenses (else they do not defend), what we see is misshaped by them, much as if we wore bad spectacles. John Dewey says that the person who rationalizes shapes the world to meet his needs by caricatured and distorted thinking. In rationalization we do not see things as they are because we are *afraid* to. If we have bought a pair of shoes that we feared were too expensive, we may say over and over, "in the long run I find it cheaper to buy expensive shoes." Repeating this shows that we need reassurance. Perhaps we were *afraid* to buy cheaper shoes, but won't face that fact. This rationalization is dictated wholly by internal conflict. Or we may fear to let others know the reason for the purchase — perhaps that it gave us a sense of superiority. In either case the statement hides the facts and is dictated by fear.

The arguments of our speeches are often dictated by fear to admit the real reasons for our beliefs. A student may give a speech against school regulations, supporting his conviction by eulogizing freedom and the need to let young people learn responsibility. These are good reasons, but they may not be his real ones. What produced the stirring energy of his speech? Perhaps the rules simply irritated him. But he cannot praise, or perhaps even recognize, so petty a foundation for a belief. For the standards out of which he has built his self-esteem do not permit him to face this real reason — to say nothing of his fear of its reception by his audience. It is impossible to calculate the amount of our speech that springs from rationalization.

Illness. One may become too ill to meet the thing he fears. There is no taboo on illness, and others comfort us when we are indisposed. Occasionally a student literally becomes too weak to leave his room on speech days, and many develop colds and throat infections. These students are neither malingerers nor liars. They simply are not "up to par," and it is always more difficult to fight fear when we are weary and low in energy. What is more, a fear-illness may have physical reactions more disabling than a cold infection. The writer has known students who, walking into speech class or by the teacher's door, became nauseated; and they did not have colds — they only wished they had. Fear-illness, of course, is a highly specialized form of rationalization.

Trial and Error Response. This is the adjustment of "blundering." Perhaps our first response is aggression, which in turn arouses the fear of not being liked. Hastily we try to correct and apologize, which in turn stimulates the fear of being too submissive. This indecisiveness is common, and is revealed in impulsive words and actions coupled with a constant retracing and correcting of statements. The mechanism of fear always stimulates the opposite behavior from the one we aim for. The more nearly equal the conflicting drives, the more likely speech is to be directionless.

These are the ways we disguise the fear that guides our talk. These are the escapes from solution. Now that we have gained some insight into speech fear, the next step is to learn the nature of its opposite, confidence, and the means of achieving it.

THE ROAD TO CONFIDENCE

What Is Confidence?

Self-confidence is the state of trusting and relying on oneself. It is a state of "reasonable" tension, tension only to the point of alertness. It is the freedom to use energy in action dictated by genuine interest rather than in exhausting concern with one's own workings. Confident speech focuses attention on what is being said, and on the effort to communicate it as well as possible. This does not mean that we take no thought for the effect we are creating; it means we focus on *communication*, the interaction between self and hearer to convey thought, *not* on *self* alone. How may this happy state be attained?

Recognition of the Problem

We do not attain confidence by ignoring self-consciousness.[11] We can not get rid of it by "thinking about something else." Nothing nourishes fear like escape. The way to fluent and well-ordered communication is through meeting the distressing situation with an understanding of the fear involved.[12] One may begin by asking, "What am I afraid of, and why?" In short, we do not overcome self-consciousness; we face it and learn to tolerate it.

Talking About Fear. Putting your fears into words for others to hear brings them to the light of day to be examined coolly and objectively as no amount of silent analysis can do. The simple act of admitting the fear reduces its dimension in our eyes, forces us to drop at least some part of the pretense it has caused us to adopt, and so helps to reduce tension. Once we admit what we are, we no longer must strive to appear what we are not; we no longer need be afraid of being found out — for we have admitted the truth. And the truth is never so horrid as we thought it might be.

---

[11] Actually we seldom, if ever, completely eliminate fear. The effect of fear is so profound and generalized that the best we can normally hope for is substantial reduction.

[12] Robert C. Leslie, "Growth Through Group Interaction," *Journal of Pastoral Care*, Vol. 5 (Spring), 1951, pp. 36–45.

As we talk out the pressure and reduce emotional stress, we gain new insights into our problems, form new associations with the speech situation, and develop new attitudes toward audience, speech, and self. We thus gradually recondition ourselves from a pattern of fear to one of equality, relaxation, and genuine interest in communication. Bit by bit we become ready for more enriched and better organized speech — and living.

Let us see how this works. A well-known poet and lecturer, at the beginning of a reading, discovered suddenly that the front row was filled with a grinning congregation of his old classmates. He stammered and came to a full stop. He looked at his papers, and again out over the footlights. And then he laughed. "You will forgive me, friends. I am afraid I am not prepared to proceed as I had planned. Though pleasantly, I have been startled to recognize many familiar faces, classmates of many years ago." He recalled old times, and talked of his pleasure and fear at the prospect of having to please old friends. As he talked his tension dropped, and he "worked" old classmates into an audience he was accustomed to. Knowing his own needs, this practiced speaker recovered from fear by talking about his fear.

Many students, though far less experienced, have learned to win confidence by the same route. Frances was at first so inhibited that her speech was a series of spurts and sputters. But after several short talks on the nature of her problem, its history, the situations that disturbed her most, and possible causes of the trouble, she began gradually to improve. Later she said one main reason for her new-found freedom was "the changed attitude of the audience." As she saw it, "Until recently people just tolerated me and, I thought, found my speech dull or irritating. Now the kids are friendly. You have no idea how much honest talk has helped me lower my tension."

Here are some starting points for a series of talks designed to lower defenses:

1. Explain a speech situation in which you have trouble.
2. Tell how fear affects you — what it does to your body, mental organization, attitudes, etc. Use examples.
3. Tell what errors in speech most disturb you. Cite two or three occasions when these errors were particularly distressing.
4. Talk on childhood fears, or your childhood view of adults. Did you wonder at the power and competence of grown-ups? What in their

bearing, dress, manner, speech, status, was awesome to you? What emotions did they arouse in you? Did you fear other children?

5. Do you fear your speech class? Describe your attitude toward it, the relation you try to establish with it. What do you want your audience to think of you?

6. From your understanding of the way fear develops, how would you explain the cause of your fear?

7. How do you adjust to fear — over-compensate, defend, rationalize? Suggest corrective measures.

Talking about Accomplishment. Truly constructive criticism has two sides; it not only seeks to discover what is wrong, but also what is right. Here are some questions to help you build constructively:

1. Consider an achievement that gave you genuine satisfaction — building a boat, quick thinking that avoided an accident, helping someone else, etc. What emotions are involved in the pleasure of achievement?

2. Describe conversations with a childhood friend. How did they give your life meaning and security?

3. If you have learned an attitude toward speaking which increased your confidence, describing it may be helpful to others.

4. Times when you achieved poise and security can be a key to your problem. At such times, do you play any central role in relation to others?

5. Discuss a person you know who has achieved an admirable adjustment. Describe his appearance, dress, interests, manner with others. Why do people like him?

6. What impressive book seems to have grown from the author's drive to discuss his feelings? What in the book leads you to this opinion?

7. Have you developed any conscious mechanisms for recovering from fear? If so, tell how they work.

Seeing Oneself Clearly

It is healthy to bring fear into the open, turn it this way and that, and seek its cure. An equally powerful means to confidence is to learn as much as possible about one's interests and abilities, to transform idealized and unrealistic ambitions into a practical sense of purpose, and to make plans toward putting that purpose into effect.

As we have seen, if conflict is the heart of fear, foolish ambition is its pulse. The relationship between confidence and ambition can almost be expressed in a formula: $\text{confidence} = \dfrac{\text{feelings of ability}}{\text{ambition}}$

If one's feelings of ability are equal to or greater than his ambition, his confidence is high, and vice versa. Obviously, there is a great difference between a person's ability and his feelings about it. Confidence is an index of the latter. But confidence can be shaken if our idea of what we can do is too far out of line with our actual ability. So it behooves us to find out as well as we can where our interests and our talents lie, and to shape our plans and purposes accordingly.

One may start the search by asking himself such questions as, "What am I good at?" "What are my interests?" "What do I enjoy doing?" The answers to these and similar questions are invaluable clues. But the answers are not always clear or easy to find. The courses that are most interesting to you and the things you most like to study will give one indication. The way you spend your spare time will give another. Most colleges and universities offer the help of skilled advisers, vocational and guidance counselors, psychologists, and teachers. Abilities may be checked by standardized tests of aptitude, personality, and intelligence, but test results should never be "swallowed whole" without the consideration of other evidence. A disappointing record on an intelligence test, for instance, if taken by itself can sometimes annihilate confidence. There is good evidence that achievement is a product of the whole personality, of which intelligence tests reflect but a part.[13]

Discussing Purposes and Plans. As with our fears, it can be an invaluable help to talk about our ambition, our purpose, and our plans. Our environment stamps its values into us before we are old enough to know their meanings, and most of us feel unhinged at the mere thought of not being "ambitious." Yet we must be free of ambition before we can recognize that our powers of self-management and productivity have already increased. Only if we become engrossed in our most satisfying interests do we recondition ourselves away from competitive attitudes. Here are some lines for exploring ambitions injurious to poise and maturation.

1. Give a talk on ambition. If you are confused about it, talking it out may help your classmates as well as yourself to think it through.
2. Take part in a discussion on the topic.

[13] D. B. Klein, *Mental Hygiene, The Psychology of Personal Adjustment*, New York, Henry Holt and Company, 1944, Chapter 16; R. DeCraecker, "L'étude Scientifique des Enfants Doués," *Revue belge de Psychologie et de Pédagogie*, 1950, Vol. 12, pp. 127–36.

3. Discuss fearful moments you have experienced that have been associated with ambition.
4. Discuss several "believed failures" that have worried you. What ambition did they thwart? Did you exaggerate them as a result of humiliation, and if so what forces caused you to do so? Were you punished? Was your standard unrealistically high? How did you develop it?

After exploring your ambitions, and cutting them down to size, it will be well to learn more about your major abilities and interests. Here are some questions which may help you in the exploration:

1. Analyze moments when you felt a sense of self-worth. What kinds of things did you do well? What courses are you taking that relate to those things? What occupations can you imagine that would allow you to do these things and be paid?
2. Discuss a person you know whose job and interests coincide. The student who is searching for his niche should remember that this is a process which everyone must go through. When you consider the thirty to fifty years most people spend in their chosen occupations, you will recognize that a few years one way or another are not so important.

Once we know the kind of activity we like, the next step is to find a socially useful end to which it can be directed. An occupation must have some meaning beyond the fact that we like the work. Only when we feel that we are a significant tool in the furtherance of a purpose larger than ourselves does a sense of personal worth and dignity develop. Thus the teacher serves youth; the lawyer, justice; the doctor, health; the social worker, welfare. We may work to eliminate war, improve government, reduce racial discrimination, or clarify student rights. The important thing is that beyond liking the work and feeling that we can do it well, we see some larger good beyond ourselves.

But it is not enough to say "I know what I want to do, my problem is solved." While millions stumble through life meaning nothing to themselves, there are as many more who know what they "mean" but cannot carry out their purpose. Dr. Charlotte Bühler, a German psychologist, concluded that the heart of the difference among people is their varying abilities to plan their lives. Most of the difficulty is in overcoming external obstacles. For the student this often means getting money, getting a quiet place to study, budgeting time, etc.

Reconditioning of Standards

In addition to re-examining ambitions, goals, and plans, it is necessary to re-form one's standards of good speech. This is particularly true for the person who is afraid he will stumble, mispronounce, repeat, or forget, and tensely guards against doing so. The reconditioning program which follows will let him climb the ladder of sub-goals until he has reached a realistic standard of proficiency which he can meet without so much tension. Since the procedure applies to all speech problems, the outline is general. The student should choose topics that apply to his particular needs.

1. After making a talk, leave the room and evaluate it. The felt need evolving from your evaluation gives you a motive for improvement.
2. Return and state to the class one feature of your talk which did not satisfy you — e.g., organization, clarity of language, eye contact. This gives you a specific goal to work on.
3. Illustrate by repeating part of your speech as you gave it. This lowers tension and lowers the drive to repeat the mistake. (See negative practice, pages 394–395.)
4. Repeat a part of your speech which you felt showed less of the fault. This strengthens the kind of speech that gives you satisfaction and freedom.
5. Restate the main point of the speech, trying to copy the good style demonstrated in Step 4. This is reconditioning; it associates the desired style with the whole speech through the central idea.
6. In your next speech, make it your main goal to apply this good feature.
7. Evaluate this speech just after giving it, following the above procedure.

When you finally feel more satisfaction in your performance than need for improvement, discuss with your audience your pleasure in achievement, again illustrating by repeating parts you feel you did well and re-stating the central idea of the talk. This kind of practice replaces standards that produce tension with a program of self-improvement. Once you have gained satisfaction and confidence by meeting your own standards, you are ready for a like program to meet those of the audience, though by the time you satisfy yourself your audience will probably have few faults to find.

A discussion group of four or five members provides a good approach to solving common problems. Here we get an opportunity to test our thinking against the observations of others. Also, as you may have discovered, you often feel freer to express views close to your life when you are in a group where others are doing the same thing. You might try this approach on one or more of the following topics, either in a "bull-session" or through a classroom panel.

1. Techniques for planning time at college.
2. The place of social life in college.
3. Effective approaches to planning a career.
4. The best ways to prepare for an examination.
5. How to deal with friends who will not let you work.

The Uses of an Autobiography

As a means of increasing your confidence, we have suggested talking freely about your speech fears, ambitions, occupational choice, social purposes, and standards. All these may be brought together in a story of your life designed to show the influences that have encouraged or injured your speech development.

There are several advantages in writing your life story. First, the concentration brings into sharp focus the causes of your behavior, and therefore gives you a starting point for directing your life more to your liking. The influences and experiences that have been good for you act as a beam of light. Second, an honest investigation of the past causes you to face those fears, humiliations, and shames which you are inclined to close your eyes to. The writing thus diminishes the power of fears and evasions. Further to reduce the harmful emotions, you should read the autobiography daily until it loses its meaning. Exhausting the emotion hastens what time does more slowly to heal any hurt. Normally, memory keeps going over a painful experience until we wear it out. But the process is haphazard, for it is mixed with intermittent running away from the pain. What we suggest is a systematic exhausion of the emotion.[14] Read your autobiography over and over until it literally bores you. Another value of the autobiography is that it may stir you to keep a diary, a running history of major impressions. To put into words what has happened and is happening to you lays a conscious foundation for improving judgments and increasing confidence.

[14] This is quite a different thing from going over and over a problem in which you see-saw back and forth on an evaluation or decision. We do not recommend this. The prolonged restraint from decision and action wears us out. When this is the difficulty we recommend a conscious redirection of attention.

SOME TYPES OF PRACTICE

One reason we do not improve in speech as rapidly as we might is that we tend to work at the problem sporadically. We can seldom speak more often than once every week or two in class, once or twice for each goal we wish to work with. This does not allow much re-conditioning, particularly when between assignments we continue to meet disturbing situations with our old habits. If we do not practice daily, even the classroom experiences may reenforce the responses we do not want. The following pages discuss some specific types of prac-tice which you should repeat again and again, outside class as well as in, until you feel thoroughly sure of yourself.

Role Playing

One of the quickest ways to gain insight into common speech situa-tions which have been difficult for you is to act them out with someone else. When you play the role you live through the situation without its ordinary stresses, and can the more readily understand the problem it ordinarily raises for you. You may feel awkward in making a request or refusing one. You may fear to ask for a job, to sell, to ask for a raise, to make a suggestion to employer or employee. You may be a feature writer for your school paper but feel awkward at interviews.

List the speech experiences you dread, from the least to the most difficult. Then each day — or as often as possible — act out one of these with a classmate, beginning with the situations you find easiest. If you can arrange to act out one of these situations in class, find a partner to play the opposite role, work out the basic situation with him, but do not plan exactly what you are to say; rather, let the con-versation develop naturally. For instance, if you are to ask for a job, decide with your partner what the job is, whether there is an opening or not, and any other necessary background information so that each knows where and how you come to meet. Each should look forward to the performance as to an actual interview. At the class meeting, the employer may take a seat before the class; you knock, enter, and begin. Such assignments should take five minutes or less.

Any role is considerably shaped by the people with whom you play it. Therefore you should play opposite different partners to learn how to adjust. The hardest test is to deal with a person who fears his role, since fear begets fear. It is a real achievement to remain poised when dealing with a person who is not sure of himself.

We fear some roles because we do not appreciate the position of the other person. You may fear to ask for a raise because you do not know how the boss will react. Playing "the boss" opposite a classmate will help you to see his problem, and thus to play your own part more intelligently.

Make a list of roles to act out, and always stay with the level of fear that you can handle most courageously. Success comes gradually; therefore never go faster than your mastery permits. If you work at such a self-improvement program day by day, success is assured. When the end of the list is reached it will seem no more difficult than the beginning.

What To Do About Physical Tension

Obviously the less tense you are before and while you speak, the better; and once you begin to speak, the sooner your tension declines the better. For those who are hypertense, who quake, move jerkily, speak rapidly, stumble, and forget, the following techniques are often helpful:

1. If you tend to become tense while waiting your turn to speak, slump in your chair, and when you feel tension developing, breathe deeply. The sigh trips off relaxation.
2. When you go to the front of the room, take time, adjust your papers, breathe deeply and slowly several times, look out over your audience, take another deep breath, and begin. After a sentence or two, breathe deeply.
3. Give your talk in an extremely relaxing and lazy posture. Drape yourself over the speaker's stand. Speak in a slow, quiet, lazy voice. Let your facial muscles fall; make no effort to show expression in posture, face, or voice. If you over-react to your audience, ask the class to slump and become passive.

Obviously, these tricks do not, at once, produce good speech. That will come later. But they will help you to associate relaxation with the speaking situation. Once you are conditioned to low tension in speech, you can begin to recondition yourself to become alert without tension. If during one of these "sleepy" talks you sense emotional quietude, then you may stand up and become more effective. Or at the close of a talk, if you feel well-controlled, you may summarize your speech in an alert posture. But as soon as tension begins to disturb your thinking or fluency, return to the lazy manner. Practice your speech in the same fashion.

A word of warning. Often students who fall into humble postures do not slump to relax and gain more composure; they slump at the command of insecurity. A man may stand on one leg and run his thumb along the edge of a desk. A girl may fall into a question mark posture and sway listlessly. These postures of misery keep feeding back to the speaker his unworthiness and reinforce his humility. Yet these are the very postures a student is going to fall into as he searches for a way to relax. The answer is to remove the stigma. When the search for relaxation causes you to be concerned for your posture, talk about your style. Tell the class how it makes you feel. This removes the shame.

Emotional stress does not always produce hypertension. As we have seen, it may produce the very opposite, hypotension. Many students become slow in action, low in voice, monotonous in pitch, and expressionless in face when they are disturbed. Their greatest need is to lower the defense. Such people profit by telling about their "tricks." If this is your trouble:

1. Give a two or three minute talk to the class explaining how you feel when you speak under pressure.
2. When you are mistakenly judged to be cool and collected in social conversation, tell the truth about yourself. Otherwise your problem remains unsolved because of the front you feel impelled to keep up. Such confessions are best tinged with humor.

The following suggestions are for both the hypertense and hypotense:

1. Get plenty of rest the night before you speak.
2. Do some vigorous walking or other exercise an hour or so before you speak. Golf, tennis, swimming, basketball, or a good run followed by a shower, are good preparation for meeting any social stress. A short vigorous walk just before class will help.
3. There are several techniques for keeping your mind from running over and over the speech as you wait your turn. Some students just listen to other speakers. If listening causes you to put yourself in the speaker's place, perhaps you can distract yourself by doodling. Some find that just naming things they see and hear occupies them. Others adopt a philosophical attitude: "This too shall pass," or "It won't

make any difference a hundred years from now." No device is valuable that you have to work on. Psychological forcing is not relaxing.

4. If there is a room you can go to for five minutes just before speaking, you may experiment with some free associational speech. Just let your mind wander. Talk about whatever flashes across your mind. Do not censor or in any way try to control the thought and speech. Several minutes of this give many students the relaxation needed for a good flow of thought.

5. During the first several speech assignments keep a record of your tension. Here is how it may be graphed:

Night Before	Waiting Time	Walking to Platform	Beginning Remarks	End of Speech	After Speech

Most

Tension

None

As you proceed through the semester your tension should be less and should decline earlier in the speech situation. If it does not, you should talk with your instructor.

6. Ask to speak alternately early and late in the hour. Speaking early puts less strain on your relaxing techniques. Conversely, if you need practice in relaxing techniques, you should sometimes speak late in the hour.

7. If you find tension associated with much of your activity, you may find it helpful to read Edmund Jacobson's *You Must Relax* or *Progressive Relaxation*. Perhaps you may wish to give a speech on the methods suggested, demonstrating the techniques.

Negative Practice for Fear Responses

The way to control a "stumble" momentarily is to try not to stumble. If one is careful and lucky he will then not make the error. This approach would succeed if it erased fear. But the long-run effect is not to reduce the urge to make the error, but rather to reenforce it. Therefore, the first step in the destruction of fear's substitutions is to do just as we do in meeting the fear to talk — deliberately do the thing feared. We should blunder purposefully, talk intentionally the way we fear to talk. If we stumble, stutter, or slump, we should practice doing these things alone, and in the situation where tension causes us to do them. These acts should not be exaggerated; exaggeration is a side-step; we should voluntarily practice the actual nervous action and voice that distresses us. We are then following the basic principle for defeating fear, doing the things we are afraid of and thereby cutting off the reward that perpetuates the fear.

The Use of Humor

A student gets up to speak. He stands stiffly, eyes shifting, his whole manner furtive. He tells a humorous story, the audience laughs, and his constrained action gives way to interesting and likeable speech. Such a student begins his speech with an indefinite feeling that he is alone and separate from the listeners. When they laugh with him, fear gives way to the security of belonging. Then his motive to share has an opportunity, for faith in one another comes of the degree to which we respond in a like manner.

Humor does not necessarily mean hilarity. We also laugh silently, and the speaker need not "strain himself." Each person has his own style; use the one that seems natural and comfortable for you. However, we generally get a better response if we under- rather than over-play the fun. People want the point of an ordinary explanation lifted out and made very clear to them, but not their humor. They like to stumble upon the twist that makes them laugh.

Perhaps more important, you should be careful not to offend your audience. Do not punish them by making one of them a buffoon. People may laugh when fun is poked at them, but they often turn the tables, and if you are put on the defensive with your humor it does little good for your social fears. At any rate you should be prepared to accept the consequences when you exploit a person in your humor. People often advise the speaker to make himself the fool. This is safer, but of no value in assignments designed to release you from fear. Fear comes from feelings of inadequacy or insecurity. Humor that plays on your own inferiority is not going to help you lessen it. The humor that will alleviate social fears is relatively free from punishment in either direction.

In sum, then, we learn to master fear by coming to know its causes and its manifestations, in others and in ourselves. Practice and frank recognition of our problem will help immeasurably to bring our fears under control and to increase our confidence in ourselves, our abilities, and our future.

QUESTIONS FOR STUDY AND DISCUSSION

1. Why should a speech course devote so much attention to the topic of fear?

2. Why does the "dumb" deer not criticize itself for its behavior? Is the deer a "coward" to run?

3. Can you explain how the nervous system thwarts good speech when we become fearful?

4. What causes us to fear other people? Is human nature treacherous?

5. What is meant by "avoidance drive"?

6. What is the cycle of a motive?

7. What are the three forms of conflict? Give an example of each.

8. What is the relation between standards and fear? What relation exists between standards and feelings of inferiority? What relationships do you see between standards and democracy?

9. What is the relation of memory to fear?

10. How does social fear begin?

11. What is the relation of inferiority to fear?

12. Discuss the prevalence of fear among college students. What are the most dominant fears? Why does youth have so many fears?

13. What are the false cures for fear? Which do you think is the least undesirable?

14. What is meant by self-confidence? What is the relation of ambition to confidence? Does confidence depend upon achievement? Is confidence more related to ability or to feelings of ability? Explain.

15. What do you think about the relation of achievement to ambition?

16. How does devoting life to a cause increase personal confidence? How is inferiority related here?

17. What is the difference between finding a cause and planning one's life?

18. Why is it unwise to criticize a person's fear responses?

19. How can you change criticism to mirroring? Why is one a breeder of fear and the other a teaching device?

20. What is negative practice? How is it valuable?

21. What are the steps in reconditioning a fear response?

22. What is meant by role-playing?

DISCUSSION TOPICS FOR PANELS, SYMPOSIUMS, AND FORUMS

1. What should education do about the grading system?
2. What are the most common fears of college students?
3. What are some of the more common incidents that cause self-consciousness?
4. What are college students afraid of when they speak in class?
5. What are some common incidents in which people punish unintentionally?
6. What are the standards of teachers that students fear?
7. What are the personality traits of the person of little fear?
8. How is ambition related to fear?

SUGGESTIONS AND ASSIGNMENTS

The following assignments are designed for specific speech problems not covered by the chapter. From the principles applied in these suggestions you should be able to devise exercises for problems of your own, if they are not dealt with here.

If You Over-Compensate

1. Watch the people at a party or dance. Do you note that some seem to overdo their parts? Do you have any cues as to what they are compensating for? How would you describe the value demonstrated in a given person's style of over-doing? Give a talk from this experience entitled "Speech Compensation." Describe the behavior. Demonstrate the behavior.
2. If you tend to compensate, tell what situations cause you to do so, and what your style is. Demonstrate it.

If You Substitute Words for Action

1. Discuss an occasion when you substituted words for action.
2. Keep a diary of occasions when you have been caught dealing with words rather than reality. What is the nature of your problem when you find yourself talking "through your hat"?

If You Substitute a Mask for an Expressive Face

In every speech class there are those with whom we never seem really to become acquainted. Generally the symbol of that personality is the impenetrable mask. If you happen to belong to this group, try to express with a mobile face as you carry out the following assignments:

1. Tell your audience what your objective is. If after a few moments your face expresses nothing, they are to shift around in their chairs as students do when it is time for the bell. As soon as you react facially — regardless of emotion — listeners are to become quiet.
2. Practice this technique with your roommate for a few minutes each day. Check occasionally with your instructor for his evaluation of your progress.

Now we are ready to reverse the procedure; that is, if you are distressed by your lack of facial expression:

1. Tell the class you are going to give a talk without the slightest facial expression. Inform the listeners that should they detect a change they are to smile. If they do, you are not to react. Whatever the subject, you should perform this assignment until you have no fear of your "opaque" response.
2. Practice this with your roommate daily during this period.

If You Substitute Rapid Speech for a More Desirable Rate

Since you are distressed by your compulsive speech let us first unload your fear of rapid rate.

1. Go to the back of the classroom where you are not seen and give a rapid two minute play-by-play description of a basketball game. Try to keep the game exciting.
2. For a daily practice intentionally speak too rapidly in a class, or in conversation with a group of students. If somebody should correct you, tell him what you are doing and say the next sentence faster yet. If your emotions rise in doing this, do it again.
3. Talk rapidly to your roommate when you are not under pressure.

But since rapid rate comes also from the fear of speaking slowly,

1. Choose a topic that calls up passive emotions; for instance, the pleasure of paddling a canoe down a lazy river, or sitting under a shade tree on a hill on a quiet summer afternoon, or lounging before the fire with your favorite magazine on a cold winter day. Or describe an experience shot through with sadness, thoughtfulness, wistfulness, yearning, sympathy, or pity.

2. To test your ability to maintain a slow rate explain slowly a topic that is exciting and makes you want to speak rapidly. Stop occasionally and look over your audience as you collect your thoughts before you proceed.

If Your Voice Is Inaudible

1. Prepare to read something very interesting. Go behind a screen and tell the listeners to call "louder" when they have difficulty hearing. You will find it easier to follow these commands when you are "further away" from your audience. When you receive no more requests for more volume, step out from behind the screen and finish.

2. For daily practice, ask your roommate to ignore your speech when he is having trouble hearing you. Ask him not to look quizzical or ask you to repeat, but to ignore you until you speak loud enough. This places the responsibility on you and makes you, by your own request, "go to him" rather than he to you. When you permit others to request repetition, your attitudes of withdrawal are being rewarded by their "asking."

Should you fear the quiet voice itself, start by lowering your fear of the voice.

1. Give a one minute talk at such a low volume that you cannot be heard past the first row. Watch your audience reactions but do not raise your voice.

2. Tell the class to close their eyes if they cannot hear you. Since you have cut the sound line they reciprocate by cutting the sight line. Do not speak louder when they do this.

3. Tell the audience to lean forward and try to hear you if your voice is too soft. Do not respond by speaking louder.

If You Substitute a Speaker's Stand for Courage

1. You may tell of one or two instances of the effects upon you when you had to speak in a situation where no stand was available. You should deliver this talk from behind the stand.

2. Determine the classroom speech situation in which you have no need of a speaker's stand. Perhaps you do not need the stand when you give a demonstration, or read an announcement, or when you have a pencil in your hand. In any case, you use the stand when you have no psychological need for it.

The above assignments are designed to lower your fear of the need. What of the fear of the way you speak without a speaker's stand?

1. List the situations difficult to face without a lectern. Beginning with the easiest, face each situation in turn. You may begin the talk explaining that you are uncomfortable without the stand. Regardless of how uncomfortable you may be, do not step behind the lectern.
2. In preparation for the above talk, practice it daily in your room, standing in the open before a mirror, preferably a full length one. Practice until you do not mind facing yourself as you talk.

If You Are Afraid to Look at the Audience

1. For daily practice, go to your room, place a pillow at the end of the bed. This is your audience. Look at it and practice a forthcoming speech. Or let your roommate help. For five minutes each day practice your speech, watching his reactions carefully. Tell him afterward what he was thinking at a given period. Tell him what your clue was.
2. When you can easily turn to your audience and remain with it, give several talks in which your objective is to demonstrate your power to do so. Announce at the beginning that you are going to speak without looking out the window. If you should fail, announce what or who caused you to become uneasy. Return to (1) and practice it for several days before coming back to this assignment.

You may be afraid of your tendency to look out the window, at the back wall, or at only one or two students. If so,

1. Give a one minute talk on what you see from the window. Do not look at your audience, even once.
2. Give a one-minute talk describing a picture, diagram, or piece of furniture in the room. Keep your eyes on what you are describing.
3. Tell about an experience of one of your classmates. Look only at the classmate about whom you are speaking.

If You Look at the Audience but Do Not See and React to Individuals

1. Look over your audience and for one minute describe the color effect you see in the room. Tell which colors predominate in the dresses of the girls; the boys. Tell how many red heads, brunettes, and blonds there are. If your minute is not up, try sizes. Who is the tallest person? the shortest?
2. Give a talk for one minute in which you read the meaning of the facial expressions and postures of various listeners.

3. Give a short talk in which you specifically try to get some overt action from your audience. For instance, you may tell a humorous story. Note the people who react and make some comment about that observation, such as "I guess that didn't go over with Jim. But it wasn't a total loss. Mary laughed and Alice almost smiled."

4. For daily practice watch the reactions of the people you are with when you feel uneasy. Observe every detail of their behavior. Keep a record of the actions of others and your attitudes toward them. After a week of recording, speak on the way you see people when you are uneasy with them.

If Your Mind Goes Blank in Speech Situations

1. Your recovery technique is to say, "Now let's see, where was I. . . . I was talking about my second point." If the idea does not take form, return to the last sentence you spoke and say it again. If this does not work, you at least can say, "Well, I guess I cannot think of it." This should be said with absolutely no shame. If you must say it in shame, repeat it.

2. Go to the front of the room and ask the students to suggest topics for an impromptu talk of two or three minutes. As soon as one "rings a bell," say "All right, I'll talk on . . . " and begin. Now you are integrating your thinking and talking. You cannot think ahead or worry about your organization or preparation. You must speak on what comes as it comes. Having the faith you demonstrate in your usual speech, you are reconditioning yourself to behave in class as you do elsewhere.

3. Go to the platform. Ask the class to give you a subject so difficult that you will probably get disorganized and lose your point. The subject might be "How Democracy and Freedom are Related." If you become so tangled that you get a mental block, try the procedure suggested in (1) above.

4. Search out, once a day, if possible, a situation that tends to cause memory failure. Observe yourself in the situation. Evaluate your behavior afterwards for your success or failure. How do you explain it? Keep a diary of your findings. Give a three minute talk to the class on this information.

If You Stumble and Become Awkward in Language

1. Give a short talk explaining how you came to have such a high regard for fluency. Tell of an occasion or two in which lack of fluency embarrassed you. Is there any similarity in these situations?

2. Give a one-minute impromptu speech on a difficult subject, one too complicated to handle fluently without considerable preparation.

402 Speech and Personality

3. Prepare a short speech in which you plan a stumble, an awkward pause, a long pause, some kind of break in fluency, at least once in each sentence. Give this speech in a halting fashion at least three times before you come to class to deliver it.
4. Keep count of all lapses in fluency on the part of your speech instructor for two weeks.
5. Give a one-minute talk in which the power of the last sentence depends upon pausing for at least three seconds before it is said. Count the seconds to yourself before you make the concluding remark.
6. When you stumble with emotion in any speech situation, stumble directly thereafter intentionally.

If You Rationalize

1. Look up the word "rationalization" in the dictionary. Develop a talk explaining how rationalization is dictated by fear. Supply some examples.
2. Give a humorous talk on the topic "My Favorite Rationalization."

If You Meet Fear With Illness

1. Give a talk on "My Favorite Illness."
2. Give a short talk with examples showing how illness may be avoidance.
3. To call yourself or another "coward" reflects primitive thinking. Can you explain with your knowledge of conflict how withdrawal can be explained in such a way that the word "coward" is not a fitting label? Perhaps you can use examples of soldiers who could no longer face battle. Do you know of the "General Patton Incident?"

If You Meet Fear With Impulsiveness

1. Explain the conflict that causes your impulsive action. Demonstrate in your speech.
2. Give a short persuasive speech. This is a challenge to your ability to take an approach and stay with it.
3. Evaluate the speech. Repeat, as before, the "blundering" parts. Then summarize, maintaining a more direct course.

. . . When I was a child of seven years old, . . .
being charmed with the sound of a whistle, . . .
I voluntarily offered and gave all my money for
one. . . . . My brothers, and sisters, and cousins
. . . told me I had given four times as much for
it as it was worth . . .

As I grew up, came into the world, and observed
the actions of men, I thought I met with many,
very many, who gave too much for the whistle.
. . .

Benjamin Franklin

20

Self-Hearing and Change

THE AUTOMATIC GUN pointer has just one purpose — to close the difference between its aim and the position of the target. It never wanders, for the information to which it is alive is the simple search for increasingly louder echoes from the target. But this simplicity of purpose is not true of all automatic machines. It is possible to build a mechanical brain that can play a fair brand of chess. If the machine plays with a consistent opponent it will improve its game, capitalizing upon its past errors. But the mechanical chess player can get "all fouled up" by playing with an inconsistent human being. It loses its ability to correct for its errors because what it is trying to adjust to has no consistent pattern. Human beings experience the same kind of difficulty in learning to talk, for so much contradictory information is communicated by the other "chess players" that we do not know what pattern to adjust to.

But this is only part of our difficulty. When the gun searches its target, it can clearly tell when it is correcting its error, by the rise or fall in the loudness of the feedback from the target. Human beings can do this only in so far as they are able to hear the difference between the way they talk (aim) and the way the audience (target) responds. Obviously, if we cannot hear ourselves, a circuit necessary to this vital adjustment is not functioning. We are left, then, with the response of the audience and no orientation as to our aim.

The problem of hearing oneself is interwoven with the problem of purpose. The human animal is peculiar in that it can identify itself so closely with a purpose that it may "pay too much for the whistle." As we begin to focus our attention upon a *purpose*, the future, we cease to live for the moment, we cease to hear ourselves, as we talk. No one will deny the value of purpose, but the fact remains that too much concern with our own purpose upsets our communication with others. Instead of hearing the difference between our speech and the needs of the audience, we hear the difference between the person we fear we are and the person we would like to believe we are. The matching process is not then such as to help us adjust to the audience. In such a case we do not hear ourselves as others do.

We need to become aware of the images that direct human speech in order to make wise choices in the search for better understanding with our listeners. What are some of these self-images?

Self-Acceptance

Randy is an unusual boy. He is president of the student body, a good student (though not exceptional), very sociable, one of the students when among them, one of the faculty when among faculty. Randy hears himself, sees the audience, and adjusts to meet others. He can make a request, register a complaint, give a word of praise,

The future self needs planning, and we
can achieve it only a step at a time.

all with the same poise. These qualities make him a very effective debater, for no matter how strongly he attacks a point of difference he does not seem to strike the opposition personally. Randy is never so adroit as when he speaks on a "foreign" campus. His introductory remarks are models of observation, good taste, and genuine human interest.

The attitude toward his own purpose that is fed into Randy's speaking mechanism is a recognition of the differences between to-day's self and the potential of tomorrow, *with primary emphasis upon the steps that lead to the self of tomorrow.* This kind of self-hearing directs attention to specific sub-goals and the actions necessary to put them into effect. Randy has faith in today's abilities and skills, satisfaction in exercising them, and a belief that they will lead to fuller satisfaction tomorrow. Since he can accept himself, he can change himself.

Randy makes mistakes and expects to make them, altering future behavior accordingly. He may or may not reach the ultimate in success, but he will go as far as his intelligence and interests carry him, and he will not be greatly concerned one way or the other. If he becomes concerned, he must change from the adaptive person he is.

The speech of the person who accepts himself and his natural interests is optimistic, zestful, and cooperative. It is as creative as his intelligence will permit. The content is honest and the delivery is not defensive. Since such a person does not live under stress and tension, his voice is calm, well modulated, and generally pleasant. He is alert to his audience and his speech therefore fits the occasion. His secret is that while his attention goes outward, he is still able to hear and change himself.

1. Give a speech describing a "Randy" you know.
2. Select a topic for debate and defend the side in which you strongly believe. Find another person in the class who believes just as strongly the opposite way. Each of you may give three or four minute speeches; then, say, two minute rebuttals. Have the class evaluate your relative abilities to speak vigorously without incurring ill-feeling. Have them tell you where you were skillful and where you "slipped." Try it again with a new topic if it would be profitable.
3. Get two pictures, one of a speaker who shows self-acceptance, the other of one who shows self-concern. Show these to the audience and explain the difference.

4. Listen to five conversations about the campus. How would you evaluate the self-attitudes demonstrated? How many cases of self-accepted speech do you find as compared to the cases of "punitive" speech? How would you describe the difference? Do you have the material here for a five minute speech?

UNREALISTIC ADJUSTMENT AND SPEECH

The Dictator Self

The poised person is unfortunately not very common in Western society. Most of us in several ways and in varying degrees create a

The Big "I" — the letter man who doesn't carry his own weight.

dictatorial image, which causes us to be restless, dissatisfied, and critical. There are several reasons for this. Exaggerated ambition in itself is sufficient cause. Another is the belief that man is naturally evil and must drive himself away from anything he is attracted to. One other cause is the very obscurity of the future and what is "right." A potpourri of inconsistent beliefs sets up the need for dictatorial speech. But whatever the cause or causes, internal conflict is usually put down by a "strong man," a kind of internal dictator.

Whether personal or political, the life of a dictator is precarious, and every defense against threatening elements in the society must be assured. To put it another way, when we cannot face up and listen to all of ourselves, we set off a part of the self, worship it, and strive to forget the rest. Anything that then causes us to hear the rest of our personal society makes us unhappy, indignant, and fearful. Obviously a dictatorial image requires techniques for convincing ourselves that it is the whole person instead of a small part. The chief technique is rationalization, which with words makes seeming reality out of make-believe.

Several kinds of dictatorship can take over in the human personality, depending upon the nature of the dominant image.

Arrogance

One kind of inner dictatorship arises from ignoring the "poor" self of today and identifying with the superior ideal which tomorrow will bring. The arrogant speaker gets set before he speaks, purses his lips, consciously rolls his coat upon his shoulders, and smiles at himself. As he proceeds he occasionally cocks his head and contemplates his position in life, snaps his head ever so slightly as he poises his hand in midair before laying it on the desk with quiet emphasis. His speech is a posture. Such a person is the victim of self-suggestion and becomes the wonderful self of his dreams.

Arrogance may take several forms, depending on what one is trying *not* to hear. The assumed superiority may be intellectual, political, religious, social, economic, artistic, or physical. Wherein his pride is, the arrogant will dream, and out of his dreams he will fashion a personality.

We all know the adolescent genius. Perhaps he is physically inferior, wears heavy glasses, is socially inept. In some way he does not feel able to cope with his world. So to compensate, he may argue, correct people on minor details, and seek points of disagreement. Since he can search in but one direction, he moves in that direction, even though the target is in the opposite one. No girl wants to hear a lecture on how reflected light tells us about the chemical properties of the moon, while the band is moaning "Star Dust."

More ludicrous is the obtuse person who becomes intellectually

*Arrogance is a monument to what
we are trying <u>not</u> to hear.*

arrogant, but he does not exasperate us as does "the brain." Somehow
it is funny to see "wisdom" made out of nothing, irritating to see
real intellect showing off — perhaps because it is not so easy to see
that the latter, too, is struggling to get away from himself.

The politically arrogant person has much to say about his many
engagements, the caliber of the people he meets and deals with, the
clubs and committees he belongs to, how important they are, how he
is pressed for advice. The world of affairs revolves about his decisions.

The religiously or ethically arrogant tries to impress us with his
fairness, his justice. Yet the care with which he "toes the mark"
causes us to question him. Seeing our suspicion drives him closer to
the letter of the law, and the more unbelievably "correct" he becomes, the more we doubt him. He is caught in a vicious circle.

The socially arrogant strives to be a Don Juan, the life of the party,
the perfect host. Dissatisfied with himself, he too tries to over-
develop what he feels are his most polished skills.

We may strive to look as wealthy as our creditors, or if we have a
bit of artistic appreciation, may press ourselves to attend the symphony, the play, or the art exhibit that we do not honestly enjoy. Suits

with wide shoulders and narrow waists, a powerful handshake, a deep or loud voice, much bustle and activity, become devices to prove to ourselves that at least in some way we are superior.

> To check for arrogance in yourself, or for that matter any other dictatorial attitude, observe your daydreams. Note the roles you dream about most often. Are there steps you can take to make them a reality? Would it be wise to do so? Do people often try to belittle you? If so what roles have you been playing?

Vindictiveness

An equally difficult master is vindictiveness, which stems from the love of power. Consider the difference between the self-images in the following two excerpts.

> When down the hoary corridors of time there echo ever and anon the deep gaunt cries of multitudes in pain and poverty, chained to the chariot-wheels of despotic government, scourged by the stinging lash of ruthless tyrants, and trembling perilously upon the brink of dark oblivion — then, then, my countrymen, it falls upon the free, God-fearing nations of this earth to hearken to the cries of the oppressed, to determine here and now to strike the grinding shackles from their fettered limbs, and deal one final, iron blow to tyranny. — Anonymous

> With malice toward none; with charity for all; with firmness in the right, as God gives us to see the right, let us strive on to finish the work we are in; to bind up the nation's wounds; to care for him who shall have borne the battle, and for his widow, and his orphan — to do all which may achieve and cherish a just and lasting peace among ourselves, and with all nations. — Abraham Lincoln

Both men are speaking about the same problem. Both are interested in eliminating the same condition in society. But one speaks from self-acceptance, suggesting love in place of tyranny; the other, speaking from the influence of a power image, would replace an old tyranny with a new one.

It is important to see that vindictive speech is that of the person who is trying to quell his fears by exercising dogma, threats, and a show of force. Defensiveness demands an enemy. Therefore, it is in the very structure of the vindictive set to make all troubles look as if they came from outside. This clears the self of fault and turns the internal conflict outward. War with a foreign enemy is always to be preferred to civil conflict, for the dictator's internal position is thereby made the more secure. All of us need to scrutinize ourselves for this self-deception, and the more we speak for "good" causes, the more we need guard against this twist. It is not a particularly pleasant thought, at first, but it is nonetheless true that reformers of the destructive type — those who would change the world by force or by destroying another's name — are victims of inner dictation trying to keep peace within by attacking a foreign enemy. Caesar, Napoleon, and Hitler are not fundamentally different in this regard from Cotton Mather, the Puritan preacher, or John Brown and Wendell Phillips of the anti-slavery movement. There is probably no lesson more difficult to learn than that attack upon others comes from mistaking our own insecurity for dangerous encirclement by external foes.

Vindictiveness. Who's doing the talking here?

Many public speakers make a career of telling what is wrong with the world. Most of us spend much of our energy privately doing the same thing. Such tirades are the evidence of a vindictive image.

1. Prepare two short speeches on a question upon which you feel strongly. In the one assume the "Lincoln" role. In the other use a vindictive approach. The second need be different only in that it constitutes an attack on somebody (specific or general) who should be punished. Give one speech at the beginning of the class hour, the second nearer the end. Have the class evaluate the speeches for effectiveness. Ask each evaluator to tell whether he favors your conclusion. You may find that those who agree with you like your vindictive speech the better. Can you explain this?

2. Select a classmate who agrees with you on a subject. Decide which is to use the vindictive and which the non-vindictive approach. Have a panel of three other classmates evaluate the two speeches.

3. Select a classmate who disagrees with you on a subject on which you both feel strongly. One of you may use the vindictive attitude, the

other remaining free of it. The difference will be easier to maintain if the vindictive speaker is second. Have the audience vote both before and after the speeches as to where they stand on the issue. Before the speeches they may vote on a three-point ballot:

affirmative   neutral   negative

After the speeches they may vote on a five-point scale:

more affirmative   affirmative   neutral   negative   more negative

So far as you can determine, which of the two attitudes was the more effective? (Other factors, such as evidence, reasoning, and delivery operate in such a decision.)

4. From an anthology of famous speeches choose a short selection that expresses vindictiveness and one that does just the opposite. Practice reading them aloud in the mood expressed in the material. Read the selections to the class with a few remarks explaining your purpose.

Perfectionism

The fluent speaker who looks silly when he stumbles over a word, the well-organized student who is not satisfied with his organization, the effective speaker who thinks he cannot get his point across, the pleasant speaker who is afraid he will hurt somebody's feelings, the slow speaker who wants to know how to slow down, the speaker with the pleasant voice who wants to know how he can correct his voice — these are all examples of perfectionistic images. Of course, we do not have to be already proficient to seek perfection, but the nature of the problem stands out more clearly when we are.

What is the end effect on speech? The speaker over-corrects himself and therefore increases the very errors he wants to avoid, as well as subtracts from the energy needed to develop other areas of his speech. He only wants to try what he already does well. He never gets enough done in his time and never does it just right.

Such an image is extremely coercive, for perfectionism enslaves a person to unrealistic standards. This does not mean he feels defeated by these standards. *Hope remains.* The two indispensable ingredients of perfectionism are (1) a *hope* that (2) *superior standards* may be

*The perfectionist can never take a
step without first taking thought.*

attained. But there is no peace in such a state of mind, for its very
nature demands standards beyond the level of performance, no matter
what that level may be.

1. Explain any perfectionistic standards in your own speech and demonstrate the errors that disturb you. This amounts to a review of pages
   375–376.

2. Describe a person you know whose behavior indicates that he is highly
   perfectionistic.

Fantasy

Consider poor henpecked Walter Mitty. James Thurber gives us
delightful flashes of his fantasy that day he drove his wife to town.

"We're going through!" The Commander's voice was like thin ice
breaking. He wore his full-dress uniform, with the heavily braided
white cap pulled down rakishly over one cold gray eye. "We can't
make it, Sir. It's spoiling for a hurricane, if you ask me." "I'm not
asking you, Lieutenant Berg," said the Commander. "Throw on the
power lights! Rev her up to 8,500! We're going through!" The pound-
ing of the cylinders increased: ta-pocketa-pocketa-pocketa-*pocketa-
pocketa*. The Commander stared at the ice forming on the pilot window. He walked over and twisted a row of complicated dials. "Switch

on No. 8 auxiliary!" he shouted. "Switch on No. 8 auxiliary!" repeated Lieutenant Berg. "Full strength in No. 3 turret!" shouted the Commander. "Full strength in No. 3 turret!" The crew, bending to their various tasks in the huge, hurtling eight-engined Navy hydroplane, looked at each other and grinned. "The Old Man'll get us through," they said to one another. "The Old Man ain't afraid of Hell! . . ."[1]

And when his wife interrupts his reverie to complain about his driving, "Walter Mitty drove on toward Waterbury in silence, the roaring of the SN202 . . . fading in the remote, intimate airways of his mind."

Mitty's type of fantasy, in its extreme form, results in the inability to tell reality from the images that float across the mind. Fanciful

It won't do just to dream how things will be some day.

speech will not see facts as they are, and makes whatever connections it wants in order to satisfy the dictatorial ego.

Dave gave a speech on the need for two years of universal military training. This he stated at the beginning. Immediately thereafter, apparently for fear he could not persuade his audience, he switched purpose, as follows:

[1] "The Secret Life of Walter Mitty," *The New Yorker*, March 18, 1939, p. 19. Reprinted by permission of the author.

Our generation must find some way of solving the international problem. We can not go on forever spending so much for armaments. The
national pocketbook will not stand it. Therefore I do not propose to
offer a solution. I am merely going to deal with the serious condition
of the world by raising important questions. First of all, what are we
going to do about atomic power? Are we going to use it for peace or
for warfare? A cupful of atomic material will drive a railroad train
across the nation. But how can we afford to turn potential bombs to
peaceful means, as long as Russia has atomic bombs? There can be no
peace so long as Russia has bombs. How can we be the leader of the
world unless we remain militarily the most powerful nation? How can
we be prepared for the bombing of our cities if we do not have every
man trained in modern warfare? How can we justify the death of so
many of our brave soldiers in World War II and the more recent war
in Korea? Did we have a right to stop in Korea before we had driven
every Communist back into China? . . . I do not propose to offer a solution, but it is clear we must find an answer.

Two things are obvious. The speaker did have an answer which
by some twist of logic he insisted, both in the speech and in the
evaluation afterwards, he did not have. Second, he digressed and he
was inconsistent.

This person is a fanciful thinker. Whatever comes to mind makes
sense to him. At first he might seem obtuse, unable to make fine
discriminations in thought. But two facts let us know this is not so.
In the first place he is intellectually too alert. He knows too much to
be dull. Even more significant, he rebels against the most gentle
type of evaluation. For instance, when the class stated his purpose
as favoring universal military training, he denied it and insisted they
had not listened. He had used a great many statistics, such as the
numbers in the American Army. We recommended that, in the interest of comprehension, he use round figures. He snapped, irrele-
vantly, "But the last man is as important as the first." If he did not
have a fanciful image that makes any thought seem true, he would
be able to listen to an evaluation of his speech, to hear himself as
others do. Bright people who act stupid are escapists; they make their
own "reality."

1. Tell the story of a person who could not find himself, a wanderer in life.

2. If your logic is often criticized, examine your daydreams. Do you play
   a vast number of roles unrelated to the circumstances of your life?

Keep a diary of your favorite roles. Do you see any relationships between these roles and your reasoning errors? Consider the motives involved in each.

3. Read for a week a newspaper commentator with whom you tend to disagree. Pick out examples of what you think is fanciful thinking. Give a short talk explaining the poor thinking in two or three of these examples. Can you determine what kind of self-image helps cause the writer to make these errors? Explain.

4. What, in your judgment, could be done in the rearing of children to make people less fanciful? What do you think is the effect of fairy tales upon the minds of children? of movies? of comic books? What conditioning process might help the child to use his imagination on reality? Can you devise a talk out of these questions?

Self-Righteousness

As an initial view of self-righteous speech consider the common character of the following statements:

"The only way to get an honest day's labor from a man is to threaten his children with starvation."

"Anybody you would want to know belongs to our fraternity."

"The trouble with most people is they are just plain lazy."

"We just don't do things that way here."

"Only the best people can get in here, you know."

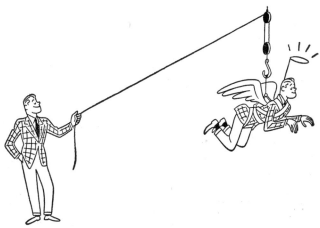

The self-righteous slave to an unrealistic image can never let go.

"How anybody can believe a thing like that!"

"If you'd give them a million, they'd be in their bare feet within a year."

"They may have things nice, but if that's the way you get it, I'll stay right where I am."

"The trouble with the European countries is they don't want to do anything for themselves. We left over there because it was a mess. Now they want us to come back and straighten it up."

"After all . . . "

It is quite possible to set up a dictator self whose purpose is to convince ourselves that, within us, things are just right as they are. As is true of all dictators, this image exists because of strife. But in this case the struggle is not to escape the person of today; rather, the self-righteous image struggles to put down any voice suggesting we are not perfect just as we are.

When we are self-righteous the most significant feature of our speech is the tendency to be extremely assertive about our beliefs and conclusions, a cut-to-order device for denying self-examination. What do we mean by assertion? It is reasoning that supports a belief by the very act of stating it. "Why am I a Republican (Democrat)? Common sense shows that Republicans (Democrats) give us the best government . . . Everybody knows that . . . Anybody should recognize that . . . Even a child knows . . . It is foolish to deny . . ." Such is the evidence of assertion. An assertion often passes undetected by the act of selecting different words that affirm what has just been said. For instance, we may say, "Let us vote for Joe Doaks. Why? Because he is without doubt our best man." We would see through our lack of examination if we were to say, "Let's vote for Joe because we have decided to vote for Joe." The only difference is that, in the former case, the insistence "What I say makes it so" does not stand out so clearly.

One cannot help recalling here these insights in Robert Frost's poem, "Mending Wall." The poet tells about a man who finds security by walling himself in, doing so because his self-god can exist only so long as he is free of the influence of other men.

> . . . I see him there
> Bringing a stone grasped firmly by the top
> In each hand, like an old-stone savage armed.
> He moves in darkness as it seems to me,

> Not of woods only and the shade of trees.
> He will not go behind his father's saying,
> And he likes having thought of it so well
> He says again, "Good fences make good neighbors." [2]

Assertion is the evidence of the self-righteous.[3]

Self-righteousness often forms an alliance with vindictiveness. The beliefs and speech of others that do not correspond to our own are mortal enemies, when we are self-righteous. Naturally enough, the source of these messages must be destroyed.

> . . . when all's said
> Right's right, and the temptation to do right
> When I can hurt someone by doing it
> Has always been too much for me, it has.[4]

It naturally follows that the less the self-righteous person is concerned with those who differ with him, the less he will have need of vindication. Serene, complacent, and secure self-righteousness depends upon learning to be a psychological hermit.

1. Listen to three conversations and write down the self-righteous comments you hear. Do you notice any physical behavior that attends this speech? In some way you will see the person pat himself on the back. Perhaps a sigh after the self-righteous remark, as much as to say, "I'm pleased with you, boy; you brush off enemies so expertly." Are there any characteristics of the voice that attend self-righteous comments? You will notice, for instance, that the quality will say one of two things: (1) "Of course, everybody agrees with me," or (2) "Anybody who counts agrees with me." When does the "smugness" change to "contempt"? Draw up a speech from your findings.

2. Practice reading the examples of self-righteous speech at the beginning of this discussion. Which are vindictive? Read the sentences in class and explain.

---

[2] From *Complete Poems of Robert Frost*. Copyright 1930, 1949, by Henry Holt and Company, Inc., p. 48. By permission of the publishers.

[3] The writer constructed a test of thinking which incorporated "assertive" reasoning. (See page 201.) The results suggested that assertion was the second most popular kind of thinking among a group of college students when they were in a situation in which they knew their thinking was being examined.

[4] "Two Witches," from *Complete Poems of Robert Frost*. Copyright 1930, 1949, by Henry Holt and Company, Inc., p. 253. By permission of the publishers.

Self-Effacement

Barbara is a tall, attractive blond. She seems moderately interested in the class and does all the work assigned, though she never contributes unless called upon. In speech assignments she is considerably less responsive than in social situations, reporting that the competitiveness of certain class members makes her feel "sort of uncomfortable." Her tension, however, is not perceptible to many, her adjustment suggesting a mixture of sadness and boredom. While she reacts warmly to the audience, her smile might be described as low in energy. This also applies to her voice which, though full, is too low pitched, and speaks little of a need to stir the listener. Perhaps the key symptoms of her image are a purposeless posture, slightly dropping shoulders, and a weak action of the lips, tongue, and facial muscles.

Self-effacing speech is guided by an extremely dominant interpersonal echo and equally low self-hearing. It is no less dictatorial

He underestimates himself; there's
more to him than he thinks.

than the other images discussed, but is such as to suggest not change or search but the uselessness of the effort. The speaker woefully contrasts the desired self with the "discouraging" reality. Such a speaker is led to say, "What is wrong with my speech?" rather than "What can I do about it?" With his attention on personal shortcomings, real or imagined, he becomes certain that these are the most pronounced features of his personality. So much do they fill his world that he is sure he can be seen by other people in no other way.

This person generally likes to be around people and reports that he gets blue only when alone. Since he conceives of himself as a relative failure, it is no fun to talk to himself. In the company of others, he seldom directs the conversation to his own internal life; his attention is directed outward.

It is obvious that this person will do what is generally classified as C work, and though he might wish for better he will seldom complain. He may even feel fortunate to do that well, for after all he has placed this label upon himself. As may be imagined, self-effacement is not conducive to speech growth. The speaker, fully convinced that his speech is a revelation of inadequacy, dissipates energy in defense that should be directed to vital communication. The consequence is unimaginative and indecisive speech, low in vitality, slovenly in delivery, and dull to eye and ear.

Occasionally we come upon a student whose speech shows all the symptoms discussed here but who is extremely concerned about his speech. This student is not quite convinced of his inability to improve. One such student did not try to change, yet he acted half angry about it, variously whining, complaining, and worrying. No matter what assignments were suggested he objected to them, only to turn around and ask for help. Somehow he seemed to think there must be a magic formula somewhere. Another student, starting a course in speech with the same feeling, gradually conditioned himself to adopt a much more aggressive image, mixed with considerable self-acceptance. He became reasonably successful as a public speaker and extremely successful as a campus politician, holding some of the most important campus offices in his junior and senior years.

1. If this description fits you, you will have mixed feelings about revealing yourself to the audience. You will want to do so because you enjoy human warmth. On the other hand, you will want to remain silent because you fear losing approval. However, your defenses need to be lowered in order to break the conflict which holds you in monotonous, low-voltage speech. Once you are rewarded for talking openly, you will be on the right track.

2. If you are disturbed by your slovenly posture and diction, follow a persistent campaign of negative practice and reconditioning as explained in Chapter 19.

Indecisiveness

Another common problem is a confused, rapid alternation between superiority and self-effacement.[5] Such a mixture "does not make sense," but human attitudes can be as contradictory as yes and no. Just as one may both love and hate the same person, so may he love and hate himself in successive seconds, or even at once. In addition, as Rollo May says, it is our conflicting attitudes toward self that cause our conflicting attitudes toward others.[6] It is common to hear

It's confusing not to know whether
you're bigger than life — or smaller!

evidence of internal attack and apology. "No, that's not so. Well, I don't mean it the way it sounds. But anybody knows. . . . Well, what I mean. . . ." This blundering and disorganized shadow-boxing is the result of mixed feelings. Each attitude brought to self-hearing gives rise to another, for the speaker does not know what he wants to hear in himself. This is just another facet of the trial-and-error adjustment to fear explained in Chapter 19. If in this explanation you see yourself, turn to the last group of exercises on page 402.

[5] Karl Menninger, *The Human Mind*, New York, Alfred A. Knopf, Inc., 1942, pp. 70–74.

[6] Rollo May, *The Art of Counseling*, New York, Abingdon-Cokesbury Press, 1939, Chapters I and II.

Means and Ends

When we accept ourselves we are concerned with means. We look upon life as a going concern, conceiving of self as the product of past experiences. We survey our present state, consider our interests, and decide the next move. The dictator-self, conversely, is obsessed by ends. The urge to divorce the imagined self from behavior that proves it false is aided by keeping attention on ends, thereby projecting out of the present, out of reality. The dictator-self is a fear structure, an avoidance of what we are at the moment.

There is just one way to find a target. That is to change the aim of the gun. *This can be done only to the degree that we are able to hear echoes of the difference between the target and the gun position.* In the speaker, once he gets the target-set, and scans with ease, the ability to alter his aim depends upon his self-hearing. Only the person who accepts himself as he is, rather than idealizing a part of himself and rejecting the rest, can develop this skill.

EXTERNAL STIMULATION TO CHANGE

The Use of Simultaneous Feedback

In Chapter 3 we discussed techniques for altering target-set, for learning to be more aware of audience needs. Now we want to arrange the speech situation to give you the maximum ability to hear yourself speak — and thereby to change your aim as efficiently as possible. What should be done, however, depends upon the present state of your self-hearing.

In order to check your self-hearing the instructor may sit in the audience at the controls of a public address system.[7] The loud speaker should also be in the audience and directed toward you at the microphone. After you become oriented and seem to be well started, your instructor will slowly raise the volume. The feedback will give you a self-hearing acuity which brings into sharp focus the role you are playing. He will search for that volume level that seems to help you function most efficiently.

[7] Many tape recorders may be used as public address equipment by turning on the speaker while recording. For machines that do not have an "on-off" switch in the speaker, it is necessary to plug in an auxiliary speaker. A large speaker is desirable, of course. Most tape recorders are designed so that the tone control does not affect the speaker during recording. As a result the quality is unpleasant. This may be remedied by having a variable choke put in the speaker line at very low cost.

You will find that a small microphone which you hold in your hand is better for the purposes of this chapter than a microphone on a stand. The very physical contact with the instrument, together with your altered self-hearing, helps you to identify yourself with what you hear. The effect is also enhanced by the fact that you will tend to speak closer to a microphone in the hand than to one on a stand.

Corrective Feedback in the Self-Hearing Circuit. If you have the right degree of self-hearing, your speech is flexible and adjusts to the needs of the situation, with or without increased self-hearing. In this case the rise and fall of volume in the loud speaker will have little effect upon you. You need no aid.

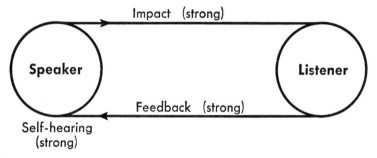

Low Feedback in the Self-Hearing Circuit. Some students find that increased self-hearing is a distinctive and dramatic aid. These persons have a self-accepting image, and hearing themselves better than usual lets them see how to change more effectively than usual.

Hearing yourself, if your voice is flat and monotonous, you will search for more varied expression. If you sense your normal low degree of "fire power," you will tend toward a more vital speech. If

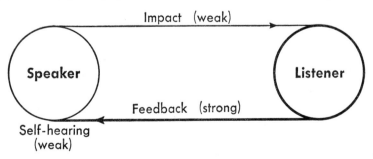

you are slow in pace, you will search for a faster movement of the idea. If you usually feel that the audience is overpowering, the increased volume will give you a sense of dominance that permits you to release your energies.

If you react this way, you need to speak a few times while the instructor constantly signals whether you are searching effectively. When you are "on the beam" he will lower the volume to see if you can guide yourself. If you seem to drift away from an effective search, he will bring up the volume, informing you that you are not hunting and at the same time sharpening your self-hearing.

After a while you will begin to anticipate the changes in volume. This means that you know when you are in or out of tune with your listeners. At this point you should inform your instructor of your increased ability to know when to hunt. In the next speech the instructor will set the volume at a level desirable to you. You may step away from the microphone when you are doing well, trying to maintain the needed circuit relations without artificially increased hearing. If you feel you are not doing well, you should move back into the range of the microphone.

By "doing well" we mean communicating with an audience. When an audience is responding with alert attention, you are on target. When you are off target, it may be for a variety of causes. You may lack a clear picture of what you want to say, your delivery may not be alive, your language may not be vital, your emotions may not generate communication, or your ideas may not organize well. It may also be that you are not well prepared or just not "up to par." At any rate, effective change depends upon hearing what you are doing and comparing it with the needs of the audience as revealed by your study of it.

Excessive Feedback in the Self-Hearing Circuit. You have probably had the experience of hearing yourself as if your voice were detached, as if it did not belong to you. If so, you identify yourself so closely with some idealized image, such as aggression, arrogance, perfection, self-righteousness, etc., that you do not dare hear your voice for fear it will inform you of your self-deception. The result is that increased self-hearing, by way of a loud speaker, accentuates your difficulties. This is particularly true of those who stumble because they try not to. Hearing themselves on the loud speaker causes them to stumble more than ever. Those who have a dictatorial standard of good speech organization react in the same way. Whatever they say in the first sentence puts them on an idea or memory treadmill. They not only have trouble getting to another idea, but cannot find the end of the one they are on. As a result they often have a compulsion to write and read their speeches, which of course they should not do. Many students with dictatorial images of good speech are literally unable to see the audience when the volume of a loud speaker is turned up. They become so immersed in themselves that the interpersonal feedback is short-circuited.

Students who cannot change because of excessive feedback will benefit from a question-answer period after their speeches. This forces

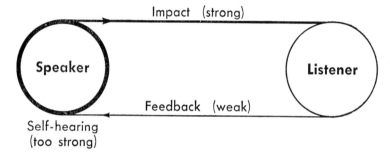

them to bring the audience feedback into relative dominance. The impromptu assignments discussed in Chapter 4 will also be of aid. To be helpful at this point, any techniques must de-emphasize self-hearing and bring the interpersonal circuit into operation. The resulting change is from a too highly idealized kind of speech to that of self-acceptance.

In Don's case, placing him close to the audience and lowering the intensity of the light was effective. He felt that the latter adjustment helped particularly. In Jane, the extreme relaxation of the audience created the optimum condition for relearning. You will find that the technique that works is one that makes you feel more intimate with the audience and less in danger of being rejected.

Separately or in conjunction with the above, it is possible to use a masking noise to lower self-hearing. Any constant noise will do. The purpose is to put so much "line noise" in the hearing circuit that the intelligibility of the hearing becomes confused. Of course noise also affects thinking. Therefore preparation needs to be good. But sensitivity to oneself is indeed lowered by an irritating masking sound.

However, those who do not want to listen to themselves should learn to do so eventually. The above assignments are intended to establish a proper relationship between attention to the audience and attention to the self. In the end, this relationship should be maintained while the speaker is highly sensitive to the impact of his words.

Again, whatever techniques produce good results need to be gradually discontinued as fixed self-control is learned.

Excessively Low Feedback in the Self-Hearing Circuit. With this difficulty the problem is not to return a habit to conscious control, as in the case of *low* feedback, but to correct for a self-effacing image.

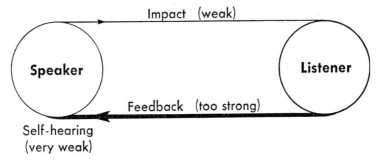

Most of the idealized images produce over-corrective hearing. But self-effacement, the conviction that the odds are against attaining the ideal, makes self-hearing extremely difficult.

If you belong to this group, you will respond somewhat to the stimulation of the loud speaker, though without much awareness of doing so, responding favorably but unconsciously. Such speakers, *when they do start* hearing themselves, improve miraculously. They become much more dominant, and often respond to audience reactions for the first time. Conversely, when the loud speaker is suddenly shut off, they literally wilt.

If this is your problem, before this dramatic self-hearing takes place you must rely on the instructor and the class to feed to you the results after each performance. You may need the volume turned up painfully high and varied considerably until you are forced to hear. Sometimes it helps to place the loud speaker to one side about ten feet away, instead of directly ahead. This causes you to hear yourself more in one ear than the other, an abnormal situation which alters hearing perspective. Or the loud speaker may be placed so that it faces a back or side wall. This sets up a delayed echo which will command your attention. Since you will have to adjust your rate in order to "live" with the echo, you will be forced to hear. Since the latter two techniques will disturb your memory, they should be used only when preparation has been good.

As you learn to hear yourself, you should pass through the "weaning" stages so that you can understand and change your speech under full self-control.

Control of the Public Address Volume by the Speaker. If you are disturbed by the prospect of having a second person manipulate your self-hearing (though few people are), the controls may be placed on the desk before you so you can adjust the volume yourself. Should you do this, however, it is recommended that you try this alone in practice a few times to become adapted to speaking while handling the controls. You will find that you can adjust, perhaps all that is necessary, by varying your distance from the microphone.

Practice with Public Address Equipment. If hearing yourself on the public address equipment strengthens your capacity to speak effectively, it is certainly desirable that you practice with it. As always in learning new skills, you will find that results vary with persistence in daily practice. Do not judge hastily whether the technique works. Time is necessary just to adapt to the newness of the experience.

If equipment is not available for such practice, you may cup your hand like a shell behind one ear. If you use this technique, you should take your hand away when you feel you are speaking vigorously and in harmony with your imagined audience. Return it occasionally to determine whether you are maintaining the desired speech.

One important word of warning about the use of increased self-hearing in preparation: *You should practice the speech aloud several times before experimenting.* If you do not, dominance of the self-hearing circuit will reduce your capacity to think and to put your ideas into words.

The Use of Post-Feedback

Thus far we have discussed devices for increasing your sensitivity to the feedback you receive as you proceed. Only as you learn to hear what you are doing while you are doing it, are you in a position to hit a moving target — which, of course, is what your audience is. Yet much can be done in retrospect that gives the set for improved simultaneous hearing on the next occasion.

The tape recorder is extremely helpful for this purpose. Record your speech and play it back a number of times — until you can learn no more about yourself. You will find that the use of earphones, in place of a loud speaker, gives much more effective self-hearing for this purpose. The loud speaker can be seen and thereby dissociated from yourself, while the earphones identify your words more closely with yourself. The first two or three playbacks may be of little value beyond getting you introduced to and acquainted with yourself. As soon as you begin to get clear reactions to the re-plays, write down what impressed you. "I like the depth and strength of my voice." "I wish I had not stumbled there." "I feel kind of ashamed of the dogma and self-importance in that statement." A study of the most impressive reactions gives you the data for appraising your self-images. For instance, "I am disturbed by the smugness of that statement" suggests that you were talking self-righteously. Hearing this gives you a "time lead" on your correction in the next speech. In practice and in delivery of this next speech, you are more likely to hear yourself if you drift into self-righteousness.

You may find that you learn something about yourself for two or three listenings, but that boredom then sets in. When this happens, turn off the machine and return to the job the next day. Upon the second occasion you will learn something new. You may find a point in the speech where you grow monotonous and make little progress, or a striking phrase, a place where the audience laughed, a section that marches with good organization, a good transition, an afterthought that came bubbling out to correct for a reaction from your audience. From these more minute observations you learn further what makes for good adjustment in speech.

Have your audience report on slips of paper all they are aware of that you aroused in them. This should be as specific and as honest a report as is possible. We are particularly interested in the images and emotions you conveyed. If you do not understand the audience reactions, you should see the listeners individually and talk it out with them, whether the comment is favorable or otherwise.

Out of your appraisal of playbacks and the comments of others, set down the particular goals you choose to work on. In each speech while you are seeking to change, concentrate upon one or two of these objectives. Tell your audience before you begin what goal you have in mind and evaluate the results against both your own and the audience responses afterward.

Beyond what you comprehend that lets you hear better in the next speech situation, you are learning to look at yourself objectively and to analyze yourself unemotionally. This is a tremendous aid in destroying compulsive images. To hear yourself is a way to find and accept yourself. To learn good speech is to grow as a person.

QUESTIONS FOR STUDY AND DISCUSSION

1. Can you explain the relation between the echoes that change the aim of a gun and the echoes that change a speaker?

2. What does the "fouled up" mechanical chess player have to do with speaking?

3. What causes us not to hear ourselves?

4. What is meant by a self-image?

5. What does purpose have to do with the self-image we develop?

6. Can you explain what is meant by self-acceptance?

7. What is meant by a dictator self? What are the dictator selves? Explain the nature of each.

8. What kind of speech problem is common with weak self-hearing? What is the device for improving the condition?

9. What kind of speech problem is present with an excessive amount of self-hearing? What devices help correct for it?

10. Describe the speech that results from an extremely low degree of self-hearing. What may be done to improve the condition?

SUGGESTIONS AND ASSIGNMENTS

As a practical device to see how many roles you can identify with yourself, give a series of speeches, each of which calls for a different relationship to the listener.

a. Tell a funny story.
b. Defend a favorite belief.
c. Give an aggressive speech.

   d. Prepare a speech that makes a plea.
   e. Register a complaint with the class.
   f. Give an informative speech.
   g. Speak in an arrogant style.
   h. Present an idea in a smug manner.
   i. Make an apology.
   j. Give a speech in a cool and indifferent fashion.

Do not tell the class what emotional orientation you are taking. Let the class label your behavior after you have finished. You will find it easier to assume a given role if the idea involved in the speech tends to arouse the attitudes you are going to express.

How many of these roles can you play with ease?

" . . . minds are made in the relationships of men . . . "

Bonaro W. Overstreet

Interaction and Personality

As WE HAVE SEEN all through this book, the focus of speech education is on the adjustment of the speaker to the target, his audience. The preceding chapter discussed the importance of hearing himself, so that the speaker will come to know when he is actually communicating with his listeners, and not just talking to himself. This final chapter describes attitudes toward the audience which further affect the speaker's relationship with his listeners.

In the telescope of the gun pointer one not only can see when he is moving toward or away from the target, but whether this movement is north, south, east, or west of the target. There are comparable, though less obvious, "directions" in speech. It is those to which we turn now.

The Three-Way Interaction in Speech

All interaction between a speaker and other persons is governed by one of three kinds of behavior on the part of the speaker, or by some combination of them.[1] As we are all too often reminded, it is possible, first, for a speaker to oppose or attack a listener or a conversant — that is, to be *aggressive*. Second, it is possible to accept another's beliefs, attitudes, or actions in place of one's own — that is, to be *submissive*. Third, it is possible to avoid a meeting or a conflict, to detach oneself from contact — that is, to *withdraw*. These simple actions, or more complex combinations of them, produce all the combinations of interaction between speaker and listener.

Flexibility and Cooperation

The most desirable adjustment is the freedom to attack, submit, or withdraw from the listener according to the wisdom of the situation.

---

[1] Karen Horney, *Our Inner Conflicts*, New York, W. W. Norton and Company, Inc., 1954, pp. 48–95; Stuart Chase, *Roads to Agreement*, New York, Harper and Brothers, 1951, p. 193.

Most of us, however, *tend* to adjust in one of these three ways more than the others. The more we tend to do so, of course, the less freedom and flexibility we have to solve the problems of living with others.

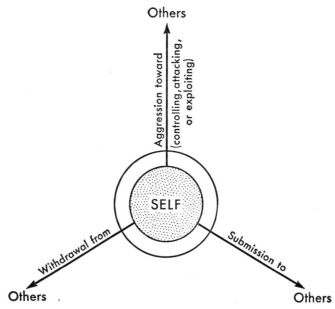

Cooperation means moving in any one of the three ways with almost equal ease.

In such behavior we act compulsively, half aware of our awkwardness and our failure to respond adequately to the demands of the particular situation.

The more a person is restricted to one approach the more he creates tension in those with whom he communicates, so that non-flexible behavior not only limits the person so impelled, but also affects others. Have you known the kind of person who would throw you a pack of cigarettes with the remark, "Here, Stoop, don't say I never gave you anything." He cannot be friendly without being rough, and the incongruous mixture of attitudes makes it difficult for you to respond freely. "What is the attitude?" you half consciously ask yourself. "Am I paid a price to be verbally kicked? If I react warmly, maybe I am stupid." As a result your reaction is awkward and conflicting. It is this sort of tension, rigidity, and limitation, resulting from dictatorial self-images, discussed in Chapter 20, that creates the need for a clear understanding of human interaction.

It should be clear from the foregoing discussion that there are three distinct kinds of action we may take in our relations with others, and that these three produce four kinds of behavior patterns. We may submit, attack, withdraw, or cooperate. The fourth pattern, cooperation (see figure on page 431), results from the capacity to shift from one to another of the other three kinds of behavior as the occasion requires. We all do this, but with varying degrees of success, and much of the difference between us depends on how far in one of the extremes our image takes us. When we are filled with hate, a kind word from the enemy does not produce cooperation; we are oriented too far out on the aggressive scale to make the shift. And some people are habitually too aggressive, submissive, or withdrawn to shift to other kinds of behavior except when shocked.

COOPERATIVE SPEECH

Occasionally one meets a person who has that remarkable balance which we praise as objective. His speech is ready but he is not excited by the need for authority, prestige, or position. His tensions are low, though arousable if he is attacked. He closes conversations and parts

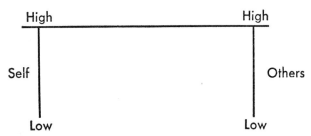

Confidence scale of cooperative speech.

company with decision and without stress. He tends to deliberate and to qualify. He is not dogmatic. His speech runs at an easy pace and is not clipped. His vocal quality is pleasant, reflecting the low tensions of his body. The pitch of the cooperative speaker usually rides a wide and varied range. Cooperation depends for emphasis upon inflection rather than on force, though the volume is adequate. The posture and body tone are good. Since the cooperative person is not compulsively self-oriented, his speech does not attract attention to itself.

Confidence

All this suggests that the distinctive feature of the cooperative person is his high confidence in both himself and others. At least three skills go to make up such confidence. First, the person is sensitive to the words, actions, and purposes of other people. Second, by "listening" to himself he is alerted to the effect of his words and deeds upon others. Third, he knows how to express his own purposes with concern for the interests of others. This mixture of self and others reflects the ego with a long radius, discussed in Chapter 18, pages 346–347.

Cooperative Speech and Democracy

Cooperative speech *divides power equally* among the members of the group, and therefore reflects the ideals of democracy. Mutual faith among people, as we have said, is the silent premise in cooperative action. Any discrediting of the average intelligence, appreciation, ability, and stability of the group is an attack upon the wisdom of democratic action in that group. Censorship of the speech of any member of the group (regardless of how repulsive it may be) demonstrates a lack of trust in the stability of the group at large. Any feeling that the co-acting of the masses is weak, ineffective, and unnatural to man indicates a disposition toward dictatorial control. We all show these doubts at times, and to the extent that we act upon them, we fail to put the democratic idea to work.

This is not a defense of ignorance or of the convictions of the least informed. But the capacity to cooperate in a group demands a respect for group judgments, and a belief that group judgments are more likely to be correct than those of any one individual.

We live in a world of intense hatred and enmity. Because of this, cooperation is often looked upon, by those oriented at the extremes, as an impracticable ideal. Cooperation may just be, however, the only road to survival. The flexibility of cooperative speech and the spirit of compromise are two views of the kind of behavior that permits those who disagree to live together. It is ideal if their cooperation can be based on mutual understanding. But as the German poet and novelist Goethe has said, a man understands only what he loves. We all know that the Christian ethic states that we should love even our enemies. Mankind at large, however, has not found it possible to adopt this behavior. The immediate hope of survival rests in the fact that a great many people are flexible enough to cooperate, to give and take, to co-exist with those they do not fully understand and appreciate.

1. Describe a person you know who is cooperative in his speech. Imitate his speech.
2. Take part in a discussion group (see pages 198–202 and 211) on the capacity of individuals to cooperate. At the end of the discussion evaluate yourself and the others in your abilities to adjust to group needs. Use specific examples.
3. If you feel considerable impatience and discomfort in working with a group, and desire to stretch your cooperative skills, join groups and allow yourself to be appointed to committees. Search out social situations. To live closely and easily with people demands cooperative adjustment.

SUBMISSIVE SPEECH

The existence of society arises from the human ability to submit to common interests. Whether this social drive arose later in man's evolution than aggressiveness is a matter of speculation. But it is clear that the tendency for modern man to join together exceeds his aggressiveness. How else explain the fact that we live in a highly interdependent society? Where man exists there is social control, which can mean but one thing — that men are willing *to give up* part of their personal freedom in order to be with others.

Men submit to control in one of two distinctive fashions, confidently or fearfully.

Confident Submission

Speech is the restless search to find our way through the problems that the ticking of the clock forces upon us. Janet illustrates in the following speech how the poised submissive person solves conflict and frustration.

Saturdays I work on the elevators at ———. Since the Christmas season has started the store has been especially busy. Usually I enjoy working when there is a crowd, but Saturday was so cold that good dispositions were at a minimum.

Because the elevators try to run separately the center elevator goes to the basement every trip, the end cars occasionally. Saturday I was on an end car. After a particularly annoying trip, being crowded in the corner, having my feet stepped on, a lady's hat feather dangle in my face while she swung her loaded handbag in my direction, a father

Confidence scale of the confidently submissive.

holding his two-year-old boy up so his feet rested on my clean uniform, and having to answer questions like "What's on the second floor?" "Where could I find something for my niece?" "Did we stop at two, Miss?" as we approached four, I went to the basement, which is usually not so busy, for a chance to pull myself together.

Standing before the elevator door in the basement was the plumpest little boy. He had curly reddish blond hair and freckles over a pug nose. He was holding his coat and cap, watching the elevators come and go. When I came down in an empty elevator and opened the door he reached out and took my hand. He was about four and he did — he really did — a big slow deliberate wink.

"Come on, Mom, this is ours." He was talking to a woman a table or two away. She told him she wasn't quite ready.

It was time for me to go up again, so I left him standing there waving his pudgy hand. When I came back down next trip he was gone. I am glad, because it made our encounter the more glowing. It was such a warm exchange. It melted the irritations of the whole afternoon.

The words confidence, poise, and dominance refers to the inclination of a person to maintain his own purposes in face-to-face relationships. As is always true of the cooperative speaker, it is quite possible for a submissive person to be confident.[2] In fact, the only distinction between the two is that the co-acting person is more capable of shifting back and forth between the role of leading and that of following.

[2] See Chapter 18, p. 362.

In contrast, the confident submissive person, more strongly oriented in the interaction of "going toward" people, sees for himself little value in leading others. At the same time, he will follow only his chosen leaders. Such followers are indispensable to a democratic order. The only leaders that can influence these people are those sensitive to their wishes.

One cannot overstress the tremendously poised position of a person who trusts both himself and others sufficiently to let others organize and execute the rules of social interaction, while he follows his more natural bents. A large number of Americans demonstrate this quality of confident submission. They do not feel impelled to rail at those who do not agree with them. They would rather follow their present occupations and in their spare time play a game of golf, frolic on the beach, study, grow geraniums, read a story, watch TV, or fall into a bull session. Stirring up fears and anxieties, or even being alert to all the "emergencies" of those who make a career out of describing the doom that is sure to come unless others listen to them, is not necessarily good citizenship. On the contrary, there is no better guarantee of democratic success than the existence of a populace stable enough to channel its energy into its own satisfying and uniting activities.

1. If you know a person who seems to be confidently submissive, give a short talk in which the class may see the behavior and speech of this person.
2. In a panel discussion before the class, assume the attitudes of the confidently-submissive. Have the class evaluate your ability to play the role. Did you find it satisfying? Why?

Fearful Submission

Those who submit out of weakness do so because they fear themselves or both themselves and others.

Fear of Self. Mary is always tensely smiling, and usually listening. Her voice is soft and pleasant, but marked by slovenly diction. Her movements are in harmony with her voice. She slumps, moves in parts and not as a unit, rhythmically and regressively swinging her arms when she is the center of attention.

The person who is strongly suggestible falls into this class. Those who believe what they are told, who easily bow to authority, who switch purposes readily under the direction of others, who stick closely to the stereotypes and values of their day, are fearfully submissive. We should not conclude that such people are dull. They do average work and would do better if they thought they could. They are not

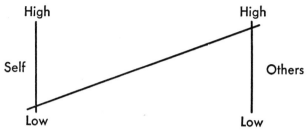

Confidence scale of the submissive who fears himself.

very effective, however, in problems of individual reasoning, for life has taught them to be uncritical. These are the conformists of society.

Such speakers are excessively sensitive to the actions of others, and the smile is designed to secure much-needed approval. It is as if their center of gravity were in others, instead of in themselves. Besides, since they are ashamed of their true selves, they present a pleasant mask so that they may not reveal the unhappy fellow within. The misfortune of this adjustment does not arise from compliance itself; all submission is compliance. Rather, it comes from the fact that the motive is fear, in this case fear of self.

While people who fear themselves are often pleasant, they are also dangerous for a democracy. These are the people who make the majority dangerous. They represent weight, not individuality, and by the number of their noses add power to the leader. Right to these people means the strongest voice in their society. Rather than fostering conformity in the many by developing strong speech in the few, the greatest need of our system is to arouse a sense of the dignity of individuality and the right of difference for all.

This is not to discredit social leadership. Society cannot do without it. But devastating harm is done in our culture by over-emphasizing its importance. In the writer's classes, 60 per cent of the students place power over others in first or second place among the things they consider worthwhile.[3] Many of these students demonstrate that they

[3] Using the G. W. Allport, P. E. Vernon, and G. Lindzey *A Study of Values*, revised edition, Boston, Houghton Mifflin Company, 1951.

have no profound interest in social organization and leadership, and they feel inadequate because they do not. Many will go through the frustrating experience of trying to find a position that will give them the power they are afraid of. What is even worse, all but a few of the remaining 40 per cent are ashamed because they do not want leadership roles. It is tragic, indeed, when men learn to believe that they must do what they do not want to do in order to gain their highest potential. Either they try to become leaders and fail, or they follow their more natural inclinations, ashamed. Both in the interest of stable democratic citizenry and of speech poise, the worth of confident submission needs to take a place nearer center stage.

The distinctive feature of the speech of the submissive person who fears himself, as we have suggested, is poor articulation and mumbling. Sometimes the image that produced the shame is still present; sometimes it is dead. If the former, the person must come to understand the falseness of his standards and to see how he came to visualize himself as he does. In short, he must learn how to cease fearing himself. Where the shame is dead but the slovenly speech persists, the habit may be broken by the use of negative practice.[4]

> Does this explanation bring to your mind a person you know? If so, prepare a short speech in which you describe this person in action. Let us see and hear his speech.

Fear of Self; Less Fear of Others. The moment extreme dependency is threatened by doubt of others, the speech changes, becoming defensive and usually satirical because the speaker is suspicious of his friends, yet needs them. Consequently, within the submissive role, he develops the skills of aggression. The humor and the smiles are a façade, and the careful observer will note the alert calculation that attends the smile. More clearly aggressive is the clipped diction, the cues of condescension, and the barbed tongue. This way he plays a role of mixed love and hate. In our culture we find such a style of speech reasonably attractive, and from the platform we love it. The fascination lies in its duplicity, and we are likely to ascribe more depth to it than it merits.

The appeal and structure may be seen in the following samples:

---

[4] As one learns to read the presence or absence of tension in speech, he may know whether submissive speech is a carry-over. If the slovenly speaker seems uninhibited we are reasonably sure that the slovenliness is habit. (See page 54.)

Confidence scale of submissive who fears both self and others.

"History is a story of something that didn't happen, told by a man who wasn't there."

"A lecture is that which passes from the notebook of the professor to the notebook of the student without going through the head of either."

"A politician is a man who meets all problems with an open mouth."

"How do they grow senators? They just club them over the heads when they are small boys."

"Philosophy is the study of less and less about more and more, until you know nothing about everything. The only hope for mankind lies in science, for the scientist teaches you more and more about less and less until you know everything about nothing."

"A freshman is a student who has not been in college long enough to become completely ignorant."

The cynicism that pervades such speech is the aggressive tool; the humor, the submissive tool. But there are combinations of aggression and submission without humor. Consider the following:

"If you loved your mother, you could not possibly behave this way."

"Why do you treat me this way when you know I love you so?"

"I know you are an upstanding citizen and will do your duty."

"I am turning this job over to you because I know I can have confidence in you."

Two of these statements suggest the feeling described here; the other two would more likely be said with cooperative or aggressive feelings. Can you sense the difference?

Perhaps you know a person who shows mixed fear and aggression. Tell the class about him. Illustrate his behavior. Can you explain the forces that have shaped his attitudes?

AGGRESSIVE SPEECH

A race of creatures with limited knowledge of the desires of others and of the right thing to do for all would be lost in total anarchy were it not for the confidence of some in their ability to direct the society. A degree of aggressiveness is therefore implicit in leadership.

Moreover, aggression mixed with the stability and socializing ingredient of love is good for self and society, as indicated in the discussion of cooperative speech. When aggression is balanced with a real concern for the welfare of others, control is the more effective, for herein lies the psychological basis for genuine tact and disarming persuasion. The listener is led to believe, by the gentleness of the approach, that "he thought of the idea all by himself." This is not a short sermon on the value of deception. It is recognition of the facts that (1) interest in the listener "cushions" control, and (2) a listener does not accept what he is on guard against. Aggression is to society what atomic energy is to the physical universe. Under control it is a great force working in behalf of man. Out of control, it spells his doom.

The essential question is, what degree of aggressive speech fits the needs of the audience and the speaker?

General Eisenhower had just returned from Europe in 1952, riding the widespread boom for his election to the presidency. He apparently interpreted the situation as one that would best be solved by pouring oil on troubled waters. But his original remarks at Abilene did not fit the temper of the day and were something of a disappointment. His followers took renewed hope as he adjusted to personality conflict.

Time magazine, reviewing the General's early campaign for the nomination, said,

> Ever since Abilene many of Ike's friends had been nagged by the feeling that his campaign lacked spirit and a sense of direction. Last week, however, things seemed to be picking up. Ike, throwing off his reluctance to deal in personalities and political maneuver, came out slugging at the Taft organization, displaying some of the hard-hitting self-assurance that Americans expect of a leader.[5]

And yet the American fighter must not get too tough.

> Candidate Taft put on the benign air of a man who has already won the decision, and is just waiting until it is made official . . . He was

[5] Reprinted from *Time*, June 30, 1952, p. 15. Copyright Time Inc.

quicker to smile, less inclined to the harsh word, and seemed to feel a little sorry for his Republican opponents. Now and then a slight sneer flitted across his face, but on the whole he was a much more appealing television personality than the Fighting Bob of the last six months, who often looked ready to eat the microphone.[6]

We can offer no formula for the proper mixture of aggression in speech. We can only observe that considerable fight is expected and rewarded in the speech of Western culture, and that this varies from situation to situation. Each speaker must decide for himself the needs of the audience, what he wants to be, and the impact he desires to leave.

Note the combination of superior rightness, lance-like force, and sharpness in a famous speech by Henry Grattan, an Irish statesman of the last century. Read this aloud with the feeling the words suggest. Appraise your voice, bodily tone, and posture.

> Has the gentleman done? Has he completely done? He was unparliamentary from the beginning to the end of his speech! There was scarce a word he uttered that was not a violation of the privileges of the House. But I did not call him to order — why? Because the limited talents of such men render it impossible for them to be severe without being unparliamentary. But before I sit down, I shall show him how to be severe and parliamentary at the same time.

The speech of open aggression is marching and incisive. The language is barbed. The speaker's rate leans to the rapid. His diction is precise. His melody tends to be in the upper register and narrow in range. His voice quality is either cold and matter of fact or irritatingly negative.[7] The latter adjustment is usually in a higher key than the former. He speaks with decided force and considerable variety.

The body tone of the aggressive person is good to tense. He gestures with decision. His step is firm. His fear — a basic element in aggression, as we shall see — is usually under control and may be perceptible only to the keen eye.

What are the attitudes that move our aim further and further in the aggressive direction?

---

6 *Ibid.*, p. 16.

7 Melba Hurd, using the Bell Inventory and teachers' ratings, found a low negative correlation (around −.24) between aggressiveness and quality, pitch, and force.

The General Character of Aggression

First, the aggressive person is one who derives a thrill in excelling others. He has a good measure of the competitive spirit. Basically, it is the love of power that drives him. Along with this essential ingredient go reinforcing elements. The leader feasts on prestige and recognition. He enjoys strategy and is ever alert for opportunities to press his advantage. If this particular feature of his personality becomes exaggerated, his whole emotional life tends to orient itself between the poles of victory and defeat. Compromise becomes a ridiculous or shameful value. Of course, when he approaches an extreme on the scale of opposing people he becomes exploitative and ruthless. As this point is approached, he loses sympathy. Sensitivity is replaced by calculation and suspicion. He puts others on guard, which in turn intensifies his own guard.

1. Fear and Aggression. The desire to control others is, in the end, the fear of being controlled and a feeling of inadequacy.

> The ability of man to make productive use of his powers is his potency; the inability is his impotence. With his power of reason he can penetrate the surfaces of phenomena and understand their essence. With his power of love he can break through the wall that separates one person from another. With his power of imagination he can visualize things not yet existing; he can plan and thus begin to create. Where potency is lacking, man's relatedness to the world is perverted into a desire to dominate, to exert power over others as though they were things.[8]

So it is that the aggressive speaker is caught in the web of his own fears, both of self and of others. We may illustrate this by a process of elimination. When we doubt only ourselves, we find our security in others, and are therefore compliant. When we fear only others, we withdraw. When we fear both, but ourselves more, we are driven to covert aggression and satirical speech. When we fear both, but others more, we express ourselves in open aggression.

2. Projection and Aggression. The openly aggressive is always more confident of himself than of others. It is therefore "natural" for him to attack others. When he wholeheartedly embraces the philosophy of aggressive speech, he breaks the conflict generated by fear

[8] Erich Fromm, *Man for Himself*, New York, Rinehart and Company, Inc., 1947, p. 88.

of self and others by identifying his distress with the external world. The more trouble he has the more hellish the world looks to him. This tendency is known as *projection.*

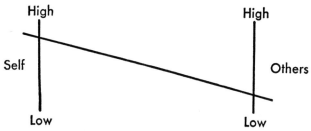

Confidence scale of open aggression.

3. *Vindictive Conscience and Aggression.* Closely allied is the vindictive image, discussed in Chapter 20. The person so driven calls it his conscience — the still voice of God. His enemies call it vindictiveness and self-righteousness. Interestingly, the voice speaks only when control is challenged or harassed.[9] When we are cooperative, compliant, or withdrawn, we are not so disturbed. The true character of aggression is further exposed by the fact that men on both sides of a fight have it.

Julian Huxley points out that vindictive conscience is that emotional supercharge which comes within us to marshal and coordinate energy when a decision has to be made out of our conflicting urges.[10] The life blood of a vindictive conscience, then, is the fear of defeat. To win is to have a conscience that pleases us with its praise; to lose is to have a conscience that shames us for having failed.

One of the most tragic of our primitive myths is that we associate God with the act of breaking out of conflict and making a hard decision. This puts all those who disagree with us on the side of the "devil." When we think this way, which is more common than not, goodness is a quality we reserve to ourselves and "our kind" in order to grasp the secure feeling that God is fighting with us. The truth is that vindictive conscience is just the barbaric cry for victory.

It follows that the greater the value of victory, the greater the need

[9] Norbert Wiener, *Cybernetics,* New York, John Wiley and Sons, Inc., 1949, Chapter VII.

[10] Thomas H. Huxley and Julian Huxley, *Touchstone for Ethics,* New York, Harper and Brothers, 1947, pp. 193–257.

to punish. The speaker who thinks that good speech is control of his listener usually finds it necessary to threaten the audience with some wholly unacceptable consequence if it does not follow obediently.

But as necessary as victory, punishment, and the prostrate opponent are to the vindictive urge, we seldom can look upon ourselves as seeking naked victory. We must cloak our aims in the robes of justice and sanctify our aggression.

4. The Cynicism of Advanced Aggression. The person who is excessively driven to control others is impressed by the belief that this is a jungle world. He therefore lives by the doctrine that the fittest will survive. For protection, he quite naturally encircles himself with friends and advisors much weaker than himself. These he "likes," for they become many pairs of spying eyes which he needs for his security. While he wants and needs compliant people around him, he despises these characteristics, particularly in himself, because they are to him self-destructive in a world of cruel and thoughtless people. Non-defensive mutuality, or love, is to him the tool of those too weak to fight. Advanced aggressiveness is the behavior of the cynic, who because he can attribute only weakness to the less aggressive, finds no true ideals save in his dictum of survival.

We have pictured the extreme. Not all, or even most, aggressive people are so immoderate. But aggression is prominent in Western culture, and much of our communication is therefore harsh. Since our personalities are shaped by communication, many persons, by the time they get to college, have been trained to believe that the central purpose of life is to "get to the top." The wide variety of temperaments found in children is channeled toward aggression.[11]

In the end it is fear of being forced into inferior roles that gives us the thirst for position and power. It is this fear that drives us to search for satisfaction in an arena where a sense of personal worth and dignity is not to be found. The tragedy is that the more we need this kind of power, the more dangerous it may be for both ourselves and society if we attain it. We cannot use it wisely, for it is not a social trust, but a fruitless attempt to satisfy internal needs. "There is nothing I'm afraid of like scared people," says Robert Frost.

[11] Gordon W. Allport, *Personality, a Psychological Interpretation*, New York, Henry Holt and Company, 1949, p. 413.

Describe a well-known aggressive person whom you admire and one you do not admire. What are the characteristics that cause your disfavor of the latter? What aggressive tendencies do you find quite acceptable? Have the class evaluate your conclusion as to "good" and "bad" aggression.

WITHDRAWING SPEECH

Jerry gave his best speech after a hunting expedition. Part of his talk follows:

> . . . After a short time, which seemed like ages, I was at my favorite spot. It was still dark. As I sat there waiting for the daylight, I saw the frost on the branches that were surrounding me like giant towers reaching toward heaven, fighting for survival. The frost glistened like the stars above. Then I wondered how such beauty could be created, and yet, destroyed by man.
>
> Finally it was daylight. I started straining my eyes for what a sportsman dreams about. The air was really cold, but, at the moment, I was too excited to notice that I was shaking — as I am right now, giving this speech.
>
> Suddenly there was a shot off to my right. . . . "

One of the writer's colleagues, remarkable in his ability to express similar thoughts and feelings, fell to recounting one of his trips to the northern woods.

> It was wonderful. I was lucky and got my deer the first day so I was free most of the time to enjoy myself. I would go out in the morning and walk until I was tired. Then I'd sit down on a rock and sun myself. All my processes would slow down; I would sort of go into a trance and imagine I too was a boulder being warmed. One day a deer came along. The wind must have been just right, for he walked up and stood within a yard of me. I could have reached out and touched him. But I didn't. I just sat there as motionless as the earth. Pretty soon he glided down over the hill and I watched him fade into the woods. It was unbelievably peaceful.
>
> Once I came up over a hill. I burst out laughing! A group of small pine trees dressed in saucy skirts of snow stood there, fixed in a frozen dance. Some awkward, some graceful, some flirting, some poising, some impishly sticking out their bustles. Gee! They were wonderful . . .

Both of these speeches illustrate the last distinctive kind of interaction, withdrawal. On the surface it does not seem like a kind of interaction at all, but rather like the absence of any, but since it concerns a maneuver in relations with other people, it comes within the scope of our concern. It should be clear that neither speech is itself withdrawing. Both are warm, slightly submissive — efforts to please. But they concern the joy of a withdrawing experience.

The term "withdrawal" is generally associated with internalized fear, though it need not be. The desire to extricate oneself from the world of social activity for the purpose of study, rest, self-evaluation, independent adventure, and creative work is a healthy response to one's own personal interests and needs. Withdrawal is a poor adjustment when it reveals a tendency to evade the solution of conflicts.

Confident Withdrawal

The withdrawing person places high value on independence or freedom. He wants to make his own decisions without advice and is willing to stand by them. Since he does not live closely with his fellow men, he tends to release his emotions in communication with the nonhuman environment. His hunting, fishing, painting, writing, carpentry,

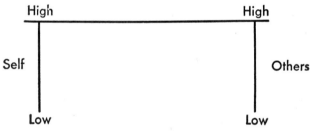

Confidence scale of confident withdrawal.

weaving, hiking, are his sources of emotional release. In essence, independent living stems from the high value a person places upon his own independent purposes.

Withdrawal is psychological isolation and does not necessarily involve physical isolation. But the person who enjoys his freedom *tends* to like the open spaces, for they are a guard against the intrusion of others. Moreover, in this frame of mind, he usually enjoys the soft voice of nature. If isolated from everything, the memory soon narrows until the same thoughts circulate again and again. The artist may paint better while intermittently looking at a landscape. Or a person who is thinking — communicating with himself — may do so better on a long walk in the woods.

Yet if one lives most of his life alone, he gradually deadens the social expression of his emotions. He appears to have ice water in his veins. His social responses come to be limited, cool, and formal. His voice is unemotional, unrevealing. He develops an impenetrable mask, and seldom abandons himself to laughter or tears. He is more likely to smile or frown.

In our culture we admire the strong and the independent. Choose such a person from your acquaintance and tell the class about him.

Internalized Fear and Withdrawal

Withdrawal is often mixed with internalized fear, of others or of self and others.

Internalized Fear of Others. When one fears others his behavior is much like the decided withdrawal of the confident person, except that it is compulsive rather than deliberate. Such a person fears his avoidance of others and develops a sort of social claustrophobia. He

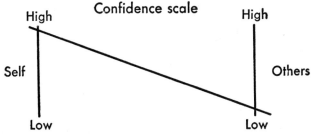

Confidence scale of the withdrawing person who fears others.

may seem to enjoy a conversation until his conversant asks a question. But at intrusion he may suddenly become indirect, evasive, and non-committal though without apparent tension. Or he may demonstrate his independence by being late wherever he goes, literally hating the control imposed by schedules. Often for such a person trains, buses, and appointments are a constant source of irritation. Of course, he dislikes committee work. At the extreme, the lone wolf has no freedom at all, for he is a slave to his own need for freedom.

The body tone, like that of the confidently independent person, is good. The manner is poised, irritatingly so to people of intense inter-action or to those who dislike these tendencies in themselves. The posture and movements are premeditatedly right. The only falseness in the manner is the lack of spontaneity.

Fear of Self and Others. Very often withdrawal develops great fear of both self and others, though the latter feeling dominates or the person would submit. The person who solves his problems inde-pendently must at the worst still have more faith in himself than others, else he could not go it alone. The fear relationship is that of aggression but his faith in himself is too low for attack.

Withdrawal, driven by this twin-engined fear, makes decisions diffi-cult. As we have seen, assured independence is marked by self-reliance. The person who fears both himself and others is no more inclined to seek advice, but he is not confident of his own decisions either. Therefore he becomes indecisive and puts off making up his mind as long as he can, perhaps indefinitely. If he decides nothing, he is fairly sure of placing no restrictions on his future behavior.

Another natural inclination of the flight from others is the tend-ency to substitute daydreams for action, replacing the urge for hu-man relations and achievements with fantasy. A girl in a speech class, in a confidential moment, related that one of her greatest joys was piloting an imaginary plane to a scene of grave disaster where she saved a life "in the nick of time," as thousands of watchers cheered. Despite heavy glasses, the girl could scarcely identify people five feet away. Her social world was not an easy one to stay in.

Since the mark of withdrawal in speech is formality, the more fearful a person is, the more precise, cool, and distant his diction and mannerisms. When speaking before a group, he tends to look out the window. When he looks at the audience, he does not see it. His rate tends to be deliberate; the melody, in a minor key. The quality is generally a-resonant.[12] The resulting speech is low, weak, and tired. This lack of energy in speech is understandable; the speaker is dis-posed to withdraw, and speech demands a certain amount of coopera-tion, submission, or aggression. The person who withdraws therefore spends great energy overcoming the avoidance of people.[13]

[12] Using the Bell Inventory and teachers' voice ratings, Hurd found a correla-tion of .72 between "retiring" and a-resonance.
[13] John Dollard and Neal Miller, *Personality and Psychotherapy*, New York, McGraw-Hill Book Company, Inc., 1950, p. 442.

While the detached person does not tend to sprawl and slump as does the fearfully submissive, his muscle tone is flaccid and gives the impression of illness or weariness.

Cooperation and confident submission do not fear. But submissiveness mixed with fear of self produces very compliant and self-effacing speech. When fear of others is also present (in which case it is less than fear of self), the speech is satirical, a calculated form of weak control. Openly aggressive speech is motivated by fear of both self and others, the fear of others being greater. A dominant self-oriented purpose and the attending love of freedom, without fear, produces an independent kind of withdrawal. Fear of others tends to accentuate the drive for independence. When fear of self intervenes, evasiveness marks the communication.

Most of us, in our speech, behave in all these ways now and then, yet we tend to find movement in one direction easier than in the others. It is best if we can keep the target, our audience, at the crosshairs in our sights, adjusting one way and then another as needed to maintain fixation on the target.

Because the human being is capable of the most complex and inconsistent beliefs and attitudes, he can take off in all directions at the same time. He may shine a man's boots and escape to a world of fantasy in which he conquers this very man. The good speaker has learned enough about himself and others to set for himself a reasonable purpose and he knows reasonably well how to attain it.

QUESTIONS FOR STUDY AND DISCUSSION

1. What are the three ways in which we interact with others? How do we account for four distinct kinds of speech with only three kinds of interaction?

2. What is the nature of cooperative speech?

3. Can you describe submissive speech? The difference between confident and fearful submission? The difference between the speech of one who fears himself and the one who fears both himself and others?

4. What is the relation between aggression and leadership?

5. What are the characteristics of aggression?

6. What is withdrawing speech? What are the three kinds of withdrawing speech? Can you illustrate each?

SUGGESTIONS AND ASSIGNMENTS

1. Select a short play or a scene from a play. With the needed number of class members, read the parts in class, after having studied the respective roles. Have the class evaluate each role and determine how well each of you suggested the attitudes of the character.

2. Select short poems or excerpts from speeches, one for each of the four attitudes toward others. Read each as you feel it should be read. Have the class determine which is cooperative, submissive, aggressive, and withdrawing. Have the class determine your ability to reveal the feelings involved in each of the four roles.

Index